Jesus

A

Master Teacher

For the 21st century

Translating Jesus' generic teaching strategies and methods from the 1st to the 21st centuries.

A meaningful transition to support teaching today.

Why was Jesus such an effective teacher?

An invitation to become more aware of his teaching strategies and methods and how they can enhance all types of teaching.

Roy Pitcher M.Ed., BA., Adv.Dip.Spec.Needs

Contact

24 Blenheim Court,
Alsager
Stoke on Trent,
Staffs.
ST7 2BY UK
e.mail: royol@talktalk.net
Tel 44 01270 875157

AuthorHouse™ UK Ltd.
1663 Liberty Drive
Bloomington, IN 47403 USA
www.authorhouse.co.uk
Phone: 0800.197.4150

© 2013 Roy Pitcher. All rights reserved.

No part of this book may be reproduced, stored in a retrieval system, or transmitted by any means without the written permission of the author.

Published by AuthorHouse   11/26/2013

ISBN: 978-1-4817-8828-1 (sc)
ISBN: 978-1-4817-8866-3 (e)

Library of Congress Control Number: 2013907579

Any people depicted in stock imagery provided by Thinkstock are models, and such images are being used for illustrative purposes only.
Certain stock imagery © Thinkstock.

This book is printed on acid-free paper.

Because of the dynamic nature of the Internet, any web addresses or links contained in this book may have changed since publication and may no longer be valid. The views expressed in this work are solely those of the author and do not necessarily reflect the views of the publisher, and the publisher hereby disclaims any responsibility for them.

Acknowledgements

Every book has a long story of indebtedness to people who have enriched the author's thinking and I am no exception. A flow of colleagues, students and pupils have enabled me to break new ground over the past decades (e.g. The Developing World Series pub. Longmans 1964-75) I am particularly indebted to Clive Kendrick for the wide ranging teaching opportunities he gave me at undergraduate and graduate levels. I would also like to thank Les Pickford (an M.Ed. student and part-time colleague) for his careful insightful thinking about leading issues in Part C. Also to Harry Chicken for his constant stream of vigorous involvement with religious ideas and aspects of matters concerned with Part C.

Graham Smith with his lawyer's mind and analytical thought has proved to be an invaluable reader whilst Mike Collett and his wife, Christine, have been my technological prop, and they have always made themselves available to solve what appeared intractable problems. Rev. Eric Challoner, who has been a treasured prayer partner for over 30 years has constantly stimulated my thinking by his breadth of vision and insights and in whom I have seen much of what is written here. But there have been so many to whom I feel particularly indebted for many reasons – such as Ian and Pat Griffiths and Trevor Condliffe and so many more who have surrounded me with their love and support. In the final stages Pastor Phil Roberts brought his expertise in desk-top publishing to bear, for which I am very grateful.

Above all, I would like to thank and dedicate this book to my wife, Olive, and our sons David, Andrew and John for the inspiration and joy they have brought to my work, without which this would certainly not have been written.

The Challenge

To translate Jesus'

teaching strategies

into 21st century practices

To Develop

Faith in teacher and self

Pereception - what is worth pursuing?

Healthy learning process

Sustained motivation / learning

Move towards known goals

Achieve desired learning

BUT HOW?

The Challenge

Jesus may be readily praised as a master teacher but that was in the context of the 1st century CE. Remarkably, despite the fact of technological change, his wealth of teaching strategies can be translated into the 21st century even when not focused on Christianity. What can we learn from his teaching style that will enhance our effectiveness? More specifically one might ask, 'Which methods would Jesus use?' His answer effectively flowed from criteria of clarity and situational requirements, plus of course personality. This relied upon oracy and demstrative actions but what can it mean today?

The *manner* in which he taught can *stand* the light of current examination and further insights can be gained by seeing the psychological principles (see Part B) and their applications to current teaching trends (see Part C). The primary goal of this book is sketched in Figure 1 that shows four modern strategies and 30 methods that bear similarities to those used by Jesus.

The philosophical validity of the task has been debated. For example, whereas Nicholas Burbules has argued for the legitimacy of transposing Jesus' methods (e.g. parables) into our contemporary situation, Prof. Terence McLaughlin has reservations. He sees Jesus' teaching as being essentially spiritual, and that his methods and message should not be separated because the spiritual concepts are integral to the methods and so override or at least question any study such as this. Although caution is needed, the view taken here follows that of Burbules and seeks to identify legitimate transfers between Jesus' techniques in Galilee and ours in the 21st century.

Jesus is an appropriate case study because:

- His generic teaching skills cross philosophical, religious and educational boundaries.
- There is an indicative core of evidence in the New Testament, despite its religious nature.
- His resources were sparse but his teaching skills show many persistent generic elements that can still unite the messenger, the message, the methods and the learners.

One Tuesday whilst teaching in Lincolnshire I had an eureke moment. I asked myself how Jesus might teach my Y7, Y8 and Y9 special needs pupils basic skills and also religious education throughout the school. My pilgrimage into teaching had begun with that one question. It became evident that his prowess could extend beyond spiritual priorities and enrich current teaching generally.

The pursuit began and has lasted over 40 years – so far! Readers will find that there are too many bullet points littering the pages, but each represents a significant step along my way. Also there are numerous charts and tables that were major advances, clarified my thinking and forced me to be more analytical in my approach. Therefore, this is not a devotional book but a sustained intuitive search that is professional – and yet more. I feel settled that the pattern of teaching based on practices displayed by Jesus are foundational and will surprise many, both in their practicality and their further scope for development. You may wish to bypass the bullets and tables and see what remains that can enhance the everyday – no matter what is taught. There is still much to say and the pursuit will continue because the wealth is so remarkable, as you may or may not agree. The decision will simply be yours as to whether you wish to be an interpreter of Jesus, a Master Teacher!

Contents

Acknowledgements iii

The Challenge v

Contents vii

Introduction ix

Part A. Illustrating the master teacher 17

Chapter 1. Teaching from his Historic Roots 17

Chapter 2. A teaching style – Traditional or Progressive 29

Chapter 3. Principles for an ultimate teaching strategy – Part A 43

Chapter 4. Jesus' teaching strategies illustrated from Matthew's Gospel ... 55

Part B. Looking at Jesus' teaching styles within social psychology 67

Chapter 5. Leadership 69

Chapter 6. Perception 81

Chapter 7. Motivation 93

Chapter 8. Memory 105

Chapter 9. Socialization 119

Chapter 10. Cognition, Creativity and Problem 133

Chapter 11. Emotions 147

Chapter 12. Ultimate Teaching Strategy B 163

Chapter 13. Teaching strategies illustrated in John's Gospel 169

Part C. Making it happen today 177

Chapter 14. Looking forward to Part C and a sketch 181

Chapter 15. Definitions of spirituality 183

Chapter 16. Eight teaching strategies 193

Chapter 17. Teaching methods in the Gospel according to Luke 227

Chapter 18. Ultimate teaching strategy C 237

Appendix Jesus and Personality Factors 261

Bibliography 263

Index 267

Mind Map illustrating an overview of the book

Figure 1. An overview of "Jesus the Master Teacher"

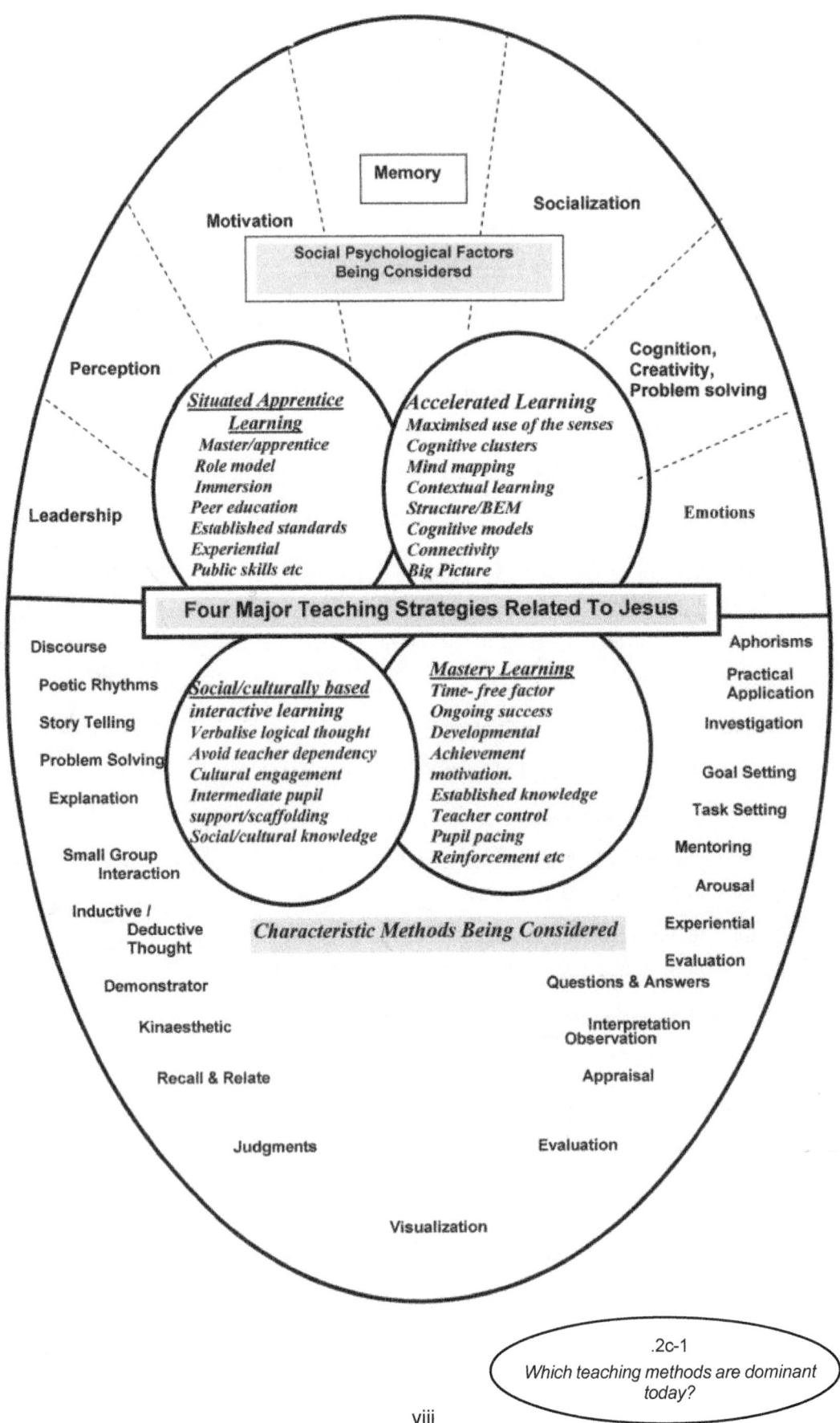

Introduction

Jesus – a master teacher for today?

It is great to be great, but it is even better to make others great. (Iroquois adapted)

Within the context of his life, Jesus was a master teacher and his life and teaching were characterized by effective long-term creativity. One does not need to be a Christian to appreciate the qualities of his methods, just as non-Muslims can recognize the effectiveness of Muhammad's methods when he established community based teaching.

Normally studies about Jesus focus on various aspects of his compassion. Whilst being glad to acknowledge this (after all it is a primary quality of any teacher) that is not the major purpose here. It is simply to see him in his role as a teacher who displayed so many skills.

Neither is it simply a panegyric of praise, but a consideration of how his understanding of universal principles that govern human behaviour caused people to say, "He knew what was in man". As such he:

- raised new realms of possibilities… personally, socially, spiritually, materially.
- responded appropriately to people's needs and aspirations.
- persuaded people about the significance of what he taught.
- promoted long-term learning.
- aroused a sense of identification and motivation.
- maximized and used people's learning skills (e.g. memory).
- took people into fresh multiple personal and socio-cultural perspectives.

People were invigorated as they watched Jesus teach! The surprises, poetry, drama and stimulating words of hope and faith raised expectations that caused listeners to run miles around the shores of Galilee to hear more, and try to make him king. Imagine the drama as the crowds leaned forward to catch every word. Admittedly it was a unique situation but the impact was memorable. Even so, which of his skills can be modified and applied today?

As we examine Jesus' methods, it is surprising that his ministry lasted less than three years, and that we only have a record of some 35 to 52 days, when we learn of fewer than 40 parables and 40 miracles amongst approximately 120 recorded incidents, which is in sharp contrast to Muhammad who served his people for 23 years and Gautama, the Buddha, who taught for 50 years.

Everybody is a teacher

Opinions about Jesus' teaching are often compressed into generalities such as forgiveness and love, parables and miracles etc, but what were their practical values as we teach one another? Everybody is a teacher from childhood onwards. A child may teach a friend to play marbles or football… a parent may teach a child to knit or read maps… a newspaper editor may… a school teacher may… He taught in order to achieve specific spiritual purposes, primarily amongst that Jewish underclass, the Galileans, but his generic methods remain. This was in the spirit of the Jewish tradition, which stated that *'everybody is a teacher led by a teacher'*.

Everyday teaching can be illustrated from a 12 year-old boy's memorable learning. It was with a builder who was a pigeon fancier. "Look at these eyes…," "These primary wing flights…," "Feel its long straight keel….," and so on. The fancier brought expertise, judgment and values to the boy with his pigeons. And so he became immersed in the world of pigeon racing and became an independent learner within a new social background! Formal teaching is publicly recognized, but informal teaching is more widely used. What might Jesus contribute to such situations?

.2c-2
Which aspects of teaching can / cannot be bridged?

The Big Idea – His purpose and ours

Teaching is not solely about knowledge and efficient procedures, but about people and their responses. Therefore, his teaching styles were imaginatively people-centred. He frequently used the environment to illustrate spiritual ideas, and so described the final judgment day in terms of fishermen cleaning their nets. He retained a high degree of teacher control by adopting processes and principles that remain such as being:

- *relevant*, both in the immediate and medium terms.
- *highly motivated* both in terms of satisfying needs and creating aspirational promises.
- *contextually meaningful*.
- *rooted* in the authority of tradition.
- based upon the authority and inspiration of his *personal ability*.

All of which provide a basis for translating his methods into the 21st century.

First thoughts about Jesus – the Teacher

Traditionally, disciples have ossified the teaching of their founder to preserve its purity, not realising that by dispensing with the teaching processes they minimize the message itself. Here the images and caricatures he used will be disentangled to re-interpret and transfer his methods into meaningful forms, and which require our controlled projection and imagination.

Though Jesus achieved much, few details remain because they were recorded in a typically succinct Jewish style, which is noted for its brevity and direct concrete descriptions. But the gospels and related background materials show embedded teaching styles with sufficient clarity to avoid excessive anachronisms when modern situations and methods of Jesus are linked and so gauge the potential transfer of his methodologies.

Figure 2

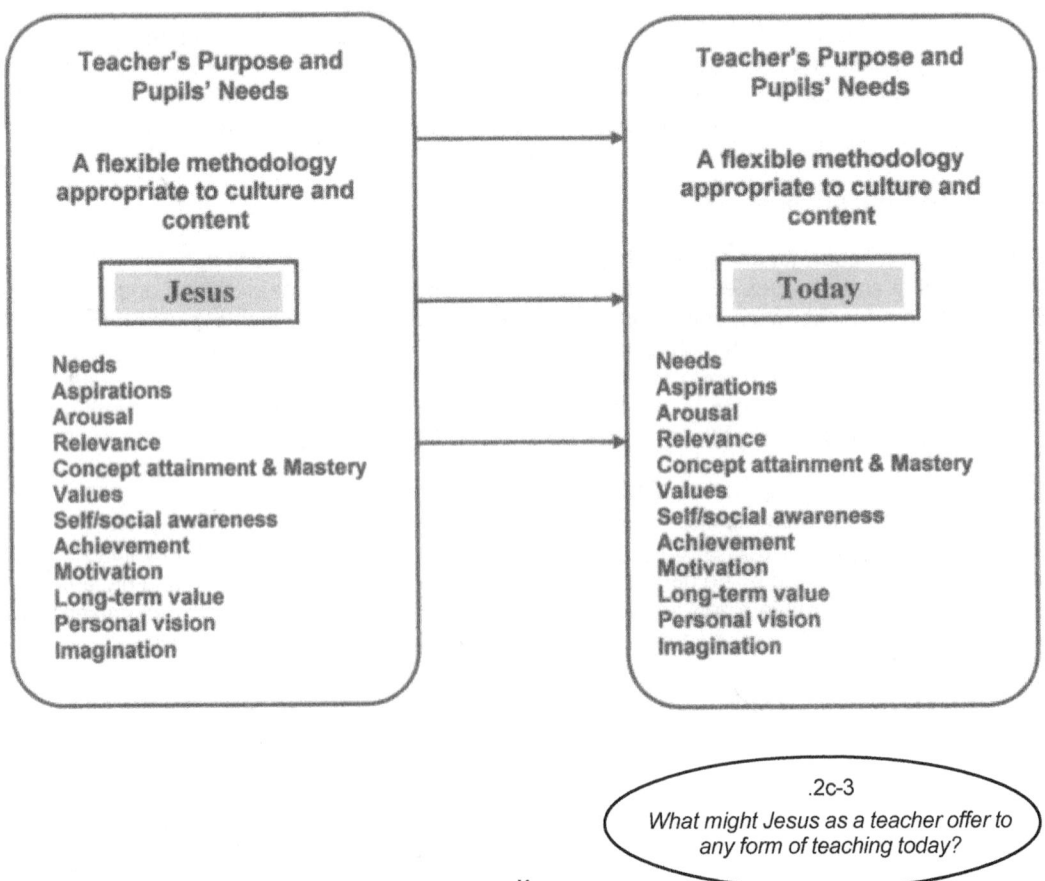

.2c-3
What might Jesus as a teacher offer to any form of teaching today?

Similar issues have been central to teaching priorities across the historic divide!

Jesus knew his audience and taught out of their culture and into their life situations. He was teaching in their world. Therefore, his relevance made them listeners. As we move rapidly from the traditional and industrial civilizations into the post-modern world we assume his teaching methods would take account of life as it is and yet retain his essential message. But how can this be achieved?

The title of 'Master Teacher' is usually reverential, and his insights did exceed the traditional three-part instruction process of:

- arousal, explanation and demonstrations
- pupils replicate the demonstrations with the teacher's assistance
- pupils do reinforcing work

Jesus used such methods but not habitually. He recognized what was worthwhile and met wide ranging demands despite militant opposition. He skilfully and readily responded to needs, arrested people's attention as he tried to change their attitude to their great expectation – the coming of the Kingdom of God. Now, as was seen in the 2012 Olympics when expectations are aroused, people can be galvanized into joyful action.

A "Toolbox" for teaching

As a carpenter Jesus used a toolbox, so the metaphor of a "tool box" aptly describes the range of methods that he used. Although his major tools were spirituality and prayer, he had for example, in his oral methods such "tools" as:

Contrast – Good Samaritan	Confrontation / conflict – Q-A religious rulers
Similarity – Good Shepherd	Deflection – Disagreement with opposition
Self conviction – the adulterous woman	Visualization – with sight and imagination
Personal identity – Samaritan woman	Involvement – feeding the multitudes

This toolbox will reveal a range of tools and their uses when developing closed instructional systems and also stimulate ideas that can be implemented (see Fig 3). These tools were varied and developed common principles such as need satisfaction, arousal, relevance etc.

Figure 3

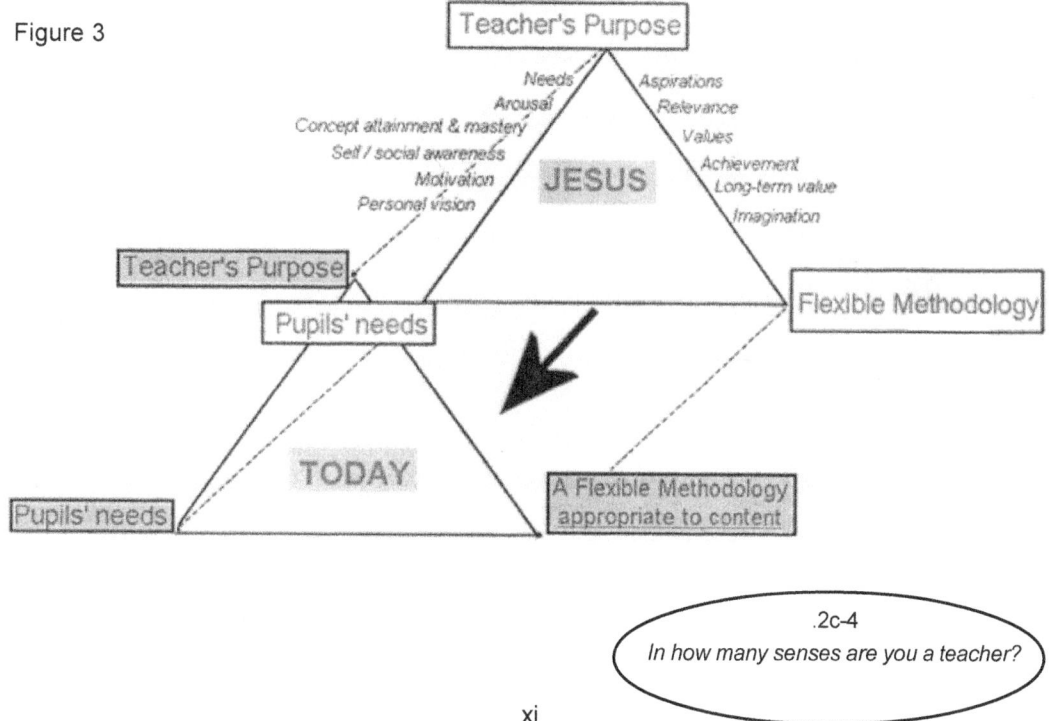

In how many senses are you a teacher?

This is illustrated further by *four central principles* of Jesus' teaching – *the Kingdom of God, the Fatherhood of God, repentance and reconciliation, plus his own Messiahship* (see Fig. 4). Ultimately this was his focus. They were developed through *core concepts* as shown in the second ring (e.g. forgiveness, discipleship etc.). These were taught through *methods* (e.g. experiential work, demonstration etc.) indicated in the outer ring that reinforced developed his core message. Evidently Jesus used many interactive methods.

These provide clues into reasons for the effectiveness of his following common skills.

- His *vision and understanding* of what he wanted to teach and how to achieve it.
- His *teaching style was* based on *relationships*.
- He *added value* to those around.
- He *saw* and satisfied *needs and aspirations*.
- He used *authority* appropriately.
- He was a long-term *role model*.
- He developed optimum *challenges*.
- He developed strong *social identification*.
- He used identifiable, comprehensible and persuasive *speech*.
- He was skilled at remaining *in touch* with 'the common man'.

Figure 4

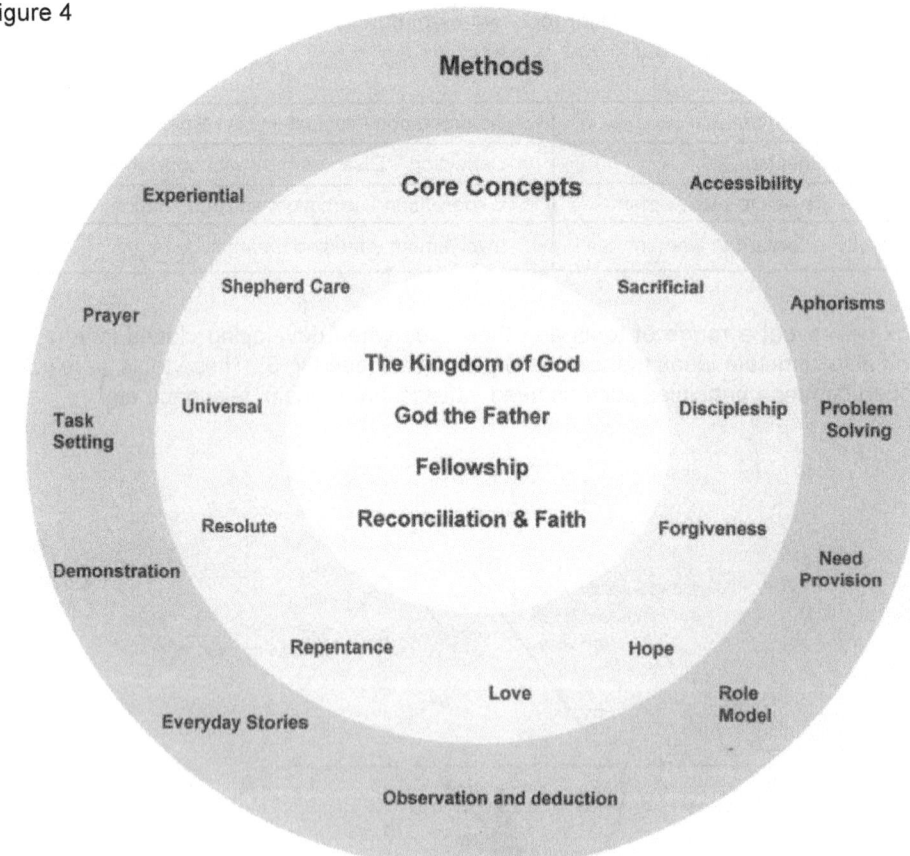

These provide insights why major learning factors (e.g. memory, perception, cognition etc.)could be developed through multiple techniques (e.g. storytelling, inductive teaching, hyperbole) – see Part B.

.2c-5
What do you regard as good efficient teaching?

Jargon or...?

As Jesus walked the shores of Galilee, his teaching methods varied but his style did not. But what might we see? Figure 6 shows elements that illustrate six/ seven influences on teaching and learning, many of which could be directly applied to him. They are partly expressed in technical language to achieve economy of space and shared understandings. For example, cell 2A emphasizes that he was their *role model* who showed them demonstrable principles of his teaching. This analysis highlights issues that are shown at the head of the table.

The intention is to enter into the dynamics of the events that absorbed fishermen etc who were not equipped to ask or answer the questions we are examining, but who provided evidence for us to achieve secure judgments. More explicitly we can identify 34 of his teaching methods as listed in Fig.5. Apart from the miraculous these are common today.

It may appear surprising that Jesus developed such an effective array of teaching methods together with imaginative and memorable content to convey the relatively few principles of faith upon which Christianity has been built, but that is not so. He inherited a rich Jewish teaching tradition (see p.12ff) that enabled him to develop prophetic teachings about God, and also pursue his unique means of changing spiritual, moral and social attitudes.

However conscious he was of the structure of his teaching is of no consequence here. What we can say is that by the age of 30 Jesus had by intuition, tradition and observation grasped the qualities of good teaching. Using these he and his later followers deftly crossed cultures and time with surprising ease and the message remained fresh, whilst being tantalizingly simple and yet profound. The following will be seen in the coming chapters:

The essentials of Jesus' teaching methods

- The person was the method.
- The bedrock values.
- The organizing principles/ concepts.
- Explicit instruction.
- Explicit promises and demands.
- Teaching a diverse range of people
- Implicit instructional procedures.
- Meeting needs and aspirations.
- Characteristic teaching strategies.
- Leading and changing attitudes.
- This servant who had authority.
- Making learning more efficient.

Effects on incoming pupils

- Personal needs.
- Personal experiences.
- Personal expectations.
- Personal attitudes.
- Personal and shared options.
- Responding to challenge
- Learning by group experiences.
- Attracted by his teaching.
- Amazed by his actions.
- Responding to his character.
- Held by his promises.
- Confirmed by his consistency.

This introduction is a *preview* that is summarized by Figure 5 where 'the Teacher's' main methods are illustrated with 34 of his typical approaches... Figure 6 lists examples of 'good practice' in modern teaching and learning. If you keep it as an aide-memoire it will become increasingly evident that Jesus' methods were insightfully appropriate, sensitive and robust. As such it acts as an ongoing *review* instrument.

Personality Factor – 1

What clues from this introduction can you begin to glean about Jesus' personality as a teacher?

.2c-6
What makes a person teachable or not?

Figure 5

Major teaching methods used	Jesus' examples	Major teaching methods used	Jesus' examples
Arousal and attention	Evidence, promise Matt 4v12 Synagogue in Nazareth Lk 4	Novelty and surprise	Nobody spoke like this The crowd /astonished Matt, 7
Brief didactic statements	The Beatitudes Matt.5 Take heart daughter Matt.9	Observation	Look at the birds Matt.6v26 Lift your eyes and see Jn4
Challenge	Follow me Matt.4v19 Foxes have holes but Matt.8	Opportunism	Zaccheus and Jesus' Lk19v5 Jesus at the well Jn4
Commands	Go into all the world Mark 16 Be reconciled. Matt.5v24	Parables, phrases, riddles	The sower and the soils Matt.13 The leaven / the loaf Matt.13
Contrasts /comparisons	Good Shepherd/ the sheep Luke15v3 The Good Samaritan Luke10	Parables – short Stories etc	The Prodigal Son Luke15v11- Rich man and Lazarus Luke 16
Conversations	Nicodemus Jn 3v1-15 The Samaritan woman Jn 4	Personal commitment /association	From servants to friends Jn 15v15 I chose you Jn 15v19
Courageous actions	Clearing the Temple John 2v13-22 So have no fear Matt.10v26	Problem solving mentoring/ counselling	Paying taxes to Caesar Mk12v14 Tolerance of others
Deeds and demonstrations	Wisdom justified by deeds Matt.11v19 Pray like this. Matt.6v9	Promises and rewards	Ultimate rewards: faithful Matt 25 Whatever you ask Jn 14 3
Discourse	The sermon on the Plain Lk.6v17 The final days Matt.24	Questions and answers	Who do men say that I am ? Matt.16 An adulterous woman Jn. 8
Discussion	Thomas said...Philip said Jn14	Reflection	Jesus withdrew Matt.15v32 Jesus withdrew again Jn 6
Experiential /expressive	Jesus sent the 12 Matt 10v5 The Lord.....70 others Luke10	Repetition	Feeding 5000 Jn6v1ff Feeding 4000 Matt.15v32
Identification and instructions	While he was speaking Matt.12v46 When he had finished Matt.11	Reinforcement	Publican standing afar Lk18 Humility Lk14v10
Interpretation/ old into new	Eating on the Sabbath Matt12 Water of life John 4v13-15	Responses to requests	Roman centurion Matt.8v5 Jesus on the water Matt14
Kinaesthetics	Washing disciples feet John 13 Mud on blind man John 9	Role-model	He who has seen me...Jn149 To be like his teacher Matt10
Meeting needs	Feeding 5000 John 6 Water to wine John 2	Use of the senses	Teaching involving sight, touch, emotons etc. John 11
Metaphors – concrete to abstract	I am the door Jn10 v9 You are the salt of the earth Matt5 v13	Using traditional scriptures	Man shall not live by bread alone Matt. 4v4 You shall not kill Matt. 5
Motivation rewards	He will repay every man for what he has done Matt.16 27	Actions for teaching	Feeding the masses John 6

.2c-7
Which of the teaching methods above would seem particularly appropriate then?

Figure 6

Common elements within teaching and learning. As you proceed note which can be applied to Jesus.

A Teacher Qualities	B Pupils	C Priorities	D Strategies (i)	E Strategies (i)	F Methods	G Method
Leadership Self – image Servanthood Shepherd	Self respect	Need satisfaction- achievement expectations success,	Apprentices - task development skills	Absolute knowledge	Short statements	Reflection and silence / quietness
Role model	Shared conscience	Sense of security	Accelerated learning	Teacher directed But non-coercive	Observation	Poetic rhythms
Character Courage etc	Positive attitude to teacher etc	Sense of success, Belonging, Affiliation Relationship	Individual mastery	Ongoing socialisation d imprinting	Situational interpretation / deduction	Paradox
Ability Competence	High expectations	Acceptable cultural norms	Clear recall reinforcement strategies	Creativity personal responsibility / initiatives	Imagination using visualization	Question - answer
Purpose Vision	Aware of personal role	Appropriate behavioural changes	Thinking skills i. Cause/effect	Systematic development of schemas	Demon- stration	Epigrams
Hope, aspirations Expectations Opportunity	Part of participant community	Continuity and change – past, present, future	ii Comparison /Classification	Scaffolding and support	Cloze /completion	Recall and relate
Appreciation Confidence in pupils	Adequate personal/ social skills	Develop corporate skills understanding	iii Analysis	Memory enhancement	Dialogue	Personal memorable experience
Motivator	Appropriate use of multiple intelligence	Shared world view /perception/ identification.	iv Synthesis	Developing concrete to abstract	Story telling	Reporting to others
Evokes personal Faith etc	Development of spiritual intelligence	High quality relationships	v Deductive- ruleg Inductive –egrule thinking	Problem solving	Physical tactile experiences	Challenge following learning and empowerm't
Makes secure judgments	Respond evaluate truth/ knowledge,	Balance - personal options / core activities	vi Contrast – similarity and difference	Decision making	Oracy	Recall activities
Appropriate Risk taking	Personal social learning	A modelled learning ethos	vii Prediction	Independent learning	Discourse	Self assessment
Shows moral and spiritual qualities eg Kindness	Use of pupils' own expertise	Freedom with commitment and rigour	viii Justification	Group learning	Dramatic personal vicarious involvement	Deliver explanations
Responsible to pupils / higher authorities	Group responsibility	Peer group learning and interdependence	ix Inference	Systematic revealed truth	Emotive projection experiences	Look for association /connectivity
Perceptive	Peer responsibility	A sense of conscience	x Sequencing	Master teacher and mentor	Aphorisms	Kinaesthetic experiences
Appropriate Innovative	Personal investigation	Inclusivity and mutuality	Community based enquiry	Informal interaction	Hyperbole	Self appraisal

The cells are not formally sequenced horizontally.

.2c-8
What makes a teacher effective in the long term?

Part A. Illustrating the master-teacher

Chapter 1

Teaching from His Historical Roots

It is frustrating that we know so little about Jesus' life prior to his public ministry. We have fragments of information from which reasonable suppositions are made. It is assumed that this intelligent, and observant Jewish boy who considered religious teaching carefully. He formulated questions about God, the Law and the prophets, developed in wisdom, and recognized his unique role in history. He was not merely an improver of the current teaching, but one who was re-interpreting the past, the present and the future. His reflective thinking and problem solving formed the basis of his personalized development – but which contained powerful traditional elements Although he lived within his culture he was not its prisoner. His vision remained intact, and so we see Jesus travelling, telling stories and performing miracles whilst also being in conflict with the religious authorities. He drew upon a dynamic mix of established traditions at a time of strife. He rose above this complex cultural situation and many of its long-term questions and practices. His principles were based on *secure goals, cohesive explicit and implicit knowledge, experiences, relationships, aspirations and a hope that transcended the frustrations of the people.* His prolonged pre-ministry development almost certainly involved such influential thought forms as shown below (Fig7).

Jesus – his self-preparation

Jesus recognized the importance of his *self-preparation*. No matter whether a person is teaching the skills of plumbing, the ways of a priest or the knowledge of the mainstream teacher. It provides assurance and adequacy. This self-preparation enabled Jesus to know himself and say, "Of the truth I say unto you…" by which he emphasized his own authority.

Childhood Learning 0-5years	Growing self-awareness 5-10 years	Home 10-12years		Observing fellow Galileans Mature manhood	Resultant aims and objectives
Bethlehem Egypt Nazareth	Personal enquiry	Prophetic strand	Personal realization	Poverty	Kingdom of God
	Rote-learning the LAW	Temple	Growing confidence	Language	Fatherhood of loving God
	Observation	Religious groups e.g. Essenes	Sense of identity	Dominated underclass	Repentance / reconciliation
	Judas' revolt	Synagogue	Purpose	Exploited	Access / Trust in God
	Traditions, Roman domination	Rebuilding Sepphoris ?	Vision	Develop John Baptist's teaching	Love/ Faith & Hope, Mercy sacrificial servanthood
		Savage retribution Romans	Committed to his call	Religious leaders/ burdens	

Figure 7 Dominant influences on the learning path of Jesus.

Therefore it can be said that….

- *He understood his own culture intimately and differentiated between its strands He respected and loved the underclass and those who were excluded in society.*
- *He had ample depth of knowledge and skills based upon the prophetic tradition.*
- *He knew himself and who he was, which was the product of long-term reflection, prayer, observation and revelation.*

Hence, he was confident in his revolutionary teaching and in himself, even to the point of death. This *self-preparation* was fundamental to his teaching methods.

.2c-9
What made his teaching fresh and flexible?

A window in time (or 'a brief calm fell upon the land')

Jesus lived at an opportune time and in a culture that enabled him to develop his teaching. He was born during a short period of relative peace following over a century of war, primarily against the Romans. Well over 60,000 Jews had been slaughtered in the previous six decades and many more had been taken into slavery. It reached a climax in Galilee in 6CE when messianic Jews rose up and destroyed the Roman administrative capital, Sepphoris, that had been built by King Herod. As usual, Galileans were to the fore of the resistance movement when a rebel named Judas gathered over 10,000 people around him. After his initial success at Sepphoris, Judas and his army were quickly destroyed and venomous reprisals followed with some 2000 being crucified. It was said that there was "grave disorder – great and wild fury spread over the nation" (Josephus). Six decades later in 66-70CE, the Romans destroyed Jerusalem and the nation was scattered. In this short period of spasmodic peace Jesus shared the common blessings of being a Jew, howbeit a Galilean Jew!

He grew up in a devout family that took their spiritual responsibilities seriously and made regular pilgrimages to Jerusalem where his inquiring mind enabled him to pose searching questions to the religious leaders in the Temple. It was said that an eminent man cannot be pious (Hillel), an idea which Jesus later modified. This demand for humility extended to the belief that people should be taught and to "let your fear of your teacher be as the fear of heaven". Therefore, as was usual he benefited from an education at home and in the local synagogue, the "house of learning". He was taught to read and write from the scriptures that were learnt by heart. Also, much teaching took the form of slogans and short sentences which became imprinted on his memory. He also noticed that the Pharisees who sat on 'Moses' seat' in the synagogue imposed burdens on the people by their elaborate regulations and petty legal details at the expense of justice, mercy and faith, even though they did not meet their own requirements. When he was about 10 years of age he probably saw the uprising led by Judas against the Romans and Herodians at Sepphoris, which was only six miles from Nazareth. As Jesus heard, observed and interpreted the suffering around him it is almost possible to hear him talking about the king who went to war. The impact of these influences is unknown but his life was typical. Like most builders, he was probably drafted into re-building Sepphoris by Herod and the Romans. If so, as he walked he saw the cosmopolitan life of traders, soldiers, travellers and Herodian rulers. But also, he would see roadside crucifixions and tragedies faced by his fellow Galileans. It appears that these became embedded in his living autobiography from which he taught. As he spoke of roadside inns, bandits, vineyard workers, sheep, wild life etc one can recognize his personal experiences.

As a pious Jew, Jesus' 'father', Joseph knew that 'he who does not teach his son a trade brings him up to be a robber'. He probably died whilst the lad was in his teens. As the eldest son Jesus undertook responsibility for the family and worked as a carpenter and builder, who together with stonemasons, were highly regarded because they built houses, and were also needed by farmers and traders. His parables were a spiritual interpretation of common observations. He watched vintners, farmers, fishermen and shepherds etc. and compared the wealthy with the poverty-stricken and developed a concern for widows and children. We find allusions to spring-cleaning, washing up, trimming lamps, observing the weather, chickens, wheat and weeds. It would also appear that he developed an awareness of number because he was frequently defining objects numerically. For example, he mentioned five wise virgins, five talents, three measures of meal, ninety-nine sheep etc.

His multicultural background fitted him for his life as a prophetic teacher. His native language was Aramaic, but he learned Hebrew in the synagogue and he possibly spoke Greek when he was talking to Pilate and the Syro-Phoenician woman. He moved amongst a mixed cultural background of Galileans, Judeans, Samaritans, Syrians, Greeks, Romans and probably others because Nazareth was close to the major trade routes, and Galilee was surrounded by non-Jewish territories. It is noteworthy that the Syrians were adept at speaking in parables. For example,

.2c-10
How might Jesus' teaching reflect our culture today?

a man wanted to borrow a friend's camel to partner his own when going on a journey. The camel's owner reluctantly agreed but made the traveller promise to care for it as if it were his own. When the traveller returned, the camel's owner noticed that it was in poor condition whereas the other camel was strong and healthy. When confronted by this, the traveller pleaded that he had treated them identically. But he then remembered that at night when he slept between the camels he did so with his head against his own camel and his feet against the borrowed camel. This parable contains similarities with those of Jesus and indicates influences on Jesus' early life. *He was a learner before he became a teacher with his own culture and experience being his powerful teachers.*

He probably dug foundations for houses before he told the parable of the wise and foolish builders. Jesus was part of his culture and yet saw beyond it and showed a wealth of understanding from which we can draw today. From Figure 8 imagine which influences were particularly important to Jesus but are hardly mentioned in the gospels. There are gaps in the texts that archaeologists and theologians have tried to fill – but even so there remain places that require a degree of intelligent infilling and which are compatible with the general tenor of the gospels. Many, but not all of these major omissions are concerned with Jesus' formative 'hidden years'. We will never know what Mary told Jesus about the events surrounding his birth, and also what Joseph may have said during their work together. How did Jesus interpret his surroundings as he grew up in the midst of a complex, fractured and yet expectant culture? As an independent, observant Galilean his assessments led to striking spiritual conclusions despite the cry from Judeans 'Galilee. Galilee – you hate the Torah!'

Being in the prophetic tradition, he used methods typical of prophets such as Isaiah, Jeremiah, Hosea, and Amos etc. There were parables about potters, vineyards and family life etc, plus observations and spiritual interpretations of nature, brief urgent commands, together with promises and warnings and allusions to the Father. In accordance with the Jewish prophetic tradition, he reinterpreted the biblical law and went beyond customary religious interpretations and traditions. Was this simply due to his unique insights? How did he develop his teaching skills? Was his teaching simply common sense or did it illustrate the understandings of a genius well beyond the first century CE? His methods were not unique, but on closer examination *in total* perhaps they were. As William Barclay noted, 'his teaching was immediate and arresting, had universal appeal, was meaningful and memorable, and met a shared sense of need and reality and was sharply provocative.'

Similarities and differences between Jesus, Galileans and Jewish leaders

The differences between Jesus, a Galilean and the Jewish leaders were decisive. For example he emphasized that:

- Formal shared knowledge of the Law was not enough.
- Tradition was not enough.
- Partial, shared culture was not enough.
- Shared hatred of any enemy was not enough.

It needed a fresh vision! But could Jesus be tolerated? Would truth and evidence be enough? Was hope and compassion enough? The prophets had spoken frequently and their message had authority but not to the same degree as the established and more formal Law of Moses that could be implemented consistently by those in control. Moreover, the religious scholars, not only controlled the practice but a[so the development and legal authorization of the Jewish faith .What hope could there be for a carpenter from the Galilean village of Nazareth who had no official authority and who was making unacceptable claims? But he was well prepared and in his own context he had good educational experiences.

.2c-11
In what way was the parable of the camel reminiscent of Jesus parables?

Consider the rich learning that Jesus experienced as a pupil.
- Rigorous thought processes of the Jewish Law and tradition (the Halakhah).
- Meditation.
- Reading.
- Observation.
- Memorization.
- Listening attentively.
- Reflection.
- Questioning current practices.
- Deduction based on a wide range of evidence.
- Parental and community religious stories, activities etc.
- Evaluating probable responses to his new teaching about the Kingdom of God.

These experiences were ideal preparations. His revelation encompassed assumptions that he modified, such as the conquering Messiah. Also, his teaching provided clues as to how he learned when, for example, he used the story of men waiting at the vineyards for work.

Figure 8

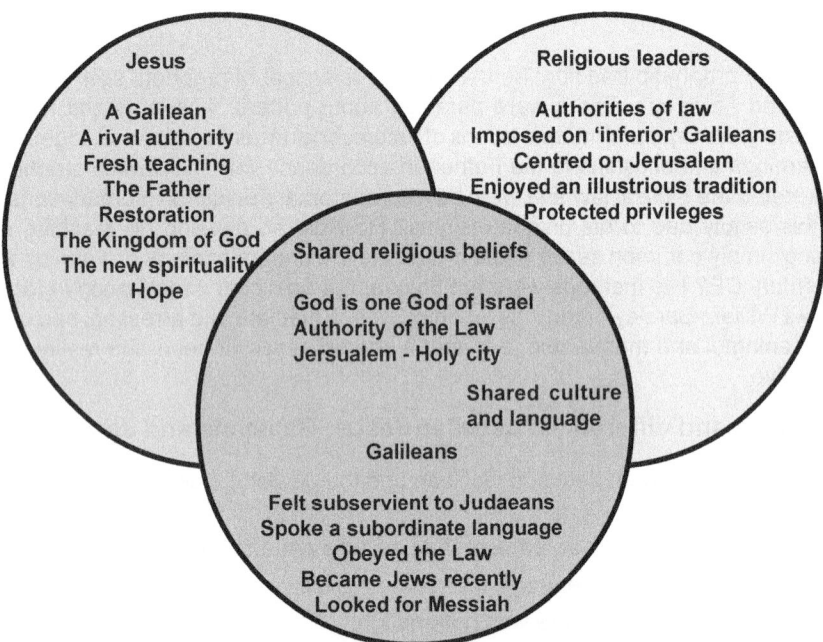

Jesus taught amongst rival religious groups. Two that offered serious opposition were rival sects of Pharisees. The followers of Shammai were strictly conservative and a rival named Hillel led those who were relatively liberal. Both parties enjoyed degrees of authority and imposed their will on the people. The Pharisees were closely associated with the Scribes/ lawyers who had an illustrious history. The scholarly scribes had enjoyed a high status since the Babylonian exile in the 6th century BCE by protecting and interpreting the traditional Mosaic Law. They maintained the purity of the written law and make it accessible to the people. From the middle of the second century BCE they had been joined by the 'separated ones' (the Pharisees) to uphold 'the traditions of the elders' and together they enjoyed high esteem. Many were crucified, when, led by Judas (the Hammer) Maccabeus in 175-165 BCE, they fought for the nation's independence. Also, they were involved in intermittent strife until 63 BCE. Consequently these heroes authoritatively made the Law of Moses relevant to national life to preserve this 'protective hedge' around the nation. There were 6000-9000 Pharisees, who were mainly town dwellers formulating new refined rules and to purify religious obedience.

.2c-12
What might be seen as rival forces that influence pupils?

These gatekeepers of the Hebrew Torah analyzed it into 613 precepts of which 248 were positive and 365 were negative. For example, 39 activities (e.g. hunting) were prohibited on the Sabbath and detailed rules applied especially in relationship to work and food. The were a self-perpetuating religious hierarchy whose scholarly authority imposed its will on the populace. In their religious debates they tended to atomize texts but once their hotly debated decisions had been agreed detail they expected everybody to conform to their conclusions. They feared Israel would become disunited, which they believed would prevent the advent of the messianic age. Although they saw themselves as the People's Party Jesus saw that it resulted in a negative view of God. Jesus' background illustrates that teaching occurs within a cultural context that influences attitudes and understandings.

The religious authorities could quell Galileans and teach them but not force them to learn! There was an appearance of obedience but many were waiting to be released. They might become wealthier but their success was rejected by leaders from Jerusalem. Jesus knew that this was not the true fulfilment of the Law because, for example, the leaders were not healing the broken hearted.

As self-appointed custodians of the truth, the Pharisees found it difficult to conceive that their perception of God was flawed. Hence, Jesus was seen as a non-conformist who jeopardized national security and religious truth by teaching practices that appeared to conflict with the Mosaic Law. The 'guardians of the truth' permitted minimal and predictable changes but Jesus' perception was rejected. These tensions were not unlike aspects of society today.

Figure 8 shows a thoroughly Jewish person living within many cultural demands. His radicalism not only questioned hereditary privileges but highlighted dangers that false prophets, messiahs and rabble-rousers had brought down upon the nation. These experiences, together with his revelations were the basis of his style of teaching. From his methods, content and handling of people we gain an insight into his biography because:
- He had learned within a working family.
- He had learned within a synagogue.
- He had learned within the Galilean culture.
- He had learned from within the prophetic tradition.
- He learned by observing the religious traditions.
- He learnt from the Hebrew Bible.

He was a decisive teacher but he was sensitive to the situation. His experiences coloured the arena of activity. It requires an imaginative leap to translate our minds to Jesus' background and adapt his holistic teaching methods to our situation but then we find that he was remarkably modern and more than a child of his time. He was thoroughly prepared because:
- He himself had a humble/humiliating birth, was penniless and became homeless.
- He had listened to and heard those who mourned.
- He had walked with those who were poverty stricken.
- He had felt compassion for those for whom he would weep.
- He saw that the people were in bondage to their own leaders.
- He had heard John the Baptist's ringing tones heralding at the coming Kingdom.
- He had a growing, radical understanding and a vision of God the Father.

These were likely situations that shaped much of his teaching...

After his cousin, John the Baptist, briefly came out of the desert like a traditional prophet protesting against the evil in the land, only to be beheaded by Herod, Jesus continued the preaching but with a vital difference. His fresh teaching about God the Father, the vision of the peaceful Messiah, the Kingdom of God and that spirituality went beyond obeying the Law of Moses and involved an

.2c-13
Select any other aspect of his background that might be important.

everyday trust in their heavenly Father. This was to be a moral and spiritual open community. Jesus had to change attitudes. But how? He displayed major elements such as:

- He was *secure* in what he was doing.
- He had *considered* every aspect and implication of his work.
- Apparently, his *preparations* had been thorough.
- He knew how he would achieve *his* goals.
- He made *clear statements* that encouraged existing expectations of those who had 'ear to hear' and offered surprises that engendered hope.
- He displayed *competences*, which encouraged people.
- He was responsive *and met needs* that fostered faith and achieved an understanding of his teaching and enabled them commoners to submit willingly to his goals.

Indeed, he encouraged those who followed him to make vital decisions. He was people centred and loved and respected those around him.

An initial crisis

After a short preliminary preaching tour, his first major crisis was in the synagogue at his hometown of Nazareth where he himself had learned to read the scriptures and to worship God. One can hardly imagine the turmoil when he uttered the following words.

> *The spirit of the Lord is upon me, because he has anointed me to preach good news to the poor. He has sent me to proclaim release to the captives and recovering of sight to the blind, to set at liberty those who are oppressed, to proclaim the acceptable year of the Lord. Today this scripture has been fulfilled in your hearing.*

He alarmed people by speaking of God blessing Gentiles. That was too bad! This young man was well thought of and yet he was committing the unforgivable sin of blasphemy! It appears that everybody, including his own family, were stunned in amazement – after all wasn't he only Joseph's son? But even at this early stage in his ministry it is possible to see certain qualities that would be repeated frequently. His teaching sources were situationally relevant. As he faced the people and the Scribes and Pharisees in particular, he quoted from their supreme authority – the Law and the Prophets. He went on to say, "Doubtless you will quote to me this proverb, 'Physician, heal yourself..........'" He then proceeded to say that God is not solely focused on the welfare of Israel. Again he illustrated this from the Scriptures – and mentioned the case of Naaman the gentile Syrian who was healed of leprosy in the days of Elisha, the prophet. He was rejected and the people tried to stone him but he escaped and went to such places as Capernaum, which became his preaching centre. His vision had been elevated to 'a call' that he could not resist. But the problem was that he was teaching people who had a different 'world view'. His was a rugged form of teaching. There were few resources; everything was dependent upon his personal impact. But how memorable would his visit be once he moved on. Exciting? Yes! But how effective?

- Would he be seen as a mere transient prophet like John the Baptist?
- Could he be a long-term leader and teacher?
- Could he be perceived as the messiah?
- Could he motivate them at into a new sacrificial lifestyle?
- How memorable would his message be?
- Could he begin to socialize them into new attitudes that were contagious?
- Could he cause some to have new minds and attitudes? Could he...? Could he...? All of this was to be achieved within the vision and practice of the spiritual Kingdom of God.

.2c-14
What advantages and disadvantages did Jesus have being a Galilean?

This was the challenge to be faced if he was to be a master teacher. His teaching style was flexible and appropriate to the situation. Elsewhere he would probably have used different metaphors and reacted differently to the authorities etc. Although he normally taught calmly even in the face of acute danger, we read of his anger and sorrow. He responded to the moment, both in terms of place and content, and taught appropriately.

He *responded to needs and created aspirations for the people.* He quoted from the historic scriptures but he did not primarily look back, but stood where the people were and taught from *their everyday experiences.* Although he demanded repentance he *created optimism, changed expectations and showed his competence to fulfil them.* This was beyond official doctrine but was within his experience. But above all was his relationship with God the Father. And so began an adventurous, peripatetic ministry moving around some of the 200+ Galilean towns and villages and passing through Samaria and Phoenicia as well as visiting Jerusalem two or three times. Although he recognized the legitimate material demands of the Galileans, he spiritualized many responses, with the forgiveness of sins and faith in God being paramount. Everything had *an ethical basis* and 'darkness' could not be condoned. Teaching encompassed knowledge, skills, and morality within spirituality.

The situation was startling. The biblical account is far from comprehensive, but it is not surprising that he evoked a popular response and made change a possibility – especially after previous disappointments. Jesus taught, confident that his vision would be fulfilled. He selected apprentices to work with him in contrasting situations. Some wanted him to be a warrior Messiah and others asked him to leave them when he healed a sick man, but many poor and needy and some liberal Pharisees saw this as an exciting revelation.

From the outset Jesus established core principles. An early eye-opening statement was "…. the people who sat in darkness have seen a great light … the light has dawned." This kernel was culturally understandable and enabled the people to sense that they were not "sitting in the shadows" but had a transforming *light and hope*. He showed how this could be realised, which contrasted with the prevailing situation. As their role model, he explained and demonstrated his core message. Furthermore, he provided memorable experiences that enabled them to solve pertinent problems. His spiritual solutions probably originated from experiencing, observing and interpreting his own social and natural environment. He repudiated many historic nationalistic beliefs and developed a lifestyle and spiritual teachings based on service and sacrifice rather than physical power and tradition. Could this succeed, either then or now, in breaking through vested interests of privilege and power? And yet it became the basis of his teaching as the people entered into this light and expectancy. This was not totally novel but it required courage, and a spiritual and moral strength and was based on three major elements.

Teaching is personally costly, but so too is learning! Jesus had to do more than teach persuasively – he had to convince people it was worth leaving home and business and even incur the wrath of the authorities. It demanded careful consideration! From this emerged a sharp focus on God, himself and those around him with their beliefs and the wider world.

Figure 9

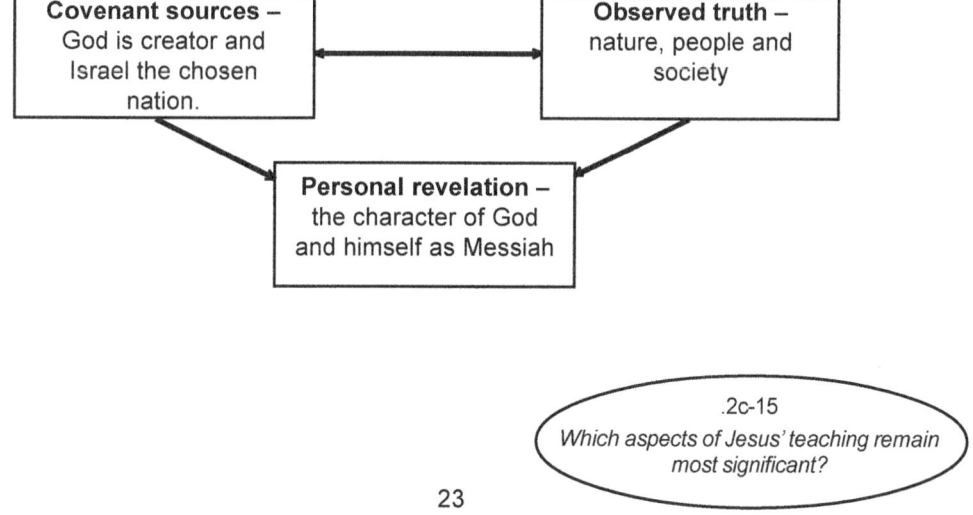

.2c-15
Which aspects of Jesus' teaching remain most significant?

'Tradition was King' and therefore one might expect to see considerable agreement between the religious leaders, the Galileans and Jesus. Fig. 8 shows there were areas of similarity between them. All said that 'the God of Israel is one God' who had given the Jews their authoritative Law, a holy capital called Jerusalem, a largely common culture and, to a lesser degree, a common language, but there were disagreements. The name Galilee could be translated 'the district of the pagans' and Galileans had only been accepted into Jewry for about a century. It was said that 'if a person wishes to be rich let him go north; if he wants to be wise let him come south'. Galilee was fertile and productive whereas Judea was a poor limestone area, but Galileans were regarded by the religious authorities as unreliable latecomers to the chosen nation who needed to be taught and watched. Might the surrounding deeply rooted Syrian culture contaminate the Jewish faith of the Galileans, who might then be tempted to stray from the historic Law of Moses?

Jesus' teaching was diverse and fresh. His expertise and calling were soon recognized. He became a role model and leader by virtue of his challenge, achievements and support. His teaching was rooted in secure relationships that went beyond repetitive conformity. His dominant verbal methods were just one aspect of his teaching. This was effective because the listeners felt accepted and there was a consistent ring to his core message as it unfolded. The elements of surprise, delight, mystery and novelty were matched with human links and personal authority. The overall pattern for establishing the scene soon became apparent.

Focus for Thought

Summary 1. This short chapter has contained analyses that illustrate Jesus' teaching styles, although their significance far exceeds any analysis.

Figure 10

Creative Problem Solving Personal Friends Outsiders Opposition	**Seven Aspects of Jesus' Characteristic Teaching**	*Core Message* Kingdom of God God the Father Reconciliation Confident faith
Interpersonal Relations Encouragement Support Appreciation Response to Faith		*Verbal Methods* Parables Discourse Conversation Question and Answer
Role Model Challenge Character Service Appreciative Leader	*Action Methods* Simple Lifestyle Parables in Action Meeting Needs Courage	*Expertize and Calling* Revelation Goals Authority Preparation

Figure 11 is a summary of major characteristics that have been introduced in varying degrees and will be developed subsequently. It can be useful when organizing information.

Summary 2. As we conclude this short examination of Jesus' background and teaching skills let us review them through Fig.11. This sketches his range of decisions and experiences. His goals reflected his rising vision that emerged during the hidden years and had been confirmed at his baptism. He knew his priorities and strategies to achieve these. He anticipated a range of responses to his vision but would not change his strategies. He knew what the vision ultimately entailed. Not everybody would be teachable but he would have a range of methods as he met various situations and 'mixed abilities' and attitudes.

.2c-16
Which aspects of Jesus' teaching (Fig 5/6/) have remained the most significant? Why?

Figure 12 is only concerned with Jesus' own learning / teaching experiences until he was at the height of his popularity. It can be shown that he went through some seven stages, each of which contained critically important issues (A-F). For example, at Stage One:

- He defined his goals and teaching strategies before he moved into the public sphere (A).
- He considered what he would do to achieve his goals (B).
- His vision of the Fatherhood of God and how to teach about the Kingdom was defined (C).
- His goals that were not changeable but were firmly rooted in this vision (D).
- He developed through teaching what was recognizable as being worthwhile (E).
- It would appear that his rising vision (Stage Two) resulted in an increasingly radical approach to religious faith (A) developed during his 'hidden years' (B).
- He developed a recognized authority that resulted in some public acclaim (C) that partly stemmed from his experiences, observations and related interpretations (D).
- He provided foundational evidence for his faith in his life's purpose (E).
- He felt his baptism personally confirmed his vision (F).
- He generated a personal trust in the Father (F).

.2c-17
Recall the Hidden Years. Which aspects were likely to be most significant?

Figure 11

General Issues	Summary 1 – Early Decisions Required By Jesus					
			c) Full understanding of the task	d) Range of likely responses		
A Goals	Goals/strategies universal but differ in their significance and effect	Examine the goals and their impact on action	Jesus' goals – clear vision plus for pupils understanding and knowledge	The goals were rooted in a long-term vision	Stable moral spiritual and teaching of recognised worth	The divine imperative of personal faith in the Father
B The rising vision	Jesus' holy radicalism	His growing awareness during the years	His vision's imperative and need to implement it	Pre-baptism experiences observations interpreted	Evidence and conviction	Baptism and confirmation of the vision
C Issues raised by the vision	The basic issues of implementing the vision	Arousing and damping popular opinion	Competences to implement the vision	The temptations - rejecting force	Rejecting spectacular signs	Reject priority personal needs
D Response to the vision	Popular expectations- excitement - needed gradual tuition	Conflict with the religious authorities, legitimate interpreters	Political authority is feared up rising	Disciples were taught, prepared to continue his work	The need for clear strategy of product and process goals	A match between his priorities and their priorities
E vision in action	Crowds needed memorable teaching causing them to think / respond	He met urgent needs	He responded to calls of faith	He created hope	Demonstrated care and love	He remained close to the people he taught
F Teach the vision	Knowledge - what shall we teach? Absolute core concepts. No relativism	Continuity with past / reinterpret traditional teaching	New / radical - the father and changing perceptions of God	The new concept of the Kingdom New attitude to the law	New focus on teaching method, Long-term interaction	Relatively little information Was taught
G The teachables	Inclusive policy	Who to teach: The underclass	The Pharisees etc – if they are 'born again'.	No test other than a sustained commitment	An intensive small group	The humble, the merciful, the poor and needy

---

Personality Factor – 2

Which influences on Jesus 'Hidden Years' may or may not have shaped his personality?

.2c-18
To what extent might Jesus really be a role model to the 'common man'?

Figure 12 (see summary)

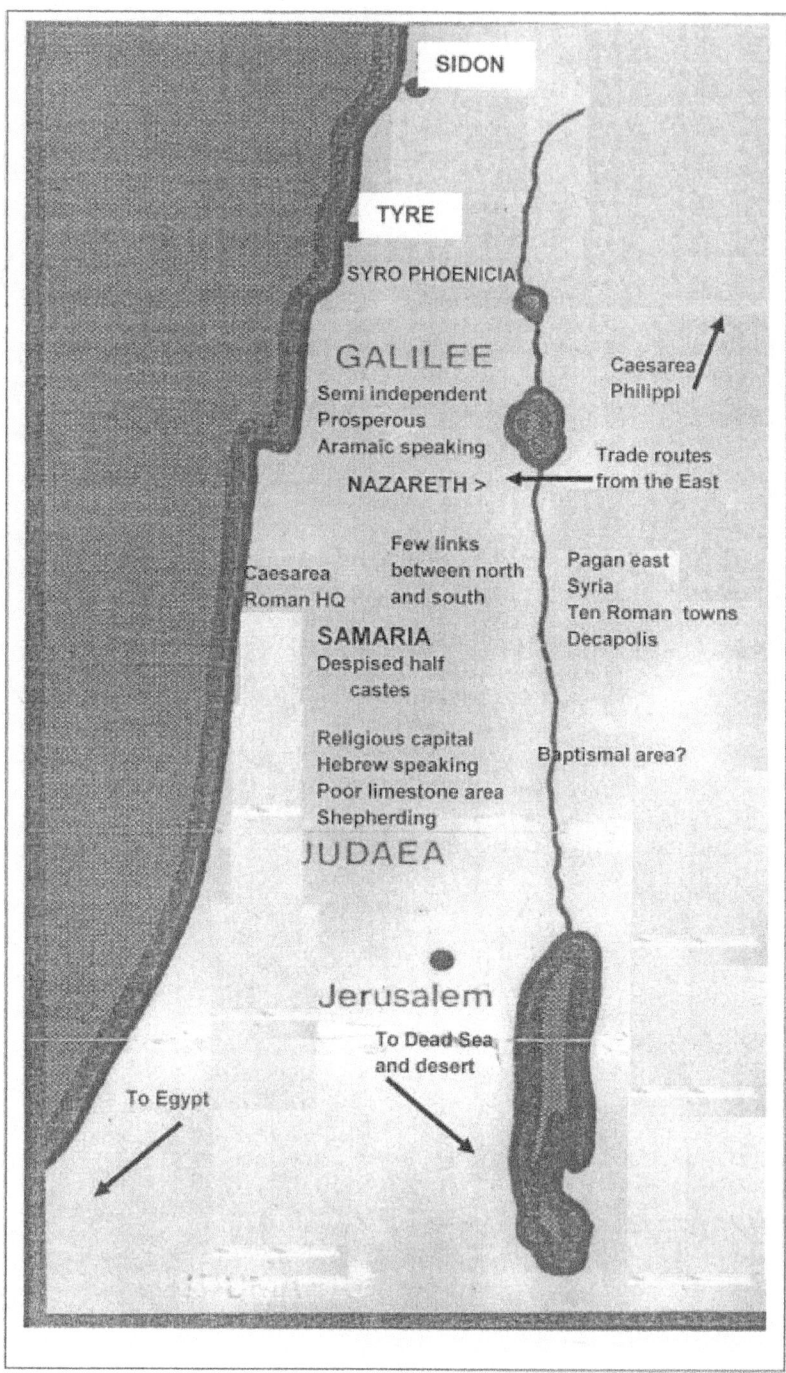

.2c-19
What advantages and disadvantages did Jesus have being a Galilean?

Chapter 2

A Teaching Style – Traditional or Progressive

We all wonder how people will react to us. For Jesus this was imperative. He had to resolve many problems. How would he persuade and motivate people? Would they learn? Let us consider some problems he faced and how his solutions are relevant to teachers today.

Teaching and learning are not mechanical processes. Ideally an interaction that exceeds traditional formulaic patterns is required. To list skills and beliefs and tell people to learn and do them is usually insufficient. Jesus knew he was not only imparting knowledge but also persuading them that it was worth staking their lives on It – a hazardous decision!

Teaching is widely related to the characteristics shown in Fig.13. Teaching is based on values and goals that may or may not be stated explicitly. From these emerge teaching, relationships and responses of those being taught... and so it was with Jesus and the Pharisees. They both followed the teaching of the Law and the Prophets and met stringent religious requirements such as pilgrimages to the Temple but there were major differences.

Figure 13

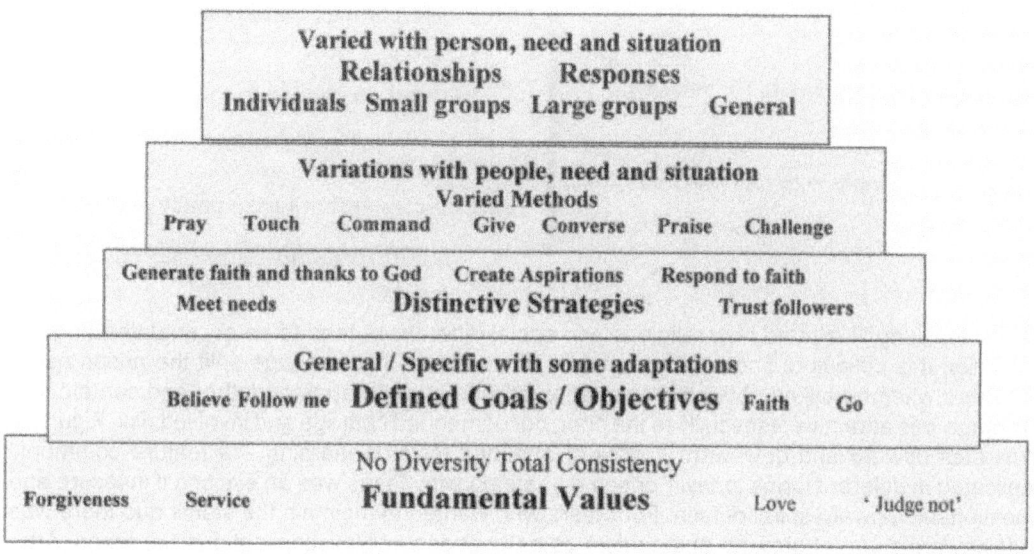

For ease of understanding these differences might be compared as follows:

Pharisaic teaching stressed conformity to corporate values + authoritative powers + established, replicable knowledge/methods/ teaching. This model appeared secure and able to generate stable learning, standards and national security that would lead to the coming of the Messiah. There was, however, a missing dimension that Jesus added to his teaching, namely freewill relationships based on love and morality.

His teaching was a new spiritual contract based upon:
- Generating hope but requiring repentance and freewill discipleship.
- Developing fresh recognizable knowledge and obedience to the Father.
- Meeting needs in various ways.

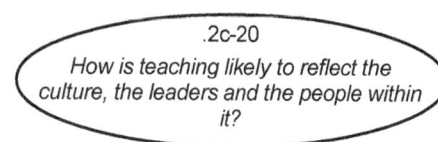

This was underpinned by a spiritual 'guarantee' – but would it be sufficient? Probably not. The guarantee was its mediation through a confident, interactive teacher/pupil relationship.

Jesus' value/spiritually based teaching required long-term commitment. He confronted people with the fact that learning, with all its promises, is demanding. He was not fazed that relatively few wanted the change for which he looked. He resolutely refused to modify his teaching but he stood where others stood and made learning attractive …but demanding!

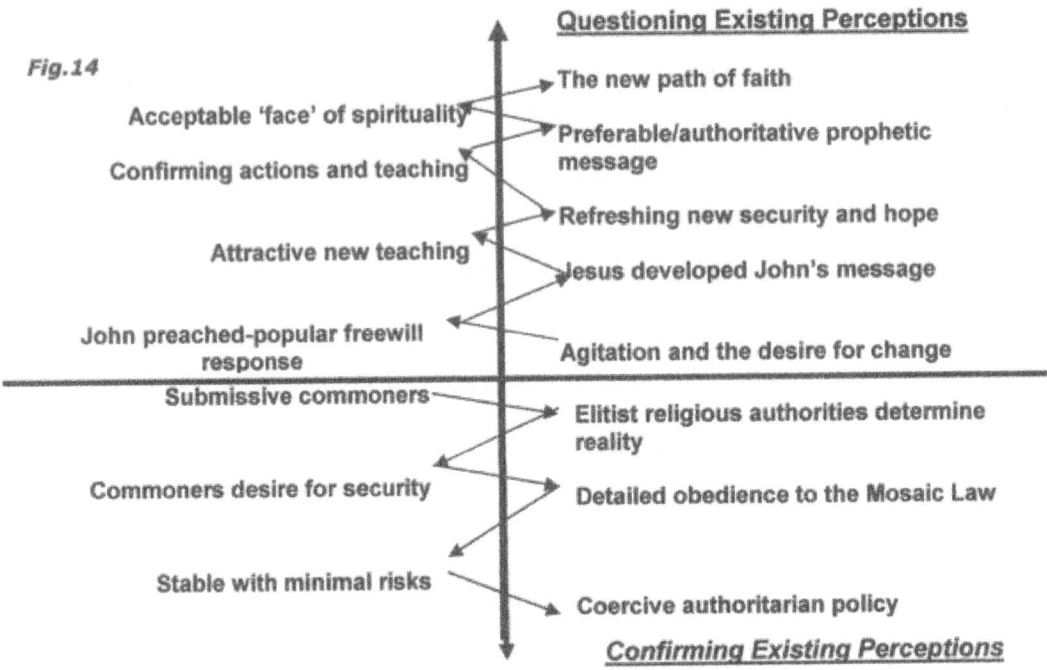

Fig.14

Jesus' teaching illustrated how religious and social differences tend to be accentuated (Fig.12-14) when it is difficult to find common ground. Jesus' dramatic message split the nation as he predicted when he talked about the separation of mother and daughter, father and son etc. His message was attractive, especially to the poor, but demanded courage and involved risk. Figure 14 illustrates upward and downward spirals of attitudes towards learning – a feature commonly replicated in different forms today. For some, learning with Jesus was an exciting if insecure and questionable upward spiral of faith. For others who wanted to maintain the status quo there was a downward spiral of growing antagonism as perceptions and misconceptions hardened. After centuries of suffering, the ferocity of the nation's guardians was understandable. Stability must prevail!

Neither Jesus' message nor the methods were completely new. The notion that the Kingdom of God was amongst them arrested attention and was memorable and motivating. He was striking at the very heart of factors that determined responses. But without actions he would probably have remained a carpenter from Nazareth in the common estimation. He gave a sense of freedom by satisfying certain needs, which granted some authority but his inclusive attitude to outsiders and the rejected had a mixed reception!

Miracles may not 'often' be performed now, but his pattern of response remains applicable. He shared their language, entered into, enhanced and created new aspirations and was somebody with whom they could relate. Thus, he enabled those who wanted to learn to do so. He knew that coercion has little long-term value and ultimately learning is dependent upon pupils' motivation.

.2c-21
How is authority achieved and maintained?

- Motivation was based on pupils' sense of acceptance, needs and aspirations being met.
- Success was derived from the quality of the relationship between the teacher and the pupils and their mutual perception needed to be positive.
- His teaching had to meet certain high priority, fundamental needs.

Not all were persuaded and motivated similarly because their priorities, personal characters and histories differed. For example, Matthew the tax collector may have heard John the Baptist's severe warning to the cheating tax gatherers, reflected on his words and so responded readily when Jesus repeated them. Simon, a Zealot, had probably been disappointed but the fire of messianic hope still burned when he heard Jesus. An aspect of the genius of Jesus' teaching was that he met the motivational requirements of his pupils. Furthermore, he not only appreciated and accepted them, but he also recognized the need for mutuality – because 'the greater needed the lesser'!

Jesus' policy of inclusion contrasted with the exclusiveness of the religious leaders. Even his own followers were shocked by his tolerance of others. Not only did he say, 'whosoever is not against me is for me.' He worked and moved easily amongst Gentiles. Interestingly, he recognized the qualities and defended a person who preached a similar message and yet did not want to join Jesus' close-knit group. Some would have destroyed the man.

Figure 15

He had rejected using extrinsic motivation (rewards etc) to attract people. Many wanted to follow him, but whilst he would not reject the crowds, he relied on those who were intrinsically motivated. He wanted people who shared his vision and did not look for material rewards even though they did not understand its full implications.

Although they might not conceive of his ideas and possibilities, they could be expected to respond to the evidence. Jesus was a risk-taker who developed confidence and obedience in pupils, That raised philosophical questions regarding control, freewill and teaching. His radicalism was epitomized by his attitude to children whom he blessed whereas they were often treated relatively poorly.

Meeting needs

Abraham Maslow was a psychologist who during the 1940's and onwards stated that all people share generic needs, which he analysed into seven hierarchical categories, as shown. He stated that most basic needs are founded on survival.. But what does that mean? He claimed that his analysis of needs can be applied to all aspects of life, including teaching. He suggested that teachers should enable their pupils to move up through the stages sequentially. This is a form of care. The principle is that needs should be satisfied at one stage before they proceed to a higher level which culminate in self-actuality (i.e. the fulfilment of one's potentials). And so needs and aspirations gradually merge. Jesus could certainly have agreed with certain aspects of this, even if not totally, because these needs are universally apparent even though they may take differing forms and priorities.

.2c-22
How might the "need" of self-actualisation be taught?

Physiological needs – food, drink and sleep

This model has been influential because of the tendency to give priority to physical needs and security, but the analysis is too neat to be true. Who would claim that love and esteem are less fundamental than physiological needs when people willingly make sacrifices? Also children can exhibit these stages concurrently at a young age? Even so, it does highlight human tendencies about teaching that we diminish at our peril. Maslow agreed that most people never pass through all seven stages and not necessarily so in strict sequence but the principle is useful. A major difference is the omission of spirituality as commonly defined.

Jesus had a different perception of man. He too recognized that people have essential needs that can be physical, social and emotional, but he saw them in the context of a spiritual dimension of human experience. Therefore, Jesus could comfortably take all strands from this and similar models and reinterpret them in the context of the Kingdom of God, which he saw as having a personal and community basis. Maslow's elements would be integral to any teaching environment as perceived by Jesus. He would, however, see them within spiritual priorities which might consist of the below, but which would not be hierarchical.

Figure 16

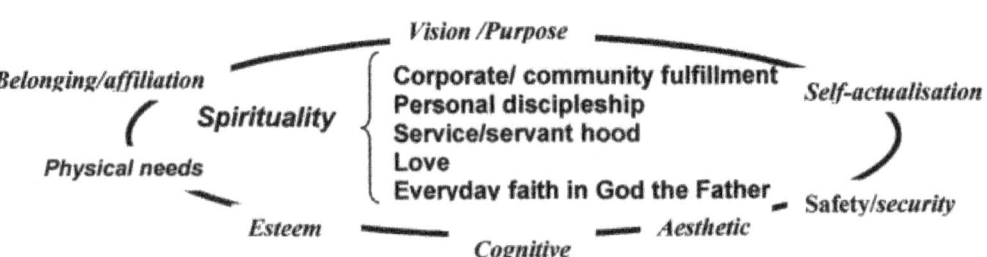

Jesus saw spirituality as the unifying feature of man's psychogenic needs. As a Jew he would have used the verse '…do justice, love mercy /kindness and walk humbly with your God.' as a defining summary. This spirituality shaped his teaching and was illustrated by his high regard for children and sensitivity to the interpersonal nature of teaching. Overall his holistic view of man brought together cognitive, emotional, personal and social and spiritual elements of life and looked for personal welfare, acceptance, belonging, achievement, understanding and knowledge. Jesus' disciples increasingly displayed an overriding confidence in the lowest of Maslow's needs being met and also being motivated to achieve the highest needs within a spiritual context. The implications of this are shown below. Fig.17. Their teaching was validated by tradition and new teachings were only recognized if they were in accord with tradition.

Figure 17

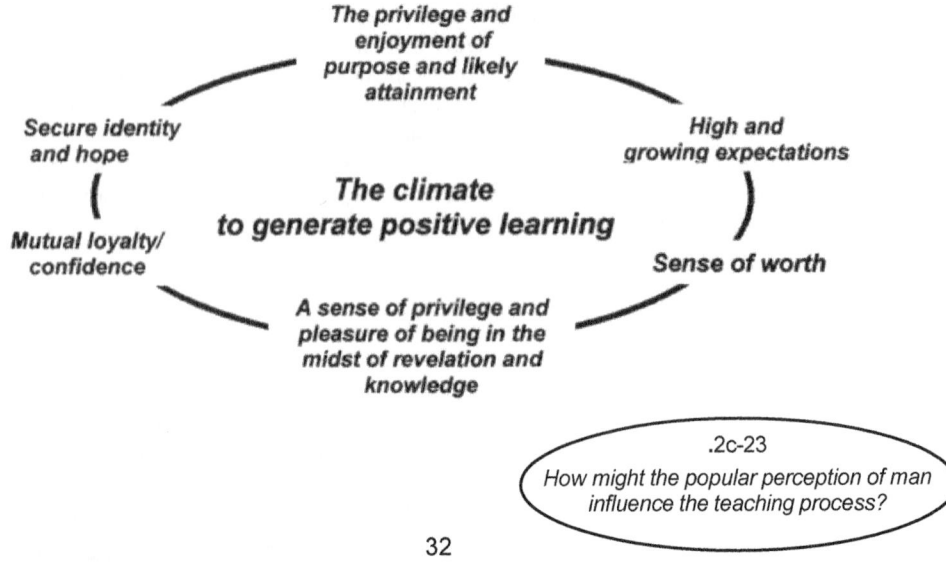

.2c-23
How might the popular perception of man influence the teaching process?

Similarities and differences

Jesus' situation reflected the persistent general life pattern of competition for food, influence wealth and power. These tensions have been particularly notable between traditionalists and progressives. Although the terms can be ambiguous they have been especially evident in teaching and learning as well as in religion and in the the distribution of wealth and power. Many people gravitate towards groups that reflect this distinction. The two extremes of traditionalism and progressivism might be characterized as follows:

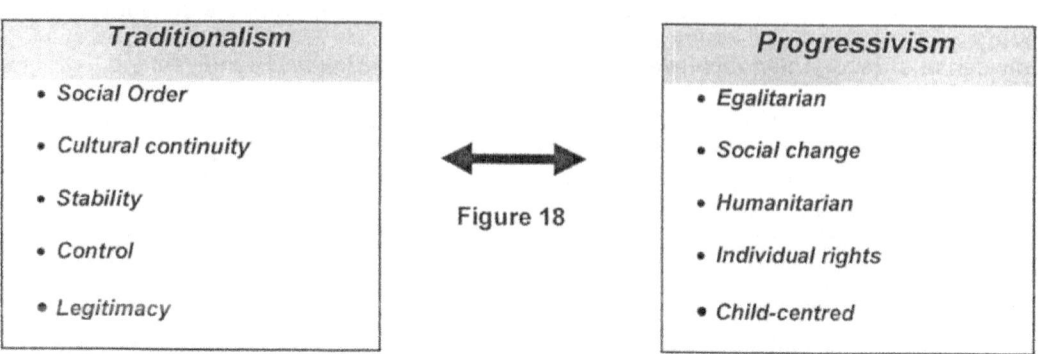

Figure 18

Traditional religious authorities generally taught through a process of didactic reception learning(see Ch.15). By this they controlled and presented that listeners learned in its entirety but it was flawed in respect of memory retention and attitude formation (see Ch.9)and left inadequate room for reflection and personal awareness. Their teaching was/is validated if they were in accord with established authorities.

Jesus too was a traditionalist because he accepted the authority of the Mosaic Law but he took it to a new level of understanding that changed attitudes and created a fresh and invigorated faith. Initially, his teaching strategy contained six major characteristics:

- He aroused hope by positive statements and actions.
- His statements could be *reflected* upon and discussed easily,
- His short imaginative illustrations were left for the listeners to *interpret*.
- His *personal authority* accentuated the distinction between his and official teaching.
- His pupils had opportunities for *experiential learning* based upon what they had seen.
- He *encouraged* people and *responded* to faith no matter what their background.

The two contrasting systems of teaching had common elements but Jesus' was a culmination of the prophetic train of thought that defended the exploited and offered a new degree of simplicity, freedom and relationship with God within an *enlightened traditional framework. He had authority without being authoritarian and was teaching them within a 21st century definition of reception learning* (see Ch.13). The contrast between these teaching styles has been notable. Jesus did not question the validity of tradition provided:

- It was not used primarily to sustain the current control /order.
- It was not authoritarian.
- It was not destroying legitimate freedoms and aspirations. It was not the restrictive tool of static doctrines.

Jesus characterized tradition by *service*. He was restating and developing the traditions of the Jewish faith. He remained true to the core beliefs, and with the central concepts secure, he challenged current assumptions of spiritual truth. This relatively progressive attitude towards tradition was and is significant for all levels of teaching. The issue was to prevent core beliefs becoming ossified and to develop a fresh spirituality. It defined knowledge and teaching in its widest sense. But what were its implications? Did it mean that a polarity such as that which developed (Figs.18,19) might occur now?

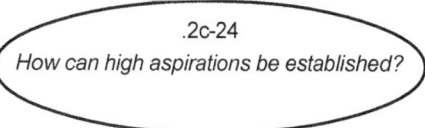

.2c-24
How can high aspirations be established?

Figure 19

Extended tradition	Renewed Tradition
Authoritarian	*Trusted friendship/ leader*
Critical imposed teaching	*Short term needs – long term values*
Irrelevant to individual needs	*Shared aspirations / expectations*
Low sense of recognition /achievement	*Recognition and achievement*
Prescribed nationalistic vision	*Universal vision of love reconciliation*
Little personal development	*Individual/group persuasion*
Few personal prospects	*Identification//empowerment*
Underlying negativity	*Positive words, actions, prospects*

Perhaps Jesus could be better described as a *radical traditionalist.*

Jesus' strategy was contrary to popular wisdom, but he insisted that it was the only way. His entry, teaching and exit strategies of love and service appeared unlikely to succeed. This high-risk strategy, and lack of recognition meant that his main resources were his vision of God, his ability to attract people as he taught and served them and his lifestyle. He did not impose his will on people but he was emphatic about the outcome if his way was rejected. His authenticity and wisdom were there to be examined by those with eyes to see.

Fig.20 shows how religious scholars modified their historic law by case law. A problem was discussed together with any fragmented evidence. When agreement was reached, they went to the synagogues where the people were expected to obey their decisions. The process was authoritative and based on an established body of revealed truth. It covered every aspect of life, especially how to keep the Sabbath. For example, people could not eat eggs that were laid on the Sabbath. This process was relatively democratic and ensured religious and social stability. Reality was defined and circumscribed within a systematic theology based upon the Torah, tradition and the Hebrew language. The Galileans accepted this, but there was a silent protest against this imposition by Judeans who were virtually foreigners to those in the North.

A Pharisees and Scribes teaching model

The general direction of the teaching – from heritage to expert to the people (Fig. 20) shows the normal pattern of authoritative teaching. This did not concern most Galileans who expected nothing else. His teaching *process* was the vital way in which he took tradition and personal vision to meet the needs of the people.

Figure 20

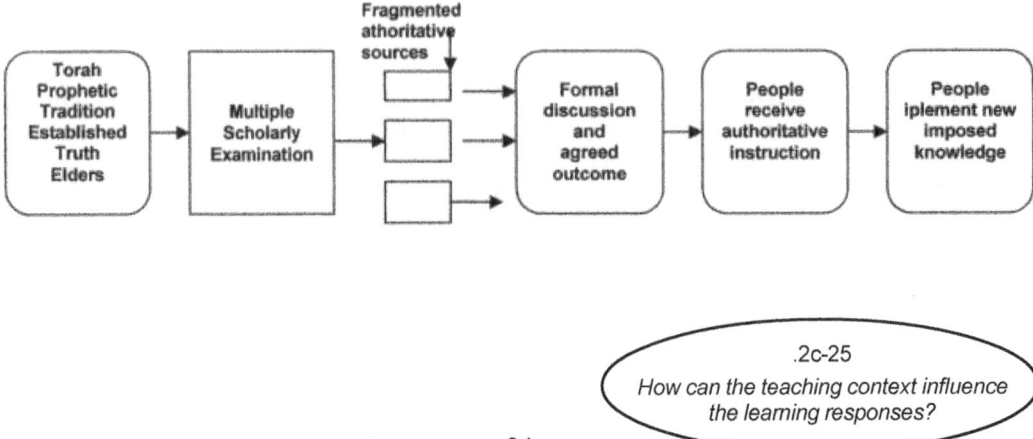

.2c-25
How can the teaching context influence the learning responses?

Figure 21

Conservative (Law Centred)	Characteristic Features Tradition / Progressive		Radical (Kingdom of God)
Desired Outcomes	Religious Authorities	Jesus	Desired Outcomes
Conformity Knowledge Information based Rote learning Separatist Content driven Standards Restrictive Established Elitism Historic / Past orientated Rules based Normative Predictable product Cultural replication/ order Tradition Authority Obedience	Control Gatekeepers National unity Official learning Personal status Formality Stability Maintenance No novelties Privilege Legalistic Linguistic Analytical Complexity Linear Formulaic	Servant hood Spiritual Sacrificial Mission Love Restoration Vision Risk taker Faith Inspirational Simplicity Relational Conceptual 'Big Picture' 'Hands on' Holistic	Trust Change Team building Humility Global Expansionist Personal development Principle / value based Forward orientated Process orientated Diagnostic Non-elitist Exploratory Challenge Confidence Service

Fig. 21 shows Jesus' pattern of authoritative teaching. This did not concern most Galileans who expected nothing else. His teaching *process* was the vital way in which he took tradition and personal vision to meet the needs of the people.

The major differences were: the relatively pedantic nature of the established teaching….

- but… Jesus' principle-based teaching was likely to result in interaction.
- The religious authorities taught from set texts and an historic perspective but… Jesus taught primarily from the listeners' situational context and the prophets.
- The religious authorities insisted upon a uniform response from the people but… Jesus accepted the likelihood that there would be a range of responses.

Teaching methods and outcomes were deeply rooted and differentiated. The two central columns compare their characteristic priorities and habitual stances. These were not mutually exclusive. Jesus, like the conservatives, was a 'gatekeeper' of knowledge and values. But there was a tendency for the values inherent in the central columns to generate teaching that approximated to the desired outcomes of the two outer columns and whose differences were increasingly apparent.

These are a caricature of tradition and an idealization of Jesus' radicalism, but the implications of these polar differences were influential. Fig.13 showed that the crucial factor was and is the value base. Although one may see teaching where there is a disjunction between methods and values, normally there is agreement. Jesus' values were absolute and deeply penetrated his methodology that fostered experience and trust. Of course, formal instruction is appropriate to teach skills such as Morse code but is less suited to lessons involving social attitudes that require discussion and reflection. Jesus' radical approach involved risk and placed responsibility on people. Would they trust his non-coercive mission?

Jesus had clear understandings about authority, knowledge, the teacher's role, the pupils' role and relationships that we recognize today. He did not impose control but rather created hope even though it appeared to end in personal failure. He did not simply impart knowledge but offered what is worthwhile, legitimate and provides a pattern for personal development.

.2c-26
Why might Jesus be considered wise to allow people so much free will?

Much of the relatively progressive attitude of Jesus has been ossified by tradition, but that does not negate the principles being explored here and which will be amplified subsequently. Jesus believed all could understand his teaching. He identified a fault in the logic of the traditionalists, namely that it amounted to an elitist imposition of control, in a similar way to Victorian landowners who did not want workers and women to have the vote.

Jesus' radical and progressive teaching

Jesus appeared to be radical but he was not progressive as commonly defined today, when it can be synonymous with humanist child-centred education. In extreme cases (e.g. Carl Rogers) the philosophy is of non-directive education based on self-motivation and effective learning coming from within a person. Normally progressive education is not taken to extremes but teaching is not overtly directive. It might be described as a sliding scale of freedom and directed tuition. Although Jesus clearly did believe that it is both possible and desirable to instruct pupils, he realized that pupil motivation must be self generated and come from watching and listening to himself, their authoritative role-model and teacher who was also their trusted friend. A broad characterization of his teaching is shown in Figure 22.

Figure 22

Authority/ Learning Structure	Teaching Roles	Characteristic Learning	Characteristic for Teaching and Learning	Assumptions
Professional gatekeeper of absolute knowledge and definitive aims. Overall control An enabling teacher High order aims and long term learning and responses Moving towards the capacity to take initiatives and make judgments	Teacher fulfils the roles of: Demonstrator Instructor Coach Mentor Role model Assumes intrinsic motivation	Pupils have the opportunity to: Listen Watch Decide Follow Replicate Discuss the new experiences High degree of interaction / involvement	Teaching based on: Core concepts Situational Opportunities Traditional authoritative knowledge updated Personal need Expressions of faith Frequent Demonstrations	Learning structure Peer-group formed at an early stage High degree of trust /interaction Ongoing discussion Intimate tuition
Traditional Highly directed		Directed instruction and personal enquiry/motivation	Non – directional High personal motivation	

Although progressivism has not been a powerful mainstream force in *public* education, it has been influential in causing children to be seen in a different light. Progressives would empathize with Jesus who regarded children as sacred, blessed them fervently and recognized that they should be seen as people in their own right and not merely vessels to be filled with knowledge., Progressives have insisted on the priority of *good interactive relationships* as a basis for teaching and learning. This might be characterized as follows (Fig.23).

.2c-27
What is most likely to want to make people learn?

Figure 23

Progressive Expectations / Relationships	Traditional Norms and Relationships
Appreciation/recognition of personal effort	Criticism/work within accepted cultural norms
Giving pupils quality time	Time is a pressured component
Promoting a quietness of spirit	Accepting that worry is an aspect of effort
Authority is felt to be personally fair	Authority and submission may be deemed unfair
Confidence/trust are based on acceptance	Rejection is likely for non-conformists
Mutual giving promotes good relationships	Relationships are unequal in power and demand
Security and exploration lead to success	Success is related to conformity to standards

This indicates that teaching and learning are inextricably linked and based upon establishing high quality interactive relationships. From progressivism flow relative values that are more fluid than those of the traditionalists and Jesus. The resultant teaching methods have promoted a higher degree of independent learning and personal initiatives. Figure 23 shows similarities and differences between Jesus and progressives in respect of attitudes children learning. For example, although Jesus' attitude had progressive traits, he saw authority and knowledge in absolute terms. He insisted that people should understand ultimate elements of discipline and authority. He accepted that people have their opinions and make judgements but his were the measure of truth. Today children often give opinions that have little or no factual basis, but teachers may not demand evidence for fear of discouraging them and so the notion that one person's view is as good as another's gains currency.

One can hardly say that Jesus had reliable relationships with crowds, hence the learning outcome was unreliable and often transient. But his interactive relationship with his followers was of a different order and had the potential to achieve high quality, long term results.

Similarities and differences between Jesus and progressive teachers (Fig.23) can be deceptive. Both the radical Jesus and progressives have used a rich array of methods to achieve intrinsic motivation but with significant value differences. Hence it should be reiterated that Jesus was radical traditionalist.

Figure 24

Common areas between Jesus and Progressives	Differences between Jesus and Progressives
Attitude towards pupil / work and achievement Experiential learning Everyday environmental evidence to support findings etc Group interaction and enablement Use of small groups Process goals (see page ix) Foster and use close relationships	Knowledge- revealed /absolute v relativism Teaching – Top down v Bottom Up (page ix) Authority – Leader v Guide Democratic basis? Direction – leadership v choice / negotiation Leader's ongoing immersion Jesus' precise product goals Relationship and response elements modify methods etc.

.2c-28
Why do some regard Pharisaic traditional teaching as doing violence against learners?

Characteristic 'progressive' priorities

Figure 25

Learning Structures	Teaching Role	Characteristic Learning	Characteristic Assumptions for Teaching and Learning	
Aims - highly flexible to meet pupils' individual needs. Psychologically based with a relative view of knowledge.	Teachers long-term role of guide and facilitator who is also a catalyst. Teachers focus on high degree of long-term personal and social development.	Frequent negotiations between teacher and pupils in content and method. Focus-decision-making, problem solving as part of the intellectual development	Ethos of co-operation and discussion regarding task formulation and completion. Teachers develop learning based on situational opportunities, pupil experiences and interests	The structure revolves around peer groups, interaction and personal responsibility within peer groups. The teacher takes on a role of a mentor or coach

The value based teaching model (Fig.13) illustrates a traditional teaching stance where the 'relationship and response' factors follow detailed planning procedures. A progressive teaching stance modifies this. The values component remain crucial but the 'relationship and response' elements are paramount and can modify the learning process.

Figure 26 indicates three teaching stances that may appear extreme and mutually exclusive. Although they highlight comparisons, they can be complementary. The 11 vertical factors indicate the range of differences between the three categories of teachers being considered and show the distinct form of decision-making and assumptions when teaching. Even so, the teaching stances form the basis of many eclectic teaching and learning approaches. Jesus' distinctive attitude and practices were in contrast to both traditionalists and many progressive teachers. These will be examined in Part C, but here it provides an early pointer to an outline ideal teaching and learning model with which Jesus would have been comfortable.

This brings us to the nub of the question. We have seen that traditionalists assumed that pupils should be controlled and instructed efficiently using established knowledge. The Jewish emphasis was on the commitment of the disciple to the rabbi. But Jesus not only reciprocated commitment, he initiated it. His unwavering commitment to his pupils characterized the impetus of the teaching/learning process.

This concept of a mutual covenant between the teacher and the pupils was the historic picture of the relationship between God and Israel. Jesus developed it and this commitment of the teacher to the pupils inspired their mutuality and illustrated that the principle goes beyond religion and acts as a basis of life and long-term learning. Progressives have tended to have more romantic ideals of pupils, emphasizing their positive motivation and responses as the natural outcome of the inquiring mind and the relationship between all participants in teaching and learning at every level. However, this is vulnerable to interacting variables.

Jesus also taught within a dynamic interacting continuum as shown below (Fig.26):

.2c-29
By which criteria do pupils judge their teachers?

Figure 26

Issues	TRADITIONAL Autocratic/ Directive Religious Authorities	RADICAL/TRADITIONAL Benevolent/charismatic/ Enabler Jesus	PROGRESSIVE Relationship Performance 'Progressives'
Authority	Absolute authority centred - imposed conformity/informatn	Absolute principled but pupil orientated/focused	Authority relative and pupil related frequently humanist
Values	Source-Revealed Law Key Words- Control, Continuity Legitimacy, Initiation Exclusion / Identity	Source- God's character Key Words- Absolute, Individual service Hope, Authority Identity / Inclusion	Source- Rationality Key Words- Enlightened tolerance Humanitarianism Personal development Relativity Inclusion
Goals	Closed / restricted path Prescription Imposition Cultural maintenance Repeat established knowledge Dependency / obedience	Point pathway-choices Strong insistence regarding best paths Powerful sense of mission / purpose	Recommended paths Maximize personal and social awareness Long term personal Independent learning
Knowledge	Revelation, tradition, prescribed Absolute –control	Revealed principles but flexible in operation Absolute pupil orientated	Relative Negotiated with Individual choice
Strategies	Teacher control Instruction Recall Repetition Memorisation Accuracy	Teacher led Teacher role model Teacher demonstration Mutual trust Short and long term challenges	Facilitator/coach / mentor Creativity Investigation Exploration Problem solving
Teaching Methods	Precise formal instruction Reception learning Social conformity Large Groups	Leader explanation Group interaction and enablement Reversible, active/ response Individual, small large groups Teacher demonstration and pupil experimentation	Democratic negotiated Generalised social values, rights Freedom Enquiry/guidance/ choice Individual / small groups Discussion/enablet
Teaching process	Top-down teacher control	Top down in principle but with responses matching pupil needs and attitudes	Bottom up with Top down guidance
Teaching Materials	Traditional sources Confined and imposed	Traditional sources plus varied everyday materials relevant to pupils	Relevant source materials vary with pupil interests
Teacher/ pupil relationship	Formal /erarchical Distanced	Orderly but close/ intimate where appropriate	Close interactive relationships
Methods	Use of standard texts Reception of scholarly established knowledge	Personal discourse Mass instruction Discussion Peer initiatives	First hand enquiry Second hand investigative learning Open discussion etc Personal initiatives Peer group initiatives
Responses	Limited freedom Linear interaction	Freewill interaction Supporting / monitoring aid Personal response to challenges	Personal initiatives Highly cooperative interactive, responsive

.2c-30
Why do some pupils 'break the mould'?

Although Jesus did not conform to either the traditional or progressive teaching models. There were common elements. Instead it can be related to modern imaginative methods that indicate:

- The teacher's authority lies predominantly in his expertise and leadership.
- The teacher has the responsibility of setting the goals for the lessons.
- The teacher is in authority without being crudely authoritarian.
- Absolute principles and knowledge can be taught within a wide range of methods.
- The pupils are willing apprentices.
- The teacher develops experiential work with pupils.

The outworking of these will be illustrated subsequently and a degree of enlightened common sense will probably evoke a nod of every day approval that says, "Of course!", which is almost beyond argument

Summary 2a

Jesus showed the following about his priorities:

- The teacher looks for and uses *incidental happenings*.
- The teacher knows that if the pupils are to learn they must be *cared for*.
- The teacher *works with* the pupils where possible.
- The teacher should *define the priorities* and pursue them *sensitively*.
- Although the teacher has responsibility for the pupils' learning, ultimately it is the pupils' responsibility to make the sacrifice to learn.

Summary 2b

Although responses to Jesus varied, they were inevitably tied closely to his approach to them. It has been indicated by Harold Belben that those who reacted positively, were drawn by the manner of his teaching. He suggested that there were at least seven distinct qualities that made him attractive and his teaching effective.

- He offered people his friendship, good relationships and love.
- He started where they were and empathized with them.
- He listened to what they said.
- He searched out the root of their problems.
- He took their questions seriously and showed respect.
- He sometimes asked favours of them.
- He did not force himself upon them.

Although these alone could not resolve problems of acceptability they did help to build an ethos of personal worth.

> Resultant aims and objectives
>
> Kingdom of God
>
> Fatherhood of loving God
>
> Repentance / reconciliation
>
> Access / Trust in God

Summary 2c

Jesus acted on the following principles:

- Although pupils' reactions and motivations of pupils are their own.
- Responsibility, the teacher enables them to come to the best decision.
- He offered prospects and aspirations that exceeded their expectations.
- He identified pupil commitment rather than previous attainment.
- He tried to meet individual needs appropriately.
- His teaching was not unduly complex but left them with expectations.
- He brought together expectations and their enablement.
- He built on the best of their established traditions and experiences.

> .2c-31
> *How might good relationships be developed in difficult situations?*

- He surprised pupils as he gave them fresh experiences and knowledge.
- His teaching was insistent on central values being shared.
- He was not diverted from the needs of others by his own needs.
- He did not make the same level of demands on all pupils.
- Any differentiation of people was based on their attitude to learning.
- He used peer education to enable pupils to explore ideas.
- He risked allowing people to have freedom to make their own choices.
- He cared for his pupils and they recognized this.

Summary 2d

Consider the validity of these 3 teaching styles and when each might be applicable.

Figure 27

Traditional teaching	Jesus' style of teaching	Modern progressive teaching
Teacher control	Teacher led initiation/ immersion	Teacher - coach/mentor
Strongly historical	Active past, present, future	Developmental - future
Established scripts and procedures	Links with/ transforming tradition	Oriented to change/individual
Learning by heart	Major ideas accepted and used	New and often ephemeral
Little deviation	Comply with authoritative values	Personalized relative values
Scholarship led	Charismatic /authoritative leader	Responsive to interests etc
Social /religious rules	Experiential/interactive	Flexibility in decision making
Didactic and formal tasks	Encouraging responsibility	Individual creativity
Standard tests /criteria/ outcomes	Principled instruction	Exploration discussion
Unified corporate learning	Aspiration /responsibility setting	Cooperation / interaction
Stable roles controlled development	Corporate outward view/	Recognize pupil preferences

---

Personality Factor – 3

In which ways might traditionalists and progressives exemplify distinctive personality factors listed in Appendix?

.2c-32
When is learning likely to be seen as particularly positive / negative?

Chapter 3

Principles for an Ultimate Teaching Strategy

Previous chapters showed that Jesus' teaching strategy initiated a learning process that created the possibility of long-term learning developing into an 'all the world' possibility, or as Jesus said, from a mustard seed into a tree in which the birds can nest. Whereas Jesus was apt to turn the physical situation into spiritual teaching, this book does the reverse and considers how his spiritual pattern can be translated into a 21st century physical reality to be developed in Parts B and C.

Figure 28

(Diagram: *Making a Framework* — How Effective? / Which Goals? / Who? Teacher / For Whom? Which Pupils? / A Template For Teaching / The Style? / Methods / An outline model?)

1 The Challenge – the Goals

Jesus faced the twin challenges of achieving short and long term goals. He responded to evident short term needs and expectations and so generated intense confidence and motivation that could subsequently promote the motivation to pursue long-term goals. His immediate actions became the basis for stories and rumours that further fostered expectations that spread rapidly. The short-term experiences promised much but in themselves they were not sufficiently rooted to achieve the complex challenge of long-term success. Both short and long-term motivations needed to co-exist and flourish. The restricted recall of limited facts could not develop powerfully pregnant meanings within the teaching and so create aspirations for higher and wider achievements. He would extend their boundaries and open broader possibilities than previously considered. Also, they would wrestle with difficult spiritual/social questions and teach widely, even to 'all the world'.

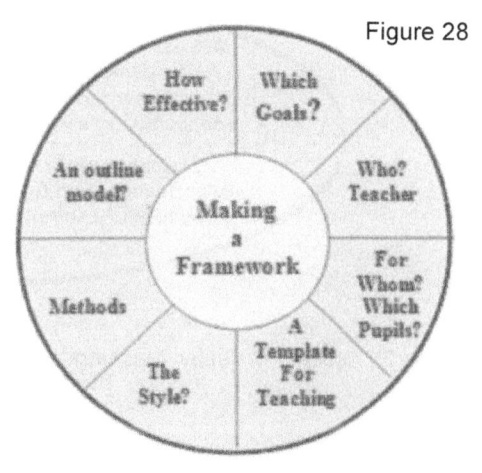

Figure 28 briefly shows the overall pattern by which Jesus achieved his goals. He was fully aware of the difficulties the existing situation presented (segment 1). But he also recognized the role of a change agent (segment 2) to generate purposeful prospects etc. At an early stage Jesus inspired people who were willing to respond with promises and authentic expectations (segment 3). The teaching built up a bank of personal memories through experiences (segment 4) that could inspire further responses (segment 5) and result in short term goals and thence longer term goals being achieved (segment 6,7) At the core were the teacher, the range of experiences and the pupils' own responsibility – a pattern that was not exclusive to Jesus and has been practised over the centuries.

There are usually close relationships between the attainment of short and long-term goals. Let us consider what this meant to Jesus and his followers (see Fig.29) and also to us in the present day. Although the diagram does not take account of complex human interactions, it does show dominant forces that enable progress to be made towards achieving desired goals. But which aspects might generally be applicable today? The two major differences are:

- The teacher and the quality of the challenge and experiences.
- The sense of corporate purpose that validates one another's efforts.

Even so a common thread is apparent.

> .2c-33
> From Figs 24a/b, what might be considered to be the most fundamental differences between Jesus and the religious leaders?

Four influential strategies by which long term success was achieved

```
┌─────────────────────────────┬─────────────────────────┐
│ Attractive instruction      │ Immersed in the         │
│ active demonstration        │ core ideas- the         │
│ with memorable,             │ Kerygma                 │
│ replicable experiences      │                         │
├─────────────────────────────┼─────────────────────────┤
│ Matching present            │ Koinonia - Bonding in   │
│ experiences with future     │ mutual support giving   │
│ promises / aspirations      │ a sense of belonging /  │
│                             │ identity                │
└─────────────────────────────┴─────────────────────────┘
```

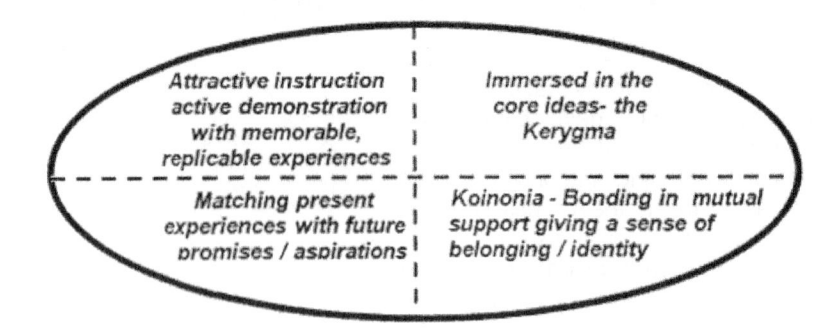

Figure 29 Aspects of Jesus' teaching to promote long-term goal attainment.

He combined *attractive, memorable instruction with active demonstrations*. These authentic *visual experiences* became their ideals. There were stories to be told and shared 'across the world'. Their universal outlook grew but it took longer than might have been expected to grasp the significance of accepting Samaritans, Romans and other Gentiles into 'the Way'. Eventually his expectations were regarded as being attainable.

Jesus majored on his *core ideas and lifestyle*. He limited himself to teaching powerful principles appropriately illustrated by word and action but with relatively few details to be learned, forgotten or disagreed about! These central principles have been called the *Kerygma*, which summarized the vision of the Kingdom of God being realised in Jesus. It focused on his *ministry, his death, resurrection and ministry to the world*. Although Jesus did not teach the Kerygma as a neat package, his followers identified the core features that epitomized his message. In effect it described and illustrated *his aspirations* and *lifestyle* that were memorable and comprehensible to a vast swathe of people. It may appear to be akin to religious sound bites but this principle of teaching for maximum effect and minimum complications was effective. They explored these understandings and skills and yet remain true to the essentials. This conceptual network was the basis of later teaching. Working from a limited number of central concepts is now common. Learners become immersed in historical, geographical, scientific etc. conceptual frameworks and use them to the point where they gain adaptable understandings. The Kerygma is one such conceptual core of organized teaching.

Figure 30

Pre-change situation	The change initiator	The initial general response and outlook	The power of memories	Inspiration of memories relived, their challenge	Short-term prospects and achievements	Long-term goals
Needs for survival Aspirations for prospects Established cultural norms	Hope Personal and group identification Challenge Purposeful prospects	Inspiration Authentic Promise	Watch Experience Inspired Demonstrate competence Personal needs met Pleasure Fresh aspirations Promises	Acceptance Fellowship Pleasure Obey Copy Secure body of teaching Changed self, Perceptions and values	High risk Individual initiatives based on experience Growing organization and planning Settled strategic developments	Eternal life, Rewards, Promises totally fulfilled

.2c-34
To whom might the stances in Figs. 24, 25 and 26 be most acceptable in the 21st century

There is power and health in *mutual support* as Jesus showed in his *community* of fellowship and practice. People benefited from learning *together* in close-knit, confident relationships. This fellowship has been called *Koinonia*. Many Christians from the lower strata of society who had nothing to lose found the love of Christians attractive and this friendship assisted long-term learning. Jesus' successful teaching and fellowship depended upon the *quality and frequency of interaction* both between himself and the 12, plus others. And amongst his followers, an *interactive group* with an *authoritative leader* caused the *community of faith* to develop an *identity that* enabled them to learn, build mutual trust and share Jesus' vision.

He provided a *secure basis*. He promised his disciples the gift of the Holy Spirit. They barely understood him, but probably grasped the notion that his spirit and vision would be given to them. As they took *ownership* of Jesus' teaching, they developed his forward-looking confidence. From these principles the long-term values and motivation developed.

Although the driving force of Jesus' teaching was spirituality, his methods did not exclude considerations typical in modern teaching. His hands-on *methods*, evident *compassion* and *commitment* to his followers and the wider population often resulted in these being reciprocated. To prepare them for impending *autonomy* and *long-term learning*, he *involved* his followers, *set standards,* created an *ethos* for learning and *trained* them to make real decisions. An emotional identification with him was developed. Further, his interest in them prevented an overly disappointment when they failed him. The learners accepted this pattern of concern and respect and reviewed their aspirations and shared his vision of *actualization and empowerment*. No longer were they an underclass and mere recipients of other people's knowledge. Both Jesus and the traditional intellectual elite defined standards, and provided security but the ethos of 'the Way' was more inspiring as he questioned cultural norms and reinterpreted the past to serve the present. A restrictive mindset was replaced by a new concept of God being universally liberating.

2 The Teacher

His message had to be uplifting, demonstrable and sufficiently flexible to make the package attractively distinctive. People responded to both the man and his teaching. He had been regarded simply as a good man until he stopped people in their tracks with his words and actions. He fostered a lighter hope rather than burdens and taught positively rather than with negative criticism – and so we see general teaching qualities to which people are likely to respond. He respected and felt for the people with a robust compassion that was fair, demanding and sensitive to the situation. He was a realist about others and as characteristics worthy of examination emerged so his purpose became their motivation.

He wanted more than correct knowledge. It required inspiration to persuade others to persevere but his regard for pupils raised the likelihood of long-term reciprocation. His moral and spiritual authority showed the 'Big Picture' which was magnetic – to some. Further, his actions were attractive and satisfied a range of interests, needs and aspirations. Interestingly, in an empire composed primarily of slaves and poor people, he chose those with whom people generally could identify to be his 'high fliers' and foundation figures.

Five common elements were integral to his teaching.

- To *inform* and *instruct* at *various levels* of understanding and commitment.
- To maximize understanding through multiple teaching methods and everyday stimuli.
- To generate long-term attitudes and faith by *personal interaction*.
- To *sensitize and persuade* people of the truth and worth of his radical goals.
- To motivate and empower his people.

.2c-35
The Kerygma is the core of what is taught – consider what might be the kerygma of something you teach.

Discipleship

But can his principles be interpreted and applied to other activities in order to:
- develop *pregnant meanings* rather than the restricted recall of limited facts?
- *create aspirations* for higher and wider achievements that would surprise them?
- *extend their boundaries* to open broader possibilities than previously considered?
- wrestle with difficult questions?
- teach for *wider applications*, even to 'all the world'?

3. Pupils in their Context

Teaching is personally costly, but so too is learning! Jesus had to exceed teaching truth persuasively. The cultural mix before him represented multiple attitudes, religious beliefs and language differences. He had to break down racial, sexual and religious barriers and develop his policy of inclusion, but for whom? He selected disciples who were mainly culturally and spiritually identified with him, plus a wider range of supporters but their cultural understandings had to be transformed. He was confronted with problems that are typical of many multi-cultural areas today. It required the long-term training of apprentices and initial acceptance and response to the wider groupings.

He recognized his mixed groupings and taught them appropriately, using their knowledge, experiences, interests and needs to develop high motivation and expectations. Their faith and ability grew to be enablers and achievers. Their 'experiential education' led them to realize the significance of what they were undertaking. As co-workers they gained ownership of what was taught and demonstrated. To this new knowledge they acquired competences to work without supervision! He took into account a wide range of variables common to many teaching situations.

4. A Consistent Teaching and Learning Template

His distinctive teaching maximized total achievement anchored core attitudes. He left the basis of a teaching template that could be universally grasped, copied and explored. This involved few mysteries but contained appropriate straight-forward practices. Figure 29 shows a skeleton of his methods from which we can identify seven principles of teaching and further simplified as below:.

- His methods were focused on his *central purpose,* the validity of which would be judged largely by whether they enabled this to be fulfilled.
- Humility, service, community etc represented Jesus' *value system*. Each person teaches within sets of values that can be defined clearly.
- Jesus, like every person, taught within a *personal and cultural context* from which assumptions and priorities can be drawn.
- There were four generic strategies involving the use of *language* in various forms, *visualization* and related *imaginative* approaches, various forms of *experiential* learning and the pursuit of high quality *relationships* during teaching and learning.

This template provides a guide for Jesus' teaching and, with some modifications, can be a useful tool in current situations. It expresses his long-term priorities and personal teaching characteristics together with an aide-memoire of major strategies and methods. For example, he restored hope and raised people from the point of failure. He used a pattern of teaching that was his undoubted hallmark but which varied considerably between teaching his apprentices and the general crowds. A simple tool such as this can still assist the maintenance of focus and ensure a balanced methodology.

.2c-36
Judas was a Judean amongst Galileans. What might this indicate about his

Figure 31

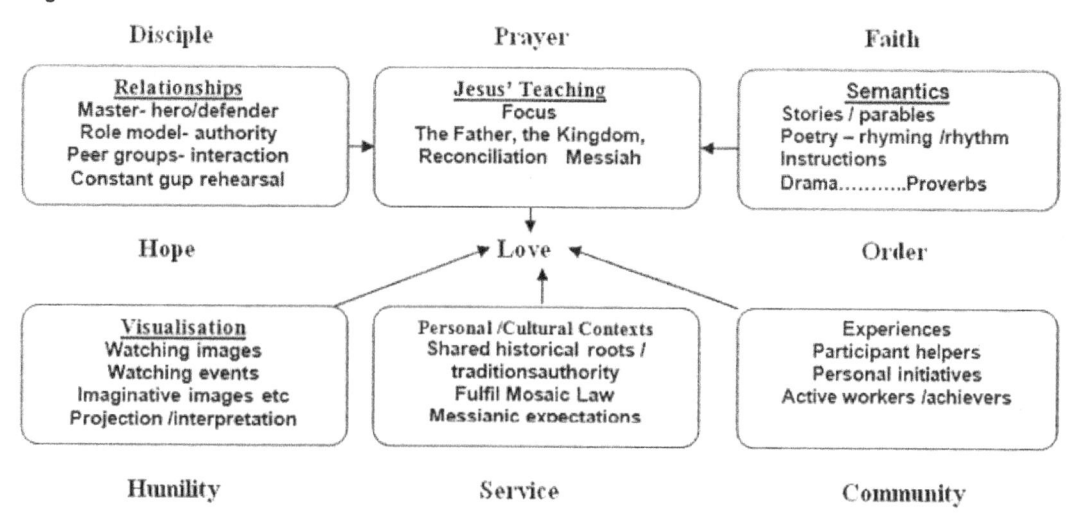

Disciple	Prayer	Faith
Relationships Master- hero/defender Role model- authority Peer groups- interaction Constant gup rehearsal	**Jesus' Teaching** Focus The Father, the Kingdom, Reconciliation Messiah	**Semantics** Stories / parables Poetry – rhyming /rhythm Instructions Drama...........Proverbs

Hope	Love	Order
Visualisation Watching images Watching events Imaginative images etc Projection /interpretation	Personal /Cultural Contexts Shared historical roots / traditionsauthority Fulfil Mosaic Law Messianic expectations	Experiences Participant helpers Personal initiatives Active workers /achievers

| Humility | Service | Community |

5 A Teaching Style

Jesus' teaching style appeared remarkably simple. It apparently followed a sequence such as: .

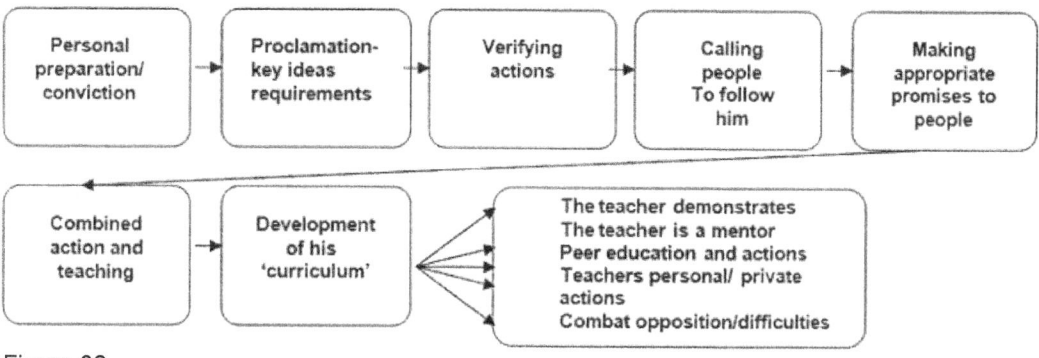

Personal preparation/ conviction → Proclamation- key ideas requirements → Verifying actions → Calling people To follow him → Making appropriate promises to people

Combined action and teaching ← Development of his 'curriculum' → The teacher demonstrates / The teacher is a mentor / Peer education and actions / Teachers personal/ private actions / Combat opposition/difficulties

Figure 32

The disciples were *attracted to the person* and his actions more than the teaching content. This reflected his treatment of his disciples as *friends and confidants.* A healthy *learning ethos* emerged. As their teacher he defined the situation, the pacing of the learning, and their transforming ongoing *experiences*. He was also a *team-orientated leader*, which enhanced their identity and was passed on to successive generations. This ownership was vital to the continuity of his teaching. He knew that aspiration alone is little. They needed *immersion* if they were to maintain their role model's qualities and vision. They were not merely listeners but *apprentices* who also became 'master craftsman' in their own right. These shared experiences, relationships and expectations anchored their learning.

The significance of the link between his teaching style and relationships was soon evident when he protected them and gave them a sense of worth. They trusted his consistency, interaction and minimum coercion. He made demands but accepted and respected them for whom they were and responded to individuals, that helped to maximize motivation. His qualities enhanced his credibility and so people became more teachable. Indeed, this policy and practice of proximity and trust contrasted with the separation of the religious authorities.

.2c-37
Why is koinonia a basis for effective teaching?

Similarly, his teaching style was reflected in his work. Although his purpose was singular and not deflected, he involved people his work. He provided an optimum challenge and teamwork and they became responsible and interdependent whilst trusting in him. He managed their stress levels, gave them real choices and expected them to at least try to solve his spiritual puzzles (or parables) that were taken from the everyday.

Jesus normally related his teaching to the people and their environment. He taught within a geographical, social and spiritual context, therefore, each step, object and place became memorably significant. Unlike the Pharisees, he referred to his surroundings more frequently than to traditional heroes. The world was seen as a living parable waiting to be told because it is God's world. His sharp observations provided him with evidence that was there for all to see. By watching, helping, copying, developing and listening the disciples developed images that became their basis to promote Jesus' teaching later. Although his teaching methods were not totally original, the manner in which he combined them was.

His requirements were *faith and motivation*. These were developed as they watched miracles, heard attractive and wise words and were readily defended from criticism. This was worth talking about! As they saw their various needs met and their dreams became reality, they felt proud to be associated with such a person. But these unlearned disciples were a high risk. They found it difficult to grasp basic teaching, but worse, they had ambitious expectations of power and leadership. With such flawed understandings, which teaching strategies could he use to ensure that his teaching didn't become a mere caricature once he left them? The crowds ran to hear him because underpinning it all was a freshness and relevance that surprised the populace, but was it a passing fad?

6. Appropriate Methods

It is too simplistic say that the methods were appropriate to the pupils' abilities, but Jesus assumed control of their learning and would not be confined by their limited aspirations as he took them to new levels of conception. He also fitted any situational evidence into his teaching which further *immersed them in this* new realm of understanding. He developed and paced the objectives and highlighted them by three aspects of his work.

- Firstly, his input was *significant* and fresh to them.
- Secondly, the element of *surprise* was memorable and eagerly discussed.
- Thirdly, the friendship groups encouraged authentic ongoing experiences and were useful as they found when they made contributions to the work – and so felt recognized and that they were *making progress*.

His methods conveyed his personal priorities as when he encouraged people to metaphorically see God in the environment. Also, he saw great spiritual values illustrated in everyday events (Luke ch.10). His use of visual symbols (John ch.10:) and kinaesthetic experiences (John ch.13) typified his use of concrete evidence to lead people on to abstract ideas. Allied to this was the central role of imagination to both develop ongoing thought and to aid rapid recall through his many examples of visualization (Matthew ch.7), using language memorably through novel stories and pithy quotes that had the effect of transforming tentative steps into a bold spiritual march. Tradition was revitalized. The pattern laid down by historic heroes illustrated both the present situation and the ultimate climax of time. His challenges were based on both opportunistic and planned evidence. This generated a high degree of relevance upon which success could be built His followers became independent enablers within his own image. Hence he assured them that solutions are always possible with the available resources.

.2c-38
How can the facets in Fig. 32 be prioritised effectively for day-to-day use?

7. The teacher's coherent teaching/learning model

Jesus did not plan his teaching and learning in a formal manner as might be done today, but rather developed the process naturally as events and opportunities emerged. One can identify those major elements that are used today.

Typically he had clear goals both for himself and his pupils, but it was a long-term process for such mixed groupings. It was not ideal for all and most did not leave their boats, workshops, tax tables etc. That meant that there had to be some flexibility and use of opportunities as they occurred, but this could not be allowed to detract from his primary goals which raised numerous problems. Those who only heard Jesus occasionally would not be expected to achieve more than a superficial understanding of a few hard words such as repentance, authority and obedience. Without wishing to exaggerate the point, Fig. 33 is a simplified illustration that shows the early progression of Jesus' ministry and illustrates features of his teaching.

Figure 34 indicates certain parallels between Jesus' strategy and a 21st century approach. Within these were.

- Frequent encouragement by word and action and a constant sense of acceptance.
- He built a body of central principles into his teaching (e.g. forgiveness).
- He met difficulties and problems in the spirit of his teaching.
- He enabled his newly built team to practice the principles that required responses.
- He realized that a golden rule in teaching is involvement.

To empower his followers they had to be co-workers and gain ownership of what was taught and demonstrated. In particular, experiential elements enabled them to recognize their gains. This required sufficient competence to reinforce the learning process and enable them to work without supervision! it is the type sequence used in some modern business, management or educational developments.

8. Teaching is both long-term and cross cultural

Although Jesus was a good *communicator* in Galilee his message had to cross cultures. It began with his own people 'the lost sheep of Israel' but then…? Even though it was fresh amongst his disciples, would it remain so in future generations?

Jesus' was teaching for the long-term and so continuity was crucial. It went beyond correct knowledge and required inspiration to persuade others to persevere through difficulties and for them to teach others with conviction. His moral and spiritual *leadership* offered a 'Big Picture' with which many *identified*. This satisfied many aspirations in an empire composed primarily of slaves and poor people. Just as his first promise was to the poor, so he appears to have given the poor prospects of which they had not dreamed. Perhaps Simon of Cyrene, a Jewish pilgrim who carried Jesus' cross and who was not poor, was a good example of growth. Shocked by his enforced involvement in the Crucifixion, he returned home to North Africa, and told his family and friends about Jesus who became followers of the Way, despite their minimal knowledge. This simplicity provided hope and dignity. The hazardous dynamics of the Way resulted in competing understandings and ample scope for people to gravitate to particular interest and fellowship groups. Despite differences and crises, perhaps the simplicity and lack of an imposed structure provided the freedom for inquiry and development and diverse leaderships under the symbol of a fish or the Cross.

This provided clues about successful teaching. The wholeness encompassed spiritual and material, personal and communal, the present and future. It was moving pupils/people from negative to positive expectations. This involved transition from being:

.2c-39
What sort of information might Jesus prioritize today?

Confused	to having orderly expectations
Anxious	to having a degree of peace or equanimity
critical and judgmental	to accepting and adopting appreciative attitudes
suspicious	to trusting
passive	to active
Wanderers	to following a specific paths

This new mindset had a spiritual basis. The teaching, like faith, was multi-dimensional and had a core not confined to religion. It provided a basis for wholeness and so enabled learning to be maximized. This, *but not the faith*, is now popularly called the art of *positive thinking* – a feature that can be seen in Jesus' own teaching methods.

He taught relatively few contentious matters other than his personal claims and a new interpretation of the Law, but strangely he left gaps in their learning. For example:

- He did not teach people how to worship. When he went to Samaria he used a nebulous phrase about worshipping 'in spirit and in truth' which left ample scope for *personalised interpretation* and *applications*.... and distortion.
- He did not teach them how to *run an organization* such as the church became.
- He did not give them a formal doctrinal agreement.
- He did not tell them precisely how to achieve *his goals*.
- But he did convey his priorities by using *recognizable methods*. For example: His ministry had many *favourable memories* and *experiences* that people could recall enthusiastically. There was a universal message that crossed cultural barriers.
- There was the ongoing stimulus of developments and achievements.

His primary task was not solely to teach people so well that they could receive all his knowledge, which had a touch of mystery. He was an *enabler* who trained people *to be enablers*. He *empowered* them and showed a *concern for and pleasure in the outcome* of their work, and so gave them a growing confidence in what he *valued, trusted and wanted* both for them and others. This gave a sense of *shared destiny* that was beyond their understanding, but even if they did not understand its significance, it would be their greatest contribution to the world.

These established foundations for life-long learning and continuity by means of a *learning package* in which there was constant interaction between the *teacher*, the *apprentices*, the *methods* and the *content/knowledge*. They copied his lifestyle as he repeated his teaching and so enlarged and enriched their understandings. The delight of *experiential* and *experimental spiritual* learning, *surprise and rising expectations* reinforced the *ongoing teaching*. But he did not confine himself to their present understanding. For example, it is doubtful if Peter understood the significance of Jesus' words, "I will make you a fisher of men" or "I am the light of the world".

.2c-40
Why do all teachers need to be opportunistic?

Figure 33 The early developmnent

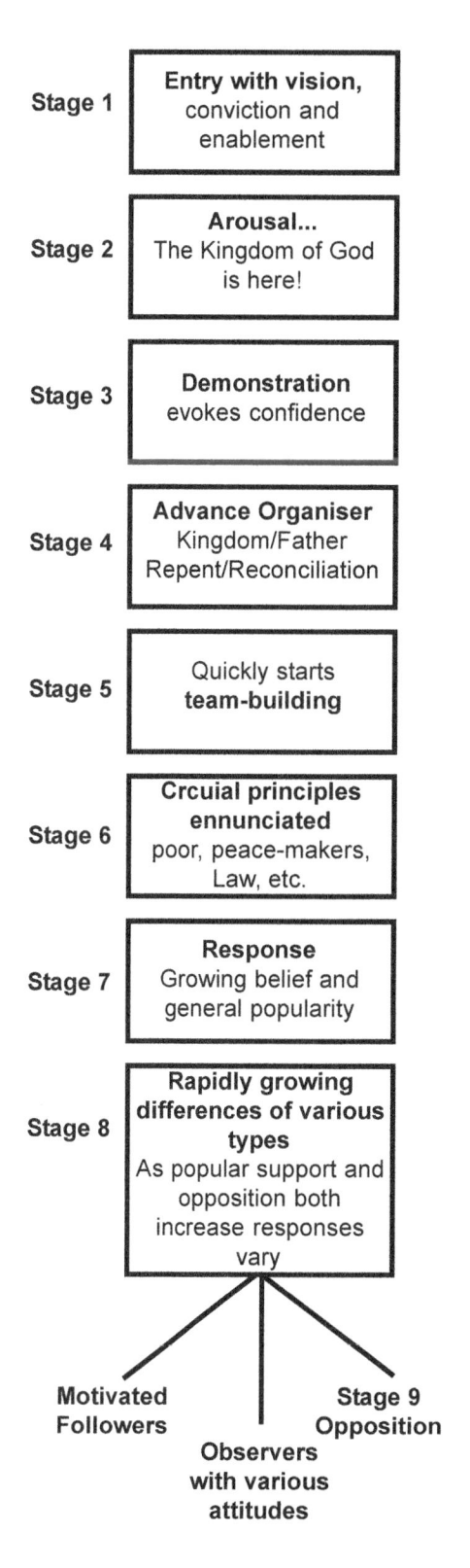

Stage 1	**Entry with vision,** conviction and enablement
Stage 2	**Arousal...** The Kingdom of God is here!
Stage 3	**Demonstration** evokes confidence
Stage 4	**Advance Organiser** Kingdom/Father Repent/Reconciliation
Stage 5	Quickly starts **team-building**
Stage 6	**Crcuial principles ennunciated** poor, peace-makers, Law, etc.
Stage 7	**Response** Growing belief and general popularity
Stage 8	**Rapidly growing differences of various types** As popular support and opposition both increase responses vary

Motivated Followers — Stage 9 Opposition
Observers with various attitudes

Figure 34 Strategic parallels with the 21st century

The 10 stage sequence of teaching stages is not surprising	The drama of Jesus' early teaching can be related to the following common teaching formula
Stage 1 His work was founded on his *enabling commitment* to his *vision*	A *goal* is clearly understood and prepared for by the teacher.
Stage 2 He stated (arousal) the *recognizable expectations* and demands of the moment.	Arousal as needs and aspirations are stated and met
Stage 3 He *demonstrated* the authenticity of his claims and so gave the people a basis for a positive response.	*Advance organisers* introduced to identify key ideas, procedures and promises (e.g. the Kingdom of God, the Fatherhood of God, a servant Messiah, reconciliation etc.
Stage 4 He announced his *advance organizer*, that is the central feature around which everything would be built.	Evoke *motivation* by meeting needs and establishing aspirations.
Stage 5 He built a *team* to meet immediate needs and *trained* them to be high performers who would perpetuate his work.	Invite pupils to *commit* to goals even before they fully understand them.
Stage 6 He devised an ideal package to take people to a new level of *expectation* and the *personal requirements* expected.	. Rapid *encouragement* by experiential learning with a high degree of participation by the apprentices and peer group tuition begins immediately.
Stage 7 His *response* to the crowds was *orderly* and he did not allow their expectations to get out of hand whilst he developed new attitudes and expectations.	Build a body of central principles into the teaching from their existing knowledge, everyday experiences, the use of their senses and by responding to evident interest.
Stage 8 *Conflict* with the existing authorities was inevitable but he remained *calm, protective and consistent* as he developed his work..	Have time for *intimate teaching* and *reflection* amongst the apprentices.
Stage 9 There were many different responses but he *persisted* despite vehement opposition. He had confidence that his claims would be *vindicated*.	Pupils have a *growing realisation* of the significance of what they were being taught and their privileged position.
Stage 10 He would *not veer* from his original purposes no matter what the difficulties and dangers	Encourage them with foundational support and traditional sources

.2c41
What are the major non-negotiable differences between the 1st and 21st centuries?

Teaching for the longer term and wider field

Jesus' disciples imitated their role model but now it is necessary to imaginatively project back to first century Palestine. He grasped this need for an *imaginative* faith that could project his teaching to have long-term applications. Remarkably, this obscure group gradually believed that they could move into the unknown on a voyage of spiritual discovery and persuasion with little knowledge. A. Einstein had the skill and the vision to translate his insights about relativity into simple understandable terms. Likewise, Jesus did not become enmeshed in detail but pushed through his 'Big Ideas' as illustrating the universal plight of man. But as Einstein said, 'Knowledge should be made as simple as is true, but no simpler.' As a teacher, Jesus knew that good methods alone were not enough. He had to incorporate the best methods with the evident worth of his Kingdom teaching so that the living principles could be applied widely. This problem and its relationship to modern situations can be summarized as follows:

- That process of continuity and development brought together the essential *spiritual message* together with what we now call *network theory* and *social movement*.
- The authoritative spiritual message consisted of a core that could be applied widely.
- It was attractive, inclusive and afforded religions and social affiliation/bonding.
- It offered prospects of personal 'salvation', needs and aspirations being met.

All this was in a favourable/ enabling situation where the Pax Romana provided some peace and a degree of freedom to travel.

Implementing his teaching

His concern was to change *people* rather than to teach methods of *religious enquiry*. Therefore, his activities were based on specific values, goals, strategies and methods that were consistent and attractive. For example, if we select any values that he inculcated, such as love, forgiveness, inclusion and servant hood, congruence was needed between them and the teaching style and methods used.

9 Training Activities

Jesus was both teaching and training his followers and one can recognize the following type of features that were included in the range of integrated *experiences* provided by Jesus for his apprentices and can be a good working basis for training people today.

- He provided a broad range of *activities* in scope and content.
- There were direct *experiences* in different settings/people.
- He fostered *affective and cognitive* facets of *spiritual* development.
- He encouraged them *to communicate* what they *knew* and *felt*.
- He gave pupils an awareness of progress and achievement.
- He ensured that all *enjoyed* the sense of *involvement* and *progress*.
- He planned *flexibility* to allow for a variety of spiritual thinking etc.
- He understood the *legitimacy* of their particular development.
- He ensured they were active participants in the learning process.
- They were able to export their novel faith, ideas and practices.
- He enabled them to *understand* a wide range of *needs and activities*.
- He encouraged *appropriate faith responses* in various situations.
- He taught them to understand that *standards* are *expected / required*.
- He taught them to see similar truths in different settings. See parts B and C.

.2c-42
Which of the training methods would be likely to be particularly important?

Figure 35

Jesus and subsequent development	The 21st century teaching situation
He was clearly a leader to follow	The teacher offers clear, worthwhile leadership.
He spotted potential 'hubs'- strong unifying people who would lead groups.	The teacher spots potential group leaders.
He provided a vision to which people could relate at various levels.	The teacher presents the 'Big Picture' and desirable, long-term patterns and goals.
Dispersion occurred through developmental visions, forced movement due to persecution, slavery, and trading.	Understanding promotes expectations of development in a conducive ethos.
The natural tendency for affiliation was effective to form hubs of activity.	Some pupils' develop the 'vision, others move and link with others, others remain dependent learners.
The strong central ideas could be stated across cultures.	Pupils form hubs or groups that reflect core ideas, methods, related lifestyle and demands.
Individual lines (or spokes) moved from united groupings or social hubs. i.e. churches.	The possibility of individual lines of study relating to the greater hub.
Alternative individuals and groups peeled off to attract and send out individuals.	There will be some will object and form alternative hubs.
People knew and had calls to maintain their links with their hubs/churches.	The skill is to cause individuals to pursue aspirations related to a community of study..
The hubs multiplied, enlarged but related and maximized the potential for expansion	Challenge pupils to look to the future when individuals and small groups may grow and relate

A review of Part A and Jesus' Teaching Style.

People responded to a positive attitude and the human touch. Jesus based his teaching upon central principles and related concepts taught by active oral teaching. He saw the plight of the aspirations of the people and from his vision and superior understanding he taught vital guiding principles. He practised the principles and interpreted or reinterpreted them in the context of the past, the present or the future. He activated his methods by using peer groups, demonstrations experiences, visualization, individual challenges, discussion, inductive thought etc to demonstrate the Kingdom of God and respond to their faith. This led them to understand and internalize his core message. This array of teaching characteristics summarized below is remarkably familiar!

Summary 3

1. The following is a selection of key words. What were their significance in Jesus' work as applied to teaching and learning.

Figure 36

Aspiration	Achievement	Affective	Authentic	Big Picture
Choice	Cognition	Communicate	Community	Demonstrate
Enablement	Ethos	Expectations	Expertise	Flexibility
Identification	Imagination	Interactive	Leadership	Motivation
Mutuality	Ownership	Promise	Relevance	Response
Spiritual	Standards	Symbols	Trust	Universal

.2c-43
What made Jesus such a special teacher then?.....Now? to so many?

2. Up to this point approximately 34 teaching methods have been mentioned to some degree. Now pause to gather these together and consider how aspects of them might be used when teaching pupils.

Figure 37

Acceptance	Advance Organizer	Apprenticeship	Arousal	Challenge
Commitment	Core Principles	Creativity	Enabler	Experiences
Interaction	Memorable	Need Satisfaction	Participation	Peer Tuition
Reflection	Reinforcement	Responsibility	Responsiveness	Role Modelling
Senses	Teacher Authority	Value	Vision	Worth

3. We have begun to see that this teacher illustrated certain essential characteristics that enabled his pupils to ultimately flourish. Match the 30 words in Figure 37 with the eight statements below
    1. The teacher had clear goals with an appropriate long-term strategy that was beneficial to the pupils.
    2. A variety of methods appropriate to the content, pupils and situations were used.
    3. At the heart of the teaching / learning were the pupil responses to enabling situations and thereby achieve a strong learning ethos as summarized by:
        - Positive emotions.
        - Expectations were high and positive.
        - Relationships were trusting and secure.
        - Meaningful and comprehensible purposes with which pupils could identify.
        - Accomplishments and attainments of teacher and pupils were high.

Personality Factor – 4

Which aspects of this review of teaching might have grated with Jesus' personality?

.2c-44

Which of the skills noted in Jesus' teaching might be used by a creative teacher in the 21st century?

Chapter 4

Jesus' teaching strategies illustrated from Matthew's gospel

The following is a chapter by chapter description of Jesus' teaching style as recorded in Matthew's Gospel. This survey is designed to *illustrate the typical principles, processes and practices of Jesus' teaching methods* that have been and will be examined in various ways in Parts A B and C. *It is not a traditional commentary.* This review of his methodology is taken exclusively from the Gospel of Matthew. There is no particular reason for using Matthew because the same principles can be highlighted in the other Gospels, which makes the conclusions increasingly secure. A similar type of analysis based on John and Luke's Gospels are found in sections B and C.

This highlights Jesus' characteristic teaching methods and related human qualities. It will proceed through the Gospel and highlight:

Decision points Matthew (ch.3 v.13-15) *Emerging and developing goals* (e.g. ch.4 v.1-11)
Particular strategies (e.g. ch.4 v.12-25) *Distinctive methods and techniques* (e.g. ch.4 and 5)

Figure 39

The person	His relationships
His self-awareness	The recognised role model with responsibilities
His authoritative personal insights	For his personal discipline and expected discipline
His unique relationship to the Father	He took initiatives for others
His long-term vision (c.f. his pupils)	He defended his pupils
The leader and ultimate decision-maker	Mutual trust
His prophetic stature was recognized	He gave pupils responsibilities but was an enabler and encourager
	Built a sense of pride and mission
His teaching strategies	**Methods**
No exclusions	Conversation
Orderliness	Didactic instructional processes/discourse
Observation	Demonstration
Using situational opportunities	Metaphor and imagination - symbolism
A core, growing message	The use of tradition
Teaching beyond understanding and a growing into understanding	Tactile
Responding to short-term needs and faith	Experiential learning - sensory, emotional, social, spiritual
Teaching through positive experiences	Environmental links
Simple language to develop complex ideas	Using crises for spiritual purposes
Teaching for growing degrees of enlightenment	Implicit recall by actions
Setting the long-term challenge	Great prophetic statements
Resolutely opposed opposition	Reflection
A thematic development	Summary statements
Brevity but with an emphatic truth element	

The nativity stories are not relevant in this particular analysis

Chapter 3

Verses 1–12 Jesus built his teaching on his forerunners and acknowledged their value that provided the foundation and an authoritative spiritual and moral anchorage for his work. He drew upon the past confidently which helped to ensure that his teaching's was recognized. He spoke to all people without favour. The message had a strong moral thrust delivered in a simple, didactic manner.

.2c-45
List 4 Major teaching skills exhibited by Jesus in these early chapters

Verse 13 Jesus identified with this foundational teaching and with the teachable listeners. *Humility* was at the heart of his baptism and became one aspect of his teaching methods. This step of *obedience* and *faith* preceded his authoritative teaching and followed existing Jewish practice.

Chapter 4

Verses 1–11 Jesus was a strategist and in the wilderness he made a three point strategic decision in respect of coercion/power, exhibitionism and self-service. Instead, he chose a strategy based upon love, simplicity and serving others.

This core passage indicates how his *aims* and *objectives* would be achieved through a precise *strategy*.

- Jesus as a teacher had a *directive function.*
- Jesus was *self disciplined and focused*. He knew that his teaching would involve a degree of pain.
- None of his work would be *self-centred or utilitarian* even if it appeared justifiable (v.4)
- He would not base his teaching methods on theatrical stunts, which he knew would not have long-term value (v.5-7).
- He would not base his work upon *coercion* when all his teaching was concerned to reveal the *character of God the Father and his love* (v.8-v.10)
- His work and teaching methods would be based upon *revitalized fundamental values* that would meet the *needs* of the people.

Verses 12–17 Jesus began his teaching with a message of *hope*. The notion of *repentance* was well known and generally accepted. It indicated that there would be a *common attitude* towards *God and authority* and *shared positive expectations* that *encouraged* the people.

Jesus gave a disciplined message – learning costs! Pupils had to know that demands would be made if they were to attain their dreams.

What he taught was current and aroused their attention. Pupils seldom understand the full significance of what is being taught or recognise what they might achieve. This beginning, based on continuity, hope and establishing clear expectations, was appropriate to his teaching. By matching actions with his teaching he established his position and their expectations.

Verses 18–22 His major teaching came through the demanding discipleship/apprenticeship *experience*s of his close pupils. Before making these demands Jesus established a reason for them. Also he had to confidently say, *'Follow me'* and for the pupils to believe that *his example,* which they had seen, would be *sustained and worthwhile*. Much of the teaching is this *personal identification* of the pupil with the teacher.

When teachers meet *real needs* it often has a powerful impact that enable crucial decisions to be made. The challenge here was for the teacher to *initially create faith* in the learning situation and for the watching pupils to *respond*.

Verses 23–25 Jesus set out his *purpose clearly, confidently and demonstrably* and he met *felt needs*. Many people may talk but at the heart of education are teachers who can satisfy these *needs*. Pupils were made to feel that what they were being asked to do was *worthwhile* and that they would be *enabled* to complete the task. Jesus set about his *faith building* exercise by demonstrating his ability to the pupils. From the outset people could see that the teacher's words were *valid*.

> .2c-46
> What differences are there between absolute and relative values in the 1st CE and now?

Chapter 5

Verses 1–11

v 1–2. It should be noted that this is the equivalent of a stilling or calming exercise that precedes lessons. It was a *routine* that was readily understood by all concerned and there was no need for the teacher to ask for silence so that he could talk. This maximizes the initial impact and indicates who is in control. If the teacher does not establish a routine that is followed by *significant content*, then the pupils will establish their own routine.

In the Sermon on the Mount major characteristics of both Jesus' teaching and his teaching methods can be seen. Although Jesus was *inclusive* in most of his work, at times he was severely *exclusive*. In an orderly way he spoke to those upon whom he would rely and who would have the greatest responsibilities. In effect, he set out his basic curriculum and *demonstrated* his characteristic teaching styles. They knew that they were privileged people. Jesus stated *positive facts* that would *encourage* everyone. He would meet them as they were and see their *positive aspects of life* and express God's *appreciation and concern* for them. Therefore, Jesus' teaching to willing learners was essentially *supportive*. In Chapter 4 he had announced the Kingdom of God, giving *hope* and *demonstrating his truth*. Similarly, in Luke ch.4 Jesus announced his ministry with positive words in a synagogue. His teaching was essentially *creative* and he recognized that *forgiveness and restoration* are at the core of successful teaching.

In the Beatitudes Jesus set out his vision of the Kingdom and its people in the form of nine unambiguous promises that were uplifting and related to everyday life. These were in contrast to the traditional judgmental teaching of the religious leaders. These brief statements were memorable and held promise for the oppressed people around them. They can be likened to the Ten Commandments. The genius of the Ten Commandments was that they were *uncluttered, brief and memorable*. Jesus, as their role model, *displayed* these nine characteristics to the pupils who would imitate him. The pupils could go down the mountain memorizing the simple statements and teach them to the needy and the oppressed. Jesus was establishing his *needs based and aspirational curricula*.

Verses 12–16. Jesus' statements were often *pictorial* based on every day *observations*. His policy of using the *concrete* to illustrate the *abstract* spiritual truths predated much of the work in the 20th century in respect of concept attainment. The disciples all knew that salt was used as a preservative, fertilizer and disinfectant, and light, lamps and the city on a hill were all *readily accessible ideas*. Clarity counted!

It was through such statements that Jesus introduced the fundamental concept of the Fatherhood of God. What could have been taught as a complex philosophical idea was taught as *a fact* which all could understand from their *everyday experiences*.

He was showing that good teaching is *memorable, relevant, essential (salt)*, gives *light*, is *public* and promotes *good works* (and brings glory to God).

Verses 17–20. Jesus' teaching was not relativistic. He taught *that morality is absolute* and *righteousness is essential* (both spiritually and socially) and to be done in a spirit of humility. Jesus was *revitalizing established traditions*.

Verses 21–26. Jesus taught *absolute values*, but he did not try to persuade people of their validity – they were established and self-evident. He was convinced that the pupils' *motivation* should *inspire* these values. Indeed, he reached the heart of his message (i.e. *reconciliation*) by *relating it to everyday life*. He regarded this and related issues as a priority for all.

Verses 27–32. His absolutism in respect of *moral behaviour* was a striking contrast with much modern morality. He stunned people by using such extreme language but it was true and memorable. Today, teachers usually work within a moral world and model characterized by relativity which pupils may recognize and understand. Although Jesus applied an absolute morality to diverse situations its validity was recognized.

> .2c-47
> To what extent was Jesus both inclusive and exclusive as a teacher?

Verses 33 – 37. Jesus began to take the *absolute laws to higher levels of application*. In verse 33 he stated the need for a person's word to be his / her bond. The *challenge* then moved to a higher plane that covered *forgiveness and generosity*. He was setting an *ethos* for successful teaching. This new absolutism was couched in reasonable *questions* but the *answers* were at a much higher spiritual level. This chapter still has far reaching implications for the teaching of citizenship and social education. He was setting higher aspirations that demand a *robust working maturity* (verse 48). As part of this moral world Jesus was saying that the teacher's *generosity* should replace retaliation and *love* to replace hate.

Chapter 6

Verses 1–4. Jesus' teaching about humility and self-effacement automatically challenged the religious practices of the leaders. Two features can be applied to teaching.

- Jesus had *faith in the pupils* to continue his teaching even before they had that faith.
- The pupils had *high expectations* of their *authoritative teacher*. Teaching and learning were seen as a result of *confident and committed relationship*. Jesus emphasized his key *revelation* of the Fatherhood of God in relationship to *everyday living* (piety) and *generosity* (alms giving). His teaching style was essentially *economical, straight-forward and instructive* where appropriate. This was in contrast to the parables that were *metaphoric/ descriptive* and had to be interpreted by the listeners. Note that Jesus differentiated between *immediate* and *delayed gratification* of rewards that was critical to all long-term learning. People need to know what type of reward they are looking for and to *pursue the long term.*

Verses 5–15 In this passage Jesus used the term Father six times. He encouraged his pupils by confidently stressing this relationship. He highlighted this concept every few words and used it 16 times in these three chapters and 12 times in Chapter 6 alone. He was reinforcing the concept in a range of contexts. His model for prayer was relatively intimate and in contrast to the religious leaders but similar to the Beatitudes with its ten memorable rhythmic and poetic phrases. It was a typical method of teaching that succinctly summarised his teaching.

Verses 16–18. These verses reiterate the principles seen earlier and provide an example of small scale *concentric curriculum* in which the core concept(s) is developed in different forms. It indicates how an established concept might be *reinforced and developed* by the technique of *contrast in a range of situations.*

Verses 19–21. Jesus' teaching style was typically Hebrew. Pupils could *visualize and identify* with the *concrete* figures of speech as he set out his priorities and purpose.

Verses 22–23. The formation of consuming priorities in any person can be difficult to explain, but he did so by using a common figure of speech…. 'the eye is the lamp of the body'. This *metaphor* was followed by two *statements* that Jesus consistently used as descriptive and analytical tools when making rational statements that pupils were expected to recognize as being self evident and true.

Verses 25–34. This critically important passage illustrates how Jesus used *observations* and *extended them spiritually*. Hence, he said,' look at the birds' and ' consider the lilies of the field' and then he extended these observations into the whole area of trust and anxiety. These *observation*s and interpretations were brought to a climax as he *rationalized* them showing two *recurring concepts*, namely the character of the Fatherhood of God and the Kingdom of God. This *link* between the *natural and the spiritual was taken to be self-evident*. More generally he showed his genius for linking the everyday with higher learning.

Chapter 7

Verses 1–6. When teaching, pupils judge teachers as surely as they themselves are judged. This may seem a negative statement but more positively it can be said, if we give them hope and faith they will probably return them as they learn.

Jesus had an evident moral authority and terse statements were likely to be obeyed.

.2c-48
By what criteria are pupils likely to judge their teachers?

Once again Jesus demonstrated the power of the hyperbole and spoken-word (log of and speck) when making a point.

Verses 7–12. The *brevity* of Jesus' statements and their total logic, which were based on established promises, were striking. *Established, unquestioned promises should be differentiated* so that other established ones are not questioned.

Jesus used the physical world as a pale comparison of the spiritual world. This similitude fits the pattern of his habitual teaching. He naturally referred to the Father with a logic that, he believed, could not be disputed.

Jesus' substantiated his teaching by using an established authority – the Father. All *teaching should be shown to be authoritative, but by which authorities?*

There was a *reasonable expectation* within all teaching situations – pupils were expected to agree with the rule that whatever we wish people to do to us we should do to them.

Verses 13–14. The narrow and the broad gates. Once again the emphasis is on *self-discipline*. The pupils can carry no baggage if they want to succeed. The simple illustrated figure of speech was taught with no ambiguities.

Verses 15–20. He applied simple *pictorial language* and logic to robust *everyday figures*. He stressed the qualities of the *teacher's character* and *abilities* if he was to succeed.

Verses 21–29. There was always a word of warning concerning *deeds being greater than words.. Sharp contrasting figures* were *memorable* but they were *not laboured*. His authority was that he had something to say which was *original* (to the pupils), gave *hope*, was *comprehensible* and *memorable*.

The repetitive analytical approach of the scribes and Pharisees appeared clever but it was not life generating to the pupils. There was a *freshness* and *immediacy* in Jesus' teaching.

Chapter 8

Verses 1–4. Jesus was not only a teacher but also an enabler. Pupils expect teachers to be change agents. One of his main concerns was to meet personal needs as they arose. As in all good teaching what had been achieved had to be verified / examined.

Verses 5–13. As a teacher *Jesus evoked faith*. Pupils recognized and *accepted authority* when they saw it *work to the advantage of others. Cross-cultural recognition* wasn't the norm – it came with *observation and needs*. Pupils can surprise their teachers by their *faith. Disciplined order* gave the opportunity for *reflection, recognition, faith and success.*

Verses 14–17. A crucial characteristic – the teacher was *available*. He met his pupils at their real *point of need. Jesus went beyond his pupil's faith*, He let him *flounder* and then *supported him.*

Verses 18–22. Success does not come cheap. Jesus warned potential pupils of the cost. Pupils who make claims and have aspirations must meet demands.

Verses 23–27. Pupils should be encouraged to take initiatives in the teaching situation. The teacher is normally greater than the pupil, and pupils expect the teacher to *resolve problems* and are delighted when he does so and *faith is enhanced.*

Verses 28–34. The best teachers have an authoritative calming effect.

This teacher did not run away from the problems.

Even *good teachers can be rejected*, especially if they make demands on non-beneficiaries.

.2c-49
How can a calming effect be generated?

Chapter 9

Verses 1–8. This illustrates certain crucial aspects of teaching.
- Jesus characteristically *encouraged* those in need. It appears that the paralytic man did not have the same degree of faith as his friends.
- Jesus responded to *pupils' confidence.*
- Peer-group learning with close teacher links is invaluable.
- The teacher was meeting tangible needs.
- He *resisted criticism* of pupils who took initiatives.
- He supported defended and justified pupils where appropriate.
- In response to pupil *motivation and faith* the mould was broken.

Verses 9–13. All can be *restored and be thankful*. Was the teacher's authority based on the pupil's *previous knowledge?* It may be necessary to *defend pupils* against others.

Verses 14–17. New developments may need radically new attitudes, but both the *old and new practices have their place.*

Verses 18–26. Teachers may need to responsively *follow pupils* to meet their needs.

The teacher was a *perpetual encourager.* (verse 22)

Pupils have *differing realization of needs* – which may be long-term.

Some teachers write-off difficult situations. Master teachers recognize and respond to faith.

Verses 27–34. How does a teacher *evoke faith*? Is it by *previous success* with other pupils?

Verses 35–38. Teaching takes place in all situations. Teachers need to be suitably *adaptable.*

The teacher is *more* than *knowledge and skills. Compassion* is a powerful *driving force* especially when pupils are harassed and under achieve.

The teacher looks for *assistance* that can be achieved through *disciplined peer education.*

Chapter 10

Verses 1–5. A teacher always needs *help!*

Teacher and his apprentices – a good example of apprenticeship *training*

Verses 6–15. The initial challenge, warnings and difficulties

The pupils as apprentices will *imitate* their teacher and *share his difficulties.*

Verses 16–23. *Jesus recognized* the *difficulties* facing his pupils

He saw that the need to be *wise and harmless* was essential.

He and his pupils would face *immense difficulties* but must *persist.*

Verses 24–33. Jesus had to face up to the *challenge* in order to *achieve* his goals. The apprentices knew that they too had to face up to the challenge like their master - and so we see the effect of a *good role model.*

Verses 34–39. The outcome of student *rigour* would be evident.

The teacher *recognized the cost* and the *motivation* of his pupils.

Verses 40–42. Do the pupils see it is worth *imitating* the role model? If so, a *worthy imitation* will receive an appropriate *reward.*

A teacher will receive a *teacher's reward.* We all have something vitally important to offer the children or any other pupils.

.2c-50
What makes a teacher worth following?

Chapter 11

Verses 1–19. Good teachers can be opposed for a wide range of reasons. John the Baptist was opposed on personal *moral* grounds.

Teachers can become *demoralized* and *question* their own actions.

Jesus showed that his teaching was validated by its *outcomes*.

Teachers are assessed by the *outcomes of their work*. Some pupils do not *persevere* (v.17) and there are always a variety of good teachers (v.18). Compare the teaching styles of John the Baptist and Jesus.

Wisdom goes beyond words and is seen in *deeds*.

Verses 20–24. Wrong-doing must be challenged variously with *wisdom and courage*.

Verses 25–30. Good students are a *delight* to their teacher and a source of *thankfulness*. Jesus knew that the students would have difficulties and that he must be thoroughly *supportive* and work *side-by-side* with them.

The pupils who responded found that 'the good teacher' is gentle, responsive and creates joy.

Chapter 12

Verses 1–8. There is likely to be perpetual *conflict* between *tradition and progress*.

Tradition is likely to be critical and may stand in contrast to the merciful teacher who recognizes what is truly *significant in and to* pupils.

Jesus *defended* his pupils against criticism. *Mercy* is at the heart of teaching. Pupils responded to this *defensive care*. Jesus knew that the pupils were *greater than the rules*. Mutual esteem grew out of this response.

Verses 9–14. The conflict between tradition and progression persisted and became an issue of conformity or need satisfaction. Jesus sacrificed established procedures for a more *pupil-centred approach*. There were always critics, even when the teacher was doing good. Many needs are self-evident and can be responded to as a matter of course.

The good teacher was (is) full of *surprises*. Good is *good* even if it breeds opposition.

Verses 15–21. This passage characterizes Jesus' manner and priorities. He *actively met every need* and showed that he had the following qualities.
- A willing servant heart.
- A person who is well pleasing and brings pleasure.
- The sense of fairness and justice.
- He was *not argumentative* for the sake of it.
- He was not discouraging.
- He gave the widest degree of *hope*.
- He *persisted* until he was successful.
- Teachers can be *driven away* by strident criticism from *lesser teachers*.
- He went into the *community* and did not remain in the official, safe 'school'.
- Again Jesus demonstrated that *mercy* (v 13) results in *motivation* (v 15).
- Good teachers are recognizable within an historic train of teachers who have possessed certain *transforming qualities*.
- Good teaching *costs* but is ultimately *rewarded*.

.2c-51
When can it be right to challenge pupils so severely?

Verses 22–37. Jesus had to defend his teaching.

Jesus' was insistent that there is a *moral basis* for good teaching.

What we say reflects who we are! Another example of Jesus' apparently simple statements.

'Out of the abundance of the heart the mouth speaks.'

Pupils recognize who good teachers are.

Teachers need to feed the heart and store good treasures that can be brought out and shared.

Verses 38–45. There is no point in being negative about discipline. Unless *goodness replaces wrong*, it will have a short-term effect.

Morality as well as spirituality comes from the heart.

Verses 46–50. Jesus *identified with his pupils* and they identified with him – but the *role model* needs to be one who can be identified confidently.

Chapter 13

Verses 1–17. This is a key chapter in respect of Jesus' teaching methods. He had to persuasively explain his concept of the Kingdom of God to people who had deeply embedded alien concepts. Therefore he had two problems.

- Prejudice.
- How to achieve this fresh understanding.

He had no books or formal organization to help them and their thoughts needed to be *memorable* and *succinct so* that people would go home and talk about the stories etc. His methods were based upon:

- Observation.
- Deductive reasoning.
- Interpreting common identifiable situations.

This encouraged people to think and answer the spiritual puzzles he posed. Amazingly, much of the understanding was left to the pupils' motivation and interpretive ability. It is a sad insight (v.12) that those who have will have yet more. He clearly showed that it is a *privilege* for people to have insights and understanding as verse 16 shows.

Verses 18–23. He was *realistic* as the parable of the soil and the sower indicates. He accepted that much learning is wasted in one way or another. He stressed *personal responsibility*. The sower and the seed are seen to be common to all. It is the soil that makes the difference, which can be related to both the context and the pupil! Jesus was *realistic and accepted* that there would be considerable differences in the levels of fruitfulness.

Verses 24–30. Another parable uses precisely the same methods in that it is taken from everyday life and is within the pupils' powers of *deductive reasoning*.

Verses 31–32. The parable of the mustard seed follows the same methodology and reflected his belief about the Kingdom of God that would have been a delightful surprise to many Galileans and a shock to the Pharisees.

Verses 33–36. These parables were *brief, memorable* illustrations taken from common life. They required deductive reasoning and established high priorities. One can just imagine the people in the crowds waiting for the next story and to see whether it would-be related to their occupation. He was *achieving attention* and relevance.

.2c-52
What does goodness and mercy and mean it in the context of teaching?

Verses 46–43. Although the parables were memorable they were not all easily understood. Wisely, Jesus was encouraging the people *to reflect and talk* before telling them the answer. He *concluded with the promise* but he also does not expect everybody to understand fully.

Verses 44–46. How brief these illustrations were and yet they were *pregnant with meanings*. This was a major teaching principle for Jesus.

Verses 47–52. This is important. In verses 51 and 52 Jesus' was reiterating that it should be possible for *traditional and progressive teaching to co-exist* even though they are distinctively different. These were significant words.

Verses 53–58. Jesus was *persistent*. He was unqualified and yet had superior *wisdom*. He was also a local person and familiarity has bred contempt. These combined to cause rejection. *Pupil faith* in the teacher is essential and over-familiarity can be a major hindrance.

Chapter 14

Verses 1–12. The death of John the Baptist hurt Jesus and he needed a time for *reflection*, which is an important principle in the teaching process.

Verses 13–21. The common people gathered around him – he had the *common touch* that was based upon his *compassion*. Note carefully:
- He faced up to *problems*.
- He did not send people away.
- He met people's *needs*.
- He maximized the available *resources*.
- Everything was done in an orderly fashion.

This was another example of *apprenticeship learning*.

Verses 22–36. A characteristic of his teaching was that *he never really left them alone*. He kept his eye on his apprentices even though they were not aware of it. He was constantly *encouraging* them (v.27). He *tested* his disciples severely but gave them adequate *support* so that they would not completely fail. Everything needed to have a *positive motive*.

Chapter 15

Verses 1–20. Jesus showed that he was a man of *reality and courage*. Again he talked in *everyday language* and *capitalized on every situation*.

He was not concerned about ceremonial but about the internalization of knowledge and the development of positive attitudes and moral standards.

Verses 21–28. Jesus, like every teacher got tired and even exasperated at times.

He kept an open ear and *rewarded* the woman who *persisted* in her faith.

Verses 29–31. He *encouraged* and yet *tested* the people's *motivations* as he went up mountain where they had to follow.

They did so because *they believed that he could meet their needs*, which is at the heart of all good teaching.

It was good that the teacher could leave the pupils and even better when they *diligently sought him*.

Verses 32–39. Characteristics of his teaching were that he had:
- Compassion and empathy.
- Met their needs.
- Did not turn them away.
- Encouraged them.
- Left them with something to think about.

.2c-53
Which particular teaching skills are notable in this chapter of parables?

Chapter 16

Verses 1–12. Cynics will criticize even eminently good things. Some people always reject the person where there are rival ideas or where their position is threatened.

He was consistently building up a tradition of valued undeniable experiences.

He talked so that *pupils needed to ask questions* and had the *confidence to do so* with him being open with his answers. Jesus had to help the pupils *recall their experiences* and *explain* them. Experiences alone were not enough – but they were very significant!

Verses 13–20. Sometimes pupils must *face hard questions*, *make decisions* and say what they *personally believe*. People can come to a wide range of conclusions even after seeing the same evidence. Jesus almost seemed surprised when Peter showed that he had interpreted the experiences correctly.

Verses 21–23. There are critical times when teachers must bite the bullet and either *pursue or withdraw*.

Verses 24–28. This represented a genuine problem. He was *the role model* that involved *personal discipline*. At a certain point *pupils* have to make *hard decisions.*

Chapter 17

Verses 1–8. *Not all pupils were equal.* Some could move on and be taken to a higher level of understanding. Jesus himself moved on and had his *faith and understanding confirmed.*

Despite the difficulties *his aspirations remained high.* By what criteria do *teachers earn the right* for pupils to listen to them? When may a pupil have a *sense of awe* of a teacher? Why? Should teachers be expected to have a *vision* for what they teach?

Verses 9–13. Is it likely that many *pupils will not understand* and *so reject the teacher?* Peer-group teaching was important to Jesus but what are its *limitations*? What are the strengths of *peer group learning?*

Verses 14–21. Peer-group teaching has its limitations and disappointments. Like any teacher Jesus was expected to *come to their rescue and encourage them on to the next stage.*

Verses 22–23. Jesus faced up to serious situations to *achieve the best goal.* In which situations is that still likely to occur for teachers? (e.g. when making *moral and spiritual demands.*)

Verse 24. Jesus met *his responsibilities*. What would that mean now in the context of teaching?

Are teaching and the of personal lifestyles plus professional methods usually totally integrated as they were with Jesus? Why? Faith is not just a religious word – what applications has it in everyday teaching.

Chapter 18

Verses 1–6. What did the notion of *humility* as part of a *caring lifestyle* means practically? What is the *significance of caring* to different types of teachers? How can teachers of all types expect to *learn from their pupils?*

Verses 7–9. When are these extreme *words of warning* apposite?

Verses 10–14. This represents a crucial aspect of Jesus as a teacher:
- Each person is of inestimable value.
- Pupils can go and get lost mentally / socially or be mentally immobile.
- Pupils should be organized to enable self-sufficiency when necessary.
- There should be joy in rescuing deviant or wandering pupils.

Verses 15–20. Be frank with the offender but leave scope for reconciliation. The issue of order and authority remains.

.2c-54
How might we generate faith in the teacher?

- Each person is of inestimable value.
- Pupils can go and get lost mentally/socially or be immobile.
- Pupils should be organized to enable self-sufficiency when necessary.
- There is joy in rescuing deviant or wandering pupils.

Verses 15–20. Be frank with the offender but leave scope for *reconciliation*. The issue of *order and authority* remain.

Verses 21–35. Jesus shows that the principle of teacher *forgiveness* is applicable.

Teaching is not unique – Jesus shared *universal principles*. The principle of *unforgiveness* and subsequent *negative outcomes* remain. Ultimately, justice is of God, but it may be worked out in this life.

Chapter 19

Verses 1–12. Jesus highlighted the need for basic *rules to protect* those who need it. Jesus accepted that not all people would receive some of his teaching because of the *hard elements* - it is not all pleasant and warm blessings!

Verses 13–15. This contrasts with the previous hard sayings. He would not allow any barriers between himself and children – his *heart has nothing but blessings for them*.

Verses 16–30. Jesus had a hard message that reflected the nature of teaching. A person with high aspirations must know this and comply with the basic requirements. It is likely to touch sensitive areas and might become more significant than the original aspirations. They need to know *the priorities and demands of the situation*.

Chapter 20

Verses 1–16. He was more concerned with the *task* than the competition for rewards. He demonstrated that people may work hard and long and yet only receive the same wages as others. The good teacher has a generous heart!

Verses 17–19. He knew that he could only share his secrets with a few. He was *differentiating* his followers yet again. The criteria would be *faith, obedience, servanthood,* compassion and the ability to convey hope. This contrasted with the normal criteria or over-ambition, privilege and control and riches and rewards.

Verses 20–28. Jesus emphatically stated that privilege/ambition is divisive. The real character is *servanthood* but it is necessary to define what this means.

Verses 29–34. He saw needs and his response was characterized by *pity and competence*.

Chapter 21

Verses 1–11. The teacher responded *peaceably to support* but did not necessarily use or rely upon it. He was aware of *degrees of commitment and permanence*.

Verses 12–17. Jesus would not be deviated. He contended for *absolute values*.

Verses 18–22. Even the strangest situations contain the element of promise.

Verses 23–27. Jesus answered critical questions with questions. He knew that argument was of little values in that situation and this revealed his *own wisdom*.

Verses 28–46. Jesus told the Pharisees a series of parables about judgment that were largely self-evident but must have shocked them. He emphatically stood for *righteousness*.

Chapter 22

Verses 1–14. The crisis between the traditionalists and the servant teacher intensified as Jesus told this third parable. When is *the traditional versus progressive conflict justified*?

.2c-55
What aspects of teaching did Jesus display during the crucifixion period?

Verses 15–22. He met *legitimate* demands.

Verses 22–33. Jesus made a *firm response* to the hierarchy who were wrong.

Verses 34–40. Jesus met recalcitrant opposition with short unanswerable statements. This was the *wisest policy* in a conflict situation.

Chapters 23–25

The situation changed. Jesus used the skills that were mastered to describe issues of justice memorably and imaginatively. He used parables to give warnings about continuing his work and maximizing achievement.

The trial and crucifixion

Jesus gave his pupils the ultimate demonstration of being the *role-model of servanthood, sacrifice and love* – the character of the Kingdom in practice. He was showing *courage, forgiveness, fortitude* as well as being full of *grace* and *truth*.

He figuratively explained the notion of rewards (ch.25 v.13).

Chapter 26

Verses 6–13. At all times there is the place for *mutual appreciation*

Verses 17–29. The teacher is also a friend and at the Passover we see *fellowship, commitment and reinterpreting* the ancient custom.

Verses 30–35. He was *honest* with his pupils even when they refused to believe what he said.

Chapter 27 The Crucifixion—The ultimate demonstration

Chapter 28 The Resurrection

Although the best examples of Jesus' teaching methods at this stage are found in Luke and John's Gospels, it does conclude with the ultimate vindication and his great commission so go and make disciples or apprentices just as he had. The teacher had both given the blueprint and inspired the pupils to do it.

.2c-56a
What sort of hard decisions might a person have to make? What might be the teacher's role at such a time?

Personality Factor – 5

Identify any examples where personality factors influence a person's teaching style

.2c-56b
What made Jesus such a special teacher then?.... Now? to so many

Part B

Looking at Jesus' teaching methods within social psychology

Good techniques are vital, but that is only a part of the story. What transforms leadership changes perceptions and motivation, improves memory, enhances socialization enables cognition to flourish and for positive emotions to raise the level of the learning ethos? How did Jesus elevate his methods to maximize such qualities and achieve long-term learning?

Social psychology can probe and enhance our understanding of contemporary teaching in the light of Jesus' teaching strategies. This will be an exploratory but useful framework to capitalize on Jesus' insights. Although most social psychology is perceived within secular/ humanist frameworks, it can be compatible with the approaches of Jesus. Like most successful teachers, he instinctively used many social psychological principles.

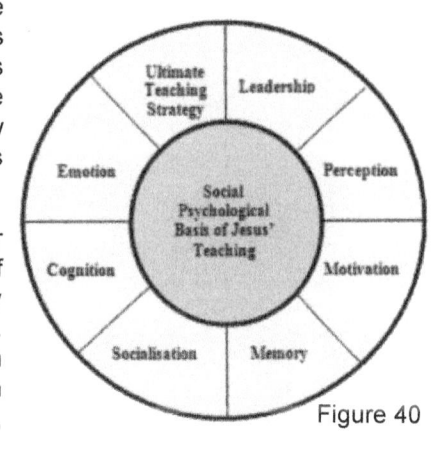

Figure 40

He developed his 'Big Picture' of God the Father etc, he taught more than one stage of his vision at a time (i.e. parallel processing) and developed principled understandings (or patterned schemas) amongst his disciples.

We can appreciate Jesus' creative and supremely high view of man. Relevant questions here, for example, are how his creative leadership produced long-term learning and to achieve his priorities? Is it possible to develop pupils' perceptions, maximize motivation and memory, develop healthy attitudes and enhance thinking skills using his methods?

A survey by United Nations International Children's Emergency Fund (UNICEF) stated that British children are poorer, at greater risk and more insecure than those in 20 other wealthy nations. This was reinforced by similar findings in 2008. Whether or not this is true, it encourages us to examine issues of teaching and learning with carefully. To do so Part B will consider aspects of human behaviour as they relate to teaching and learning. The following sections reveal man in an holistic sense but also consider seven major themes involving Jesus' teaching techniques and modern analyses. The themes are:

Leadership	**Perception**	**Motivation**	**Memory**
Socialization	**Cognition**	**Emotions**	**plus Ultimate Strategy B**

Of course, none of these components are isolated, but each is influenced by the other themes to varying degrees (there are a minimum of 175 interactive nodal points and 'infinite' variations within the 7 themes!). Even so the 18 point matrix at the opening of each theme highlights major issues to some degree.

To make the process manageable, eight major questions summarize these themes in the light of Jesus' practices and modern developments.

Q1 What is meant by high quality worthwhile teaching and learning?
Q2. What might characterize a good teacher who is also a leader to learners?
Q3. How do learners perceive their long-term learning prospects during current teaching?
Q4. What are the most worthwhile and reliable means of motivating pupils?
Q5 How can learning be made memorable?
Q6. Which patterns of behaviour and attitudes are likely to gratify pupils in the long-term?
Q7 Which patterns of understanding, cognition, creativity, imagination and problem solving might aid pupils in the long term?
Q8. How should teachers be developing and using the emotions of their pupils?

.2c-57
What makes high-quality teaching worthwhile?

Chapter 5

Leadership

Leadership across the themes

Looking forwards: Leaders as teachers? ...Covey's ideal model and questions... Leadership characteristics... Greater goals of leadership...Five particular practices...Kouzes' and Posner's ideal model... His pattern of leadership...Top down/bottom up leadership...A significant other...The leader/master craftsman...This servant leader... Expectations/modern applications.

Prior to every chapter there is a matrix of questions that relate the theme to the six other themes. These pose questions about the social psychological issues, how they raised issues for Jesus and their implications for today. A summary matrix follows (ch.12).

Indisputably Jesus was a defining leader from whom inspiration flowed, but what might the insights from social psychology indicate about him as teacher and leader and how might they relate to the other six themes? The questions in the overarching themes are addressed and summarized in the text and in Part C.

As stated earlier this is not suggesting that Jesus had a precise technical understanding of leadership (or teaching) methods, but it does appear that he intuitively used generic methods that we now regard as modern.

Figure 41

THEME	Issues particular to the theme	Relating the theme specifically to Jesus	Relating the theme to teaching generally
Perception	How does a leader perceive the task, people and situation?	How did Jesus perceive his leadership role?	How is a leadership perceived when teaching?
Motivation	How is the leader both self-motivated and able to motivate others?	How did Jesus as leader motivate others?	How can pupils be motivated to learn?
Memory	How does a leader choose what is memorable?	How did Jesus choose and make material memorable?	How is teaching made memorable?
Socialization	How does a leader socialize his followers?	How did Jesus socialize people into his chosen ways?	How does a teacher train pupils into appropriate behaviour?
Cognition	How does a leader understand his tasks etc?	How did Jesus learn and teach others essential understandings?	How can effective learning procedures be achieved?
Emotion	How do leaders use emotions creatively	How did Jesus use emotions to maximize learning?	How does a teacher use emotions discriminately?

.2c-58
How did Jesus relate his aims to the pupils' aims?

Leadership Qualities

Below are 16 of the qualities that might be found in leaders. In the case of Jesus, which stand out and what is missing?

Leadership Qualities

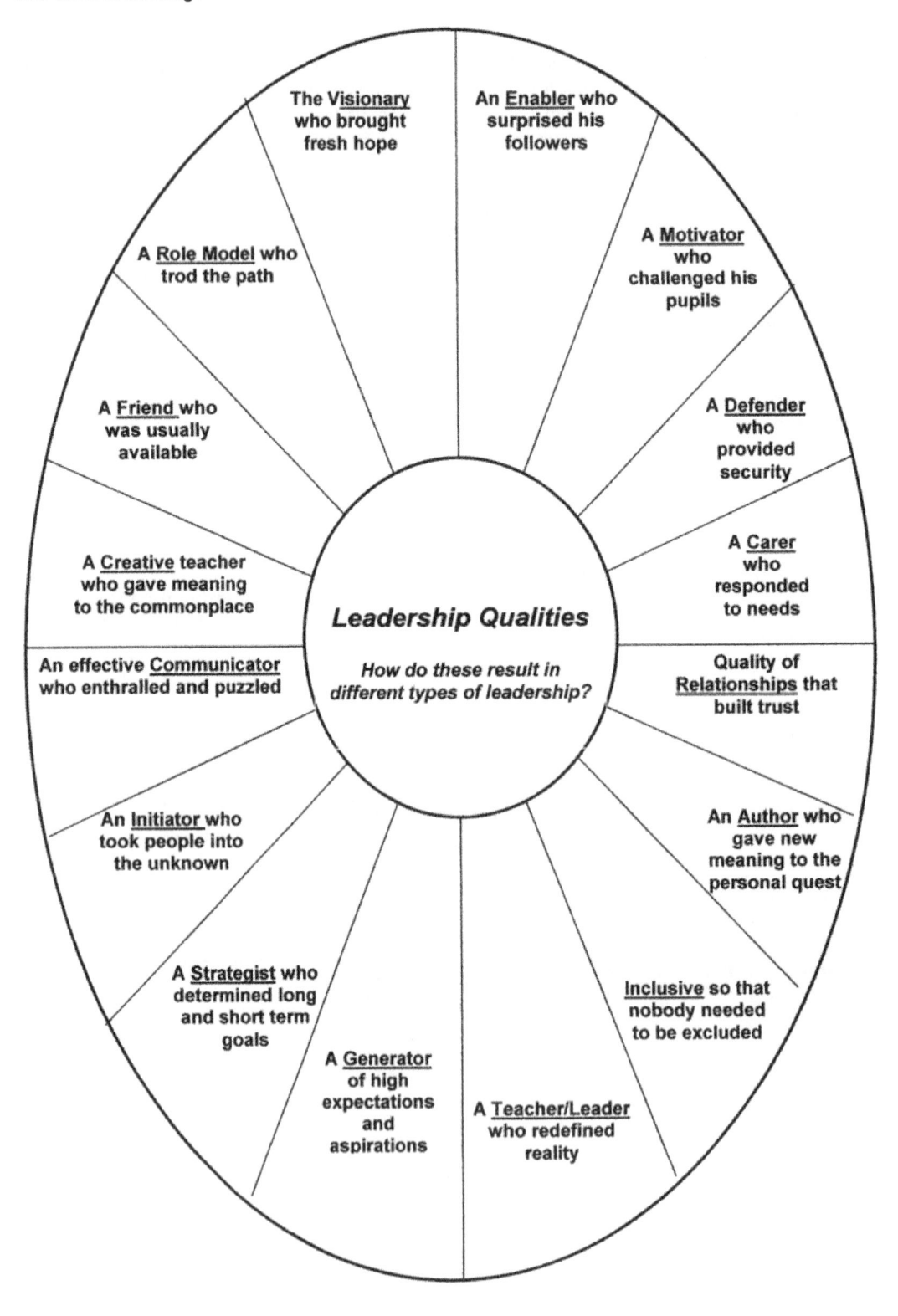

How do these result in different types of leadership?

- The **Visionary** who brought fresh hope
- An **Enabler** who surprised his followers
- A **Role Model** who trod the path
- A **Motivator** who challenged his pupils
- A **Friend** who was usually available
- A **Defender** who provided security
- A **Creative** teacher who gave meaning to the commonplace
- A **Carer** who responded to needs
- An effective **Communicator** who enthralled and puzzled
- Quality of **Relationships** that built trust
- An **Initiator** who took people into the unknown
- An **Author** who gave new meaning to the personal quest
- A **Strategist** who determined long and short term goals
- **Inclusive** so that nobody needed to be excluded
- A **Generator** of high expectations and aspirations
- A **Teacher/Leader** who redefined reality

Figure 42 More than an enforcer!

.2c-59

Can there be a balance between coercion and free commitment?

Principles of Jesus' Leadership

All leaders may not be teachers, but all teachers are likely to be leaders to a degree and some are both leaders and teachers – of which Jesus was one. Indeed, without leadership qualities it is doubtful if he could have been a successful teacher. But what were his leadership qualities? After years of reflection, a disciple, John described Jesus' leadership and character as being full of grace and truth. But how far can that take us in his practical tasks that lay ahead? Also, what relationship can there be between common religions and teaching leadership styles and any guidance it can provide generally.

Figure 43

	Personal Finding One's Voice		Corporate Inspiring others	
Mind	Vision Possibilities?	Creativity Thinking strategically Reflection	Common vision	Shared vision Pathfinding
Body	Discipline Requirements to achieve vision	Ability to take action Consistent to	Effective systems	Implement common vision Focus energy Aligning
Emotions	Passion Conviction and drive to sustain discipline	Commitment Hopefulness Courage	Empowerment	Whole hearted commitment and dedication to others
Spirit	Conscience Inward moral sense Guiding force Vision, passion Discipline	Responsibility Wisdom Respectfull Compassionate	Conscience modelling	Follow willingly

Links between Jesus' teaching and leadership were direct and observable. The religious authorities expected deference, but their leadership needed to be *imposed.* Jesus knew that his authority needed to be freely recognised and so rejected coercive control and saw his teaching as integral to the concept of servant-hood. This authority was based on his words, actions and lifestyle. But could his leadership generate an ethos to which pupils would respond positively in the long term? In contrast to the religious authorities, Jesus' informal authority was vulnerable because it relied upon his personal authority and expertise being *voluntarily accepted.*

The mind map (Fig.42) shows a range of qualities that might be expected in such a leader as Jesus. As his followers gained confidence so their expectations rose. Leaders may be limited to particular specialisms, but he was multi-skilled and cut a fresh path that motivated and enabled his followers to thrive within his personal and corporate abilities. His spiritual and moral basis provided people with grounds for believing in the fulfilment of his great promises. A succinct analysis of such leadership qualities (Fig.43) has been structured by Stephen Covey. This model, 'the Four Dimensions of Man' is not a religious analysis of leadership but one can envisage Jesus *'finding his voice'* during the 'hidden years' and then 'inspiring others' He built lives as if they were works of art.(Heschel). Even so, the question remained - how to transform the aspirations of his fellow countryman, and others! He was an *encourager and enabler* rather than an enforcer.

From the outset the issue of authority was dominant. There could be no compromise. He was tolerant but insisted that ultimately his was the only way. This leader's code of practice provided *Positive* learning that was *Authentic* and attractively *Creative* as he taught his vision of the *Truth.* The popular belief in his dual role of teacher/leader increased as his 'heroic activities' met needs and raised aspirations but relatively few entered into the total teacher- pupil involvement Jesus required, but he would not be deviated. His leadership required both truth and pertinacity and for

.2c-60
What should be the priorities of a good teacher/leader?

people to freely enter *his* world and for *his vision* to become *theirs'*. Perhaps people were waiting to be liberated. He worked alongside them telling recognizable stories and was visible during times of uncertainty. Not surprisingly, they turned and listened to an admired master. They appeared to be agreeing a *PACT* voluntarily.

Jesus' challenge was awesome given his starting point, but although he was distinctive from conventional religious leaders and conquering generals, politicians or business entrepreneurs he shared major leadership characteristics. He inspired followers to believe the worth of his teaching and to trust in his courage and acumen as he displayed heroic qualities and abilities. These generated sufficient confidence and admiration for them to identify with him.

Jesus' spiritual leadership involved a commitment to destiny with powerful 'ideas'. He created dreams and whilst he did not command allegiance, he inspired it. He did not lead an army, but he enabled many others to achieve alternative conquests. He exceeded their expectations. He seized the initiative, created change and challenged followers to imitate him. They would look at the world with fresh eyes and expect to find new opportunities. He wanted fundamental changes and created unforeseen possibilities. But what does this indicate about his teaching style, and what are the implications for the current situation?

It is commonly held that successful leaders do not say 'I' but enable others to say 'we'. Although Jesus was the dominant 'I', he transformed others to feel stronger and more capable than previously thought. Essential priorities of this teacher/leader were his *relationships* and *interpersonal skills*. Furthermore, his leadership flourished as he *demonstrated* his teaching and said, "Believe me for my very works sake". As he moved from town to town his followers became his apprentices, but he was not sidetracked from his greater goals because 'the good could be the enemy of the best'. Both his message and teaching methods reveal aspects of his leadership role:

- He *observed the qualities* of potential pupils and *invited* them to 'come and see' his work.
- He entrusted his vision to people who would *look, see, judge and act,* and become his long-term 'graduates' – a far cry from the prejudices of the authorities and the unreliable attitude of the crowds.
- He realized his pupils' *potential* exceeded their *apparent present capabilities*.
- The *pupils would do greater things* than he. This is reminiscent of a Jewish rabbi who bowed before students at the beginning of every lesson because the potential for the future lay in them.
- He was their role model who translated intention into reality and sustained it.
- His character and singleness of mind developed motivation and expectations.
- Jesus exceeded stereotypical learning. He needed *creative, adaptable people* to move into new, unknown situations because the world was their goal! But how could he train them?

In 2002 Kouzes and Posner published a business management leadership model (see Fig.44), which although not based on Jesus' example, closely reflected what he did. It is as though Jesus said to himself, "I will be their role model and inspire my shared vision. To achieve this I must encourage my followers."

Kouzes and Posner's course *Five Practices and Ten Commitments of Leadership* cut new territory in management training. Of particular interest is the fifth practice *'Encourage the Heart'*, which was what Jesus did and what the disciples copied. These five practices are achieved through the ten commitments. This aligns personal and shared values with appropriate actions, envisions the future, and attains its climax as it recognizes personal contributions and celebrates corporate achievements. Jesus was changing established mindsets and creating "an awareness beyond dreams" (Greenleaf).

.2c-61
How might a teacher/leader 'encourage the heart'?

Five Practices and Ten Commitments of Leadership	
Practice	*Commitment*
Model the way	Clarifying your personal values
	Set the example by aligning actions with values
Inspire a shared vision	Share the end vision and future possibilities
	Enlist others in a common vision
Challenge the process	Seek innovative ways to change, grow and improve
	Experiment and take risks - generate small wins and learn from mistakes
Enable others to act	Foster collaboration with co-operative goals and building trust
	Strengthen others by sharing power and discretion
Encourage the heart	Recognize and appreciate individual excellence
	So achieve the great values and victories by creating a spirit of community

Figure 44

Teaching is based on values bonded by shared tasks that provide achievement, pride and a sense of identity. But not everybody wanted or could follow this pattern, even though Jesus was willing to serve all and provide privileged responsibilities to those who wanted it – sufficiently! Jesus breathed life into exciting possibilities so that their dream for the common good could be achieved. But they needed to work with their 'heart'. Kouzes and Posner's leadership model was originally designed for commercial uses but it is applicable to teaching and matches not only Jesus' own practice but much modern teaching.

Many leadership analyses have been applied to Jesus. There is no doubt that at times he was autocratic and directive because that was appropriate to the situation. But whilst he was authoritarian, this charismatic motivator was also a benevolent enabler who laid great store on creative but disciplined relationships. Therefore, Jesus had a flexible and multi-style leadership that and was adaptable to the situation. This was appropriate and matched the dynamics of the leader's power, the relationship with group and the task requirements. Not all would be such flexible leaders/teachers but all could make decisions about priorities of goals, content, relationships, methods and definitive roles.

Jesus' leadership touched something identifiable in people. Although he drew upon the best prophetic traditions, he convinced people by his presence (Whitman) and the fresh hope he generated. It was inclusive and had universal applications that enabled him to move easily between cultures without making many racial demands. At times he was vulnerable and only protected by his popularity amongst the common people. Even so he knew that their shouts of support were unreliable. His demanded commitment and understanding, hence he invested a high proportion of his time on his close followers. The issue remained – what could they expect from him and he from them? They realized that he did not exploit the poor but was a teacher who held himself responsible for both his and their actions and fearlessly met any challenges. Therefore, what began as an informal authority quickly became formalized in the eyes of many who regarded him as an authoritative rabbi without formal qualifications. What emerged was a personal vision expressed in tangible attitudes developed through a variety of hands-on methods. And so his pattern of leadership emerged (Fig.44).

> .2c-62
> *What are the relative advantages of top-down and bottom-up decision- making?*

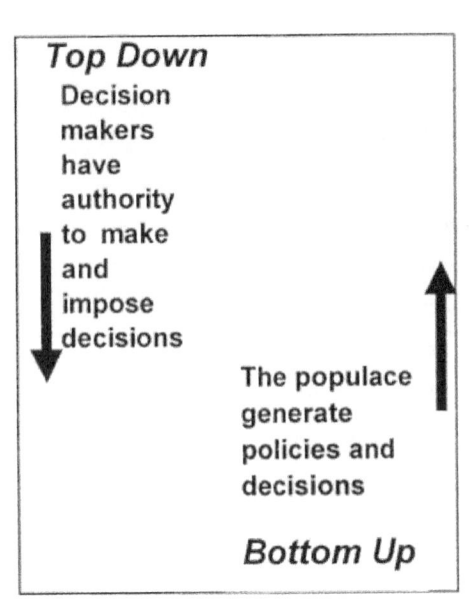

Top Down
Decision makers have authority to make and impose decisions

The populace generate policies and decisions

Bottom Up

Figure 45

Both Jesus and the religious authorities adopted a *top-down* leadership based upon their knowledge and expertise, with very little scope for *bottom up* (or grass root) decision making and this resulted in led instruction teacher (Fig. 45).

It was clear that as a top down leader who made all the major decisions that he needed to have a total overview of the scene that involved goals, knowledge, methods, relationships etc. (Fig.46) and that these should be expressed to and received by his followers, especially as he was preparing them for his departure. The would then become the new Top Down leaders, but within the authority of their greater Top Down leader.

Figure 46

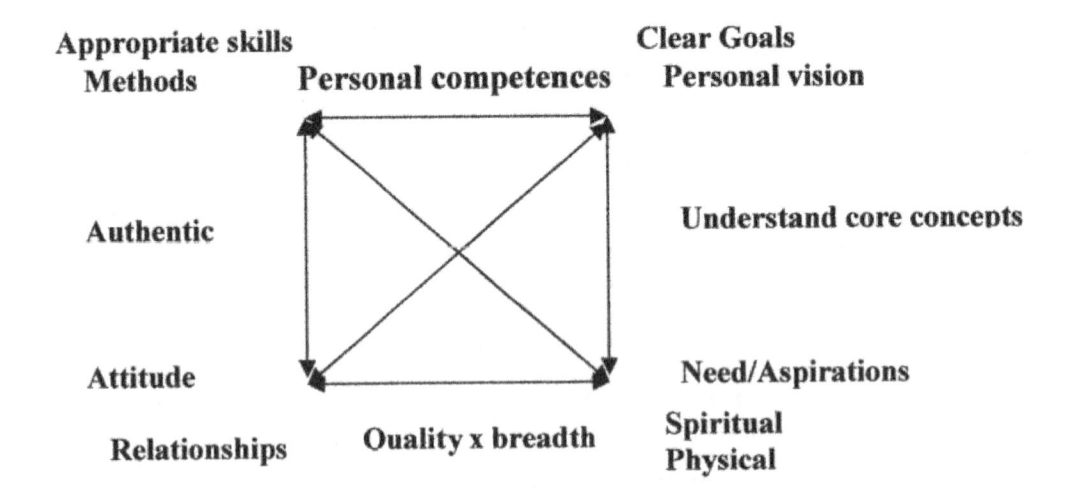

Appropriate skills / Methods — **Personal competences** — **Clear Goals / Personal vision**

Authentic — **Understand core concepts**

Attitude — **Need/Aspirations**

Relationships — **Quality x breadth** — **Spiritual / Physical**

Although he set the total agenda, the *relationships* that enabled people to work willingly within the situation was their choice. He knew that he had to trust the people, even to the point of letting them go. As he was watched them he knew that he too was being assessed! This could result in doubts and rejection of what he taught, but Jesus provided a sense of progress that influenced people for good and took them beyond unsatisfactory traditional answers. Ultimately he trusted the untrustworthy to the point of failure that proved to be highly significant. He achieved his goal as they yielded their autonomy to him. He had recognized their potential before they recognised it in themselves as they ventured out taking initiatives! They were seeing something new which caused people to listen and believe that old and ongoing problems would be solved. Furthermore sustained links were being developed with people that might ensure the continuity and clarity of the values being taught and lived. This was aptly summarized by Alan Keith in the words *'Know yours and their values, be willing to take a risk and lead from the heart.'*

Jesus' teaching methods were inextricably linked to his pattern of leadership. Hence, his favourite metaphor of a shepherd with his flock was appropriate as he led and protected those who wanted to follow him, but his commitment was shown in his determination to rescue any who lost their way.

.2c-63
What are the likely effects when 'leading from the heart'?

Jesus – the leader/master craftsman

As their role model Jesus followed an ancient tradition of the master craftsman teaching his apprentices. One can see twelve characteristics of Jesus' leadership/teaching model. After considerable *self-preparation* he was *confident* in what and how he would teach regardless of the response of the people. He was the *'Master Craftsman'*.

- He *told* the people about the Kingdom, and *demonstrated* its characteristics.
- The master carpenter became *recognised* as a spiritual 'master craftsman'.
- He gave *assistance* to those who stayed with him and had faith in him? They persisted, watched and helped him in a wide range of situations.
- He sent them out in pairs to provide *mutual support* and *work like he did*.
- They *replicated his work* and found that they could do it!
- They were encouraged by the fact that they had a new found competence..
- He then further developed their knowledge.
- He promised that they would *do greater things* than he, the master, had done.
- He promised them continued assistance, guidance etc
- Leadership reflects the personality and the role of the person concerned. This was so with Jesus. His robust leadership then *produced his masterpiece of creativity* to set the standard of the Kingdom of God.
- His leadership qualities can be summarized in Figure 47.

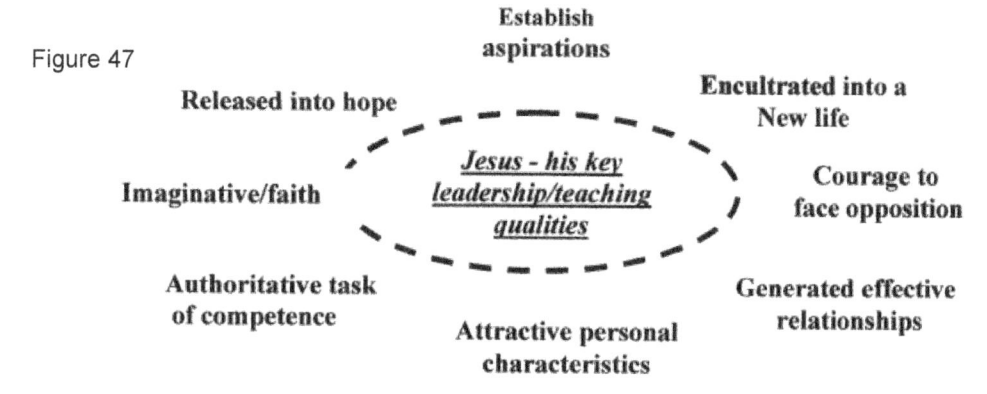

Figure 47

Jesus - his key leadership/teaching qualities

- Establish aspirations
- Released into hope
- Encultrated into a New life
- Imaginative/faith
- Courage to face opposition
- Authoritative task of competence
- Attractive personal characteristics
- Generated effective relationships

Many learners were awe struck. Whilst his teaching could be construed as delightful and comforting and provided the possibility of freedom, his actions and the serious tenor of his teaching determined the nature of their relationship. He was responsible for what happened and opened new avenues for his followers, but as he challenged the ruling class and the exploitation by the Temple traders, the two-way commitment became increasingly evident. When Jesus said, 'he that has ears to hear, let him hear' what would the response be?

Jesus did not fit easily into any leadership model. He was not totally autocratic, demanding absolute obedience because he let people leave him without any criticism. It would appear that there were followers who believed but who came and went. For those who remained *his vision became their vision*. As the guardian and definer of the vision, he enabled them to move authoritatively in his name. Also, it was not a case of them democratically conferring leadership upon him, but rather them voluntarily accepting his leadership. Similarly, his was not a *laissez-faire* leadership because although people could come and go there was no doubt who was in control and made all major decisions. His leadership had to be recognised and obeyed and a degree of separation accepted for long-term learning to occur. Although he was the undoubted leader, when people began to desert him he asked Peter, "Will you also go away?" Peter replied, "To whom can we go?" *Mutual dependency had been achieved.*

This Servant Leader

Leaders are recognized by their values. Jesus constantly depicted himself and his followers as *servants*. The implications of this for the servant

.2c-64
How can values indicate a possible leadership style?

leader/ teacher were far-reaching. This was an emphatic, non-negotiable statement - but what does it mean in practice as it counters the common view of authority, and might even be perceived as weakness. Covey stated that leadership derives power from values and principles. An assessment of what this might have meant for Jesus is listed in Fig.48. From it we can say that his style was built on character and humility together with the willingness to learn. This servant was being observed and subliminal messages were being conveyed. Followers could see that to Jesus servant hood was not a belittling term but rather contained fine qualities. He was accessible and both affirmed and empowered others. He provided a calm strong centre of warm persuasion and recognised the potential attainments of his pupils. Above all, this was a creative leadership. Figure 48 Jesus' leadership valuesleader, when people began to desert him he asked Peter, "Will you also go away?" Peter replied, "To whom can we go?" *Mutual dependency had been achieved.*

This Servant Leader

Leaders are recognized by their values. Jesus constantly depicted himself and his followers as *servants*. The implications of this for the servant leader/ teacher were far-reaching. This was an emphatic, non-negotiable statement – but what does it mean in practice as it counters the common view of authority, and might even be perceived as weakness. Covey stated that leadership derives power from values and principles. An assessment of what this might have meant for Jesus is listed in Fig.48. From it we can say that his style was built on character and humility together with the willingness to learn. This servant was being observed and subliminal messages were being conveyed. Followers could see that to Jesus servant hood was not a belittling term but rather contained fine qualities. He was accessible and both affirmed and empowered others. He provided a calm strong centre of warm persuasion and recognised the potential attainments of his pupils. Above all, this was a creative leadership.

Figure 48 Jesus' leadership values.

No.	Characteristic values
1.	His teaching was value based e.g. John 8 v1ff.
2.	He built on existing spiritual and moral teaching.
3.	Basic criteria in his teaching - e.g. the fatherhood of God, restoration, service etc
4.	He worked within an historic continuity - past, present, future expectations.
5.	Universal values such as honesty and compassion permeated his teaching.
6.	He set out to change people's spiritual and mental values
7.	He taught for both behavioural and spiritual change.
8.	His principles of living were his teaching of the Kingdom of God
9.	His central guiding vision was love
10.	His attitude of acceptance, forgiveness/ restoration, inclusion, sacrifice etc
11.	He followed a heightened teaching of existing cultural norms
12.	Each person has a wider responsibility e.g. the salt of the earth etc
13.	He sought to establish a shared conscience
14	He esteemed a life of simplicity greater than that of greed
15	He taught the virtue of humility as against ambitious rivalry
16	He looked for trustworthiness/faithfulness
17	A respect - self, others, the environment and the wider world

.2c-65
What is the wisdom and the notion of being a servant leader?

Jesus knew the wisdom of prophetic leadership and that of the servant-like Moses. The prophet Isaiah had described the ideal leader as a suffering servant, which Jesus demonstrated to his followers. It stood in sharp contrast to servility. This servant would raise others to a higher level and both empower and enable them to be 'true selves'.

Servant leadership is not necessarily religious, but it is essentially moral with a defined attitude and spiritual framework. The dignity and empowerment rests with the server. The one being served experiences this, which is then, ideally, reciprocated and becomes part of a new lifestyle. This Servant Leader brought new values to others. Jesus could not serve that 'old fox' Herod but he could serve one of his noblemen and a courtier. He could not serve Pilate but he could serve a centurion.

There is a moral and spiritual imperative at the heart of servant hood. Indeed, the one who was to be served had to make the process possible for the waiting servant to act. Jesus could not serve the aggressive Pharisees and he neatly told one of them that they had to' be born again'. He could wait, he could turn the other cheek but the person had to be willing to be served and become a servant. Although Peter protested at the thought of being served by his Master in the Upper Room, Jesus had been serving him for the previous two and a half years. One can speculate that when he used the metaphor of the camel going through the eye of a needle, he was teaching both about humility and the desirable conditions for being served. The normal pattern of the lesser serving the greater was reversed, although ultimately the ideal would be that all could humbly serve each other with equanimity. We do not know how Jesus arrived at this great principle, but he would certainly have conceived that even God the Father has the heart of a servant.

It will be shown in Part C that this elusive concept of servant hood can be related to the *apprentice teaching model* rather than to a highly structured efficiency strategy. The principle was and is that its implementation is dependent upon a mutual humility.

The notion of conquering servants seemed contradictory and reversed customary practices. Leaders normally assume rights, privileges and powers over their electorate etc. These often increase as the period of leadership lengthens and the subjects remain tolerant of impositions made upon them. In contrast Jesus simply walked the streets, meeting needs, and asking nothing in return. This generated faith in such people as a poverty stricken woman who was healed when she touched his garment amongst the milling crowds. Jesus regarded her as a 'daughter' of the Kingdom. This was in essence his message of open, access to God and a judgment on leaders who separated themselves from the weak, the sick and the needy. He, the Servant Leader. He did not fear that this would undermine his authority – in fact quite the reverse. As he washed his disciples' feet, he knew that he was further establishing both the norms of the Kingdom of God and ultimately enhancing his own authority. This same attitude has been shown to be effective by both Christians and non-Christians such as Teresa of Calcutta, Dr Martin Luther King, Mahatma Gandhi, Nelson Mandela etc who have been servant leaders amongst the people. Jesus believed that he himself was under the authority of God who would ultimately vindicate him. Robert Greenleaf expressed the notion as follows.

> *"The servant leader is a servant first. It begins with the natural feeling that one wants to serve. Then conscious choices create aspirations to teach. The best test is: do those served become healthier, wiser, freer, more autonomous and more likely themselves to become servants?.... Such a person is a listener before being a talker, empathetic rather than a judge and a healer rather than hurtful, a persuader rather than an instructor as a community of faith is built. At the heart of this notion of this servant—leader—teacher is the commitment to the growth of others which can be seen in Jesus' ministry." (The Power of Servant Leadership' by Robert Greenleaf)*

.2c-66
Many leaders are not really leaders! Why?

This concept requires inner strength to see the possibilities in those being served, and having the faith and understanding to serve. And so a coherent pattern of leadership emerges and reveals aspects that are normally rejected because of excessived emands.

This view of servant leadership sharply identified Jesus' priority when developing others. His creative leadership was expected to produce creative problem solvers in his own image. It was a fundamental statement about the nature of leadership and would be brought together with motivation as illustrated in the parable of the talents, thereby producing a creativity characteristic of the Kingdom of God.

Let us look at eight principles and translate them into appropriate teaching. (Part C)

- Develop an *empathetic work/ learning environment* that enables pupils to know that the teacher is supportive and 'leads from the heart'.

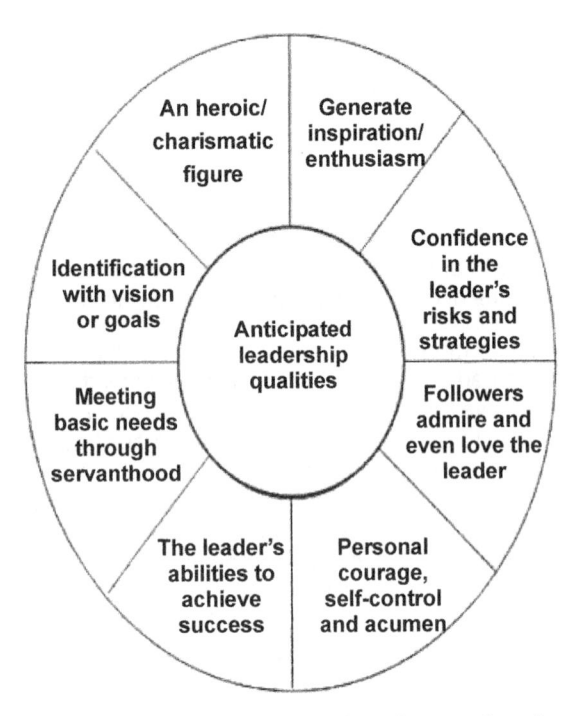

Figure 49 Strategic principles of servanthood

- There is room, time and proximity to imitate and learn from the role model.
- There is a total sense of *acceptance and inclusion.* (Greenleaf).
- The teacher is a *participant leader*, which requires competence and humility when pupils know more than the teacher.
- The leader *inspires and serves* all with appropriate opportunities and challenges.
- Jesus was big enough to hide behind and provide *security*.
- The principles are applied across the board 'from literacy to lifestyle'.
- The teacher *leads into* situations that may be surprising.

The Servant's methods for leading and teaching

Jesus might be seen as a craftsman-leader who tends to handle his materials with pleasure and pride – and this is probably how he handled his followers!

- He *responded spontaneously* to achievements.
- He *responded* according to needs and situations (Lazarus and Jairus).
- He faced up to the *priorities* of the occasion (John ch. 6).
- He used *dialogue* to take pupils to a higher level than expected (John ch. 4).
- He *delighted* and provided *surprises* that became topics of conversation.
- He *listened* as people struggled to answer the riddles he set before them.
- *Instruction alone is inadequate* and that learning needs to be active.
- He used *wide-ranging experiences* to bring learning to fruition.
- He gave pupils *leadership roles*.
- His *shared their heritage,* and *achievements were interpreted and used* as a forward indicator.
- He *minimized disappointment* (except at the Passion), and gave a sense of *moving* into the unknown.
- He *watched* them work and saved them *from failure* by opportune intervention.

.2c-67
Is servant leadership a viable style in teaching situations?

Jesus posed a well-known problem... he was emphatic that he himself was under authority and that yet he was in authority. Similarly, this servant was the shepherd who knew which path to take and who expected the followers he served to obey him. This highlighted that whilst the leader must lead, followers need to sense that they are pursuing worthwhile goals and that the leader will ensure they can succeed. But what did and still do people expect from a leader?

On three research programmes people were asked to prioritise 20 leadership characteristics. The four most significant James Kouzes and Brian Posner conducted research across six continents involving thousands of people to ascertain popular primary leadership expectations. The pattern of results showed a remarkable consensus of priorities were.

The qualities that were judged as being less important were in order of priority:

Inspirational	Honesty	Competence	Forward looking
5. Intelligent	6. Fair-minded	7. Broad-minded	8. Supportive
9. Straight forward	10. Dependable	11. Co-operative	12. Determined
13. Imaginative	14. Ambitious	15. Courageous	16. Caring
17. Mature	18. Loyal	19. Self-controlled	20. Independent

Figure 50 Jesus — the qualities of the leader:

These findings were surprisingly consistent, but Jesus displayed these four major leadership qualities, together with many less significant ones. One suspects that this was in contrast to many religious leaders. If people's judgments in first century Galilee even had a semblance of similarity to our understanding, then Jesus' leadership powers were not surprising. For example, no matter whether it was a Roman soldier or a Samaritan woman at a well, he met needs that covered physical, social, emotional and spiritual aspects of life etc. Furthermore, he revealed these characteristics and raised their historic aspirations.

Modern applications of Jesus' leadership/ teaching.

Jesus' holistic approach to teaching involved 10 fundamental principles:
- *Confident relationships* were incorporated within instructional techniques.
- He provided *success* that was built upon his own and their efforts.
- The pupils felt *proud and secure* to be associated with the teacher.
- Jesus taught from and into their *common experiences and needs.*
- Pupils enjoyed the sustained, tangible *achievements.*
- When failure occurred there was the opportunity of face-saving *reinstatement.*
- The pupils enjoyed the rising expectations based on *demonstration and reality.*
- There were *crises* but the teacher *resolved* them.
- The pupils made *real decisions.*
- The pupils learnt to translate the physical into the spiritual *like their master.*

.2c-68
Which of the leadership qualities listed above, or others, would you look for in a teacher leader?

Summary 5

1. This may appear to be an idealized view of Jesus, the leader/teacher and one that has not been generally copied over the centuries but it was his purpose to create a faith that would have these effects on his followers. Namely, he
    - Was essentially *principled*.
    - Was driven by a unique quality of *vision and purpose*.
    - Was in focused *control*.
    - Had unequivocal criteria for *decision-making*.
    - Displayed consistent criteria for *worth*.
    - Defined personal *wholeness* to include *spirituality*.
    - Resolve personal *needs* within declared *principles*.
    - Took on a role model of *servant-hood*.
    - Promoted and validated the blend of *experiential and reception learning*.
    - Recognized that individual learning incurs *sacrificial costs*.
    - *Enabled* his followers to become *high achievers*.
    - *Consistently* supported and *encouraged* his followers.
    - The leader had *authority* based upon *vision and competence* to take followers forward.
    - The overall long-term view was to be *comprehensible and desirable*.
    - The leader teacher had responsibility for *guiding choices and planning*.
    - The leader teacher should have an optimum degree of *identification with pupils*.
    - The leader teacher needs to be aware of the *scope and uses of his abilities*.
    - The leader's authority is based on *the pupils' desire to follow* the teacher's leadership.

2. Consider the following characteristics of Jesus. Prioritize them as they leadership.
    - He was sure of his calling.
    - He cared about unwanted individuals.
    - He was slow to condemn.
    - He saw people as they might be.
    - He did not give up easily.
    - He saw them as whole people.
    - He gave up everything for others.

3. To summarize, Jesus showed that at the heart of the servant leader/ teacher are:
    - commitment to the growth of others.
    - a competence which evoked confidence and expectations in his followers.
    - a progressive clarification of his total strategy.
    - clear personal boundaries.
    - defined ethical, spiritual and social standards.
    - a distinctive and secure spiritual base.
    - courage to confront dominant views.

Personality Factor – 6

Which personality factors were particularly apparent in Jesus' pattern of leadership?

.2c-69
Which leadership qualities listed above would you look for in a teacher / leader?

Chapter 6

Perception

Looking forwards...Significance...Perception and World View...Man – the Interpreter...Jesus-perceiving the people...Teaching for perceptual development...Changing perceptions...Jesus and perceptual change...Major dilemmas...Summary.

> "We see things not as they are but as we are" E. Kant.

Perception is an observation that results in a discernment /awareness of an object, situation or person that is interpreted mentally to produce insights, 'knowledge' and intuitive judgments. It may be an intuitive recognition of what is true or false such as an identification of the particular qualities of an object, a person, situation, values or causal effects.

Figure 51

	Issues particular to the theme	Relating the theme specifically to Jesus	Relating the theme to teaching generally
Leadership	How does a leader perceive the task and situation?	How did Jesus perceive his leadership role?	How might a teacher perceive a leadership role?
Motivation	How does a person perceive a situation as it motivates ?	How did Jesus see situations and people so that he was motivated to act?	How do T/P perceptions motivate them to teach and learn appropriately?
Memory	What does a person perceive as being significant to remember?	How did Jesus recognize and regard what was or not memorable?	How is T/L made to be perceived as worth being memorable?
Socialization	How do people perceive what is the best form of action in any situation?	How did Jesus perceive what was the best form of action in the Kingdom of God?	How do T/P perceive what is the best form of action in the T/L situation?
Cognition	What is the difference between perception and cognition?	How did Jesus perceive if people did or did not understand his teaching?	How do T/P perceive what is being taught/ learned?
Emotions	How do T/P perceive the emotional state of the P/T when T/L?	How did Jesus interpret the emotional state of the people around him?	How can the interpretation of the T/L situation be influenced by the emotions?

This theme is also developed in the other six themes. Such questions in the overarching themes are addressed within the text itself or summarized at the end of the theme.

> .2c-70
> *What is the most vital stage of changing people's perceptions?*

The Struggle for Perceptual Control

Perception is critically important because it is the basis of our judgments and human understanding generally! Every day we experience the powers of persuasion trying to influence our perception about anything and everything. It can be a small matter of retail advertising or a highly significant battle of competing ideas, priorities and actions ...and so it was with Jesus as he tried to change people's perception of God. His spiritual and social perceptions indicate how people arrived at judgments about him and how he saw himself, his teaching and those around him, but it goes beyond that.

Perceptions change – but how? The table below (Fig.52) shows a skeleton of perceptual change and the constant struggle to control people's perceptions within society.. Perceptions can originate and be rooted in the past so that tradition is virtually equated with truth and assumes considerable authority. But thereafter it is likely to be challenged, the strength of which may depend upon the prevailing degree of contentment, the presence of a rival ideology or such like (or any other competing force). These determine the historic pattern of power and highlights the present competition to control the acceptable realities. These consist at the present time of such forces as globalization, political and social aspirations and the challenge of industrial development and global warming. These various forces can variously strengthen, fade or become distorted and new dominant perceptions probably emerge. Excellent examples of this can be taken from the war in Iraq and the rising confidence of Islam. Saddam Hussein was nearly killed in the first 10 minutes of the Iraq war. if successful, that may have resulted in a different perception of the invasion by the USA and Great Britain in particular.

Figure 52

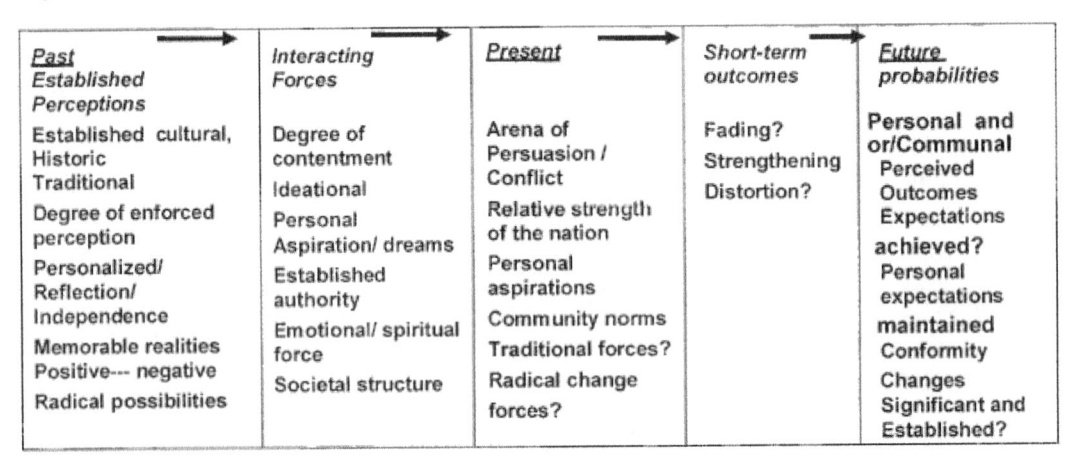

Past Established Perceptions	Interacting Forces	Present	Short-term outcomes	Future probabilities
Established cultural, Historic Traditional	Degree of contentment	Arena of Persuasion / Conflict	Fading? Strengthening Distortion?	Personal and or/Communal Perceived Outcomes Expectations achieved?
Degree of enforced perception	Ideational	Relative strength of the nation		
Personalized/ Reflection/ Independence	Personal Aspiration/ dreams	Personal aspirations		Personal expectations maintained
Memorable realities	Established authority	Community norms		Conformity
Positive--- negative	Emotional/ spiritual force	Traditional forces?		Changes
Radical possibilities	Societal structure	Radical change forces?		Significant and Established?

The Jews had a powerful historical tradition that had shaped their self-perception as the 'Chosen Nation' with Yahweh leading them ultimately to a great messianic age. This resulted in a national unity based on the authority of the religious law, the prophets and the religious authorities.

At the time of Jesus, radical change forces existed and the Galileans/ Judean link was not as strong as the Judeans wanted. What would happen after Jesus – would his revelation have faded, strengthened or become distorted? How would his followers' perception change? What would happen to Jewish national identity and messianic expectations?

The ultimate issues were credibility and trust without which there was little chance of persuasion and success – how would Jesus persuade people to recognize/perceive him as the Messiah?

    Q1. Which dominant forces would establish perceptual reality?

    Q2. What were the relative strengths of the various perceptions about Jesus in the land?

.2c-71
Which problems of perception do teachers and pupils face today?

Q3. How could Jesus change people's perception of him?

Q4. How could the authorities resist the changing perceptions amongst the people?

Q5. What were the likely perceptual outcomes amongst all concerned?

Q6. What were the long-term effects of the perceptual differences about Jesus?

All of these questions are universally relevant

To be an effective *leader* a person must be perceived as one. A person is usually *motivated* when the opportunities presented are *perceived* to be beneficial. *Memory* is activated sharply by incidents and facts that are perceived as significant. The same principles governing perception also influence *socialization, cognition and emotions.* Its importance is boundless. Also it determines the effectiveness of teaching and learning as the participants look at each other with varied degrees of trust, admiration and anticipation. Therefore, ongoing perceptual differences in respect of priorities, interpretations and predictions have extensive effects. Could these cause rebellion or negativity and so become a sub-cultural norm? Similarly, it is not surprising that the Jewish religious leaders perceived Jesus, the peacemaker, to be a rebellious troublemaker. How could he convince people that his was the correct perception (or truth) of God? It went beyond claiming to teach the truth. The question became whether they recognized each other's valid expectations. Jesus had to earn his authority by his actions and words. But would they perceive him to be the Messiah as he himself perceived it. Howbeit, when they did see him as such their particular perception was erroneous. His message stirred deep *aspirations* in many and his *actions* were recognized as signs by some *to* prove his credibility. Even so, there was no guarantee how any person would perceive Jesus – even amongst his followers.

A major task facing teachers, Jesus included, has been to ensure that pupils see the world and knowledge similarly to the teacher. If this similarity of perception cannot be achieved learning can be minimal or even counter-productive. Also, did Jesus perceive his disciples and the crowds so differently that he could wash his disciples' feet but not those of the crowds generally? We do not know but the implications are considerable. Each person may physically *see* objects and situations (i.e. *the sensation*) and yet *interpret* them (i.e. the *perception*) differently, and so we find ourselves in a web of rival perceptions that can be contradictory. The issue, therefore, becomes who is correct and can perceptual differences be tolerated or changed?

We occasionally look at illusions involving diagrams and pictures that we interpret individually. Although this can be a game the underlying significance is serious. This principle extends to our socio-cultural environment where we interpret what 'we see' as what we *'expect to see'* based on previous experiences. We look / see / think / experience and interpret what has been seen (visually or mentally). This may be true or false but is still used to arrive at 'rational' conclusions.

This characteristic may result in *'perception in terms of the probable'* (James) and develop into common stereotypical understandings. These develop into a *'world-view' (WV),* which becomes the basis of judgments. Our dynamic world-view may be stable and yet continually developing and making adjustments between expectations and actuality. These can compete or combine to modify our 'world-view'. This is especially seen when pupils do not perceive learning as worthwhile and decide not to invest time, energy and social relationships to it.

Our perceptions constantly meet new situations where they are gathered, selected and interpreted within a new 'mix' and so possibly arrive at rapid and even rash, habitual conclusions. Therefore, it might be said that each person is an *interpreter* of experiences. We do not see things precisely as they are, but as the mind develops mental patterns (see ch.11), so everything is interpreted. The trained eye is more perceptive than the untrained eye, but is maybe more conformist because it predicts what will occur based on past experiences. The principle of perception was fundamental to Jesus' teaching, and might be regarded as the key to understanding him. Although there were many travelling preachers in Galilee, he provoked a degree of concern amongst the leaders, because he and they were teaching within different perceptions of God. This competition between

.2c-72
Why might perceptions be regarded as anchoring points for new knowledge and experiences

rival perceptions was seen in his own family where at first he was disowned because of his claims. Gradually their perceptions changed and his brother James later led the infant church in Jerusalem. Similar conflicts occurred throughout the nation when some wanted to make him king whilst others finally crucified him.

As Covey's model implies (Fig.41), Jesus had 'found his own voice' during his 'hidden years' and his perceptions of God and the world were unified in mind, body and spirit. Jesus' settled perception that this is God's world meant that he saw the hand of God and actions of man in relation to God everywhere. He wanted people to share his faith and interpret actions accordingly. We are told that Jesus constantly taught through parables, which were a form of spiritual perception. Although he criticized the legalistic burdens, his use of parables minimized debate about the Mosaic Law. Instead, people were shown the surrounding reality of God. His coherent perception contrasted with prevailing views. He recognized that people had not been given God's loving respect for them. Therefore, perception was central to understanding the nature of Jesus' teaching. His ability to reliably perceive individuals crowds and situations was a major skill, He knew that they too were trying to perceive who he was.

Perception goes beyond the 'simple' matter of truth. Consider the responses to Jesus and the religious authorities. Some focused on the personal and charismatic authority of Jesus whilst others were influenced by the Pharisees' legal standing. This generated vastly different moods. There is a tendency to idealize and over simplify the complex dynamics of Jesus' situation where the interacting perceptions varied to the point where they became incompatible. Similar complexities can pose difficult problems for any teacher. The basic questions such as, "Who are you really?"... "What are you trying to achieve?" lead on to questions of how, why, where and when. One can imagine that Peter's perception of Jesus may have been somewhat different from that of his wife when he left her to follow Jesus.

It is possible to restructure a stimulus in order to alter a perception. Jesus drew upon common experiences, such as inconsistent Sabbath laws. But would people be willing to consciously restructure their existing perceptions? Many were reluctant or unable to do so, for various reasons. This difficulty of persuading pupils to modify existing perceptions is familiar to everybody. Impressively Nicodemus the Pharisee, weighed up the initial evidence, fearfully came to Jesus, listened and considered the claim and then gradually changed his perception of Jesus. But this does not appear to have happened often.

How would Jesus resolve the problem of changing people's perception of himself as a carpenter to that of the Messiah sent by God. Despite their discontent people had powerful, stable religious beliefs and lived within a social class. Inertia prevailed and so how could he change this and enable them to share his perceptions of God? Apart from Jesus' evident courage and attractiveness, those who responded positively could base their new perceptions on the following.

- His teaching was acceptably rooted in the authoritative common religious heritage of theTorah. e.g. The Golden Rule, laws regarding the Sabbath etc.
- His teaching was applicable to the poor, mourners, widows, farmers etc.
- He used common figures of speech to which people could relate. e.g. sparrows, builders.
- He used comprehensible self-descriptions. e.g. the Shepherd, the protective door.
- He met many fundamental needs.
- His teaching was non-judgmental.
- It offered a rich vein of attractive promises and aspirations.
- It stood in striking contrast to the prevailing teaching.

In effect, Jesus and the Pharisees trained people in perceptual awareness that led to two different established beliefs and value systems. Jesus' teaching was firmly principled and yet flexible to the situation and the people involved. The Pharisees preferred a stable, patterned style of thought – that of teaching within a closed biblical circle that involved virtually no risk, could be replicated

.2c-73
Pupils often recall more about the teacher than what is taught. Why?

throughout the country and passed on faithfully with minimal change across the generations. Whose perception was right? In every teaching situation differences in perception of the teacher and the learner lead to frustration or ridicule and so the skill of minimizing perceptual differences becomes vital. Although perceptions are based upon *values, defence mechanisms, acceptance and rejection, aspirations and continuity*, changing them within effective teaching methods demands that we *look at people afresh*.

Teaching for perceptual development

From the outset Jesus' purpose was to develop and change people's perceptions about God and man! The principles used, however, can be discriminately applied today. He needed to consider three distinct groups:

- His close followers who were open and committed to his teaching.
- The crowds and those with general interest.
- Those who opposed him.

Perception involves persuasion, interpretation and generating different moods. Therefore, major problems arose from varying degrees of perceptual rigidity within society. This often demanded a process of 'unlearning' long-held perceptions and developing new mental sets based upon his concept of spirituality and truth. This required more than a brief explanation, but rather a process of retraining which enabled them to develop a new habitual perspective to which new situations could be related. This training demanded both time and trust if the former perceptions were going to be displaced permanently. The teacher needed authority and to generate an expectancy that they would understand. Let us look at the following ways by which Jesus changed people's perceptions.

The role-model: It has been emphasised that an authoritative role-model who has expertise and promotes personal confidence is most likely to change perceptions. One sees in the gospels that where Jesus is the role model learning by imitation occurs. But where this was not so perceptual change was either temporary or rejected. This was shown at Capernaum where despite the evidence of numerous miracles the people failed to reappraise their perceptions in the light of Jesus' teaching and so brought severe warnings on the town.

The training process: In effect Jesus said, "Look, consider this and do it my way." but this required time and ongoing reinforcement. Therefore it is unlikely that many could attain perceptual changes like his friends. He did, however, identify dominant points which could be remembered and so usefully contribute towards new perceptions.

Planning: Although Jesus did not appear to plan his teaching, the on-going incidental observations provided situational images that coloured their growing range of insights. This increased the validity of his teaching that was not narrowly linear, but generalized, multi-dimensional and applied to contrasting situations

.2c-74
In what ways did Jesus' perception of work become the basis of his teaching?

The media used: Although Jesus was restricted by the media at his disposal, he brought together investigative, memory, inquiry and critical thinking skills through visualisation, kinaesthetics and verbal descriptions that enhanced their powers of perception. The reality of personal experiences enhanced the process of authenticating perceptions.

Every day rationality: People tend to make bi-polar responses about people and situations. This includes seeing a person as good or bad, warm or cold, friendly or unfriendly. This principle was seen when Jesus taught a positive perception of God. The total range of stories could not provide a complete picture of God, but listeners could link them and insert additional details. The central idea was inviolate but contributing figures and situations complemented the picture. Although some details might be erroneous the central perception remained consistent and flexible to other situations and totally memorable.

Attitude: Attitudes to Jesus varied greatly as did his teaching styles to those concerned. He appears to have preferred to teach his supporters privately, where he might criticize them. Although he loved his enemies, he recognized that some needed to be a confronted so that all could understand their disagreement, even if it hardened their perception of him.

The rich amalgam of past and present colour our perceptions and responses as we see through our pre-focused values and experiences. Many major problems facing the world occur where conflicting perceptions can be legitimatized and evoke a rivalry and hatred which develops and persists. But how can they, or conflicts in teaching, be changed?

Psychologist U. Neisser (1976) assessed how perceptions might be changed. He saw people holistically with their experiences, emotions, memories etc interacting with incoming stimuli to form fresh perceptions. He realized that people respond simultaneously to a multiplicity of rich sources of information and experiences. He produced a cyclical model he described as a continuous process of experience, re-examination and possible change. By so doing perceptions can be either changed or confirmed (see Figs.52, 53).

Let us briefly follow the cycle through its various stages. Imagine a person has an established perception of a crowd of young people.

- Fresh worries grow as they watch young people with concern.
- There are initial reactions to the new stimuli, which are accepted or rejected.
- The stimuli of the people are related to *past* experiences and to the *present* situation and what they anticipate their *future* impact might be.
- This develops into an overall meaning for the person concerned.
- The person explores the degree of acceptability of this new meaning.
- The degree of acceptability evokes a direct response- anxiety or pleasure etc .
- The person's perception of young people may be modified/or not.
- This new or confirmed understanding may provoke some type of action/or not.
- The person now has a revised 'world map' to interpret fresh information.

.2c-75
Why might Jesus' Hidden Years have been so vital in respect of perception?

Figure 53

Neisser's spiral/cycle of constant perceptual adjustment

1. Initial established perceptual scene
2. Incoming stimuli
3. Samples accepted/rejected
4. Stimuli are translated and related to past, present and future expectations.
5. An overall meaning developed
6. Explores the degree of acceptability
7. Makes a direct response
8. Modifiers/or not the existing cognitive map
9. Action
10. Revised cognitive map receives fresh information and responds accordingly

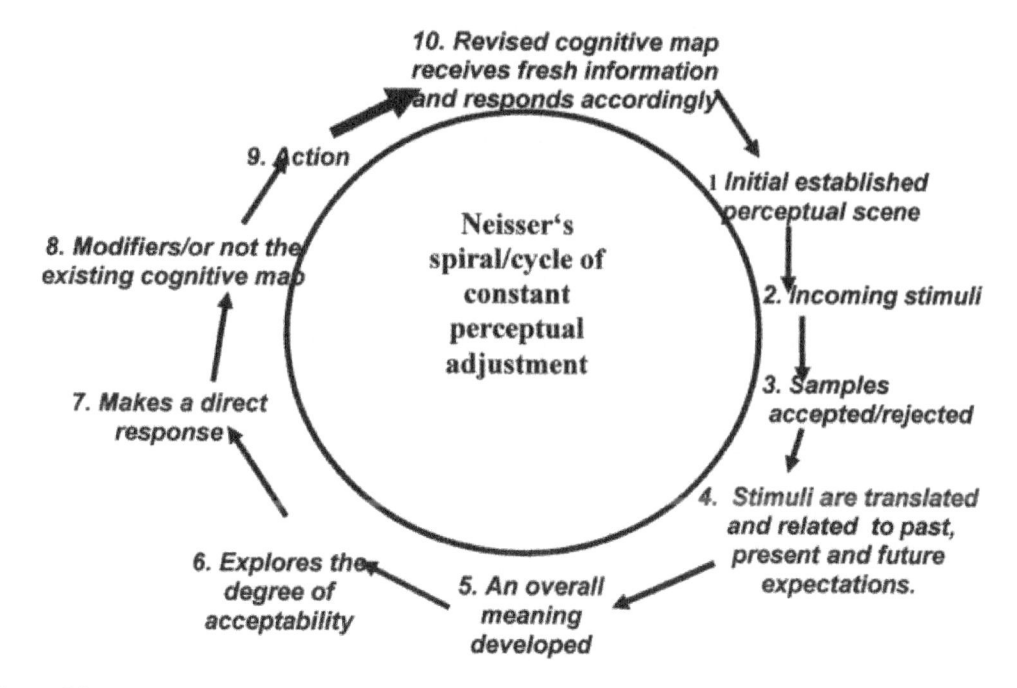

Figure 54

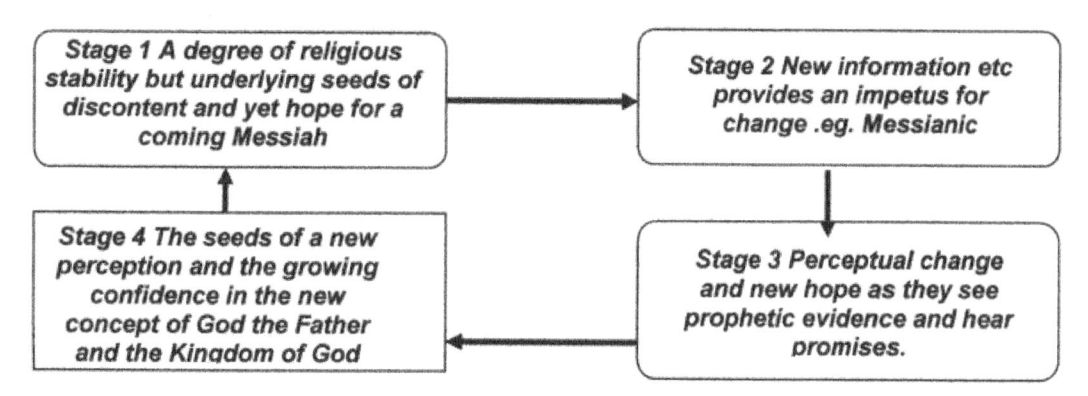

- **Stage 1** A degree of religious stability but underlying seeds of discontent and yet hope for a coming Messiah
- **Stage 2** New information etc provides an impetus for change .eg. Messianic
- **Stage 3** Perceptual change and new hope as they see prophetic evidence and hear promises.
- **Stage 4** The seeds of a new perception and the growing confidence in the new concept of God the Father and the Kingdom of God

This cycle illustrates that information is interpreted in ways that are useful and make sense of experiences in an ever-changing world. We choose what we will attend to and our response is based on our past history, our present situation and an anticipation of relevant future outcomes. We are active decision makers who make choices that may be conscious or not, but which can make significant perceptual changes that may have far-reaching effects. We tend to select that which is personally relevant and ignore the unimportant but of course some may be more prepared to receive certain stimuli than others (e.g. mountaineering). Neisser's cycle of perceptual change can be modified and applied to Jesus' situation as follows.

He presented a distinct perception of God. Some preferred the order, control and stability of the traditional view. Jesus' teaching, however, did not slot conveniently into the existing pattern. It required a change of mind and involved risk, the worth of which was questioned. For others, however, this was a release. They were being given a new attractive perception that showed God wanting to respond keenly as any human father would. Follow an event such as Peter's conversion. To what degree did his experience match that indicated in Neisser's cycle, or else relate the cycle to a personal incident involving confirmation or change in perceptions. Which catalysts enable perceptual change to occur given that *perception is the manner in which we build and make sense of experiences*. See Figure 55.

.2c-76
What have you found to be the most powerful determining factors in the development of self perceptions?

Column A emphasizes the traditional order in the development of Jesus' perception of the Kingdom of God and his own role as the Messiah. It minimizes everyday personal conflicts and crises he is likely to have experienced. It states clearly his major teaching, attitude/world view, his own self-image and that of other people.

Column B begins where he realized his unique position and presented an attractive message that he validated. He stated his message that contrasted with his later more developed teaching. He spoke in their vernacular language and used their existing understanding. His confrontation with the religious authorities left the people in a state of indecision. Views hardened and there was little agreement.

Column C considers a typical school based strategy in which the teacher controls what is deemed to be valid and seeks to evoke positive pupil views by promises of worthwhile results and rapid initial experiences. The Big Picture is shown to be worthwhile. It is then well-organised and taught to maximise initial success and show that promises were being fulfilled.

This perception of God's priorities (Column A) shocked the religious leaders. Their world-view acted as a personal truth and reality check. Jesus had developed a coherent pattern of understanding about God, but so too had the Pharisees and the common Galileans but they were not compatible. Similar tensions exist today (see Column C) and can result in teachers' attitude to fresh ideas or even for pupils either finding it difficult to learn within a particular style of teaching or else 'writing off' their teachers. The differences may be due to cultural or educational expectations regarding future outcomes.

Our visual, auditory, kinaesthetic and tactile experiences extend into many different forms of perception and influence everyday affairs. Impressions can extend socially where judgments are based on our perception. First impressions can have powerful effects on ensuing attitudes, interactions, and judgments even if they have little foundation. This selective bias influences reactions that can persist and become confirmed. Judgments based on scant evidence can result in social perceptions becoming fixed and stereotypes are formed.

Jesus and perceptual change

Jesus' perceptual development shaped his teaching methods. Although we have few details of this, Fig.55 attempts to show that Jesus had diverse formative experiences during his 'hidden years'. He undoubtedly reflected on these and related them to bodies of existing, authoritative knowledge. The total combination of revelation, prayer and reflection resulted in him developing a stable, coherent 'world view'. It was a spiritual shorthand that did more than provide him with a view of right and wrong. It resulted in his central overriding perception that this is God's world and that God's kingdom would reflect the will and mind of God the Father. His perceptions were, therefore, organised around this principle of faith It is not surprising that his early teaching focused on promises to the poor, the merciful, the peacemakers and the righteous etc. This was his Big Picture of God and the 'Kingdom' (see Fig. 54 column 1). Therefore he confidently questioned established teachings and practices of the Mosaic Law and denied that the Gentiles were the fuel for the fires of hell, but were loved by God. Is difficult to realise what a radical shift this and related teachings were.

When Jesus' cousin, the ascetic John the Baptist, emerged from the desert many responded to him readily partly because he matched their perception of an authentic holy prophet. Jesus the carpenter was not so readily identified until he began to perform prophetic *actions*. When John the Baptist was imprisoned, he too had doubts about Jesus. Had his initial perceptions of Jesus been wrong? Jesus' reply was to tell John's disciples to give him *evidence* of what he was doing and then he would recognize the truth. Facts alone were not enough – the perceptions coloured the process of interpreting situations. The majority of people perceived obedience to the Mosaic Law as being equated to holiness. This shared belief of holiness provided a basis for understanding – even if they were wrong. Similarly pupils may perceive what a teacher ought to be like and if this match does not occur it can make life less credible.

.2c-77
What is the fundamental idea behind Neisser's thinking?

Figure 55

A. Jesus' developments A traditional model	B. Jesus changing people's perceptions – an analysis based on Neisser's cyclical model	C. "Our World" Examining perceptual developments based on different views of learning
The young boy begins to see life in the context of God the Father	He was amongst an expectant but frustrated people.	Aims stem mainly from teacher's WV/Professional View
The young man sees the burden which strict religious observance laid on people.	He entered with a traditional message that brought together and met needs and aspirations of common people.	Establish what the 'pupils' expectations are.
The Galilean man sees the aspirations and shares the hardships of other Galileans.	The teacher – Jesus established spiritual and moral excellence that could hardly be disputed	Understand the WV of the pupils and their priorities and any necessary changes needed.
His mature recognition of the spiritual Kingdom of God, the character of his Father, the active creator and restorer in this world.	Presented a sketched "Big Picture" that was traditional, novel and offered hope and could be recognised and partially understood.	Look for links between pupil and teacher WV's
His coherent conception of love, forgiveness, sacrifice etc	He used existing understanding to develop new overall meanings within their existing schemas	Enhance pupil expectations Create positive experiences. what might be expected, is right Cause pupils to analyze their Big Picture.
This was his cognitive / spiritual basis against which he perceived people and situations. Examples:	He faced the authorities confidently and established a zone of conflict.	
a. His recognition of potential qualities in such people as his disciples.	He made a direct response to the people and demonstrated the truth of his teaching by word and action.	
b. His perception of such people as 'the rich young ruler'.	He sustained his teaching with promises and provided a coherent 'Big Picture' or cognitive map against which things were to be judged. and would not be modified.	Establish the pupils' world view aspirations, recognizable responses, shared schemas? – self- realisation (inductive)
c. His perception of the Pharisees, Herod etc	A period of action that brought people to varying points of decision from which perceptions could be changed.	Hone and improve
d. His perception of people such as Nicodemus etc	He gave them a experiences of success.	Gave pupils ample opportunities to test the truth and build up new WV and perceptual mind map - a new pro-learning culture of fulfilment / trust, success and learning
	He consistently demonstrated his core conceptions despite constant opposition from the authorities.	
	He developed the scope of the perceptual patterning to cover all aspects of life.	
	He upheld people as doubts developed	born based on promise
	He proved the validity of his teaching.	recognition of their value added
	He provided aspirations for the future in accord with his perceptual mind map.	
	Conflict escalated outside of Galilee.	

Major Dilemmas

This process of developing perceptions is usually a search for the most satisfying interpretation of the available data rather than simply responding to the incoming stimuli. In other words, Jesus had seen the poor and the suffering all his life and had from a very early age adopted the prophetic teaching about God and the poor.) Therefore, he developed this particular way of 'seeing' and understanding both the world and God. This was an ongoing process and as he grew he refined his understanding of spiritual realities and the Kingdom of God. He was observing and weighing from a mass of possibilities what God wanted, and so through prayer and meditation he established firm, 'habitual mental/spiritual sets' or attitudes that caused many religious leaders to harden their attitude to Jesus. Therefore, personal interpretation and insight are not all of equal significance or necessarily based on truth. Ideally, with greater knowledge, skills experience all should become more discriminating but people's personal expectations and perceptions can become stereotyped and make change difficult.

.2c-78
Compare the three columns in Fig. 55. What differences can you note between them?

"We learn what to perceive" but perceptions are also based upon the emotions, desires, social experiences and the social norms as well as facts. Therefore, Jesus had to both state the truth in recognizable forms and enable people to *feel* the truth and identify with it. Hence his principle of a *small group receiving, long-term training* to modify their perceptions was justified, although this notion of long-term stable tuition is usually deemed uneconomic and logistically inoperable.

Agreement between a person's private world-view and the public world-view normally results in stable perceptions about acceptable lifestyles. Serious problems can ensue where there is conflict between *private and public world-views* with their varying powers and authority. This was so in Jesus' life just as it is for many today.

It has been indicated that perceptions develop as a total resultant of:
- the perceiver's relative stability,
- the wider context of social life,
- forces acting upon the personal history, situation and expectations of the perceiver,
- the relative legitimacy and force of group definitions.

These can result in either an inward looking self-image or an outward world-view. A good example of this was Jesus' self-perception of himself as the Good Shepherd. This builder had probably never had sheep but it was central to the idealised prophetic tradition that he had visualized on the hillsides in Galilee. Similarly, imagine how Jesus was perceived by the studious Nicodemus, or James and John who were commonly known as the Sons of Thunder, impetuous Peter, the contrasting sisters Martha and Mary, Lazarus, the adulterous woman and the rich young ruler. All had views of Jesus that had been changed but others who resolutely opposed Jesus were not. Why was this? Also, what were Jesus' perceptions as he praised God, wept over Jerusalem and for the people who played pipes and danced. Similarly both teachers and pupils use self-images that may or may not be justified or recognised by others.

Our world-view may be stable and yet it can also be continually developing and making the adjustments between expectations and actuality. These can act as competing forces or move harmoniously to determine any modifications of our world-view. Take for example the religious leaders' perception of Jesus. He was a Galilean, a commoner who might be regarded as an unauthorised teacher, a danger to national survival and one who challenged the traditional stability and structure of the nation. Stark comparisons such as these made mutuality difficult – a feature that persists in the world's communities today.

A major task for Jesus was to teach so as to achieve perceptual change amongst the people. The shift in recognition from being a carpenter, to a leader, prophet and rabbi, and being recognised as the Messiah and ultimately evoking the exclamation from Thomas, 'My Lord and my God" shows that his teaching was successful... amongst some.

In reality he was pursuing many normal teaching processes, howbeit, at a somewhat different level! The underlying principle was that to achieve perceptual change he put people in practical positions of *learning to see and question over a prolonged period of time*. His followers gleaned evidence from relevant information and developed rational explanations from a mass of possibilities. Therefore, when they saw a field of corn, it possessed a dynamic perceptual symbolism of a spiritual harvest. Gradually a coherent perception that was in line with Jesus' teaching about the Kingdom of God was established.

.2c-79
How could people decide who had a true perception of Jesus?

A major problem in society is that so many people base their perceptions on erroneous stereotypes and so make judgments that are fundamentally flawed. Therefore, in schools and youth centres, drama is often used to provide experiences that enable them through projection and role reversal to move from the actual situation to anticipated outcomes and changed perceptions. It is based on the assumption that people are sufficiently rational to be able to compare the relative validity of rival perceptions when placed in alternative social roles.

Although Jesus was often acting on flows of incidental situations, it did enable people to build up what might be called a perceptual vocabulary that not only consistently recognised perceptions but on the basis of that evidence made rational deductions and anticipated probable developments.

At first the people wanted to kill Jesus but then they wanted to make him King. The basis of the people's changing perception of Jesus was quite straight-forward and can be visualised today. This teacher was *effective* and strangely he had a *confidence in them*. His *personal qualities* such as *courage, tenacity and an accepting manner* were allied to his *fresh knowledge and wisdom* and resulted in him receiving *authority* even though the people found it difficult to grasp the implications of what he was saying. He was giving them time to *reflect*. This will be further developed in Ultimate Teaching Strategy B and Part C.

Summary

From the above it is possible to identify how Jesus used his perceptual skills both in his own development and in the way in which he taught others.

- He accepted that there were many perceptions of him.
- He presented a *stable image* of himself so that people had the opportunity to adjust their perception of him.
- He had total confidence in his own world-view.
- He recognized that the perception of friends and followers would be related to both his *character* and the degree to which *he met their needs* and *aspirations*.
- Perceptions are closely linked to the *outcomes* of *learning experiences.*
- The perception of his followers was more *individualized* and related to their *interaction* with *each other* and *Jesus* himself.
- The perceptions of outsiders who were resolutely opposed to Jesus were not significantly influenced by their learning experiences with him.
- Jesus tried to relate his new teaching to a range of *established perceptions*, such as their shared heritage, common environmental experiences and 'certain' messianic expectations.

These points can be related to everyday situations as the following shows.

The intense crises Jesus faced indicate powerful differing perceptions. The principles he used to resolve critical problems have practical validity in the 21st century. In schools there are wide ranging factors that cause and resolve crisis situations. These flourish especially where negative pressures and disillusionment prevail and people look for alternative outlets to satisfy their varied needs or else withdraw into the relative safety of their own domain. This raises questions regarding the necessary conditions for a person to want to become co-operative. Jesus would not have thought that perceptual change was more important than improving the management style.

Crises are commonly related to perceptual choices and decisions. In Fig.55 some questions that teachers and pupils might consider are listed. People need to know who will benefit. Will any underlying animosity remain and any conformity be superficial? The cardinal question will be, *'What is in it for me?'* (WIIFM). Jesus was the servant leader whose major concern was the welfare of others. He was *living the part,* and not using the situation selfishly. This teacher had *values* which were adhered to both by himself, their *role model*, and his followers.

.2c-80
On reflection which perceptions have led you to make a questionable decision?

Figure 56

Major perceptual questions/issues	Teacher percept'n	Pupil perception
The teacher's perception of pupils Do the pupils want to learn? What is the character of pupils? Which problems do they bring? What are the effects of their social background? **The pupils' perceptual questions of the lesson** Will it all be worthwhile? Do I feel interested/making progress/good? Are my needs being satisfied? Will it help me to do well? Will the teacher be able to resolve problems? Does the teacher enjoy what he is teaching? How relevant is this to me? Is all this pointless? What are my friends think? Will the teacher persist with us patiently? Will the teacher be fair? Does he really like us? Does he really understand that I'm better than he thinks? Can I see where all this is going to lead me? How will past help equip me to do this? Who decided precisely what I would do? Are any of us going to be left out? Will he be pleased with my efforts? Will I be expected to do everything by myself? Will the lesson be personally useful and successful?		

They created an ethos knowing that watchers were critically monitoring them. Would they want to pay the price of committing themselves to him? Would his authority be more satisfying than that of existing authorities? Would his positive discipline of forgiveness, acceptance restoration and sacrifice be superior. Would his confidence in them remain even when they failed or would he make withering criticisms? What would their perception be?

Also, would he give them *stability* if they entered into his promises that involved a distinctive *lifestyle*? Would he *persist* and regard their *good* to be of greater significance than himself? Would he prove by his direct action that he could *support* them and be their *enabler* rather than an enforcer like customary leaders? In fact, did he really *want and respect them*? And did they have a *group* to which they could belong and identify?

These issues of expectations, stereotyping, worth and expertise are ever-present. As Jesus led from the heart and appears to have strengthened people's strengths rather than criticize their weaknesses, so their view remained fresh. His followers trusted him, even when trouble occurred. Their perception was settled!

.2c-81
How might Jesus resolve a problem of which you know?

Personality Factor – 7

Which indicators from Jesus' personality factors provide a better understanding of how he perceived the world and the people?

.2c-82
Which incidents do you imagine most profoundly influenced Jesus' early perceptions?

Chapter 7
Motivation

Looking forwards:

Motivation defined...Influences...Range of motivations...Effects of motivation...Jesus the motivator...Intrinsic motivation...12 positive motivations...God—a noun or a verb?...Murray's taxonomy...Motivational structure

Jesus was not only motivated himself, he was also a master of motivating others as befits a master teacher. But how? How might the master teacher's methods help teachers to motivate pupils today? This vital theme is further developed in the rest of Part B. These issues and the cross thematic questions are addressed either in the text or at the end of the theme... or elsewhere as indicated.

Figure 57

	Issues particular to the	Relating the theme specifically to Jesus	Relating the theme to teaching generally
Leadership	What motivates a Leader? How does a leader motivate?	What motivated Jesus? How did Jesus motivate others?	What motivates teachers and learners? How are teachers and learners motivated?
Perception	How does a person perceive a situation? How does a perception motivate?	How did Jesus regard motivation?	How do teachers and learners regard motivation?
Memory	What motivates a person to remember?	How did Jesus motivate people to remember?	How are teachers and learners motivated to remember?
Socialisation	How are people motivated into behavioural action?	How did Jesus motivate people to develop patterns of behaviour?	How are teachers and learners motivated to be socialised?
Cognition	What motivates people to think in certain ways?	How did Jesus motivate people to think in his manner	How are teachers and learners motivated to think in certain ways?
Emotion	What motivates people to give priority to certain emotions?	How did Jesus use and develop emotions?	How might teachers and learners use and develop emotions?

.2c-83
Examine columns 1 & 2 below. Which motivational priorities would you consider most important?

Figure 58 Motivational influences

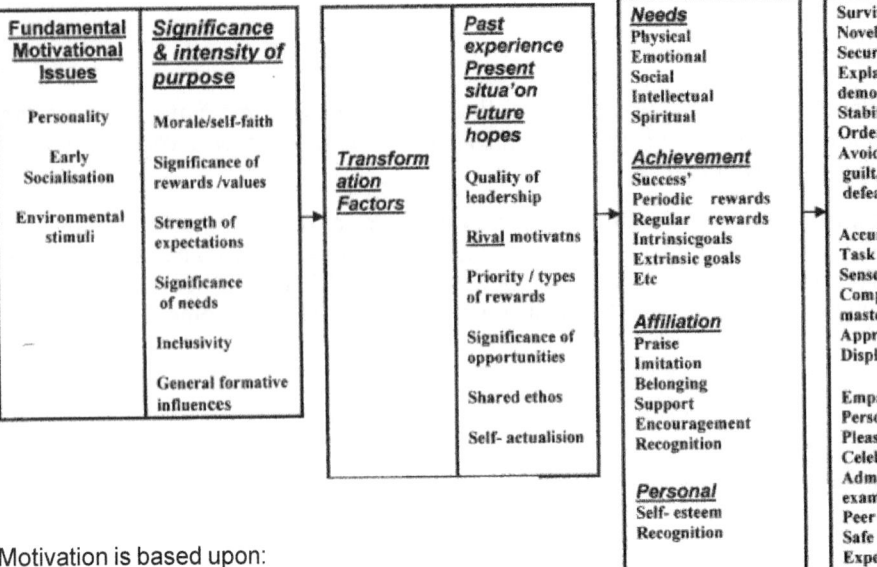

Fundamental Motivational Issues	Significance & intensity of purpose	Transformation Factors	Past experience / Present situa'on / Future hopes	Needs	
Personality	Morale/self-faith		Quality of leadership	**Needs** Physical Emotional Social Intellectual Spiritual	Survival Novelty and freshness Security Explain and demonstrate Stability Order
Early Socialisation	Significance of rewards /values		Rival motivatns	**Achievement** Success' Periodic rewards Regular rewards Intrinsic goals Extrinsic goals Etc	Avoidance of blame, guilt, failure, hurt, defeat, rejection
Environmental stimuli	Strength of expectations		Priority / types of rewards		Accumulation Task completion Sense of being correct Competence and mastery Appropriate challenges Display
	Significance of needs		Significance of opportunities	**Affiliation** Praise Imitation Belonging Support Encouragement Recognition	Empathy and altruism Personally significant Pleasure and fun Celebration Admirable model / example Peer group support Safe to make mistakes Expertise of the leader Full acceptance Admiration Affection Dominance
	Inclusivity		Shared ethos		
	General formative influences		Self-actualisation	**Personal** Self-esteem Recognition	Personal relevance Curiosity and discovery Experiment and creativity Sense of being cared for/caring Problem solving Inspiration Wonder and awe Privilege Sacrifice

Motivation is based upon:

- Natural physical and mental generic features.
- Early socialization experiences.
- Multiple positive and negative inputs that shape motivation generally.
- Powerful motivational experiences that can alter motivation significantly (e.g. needs, aspirations).

.2c-84
Which influences might a trainee electrician especially appreciate?

A Driver

Motivation drives us! No matter whether it is to achieve particular successes or to conform to expectations, motivation is that which spurs or drives people on to achieve their desired goals – for good or for bad, out of confidence or fear. What motivates and the degree to which it motivates distinguishes every person – Jesus included. But what motivated him and how did he use that motivation to motivate others? And which aspects of their motivation can be applied to the innumerable teaching situations in which people find themselves in the 21st century?

Motivation indicates the direction (i.e. goal), intensity (i.e. effort and concentration) and persistence (i.e. pursuit) that drives people to achieve their worthwhile goals, with *values* often being the basis of motivation. Without it, abilities seldom achieve their potential. It drives people to all types of excellence, but can also cause under-achievement. It is multi-causal, therefore, just as everybody is a teacher so everybody is a motivator and Jesus had to motivate people. What can he teach us about motivation? Jesus' own motivation was a driven passion to do God's will. But how could he motivate his apprentices to share this vision, which made the process of inspiring others imperative (see Covey Fig.41) The latent potential of his countrymen depended on their motivation…but perhaps they were waiting to be motivated!

Motivation is often regarded as a linear process of creating rewards or success that translate into higher motivation. Jesus would have rejected this concept. Learners may respond to this token/ reward system of motivation in the short term but once the constraints of instruction are removed and the rewards are satiated, it can decline. To maintain motivation rewards might be constantly inflated. And so the problem of developing lifelong learning or active work participation can remain. Although such words as expectancy, relevance, reward etc can be applied, motivation usually involves the whole social/ emotional/ intellectual being with many possible but uncertain outcomes.

Figure 59

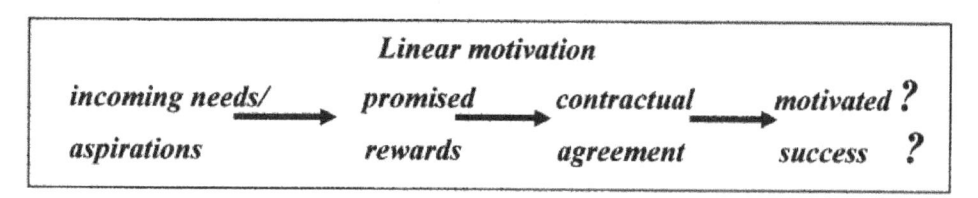

Linear motivation

incoming needs/ aspirations → promised rewards → contractual agreement → motivated ? success ?

Frederick Herzberg (1966) suggested that workers fall into two categories – satisfiers and dissatisfiers or intrinsic and extrinsic motivated workers.

This contains no surprises. It contrasts modern commercial developments in which workers have personal involvement and responsibility with situations where the workers' major concerns are the rewards of their wages. This reflects the comparison in schools where pupils, students, trainees etc become involved in their own studies and the development of their school or college, with those solely focused on formal learning. What is the role of the student? How can long-term motivation be maximized

Figure 60

Satisfiers	Dissatisfiers
Achievement	Organization, policy and administration
Recognition	Heavy handed supervision
Job interest	Poor interpersonal relationships
Responsibility	Inadequate salary
Advancement	Uncomfortable working conditions

.2c-85
What are the major motivating features you would expect to find in a primary school?

Fig.58, 59 indicate influences on motivation. There is truth in the linear model, but the multi-causal explanation illustrates recognisable complexities of life. Moving from the left column, at the entry stage the significance of anticipation, morale and needs commonly reflect early personal differences. But modifications occur at the transformational stage and significant differences such as past experiences, the present situation and qualities of leadership all influence motivation. At the third stage these differences are accentuated by influential priorities. Blaise Pascal echoed this when he wrote, "The heart has the reasons that reason alone does not know."

Motivation encompasses efficient rational planning and cognition and also *affective, social and emotional identities*. Jesus recognised this holistic approach. As he taught, so aspects of people's motivations were revealed. Often where there is no satisfactory motivational mix a person is likely to seek alternatives – for good or for ill. This then becomes the story of how needs and aspirations are pursued. Jesus motivated people by creatively maximising people's personal significance, purpose, and self-actualization. These energised desires that activated hidden qualities.

The analysis in Fig. 57 indicates identifiable elements that motivated Jesus' followers. These were, for example:

- enjoyment of the qualities of *the leader* who they *wished* to *copy*.
- relating the new to past experiences.
- enjoying the likelihood of *success*.
- sensing that they now had *the correct solution* to their *problems*.
- enjoying a *creative vision* which went beyond expectations.
- enjoying clarity of aims, strategy and progress.
- enjoying the sense of *privilege* of a new message, leader and prospects.
- having a sense of acceptance, identity and significance.

These positive motivational features were transforming!

Jesus' own motivation and his motivation of others

He acted to secure a match between the motivator, the motivated and the message that needed to be clear, positive and secure. Fig.57 also illustrates how Jesus exemplified intrinsic motivation in his personal and social life. It was consistent, as was his motivation of others, although he allowed them a degree of latitude. Even so, he expected this intrinsic motivation to distinguish them from others. The extrinsic motivation as seen in their desire for privileged positions persisted until the last week in Jerusalem but it gradually gave way to their intrinsic desire for 'the pearl of great price'. This challenge for people to turn their thinking around was a major theme in Jesus' teaching and is still a distinguishing factor of much long-term learning which can withstand disappointments and persist in following 'the dream'. In the third column of Fig. 58 the characteristic elements drawn from Jesus' life demonstrate that they can enlighten teaching today.

Jesus' words and actions were motivating, but not for all. They were drawn to a cluster of methods and a core message that achieved a balance between:

- learning and serving.
- belonging and self-esteem.
- curiosity and discovery.
- wonder and awe in a non-judgmental ethos.

Perhaps he presaged the constant challenge in schools to create pupil motivation. To what extent can a teacher motivate a reluctant learner or has the learner a responsibility to be self-motivated? Jesus' message and actions brought together relevance and challenge but people were motivated to follow him they found that he was 'developing what was alive in them' (Kouzes and Posner) which contrasted with false messiahs through whom hope had been damaged.

.2c-86
In your situation what are the major motivators and dissatisfiers?

Jesus demanded that challenges were met. His pupils had to make decisions and stand by them. Their guarantee was the security of their faith in God and Jesus and the satisfaction of spiritual achievement as he encouraged them to believe and respond to a new lifestyle in order to realise their dreams. From the outset the issue to be decided was self or altruistic service. They felt privileged and rapidly saw that their expectations were exceeded as they established new horizons.

Jesus' motivation must be seen within the context of his *spiritual* vision. Many principles upon which every day motivation is based were in essence shared and used by Jesus — but were given –piritual interpretation. First and foremost was his desire to *obey God* that reflects the balance in the 10 Commandments.

- What is of *value/worth* to God, himself, themselves and others?
- What are the *primary needs* and *expectations* in the Kingdom of God?
- What were the *significances* of the *goals/ achievements* he was setting?
- What would be the *costs* to them?
- Would they *believe* in the final analysis that *truth and love* must win?
- Would they attain the *essential skills,* faith, obedience and discipline?
- How *driven* would they be to *explain* and *demonstrate* his work?
- Would they *develop* from being fearful to having a *lifestyle confidence?*
- What they see the priority of *intrinsic rewards?*
- Would they accept delay of gratification?

Consider the stages adopted

Jesus initially *demonstrated* his own *competence,* showing an authoritative understanding, meeting personal needs with courage. This provided a *secure* basis to motivate others as he established *new aspirations*. These new *prospects* created a *confidence to join* with Jesus in the ardent *pursuit* of new goals. Many left when it became evident that there was a cost to pay in terms of hardship but those who stayed responded to a motivating novelty of being released from the old and developing new prospects as they *practised* and *helped* Jesus and saw the Kingdom of God in action. The quality of the relationships developed so that when he offered them the opportunity of leaving him, their response was 'to whom shall we go?' When they were *sent out in pairs* to *replicate* the work of Jesus and returned with stories of *success*, their motivation moved on to a new and higher plane. His high-risk strategy was proving successful even though it required long term sacrificial commitment to a revolutionary new concept. The distinctive features were leadership, confidence and sharply positive prospects.

Jesus' ministry showed many classical motivational practices and that he was not relying on a totally novel approach. Twelve of these positive motivations were:

Figure 61

Inspirational role model	New knowledge and truth	Prospects /expectations	Secure relationships
Personal relevance	Success	Inspired transmission	Challenge
Enhanced competences	Memorable demonstrations	Experiences and achievements	Promises

.2c-87
Find instances in Jesus' life and as reported In local newspapers where the motivations in Fig.61 were apparent

Jesus took the best practices, raised them to a high level and made them appropriate for his purpose. He arrested and virtually propelled people through many memorable experiences.

Although not all are regularly used they are recognizable with special emphasis being given to relevance, success and enhanced competence that contrasted with many customary de-motivating practices. This dichotomy still exists as learners reject established paths that appear to have little value. But there is a balance. Whilst it was the responsibility of the teacher to restore the 'lost sheep' and not leave it to its own devices, individuals had the responsibility to 'buy the field containing the treasure' and maximize their talents.

The criterion of worth normally determines people's motivation. Minimal motivation is demonstrated where everyday teaching / learning becomes like a barren desert. In contrast, Jesus' vision offered hopes that were beyond normal expectations and so followers were given a sense of *value/worth* and were motivated. He also *sustained their* motivation. Although they were excited by Jesus' unfolding ministry, the distance between their expectations and Jesus' goals was great and their learning progressed slowly. Even so, as the group improved so the *resilience* and *task commitment* became more *secure*, and ultimately they shared his motivation as they became more comprehensible. This was achieved by the following:

- His work was of both *long and short-term relevance* to the people.
- He met people's *needs* and developed their *dreams* for the future.
- His *demonstrations* showed that their dreams were *attainable*.
- His attainment required *commitment* and did not come cheap.
- He developed his work *imaginatively* so that it held people's attention.
- He brought considerable *variety* into his work - what would happen next?
- He *paced* his work to cause to reflect about an important *fact, promise or idea*.
- The motivation was sparked by creativity, surprise and attainment.

And so motivation might be reduced to these few key words. But motivating for whom?

Primary motivating drives usually powerfully satisfy physical, social and emotional needs and the desire for achievement. These drives encompass other powerful motivators. It might be said that the most universal motivation is expressed in the letters WIIFM – what is in it for me? that expresses that *self* is a powerful common motivator. But Jesus had to turn WIIFM into WIIFO – what is in it for others? Hence, he re-defined motives. Most can be seen as being inward-looking. For example, achievement might be seen as accumulating wealth but to him the motive that caused the widow to give her mite was greater. Jesus wanted his disciples to be great achievers by being selfless and outward-looking.

Transforming modern analyses

In the 1930's the psychologist, Reuben Murray, defined what he regarded as universal human needs and related these to motivation (see Fig.59 col.1). He did not include a spiritual dimension but listed six areas of human drives. A spiritually based analysis by Jesus (col. 3) might be compared with Murray's humanistic analysis and might be related to everyday applications (col. 2). Murray's taxonomy is a neat analysis of human tendencies, but Jesus' purpose was to transform human behaviour. For example, aggressive tendencies that are exhibited in many physical, social, emotional and economic forms could be translated into spiritual terms and take the form of fighting for righteousness and peacemaking. Similarly abasement is not seen as negative servility but as a positive aspect of repentance before God.

Needs based motivation is neither negative nor limiting because it can cover the whole range of human experience. It does, however, necessitate re-defining needs. His actions imply a belief that learning is based on the pupils' desire to learn and therefore he let potential students go rather than foist himself upon them. His pupils could freely enter into his goals.

.2c-88
How might learners be given a sense of motivating long-term worth/value?

Figure 62

Jesus the Motivator	Jesus the Motivated	Motivational factors
Providing the longed for vision and possibility of success Allowed extrinsic motivation to remain Stimulated affection & loyalty (N.Aff) to develop a working personal relationship Giving a sense of awe and hope – extrinsic? Making the process relevant to the person His character was inspirational Transmission of vision by word & action Developed a personal vision in 'pupils Demonstrated & inspired – imitate to serve & achieve Raised their sense of competence and empowerment Enabled them to meet challenging situations Led them in the faith drive and achievements (N.Ach) Clarifies cost but high expectations of rewards Created aspirations with clear goals of high worth Move pupils from 'legalism' to spiritual understanding Develop positive acceptance and sense of achievement Challenged the brain to think and explore Imparts passion, vision & action- high expectations Provide direction, expectations & pursuit of energy Time for involvement in his (role model) action Mystical promises	Intrinsic motivation / interest Growing conviction / inspiration internalised Learning and formulating his vision / goals / strategies Commitment to God/people Sublimating existing beliefs etc regarding the Kingdom of God Demonstrate the nature of the vision Explaining the nature of the vision Develop his conviction and skills in others Face opposition / difference with insight and fortitude Be the motivating role model for others Facilitate the development of others The ultimate sacrifice	Support and encouragement Praise Ensure competences were gained Memorable occasions #High degree of personal relevance Being an admirable model / example Generate hope Meeting needs and aspirations Generating inspiration Promoting a sense of wonder/awe Create appropriate challenges Create positive expectations Give Enjoy a sense of success them a degree of mastery Create and satisfy curiosity Promote security and confidence Give a sense of novelty/ fresheners Show expertise as a leader Promote peer-group support Provide positive self-esteem Provide acceptance and belonging Provide hope of long term rewards Provide a sense of being cared for Meeting or a full range of needs - (physical/emotional/social/spiritual) To discover the unknown They would become significant They had great pleasure It was safe to make mistakes They could imitate their charismatic leader They were cutting new ground - an exploration in faith

In Fig.64 Murray's taxonomy is listed in three of the four quadrants but the key is in the first that contains Jesus' major concepts and in the remaining quadrants Murray's taxonomy has been reinterpreted. The claim raised here is that analyses such as Murray's are sufficiently flexible to be applied to all types of learning, with appropriate modifications.

Jesus' priorities in respect to motivation can be related to the simple six stage taxonomy by Rath (Fig.65). This cluster of generalizations certainly resonates with Jesus' priorities. Whilst Jesus would not have accepted some of Rath's humanistic definitions of freedom from guilt etc there is an affinity as regards man's innate priority of needs. Jesus, however, saw these principles within a spiritual context. Therefore, whilst Jesus would not have denied crucial elements in the findings of Maslow, Murray and Rath etc. he could not have shared their view of man because Jesus envisaged the basis of motivation to be God the Father.

.2c-89
What is the distinguishing feature of common motivation from Jesus' point of view?

Figure 63

Murray's taxonomy	Everyday Activities	Jesus' strategies/methods
1. Needs and Inanimate Objects Acquisition – gain possessions Conservation – collect & preserve Orderliness – arrange & organise Retention - retain possession Construction – organize and build	Collecting objects (eg. .stamps) School displays Curriculum, timetable, library, Literacy games Model making	Jesus neither acquired or gave possessions but he did give the spiritual equivalent of memorable stories, incidents and sayings which were collected, arranged, organized and treasured. Basic physical needs could be left to God
2. Ambition, willpower, prestige Superiority, excel, achieve, recognition Achieve- overcome, exercise power Recognition-excite praise/ condemnation? Exhibition- excite, thrill others Inviolacy-not dishonoured, self image Avoid inferiority- failure, ridicule Defensiveness- self-justification Counteraction- overcome defeat	Examination success etc Excel (most activities) Problem solving Rule keeping Mastery learning, contract learning Self evaluation techniques, review Sporting competitions, reporting etc	The notion that they were unique ambassadors of the Kingdom of God gave a profound sense of privilege and excellence. They enjoyed a degree of prestige as they worked with Jesus and then ultimately exercise power and overcame ridicule and defeat because they have the Supreme, prestigious task of heralding the kingdom of God
3. Human power and resistance Dominance Deference- admire, serve gladly Similance- imitate, agree / believe Autonomy- independence Contrariness- be unique,	Hierarchical organisation Prefectorial systems, initiation Faith school, socialisation, life skills Independent studies Self pacing,	Jesus set out to transform humanity, and that all power ultimately belongs to God, His way was service, not dominance. Also, within this there is deference (humility) as they imitate Jesus, resist evil and depend on the heavenly Father.
4. Needs and injury Aggression Abasement Avoidance of blame	Physical sports, physical discipline Apologies Excuses, conformity	Aggression is sublimated to become boldness for righteousness and yet humble repentance and hence forgiveness before God.
5. Affection Affiliation Rejection- snub, ignore others Nurturance- protect and aid Succorance- seek aid, be dependent	Inclusion policies School exclusion Counselling School's formal control Team and group activities, drama etc	This was central to Jesus' teaching strategy. Characteristically it involved Fellowship, love, acceptance, nurturing/protecting others etc
6. Socially relevant needs Play – relax, diversion Cognisance- explore, ask questions, curiosity Exposition, demonstrate, explain, interpret	Break time, extra- curricular activities Fieldwork, guided enquiry, experiment Discuss /debate / written work /exhibits	The Kingdom of God was displayed through all types of informal fellowship, by confident prayer (ask, seek and knock), and by both demonstrating and teaching about the Kingdom in various ways.

.2c-90
What general point in Figs. 61-63 can be applied to Jesus' teaching?

Figure 64

Converting Murray's Taxonomy to relate to Jesus' motivational thrusts	
Meeting Personal Needs *Trust for God's provision Freedom from fear - a new confidence Freedom from guilt - forgiveness Belonging - a new community Sharing pleasurably Achievement of a special type Understanding and knowledge*	**Personal Qualities - Positive** *Cognizance - exploration Nurturance - protect and aid Affiliation - friendship, community Similance - imitate, agree, believe Deference - admire, serve gladly Achieved - overcome, exercise power*
Key Unique Concepts – Foundations *The Kingdom of God The Fatherhood of God Repentance and reconciliation Salvation and the mission Servant-hood and discipleship Jesus - Messiah/authority*	**Transformation to Spiritual Norms within the Kingdom of God** *Acquisitions - spiritual rewards etc Construction - build Inviolacy - self-image Aggression - extend the Kingdom Abasement - submission Superiority - the truth as perceived*

Figure 65

Rath's taxonomy of Psychogenic needs	Examples of Jesus' spiritual sublimation of Rath's taxonomy
Love and affection	This was fundamental to his whole strategy and is shown in his attitude to children, the needy and his disciples etc.
Belonging	The disciples felt that they belonged to a highly privileged group with unique access to their teacher
Freedom from guilt	The central notion of forgiveness is clearly exemplified in the adulterous woman, the prodigal son, and Peter.
Achievement	The sense of challenge and success was exemplified when the disciples were sent out in pairs.
To share	Jesus had to share possessions and the notion of sharing was characteristic of his community.
Freedom from fear	One of Jesus' characteristic phrases was, 'Do not fear' and this was illustrated in the parable of the prodigal son
Understanding and knowledge	Jesus spent a considerable time explaining the meaning of parables and his more intimate prophecies to disciples
Economic security	Jesus did not promise economic security but he did pray that just as he had kept them, so God would keep them

Teachers are usually torn between the ideal and the possible, and between the desirable patterns for the individual compared with those of larger groups. Figures 59 and 60 show how certain ideal characteristics of psychologically based motivations are matched or differ from those in a good working situation. One not only notices the degree of overlap, but also how Jesus' own motivations can be related to them.

These were typical issues (seeFig.66) raised at a brainstorming session in a curriculum planning group in a school that needed to urgently enhance pupil motivation and improve attitudes partly through a personal and social education course. The staff started with a brainstorming session (column la) and then refined it to a working planning session (column B). What are the major differences? How might they relate to this chapter? The best in motivation is often sacrificed to management constraints. Perhaps it illustrated what Jesus already knew, that it is difficult to motivate a large number of pupils over a short period of time, and so he taught a relatively small group of disciples and friends for three years!

.2c-91
Which aspects of Jesus' motivational skills might be applicable to you?

Summary 7

1. It has been shown that Jesus' teaching enhanced motivation but like all teaching it posed certain questions because types of cost, commitment, attitude, effort and opportunity are required by pupils. The most general of these questions are:

- Does the teacher enjoy a *recognized authority* amongst the pupils?
- Are the pupils motivated by *the competence* of the teacher?
- Do the pupils accept the principle *of delay of gratification?*
- Do the pupils see the priority of *intrinsic rewards*?
- Can the pupils enjoy *a vision* that goes beyond expectations?
- Can the pupils enjoy the likelihood *of success*?
- Do pupils have a degree of *personal choice*?
- Do pupils enjoy the sense of *privilege* and *discovering* new understandings?
- Do teachers meet *felt needs* and provide a sense of *enjoyment /satisfaction*?
- Are *purposeful aspirations/prospects* provided that relate to pupils' interests?
- Is a *value basis* provided to the work that *pupils understand?*
- Does it provide a pathway to success that is understandable and attainable?
- Does it provide a sense of ongoing attainment and progress?
- Are there tangible goals, strategies and methods that pupils understand?
- Do pupils' sense *acceptance, approval and appreciation* – even during failure and adversity?

2. Jesus provided a motivational structure that can be applied to all teaching. The constituent parts listed below will be considered in greater detail in Part C.

- The provision of *goals*.
- The satisfaction of *needs*.
- Raising *hopes and aspirations*.
- Offering *superior and positive learning paths*.
- Providing a *replicable process*.
- Providing the possibility of *rewards*.
- Setting *attainable challenges*.
- Showing *valued commitment and persistence*.
- *Encouraging initiatives* and enjoying *success*.
- Providing the opportunity for *peer-group development*.

.2c-92
Why does motivation vary between people?

Figure 66

Ideal need / aspiration based motivations – the brainstorm	Common teaching / learning motivation – the planning priorities	Motivational priorities alluded to in this chapter
Acceptance	Activity/construction	Acceptance
Achievement	Care	Achievement
Affiliation/friendship	Challenge	Affective
Avoidance of hurt	Choices are limited	Aspiration
Avoidance of failure	Competition	Challenge
Celebration	Compliance to a group	Change
Change/development	Custom	Cognition
Choice	Generalized instruction	Drive
Competition	Grouping – regular	Expectation
Co-operation	Identification	Experience
Creativity/problem solving	Imitation/hero-worship	Goals
Curiosity	Life chance promises and prospects	Identity
Self-esteem/confidence	Needs imposed - goals short and long-term	Intrinsic
Experiences	Personal opportunities	Memorable
Focused personalised instruction	Personal Interest	Needs
Habitual/moral basis of work	Rewards – extrinsic	Pleasure
Initiatives	Rewards – intrinsic	Praise
Leadership opportunities	Risk taking	Prospects
Mastery / success	Security	Relevance
Novelty	Stability - higher prediction	Replicate
Personal ownership and development	Structure – high	Reward
Progress awareness	Success - mastery or minimal failure	Security
Risk-taking	Survival	Values
Security	Task completion and closure	Worth

Personality Factor – 8

Which personality factors might hold the key to understanding one of the motivations of: Jesus…. His close followers….Enquirers….Crowds… Religious authorities

.2c-93
Select what you consider to be the 4 most powerful motivating forces?

Chapter 8

Memory

Looking Forward

Multi-causal memory...Three hypotheses of memory...Maximising the use of memory Memory building skills...Arousal and retrieval...Experiential learning...The use of language...Semantic memories...Peer-group memories...Flashbulb memories...The teacher and memories...A pattern for memorisation...A summary for efficient memorisation...An analytical aide-memoire of factors influencing the memory.

The power and necessity of personal and corporate memory can hardly be gauged! This was especially so prior to the emergence of the mass media when the histories of civilizations such as the Incas were virtually wiped out because written records were sparse. Although the Jews had a fine written record of their history and religious faith, Jesus followed the Jewish tradition of relying heavily upon people's efficient memory to perpetuate his teaching. Throughout their history memorization had been commanded and practised, not much of which was authoritatively sacred. We can now appreciate how successful Jesus' teaching methods were in passing on his message, even though they were not written until decades later. When one considers that the decay of personal memory is usually 80 per cent in the first day, the success of relating his teaching through memory efficient methods becomes evident. Without them there would probably be no Christian faith in the world today. But how can this help the teaching and learning process now?

Figure 67

Themes	Issues particular to the theme	Relating the theme to Jesus	Relating the theme to teaching generally
Leadership	What motivates a leader's memory?	How did Jesus control memories?	What is likely to be at the fore in memories when teaching and learning?
Perception	What does a person perceive as significant to remember?	How did Jesus perceive what was memorable?	How might teaching and learning be made memorable?
Motivation	What motivates a person to remember?	How was Jesus motivated to remember key facts etc	What motivates teaching and learning to become memorable?
Socialisation	How are people socialized into memory patterns?	What was the social basis of Jesus' memories?	How are memories related to the socialization process?
Cognition	How are memories formed and developed?	What was the basis of Jesus developing memories?	How are memories maximised?
Emotions	How are memories influenced by emotions?	How did Jesus use emotions to develop memories?	How are memories related to emotions in teaching and learning?

Note to Fig.68: The power and yet frailty of the memory are proverbial, but it was a tool upon which Jesus depended. Fortunately he maximized its effectiveness to a remarkable degree – but his memorization methods were not supernatural or beyond normal practice. The permanence of memories are often related to:

Their personal significance.

Situational links and their significance.

Needs and aspirations.

The significance of the source of the stimulus.

The compatibility and patterning with previous experiences/knowledge.

Contrast and habituation.

Language.

Emotional significance.

.2c-94
What makes your memory particularly good or poor?

Figure 68

Four Distinctive factors in Memory Formation and Retention

Generic sources	Stimuli	Universal methods of memory development	Typical Jesus related memories
Cultural/Historic	Arousal	Response to /of authority	Parental memories
Personal experiences	Novelty	Language	Observing local people and situations
Crises/ Pressures	Surprise	Cognitive development	Admiration of John the Baptist
Cognitive inquiry	Patterning/ relationships	Observing demonstrations	Traditional memories
Sensual experiences	Pleasure principle	Thinking skills e.g. cause and effect	Synagogue memories
Imagination	Experience/ previous learning	Elaboration	Self referencing memories - the Son of Man/Messiah
Current contextual stimulation	Needs /Worth	Networks/schemas	Critically important experiences e.g. his baptism
Observations	Anticipation/ promise	Rehearsal/recall	Group interaction memories e.g. The Passover
Emotions	Associative memories	Primacy	Repetition e.g. feeding 4000
Values	Critical experiences	Recency	Emotions e.g. weeping
	Affiliations	Retrieval	New works and schemas .e.g. fulfilling the Law
	Purposeful creativity /construction	Self- referencing	Affiliation experiences e.g. the transfiguration
	Group interaction	Interpretation of situations and emotions	Language memories e.g. the Sermon on the Mount
	Flashbulb memory	Visualisation	Action and memories e .g. washing the disciples feet
	Previous knowledge	Kinaesthetic	Affiliation memories e.g. the call of Peter
		Auditory	Patterning relationships e.g. appointing the 12
		Projection	Purposeful creative memories e.g. the blind man in Jerusalem
			Flashbulb memories e.g. *Lazarus*
			Sensual experiences e.g. water into wine
			Sorrow - the Crucifixion
			Joy – the Resurrection

.2c-95
How might each of the memory stages listed above affect each other?

Memory is not magical

Jesus' teaching was memorable – but how could he have been so effective that his teaching remains in a coherent inspiring form. Also how might his methods be relevant today? These and the cross thematic questions are addressed either in the text or at some other indicated place.

Memory like perception is interactive and can vary with the context. Like all great teachers, Jesus recognized the power of using the visual, auditory and kinaesthetic senses together with visualization etc to establish powerful memories. The mind map (Fig. 63) shows the complexity of memory with its many causal operations. It illustrates three major aspects, namely its *generic sources, specific stimuli and universal methods of development*, which together show causes, processes and outcomes of memory formation. Typical examples of these in the gospels are shown in the right hand column. A brief glance at the generic sources shows how they were and are mutually stimulating. For example, when Jesus was in the cornfields defending his disciples against accusations that they were harvesting and eating bread on the Sabbath, He drew upon:

- Cultural / historic sources (King David).
- Use of sensory experiences (hunger).
- Current contextual stimulation (cornfield).
- Creating comments based on an authoritative source (the Scriptures).
- Direct personal interaction.

The crisis was transformed, values questioned and emotions released. Powerful memories were intensified by a complex mix of emotions such as fear, surprise and anger that were channelled through language, observation, visualization, kinaesthetic and auditory experiences – and so powerful memories were secured for posterity. Furthermore, the group had something important to talk about and sharply memorize. Also they could take pride in their teacher's ability and identify themselves with him in a reasonable confidence that he would protect them.

The mind map (Fig.68) shows that the memory uses interacting and changing stimuli that produce personalized memories – after all, in the cornfields, the memories of the religious authorities and the disciples no doubt differed. Memories are modified as new stimuli elaborate them, or remain relatively stable when earlier memories powerfully subsume them or if they become caricatured. Like perception, motivation, learning and emotions, the memory is dynamic, selective, interpretive and ever likely to be influenced by particular contextual situations and senses involved. Therefore, memory's complexity raises problems regarding its accuracy and influences the level of performance of both teachers and pupils.

Three contrasting explanations of memory can be briefly summarized as follows:

Hypothesis No.1

During the 1960's psychologists led by Richard Atkinson and Richard Shiffrin claimed that memory takes the form of a three-stage process. The sensory register swiftly responds to new stimuli for a minimal time. It makes an immediate reaction and is particularly important when issues of safety and avoidance are concerned. Part of the information is sifted and passed on (or encoded) to the short-term memory where it remains for approximately 15 seconds. Some is consciously retained as being significant but much is lost by memory fade and displacement. That which is retained then passes on to the long-term memory where in may remain for a lifetime. The short-term memory can retrieve knowledge from the long-term memory when necessary. Hence, if a person has learned that 15 x 15 = 225 that knowledge will be accessible even though it is not frequently used. Also, the knowledge in the long-term memory can be honed and renewed with relative ease so that it can be retrieved and used habitually. Jesus' standard methods of teaching were based on mutually supportive principles and concepts being developed through multi-sensory experiences which maximized likelihood of the teaching being retained and made available in the long-term memory.

.2c-96
Yesterday is today's memory and tomorrow's dream. What clue might this give about memory?

Figure 69

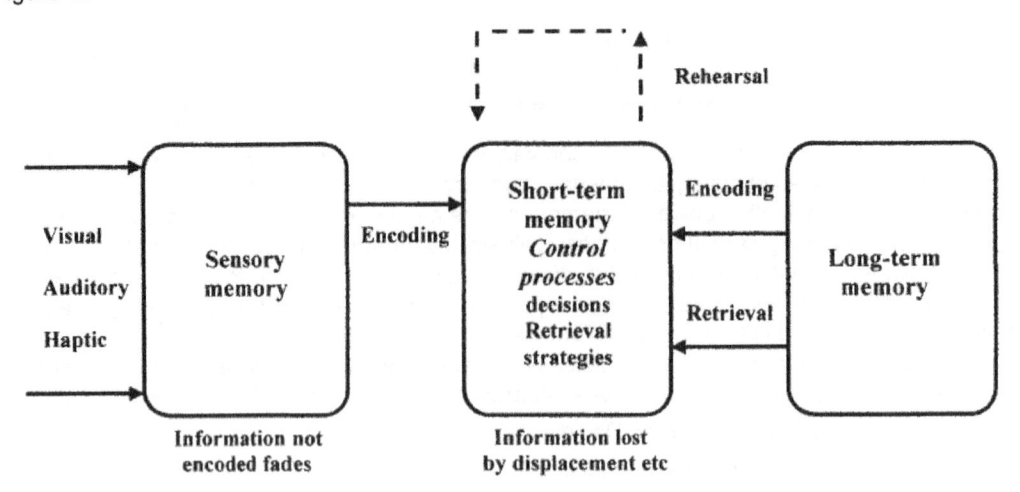

```
Visual ──┐                          ┌─ Rehearsal ─┐
         │                          ▼             │
Auditory ─→ [Sensory  ] ─Encoding→ [Short-term ] ←─Encoding── [Long-term]
            [ memory  ]            [ memory    ]              [ memory  ]
Haptic ──┘                         [ Control   ] ──Retrieval→
                                   [ processes ]
                                   [ decisions ]
                                   [ Retrieval ]
                                   [ strategies]

         Information not            Information lost
         encoded fades              by displacement etc
```

Hypothesis No. 2

In the early 1970's A D Badderley and G Hitch popularized the concept of the working memory. The claim is that new stimuli are related appropriately to material from the long-term memory and so allow several pieces of information to be held in the mind and be inter-related simultaneously. It is envisaged that a central executive creatively uses this material from visual and verbal sub-systems. This notion of a dynamic working executive assumes that there is a limited storage capacity that can be temporarily exhausted. It is then difficult to perform information processing tasks simultaneously. Memories may not be recalled in the form they were received and stored. The working memory is seen as holistic and dynamically searching for meanings, storing, recalling and modifying memories as new experiences occur. The central executive can modify memories as it draws upon the past and selects new memories to embolden them. This is a particularly useful explanation of how Jesus' teachings were enriched by the process of reflective and meditative thought as the various stimuli interacted in the working memory and so could be both strengthened and transformed, a feature which is a common experience and which influences expectations and decisions.

Hypothesis No. 3

A view propounded by F Bartlett in the 1930's is closely related to Chapter 6 (perception). Bartlett stated that the mind builds schemas or typical patterns of thought and understandings. It collates similar ideas and so develops memory patterns that we call scenaria. An interesting point to note was that Bartlett found in his experiments that people frequently imposed their own meaning on memories. For example:

- They may yet change some details.
- They may change the order of incidents in an action.
- They may give personalized emphasis to some aspects of a situation.
- They may impose personalized reasons/ meanings on a story or situation.

.2c-97
How can you maximize your memory?

Memory is seen as selective, interpretive and ever moving as it can vary with the senses involved. Therefore, its accuracy and reliability can be doubted. Any model of memory must recognize the effects of multiple inputs, usage and a person's existing knowledge. Memories may be distorted due to reordering and rationalisation of knowledge, omission of detail and undue emphasis given to particular facts. Also the influences of emotions such as fear and love, excess or lack of enthusiasm and interference from other learned material etc are influential. Hence memories may reconstruct reality.

These hypotheses pose three immediate and relevant issues:
- Can knowledge be *recalled* reliably and efficiently?
- What happens as knowledge is actively *received* in relationship to prior knowledge?
- How is knowledge *interpreted* and what is the resultant memory?

The question therefore is how Jesus' teaching style maximized the possibility of long-term memory, reinforcement, retrieval and reflection and also generated a consistent conceptual image that could become a shared perception/interpretation.

A consideration of how Jesus maximized the use of the memory

We know that *active/ positive sentences* are processed more quickly and reliably than those that are passive or negative and that *short visual statements* are more reliably remembered than long abstract accounts. The Sermon on the Mount is a good example of the use of short sentences, sharp illustrations and personal relevance. But how would Jesus be remembered? Even when experiences are similar, memories differ in their intensity, priority and meaning. But it is reasonable to assume that Jesus' followers experienced sufficient *repetition to retain and develop memories*. When he taught in successive villages they heard similar teaching in various forms that they could discuss. Their memories were constantly renewed but those of the crowds who had only heard snatches of his teaching were probably distorted. The energizing experiences provided a flow of visual, auditory and kinaesthetic experiences that became embedded and transformed in the working and long-term memories.

The *cumulative* effects of these memories over three years resulted in a secure impression of Jesus and his mission. This *immersion* in Jesus' teaching provided norms and perspectives that became the basis for *new information to be received into meaningful mental structures as anchored memories and*

'to those who have shall more be given.......'

Jesus understood that the past can cause the present to interpret its experiences and to anticipate the future. It is likely that both A D Baddeley and F Bartlett would recognize that Jesus' teaching style exemplified aspects of their working memory and interpretive memory hypotheses.

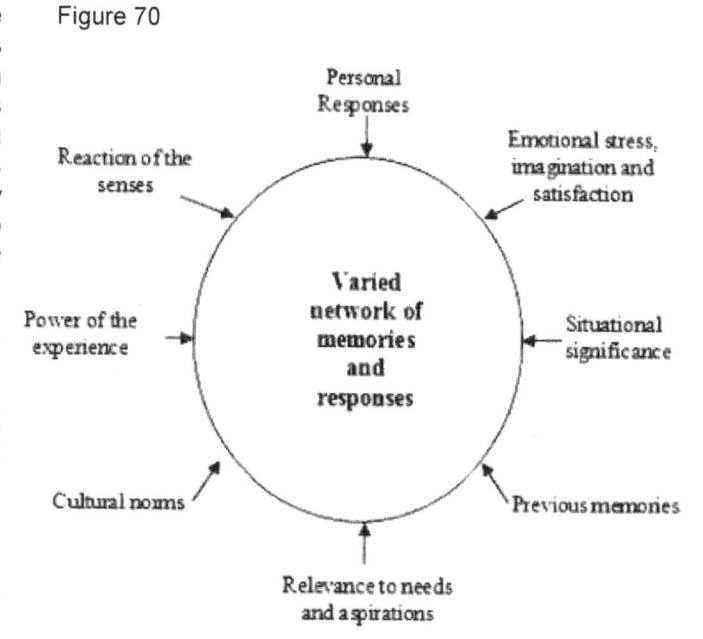

Figure 70

Varied network of memories and responses — with surrounding factors: Personal Responses; Emotional stress, imagination and satisfaction; Situational significance; Previous memories; Relevance to needs and aspirations; Cultural norms; Power of the experience; Reaction of the senses.

.2c-98
Which insights from the three hypotheses could help when teaching?

Figure 71

```
┌─────────────────────────┐
│    High Level           │
│    Memorizsation        │
└─────────────────────────┘

    Pleasurable Emotions


    Constructive Peer Group Activities


    Popular Language


    Meaningful Learning Experieces


    Linked Knowledge


    Perceived as Relevant, Worthwhile

    ╭─────────────────────╮
    │  Entry Impressions /│
    │     Expectations    │
    ╰─────────────────────╯

    Low Perceived Relevance etc


    Fragmented Knowledge


    Chalk, Talk Instruction

    Unpleasant Instruction

    Professional Non-friendly Language


    Isolated Instruction


┌─────────────────────────┐
│    Low Level            │
│    Memorization         │
└─────────────────────────┘
```

Their concepts of memory being a processor that constructs patterns or networks based on incoming stimuli and existing memories would match Jesus' teaching style, as exemplified when a paralysed man was brought to Jesus by four friends in Capernaum. Something similar to Fig.68 probably occurred. The varied stimuli produced diverse experiences, but a core memory developed.

Jesus made simple statements which everybody could receive and retain, but because of their past experiences (e.g. the Pharisees) their understanding and responses differed. To some Jesus became a 'star' who was worth following. The effect of the fast-flowing memories differed in their priorities. Hence the only miracle recorded in all four gospels, the feeding of the multitude must have been powerful and interpreted with varying degrees of spiritual meaning, whereas the healing of Peter's mother-in-law was a relatively private expression of compassion, care and competence.

Jesus was a memory maker who also drew upon his own memories and those of his followers. His cumulative experiences must have been a major factor in his vision and work. His personal memories together with his historic culture and observations provided conditions to construct meanings that became lifelong memories and purposes. These were not simply actions in the past tense, but evocative experiences that people found worth sharing and acting upon in the present and the future.

Memory is usually related to the authority of the teacher as perceived by the pupils. As their role model, Jesus possessed validity and authority, but often the pupils' memories *preceded* their understanding. Even so, the memories were building blocks for subsequent understanding and his words became treasured memories. He was organizing and interpreting principles freshly in terms of traditional knowledge that provided 'memory hooks' for listeners and watchers, and established a sense that their needs and aspirations would be met. Although they did not understand precisely where he was leading, it promised to be a memorable journey as he opened new vistas. Therefore, his teaching was rooted in his own person and the people's view of him. For example, one wonders what the boy who gave his lunch to Jesus remembered of that epic day. The teacher fostered *motivated remembering* rather than incidental or motivated forgetting as is sometimes the case amongst reluctant learners.

Jesus linked old and new memories in people's imaginations that heightened their variously interpreted memories. He stated succinctly what was to be remembered. As he related historic events to his present

╭──────────────────────────────────╮
│   .2c-99   │
│ Analyse the diagram (Fig.71) of │
│ tendencies to form positive or │
│ negative memories in respect of │
│ learning. How might it be made │
│ more attractive?   │
╰──────────────────────────────────╯

and to the future, it gave them an authority similar to that of the traditional events themselves. He had to foster both *affective* and *cognitive* memories if people were to develop a personal commitment to him. The gospels contain innumerable examples of people with an affective commitment to Jesus but whose memories were of greater significance than their understanding. That has been the norm throughout the centuries of much Christian worship.

Affective memories constantly set the tone and quality of learning that would otherwise be inadequate and possibly short term. People might remember good things that were incidental to the teacher but be distinctive and relevant to the learners. Hence, memory promotes the deep processing of knowledge and the elaboration and distinctive personalisation of learning experiences. Perhaps, a feature of his teaching techniques was that he was able to establish.

Memory building skills

Examples of memory building skills	
Common memory making skills	*Examples of Jesus' uses*
• Elaboration • Critical experiences • Organizing knowledge coherently • Constructing meanings • Arousal /retrieval • Novelty • Patterning in the past • Relating the past to the present and the future • Demonstrations • Using the senses • Purposeful cued memory • Personal response • Overcoming opposition • Creating associations and privilege • Deep explanations / cognitive processing	• Historic memories -------Jonah • Personal experiences • Observations • Logical outcomes • Crisis • Visualization • Auditory experiences • Achievements • Kinaesthetic experiences • Compassion • Stories • Sound bite teaching • Strongly affected actions • Various forms of repetition/development • Poetic rhythm

Figure 72

His wide array of memory building skills were such as those listed in Figs 66 and 70. Let us consider some in more detail.

Elaboration: (This does not imply a fictional elaboration)

The implicit patterned structure of memories in Jesus' teaching was based upon a limited number of organizing principles. This can be illustrated by a process that we will call *elaboration*. He reinforced existing ideas with new knowledge that were 'woven' together to create 'patterns' with rich, potent meanings. These were elaborated by further incidents, words and situations that maintained an ultimate focus. By this Jesus retained the original core (e.g. the Father and care) and developed it opportunistically. And so a cumulative 'picture' of memories of the Kingdom life emerged. Through observations and discussions their faith could be likened to a banner or tapestry that was readily recognised, attractive and comprehensible. This 'elaboration' was a more powerful form of learning than rote repetition and their powers of recall increased with the potential for further elaboration based on related novel actions and stories. For example, the principle of servanthood was 'elaborated' with memories as he served them. He *chunked* the ideas into small components and consequently, over a three-year period the disciples' knowledge, though lacking precise details, was elaborated into a meaningful pattern that could be visualized. In total this produced memorable long-term corporate learning and understanding. This process can be traced in the synoptic gospels as follows:

.2c-100
How might the process of elaboration be used to aid memorisation?

- The fundamental statement was set out as the basis for the whole picture.
- An outline' sketch' illustrating the principles of the statement was inserted.
- Detailed 'drawings' illustrating the statement in action and bringing it alive.
- Further 'sketches' illustrating the problems in the initial statement.
- Background materials based on the parables were inserted.
- Climax 1 – Peter's confession at Caesarea Philippi.
- Climax 2 – the Transfiguration.
- Climax 3 – Growing problems facing the initial statement.
- Climax 4 – Jerusalem…. Popularity v Problems.
- Climax 5 – the fundamental statement destroyed?
- Climax 6 – the fundamental statement justified.

The principles of elaboration are coherent development, continuity and clarity. This process requires teachers to develop the overriding principles whilst retaining the core idea. Teachers might link successive topics by common concepts or by taking a major situation/problem to which organising concepts are introduced. Alternative approaches to using the principle of elaboration are shown in Part C.

The process of elaboration might be likened to a 10 stage 'R' sequence.

Take a *Relevant* issue/situation/problem.

Reception – ensure new knowledge is compatible with pupil understanding.

Relate the pupils to the problem.

Recall any previous appropriate knowledge.

Reconstruct what has been learned with slight variations and assess which new knowledge is required to achieve flexible understanding.

Research to acquire any necessary new knowledge.

Relearn the initial ideas and apply them into the new/modified situation.

Repeat into a situation with significant differences.

Reinforce the knowledge by a parallel reconstruction based on a new situation.

Revive and *refresh* the whole process periodically.

Why might this be 'memory efficient'?

Arousal and retrieval:

Memory needs focused arousal and retrieval and not be sidetracked into forgetting! Jesus effectively did this by arousing memories almost incidentally and linking his teaching *to the established past, by meeting particular needs of the moment and by creating hope for the future*. This was powerful because memory responds readily to positive, relevant incidents that have given pleasure and provide hope. The bulk of Jesus' teaching in Galilee was encouraging and was memorable on the Pollyanna principle. This states that we remember pleasurable incidents most readily. It is estimated that 50% of recalled memories are pleasurable, 30% are disconcerting and 20% are neutral. Therefore, a wide range of pleasurable memories together with the extreme emotions of Jesus' suffering generated many common, powerful memories. Their achievements, proud identification of being with him, allied to a sense of awe, maximized the ready recall of memories amongst the disciples. The danger was always that memories could be embroidered with repetition.

.2c-101
Can you find it any evidence to suggest that the Pollyanna principle is correct?

Arousal and retrieval are ongoing necessities. Attention normally declines as the mind and the senses continually look for fresh stimuli. Also, frequent retrieval or renewal is important if the learning is to be permanent and capable of creative developments. This does not always occur but it normally did for the disciples. Arousal and retrieval therefore were closely related. Also, it has been found that the most memorable stages of teaching are normally the beginning and the end, with the middle section susceptible to decline and difficult to recall. This is known as *primacy* (the first thing heard) and *recency* (the last thing heard). Jesus' stories were short and had a minimal middle stage. The strong beginning and end enhanced the likely secure memories of his teaching. Linked to this, the *strength* of the *initial experiences*, plus the sense of the *significance of the learning*, the impact of the *emotional stimuli* and certain agreed *group values* together ensured that memories were sufficiently intense and focused to be retained in the memory. One can only imagine the frenzied excitement aroused around Galilee when the news came that he was on his way. He had something to say that was important to them. The arousal that Jesus' teaching could evoke was not only that it was purposeful, but it also contained novelties and surprises. Imagine any situation such as healing a leper, or a blind man or rebuking religious leaders and one can visualize people running to talk about this new prophet and running back to hear more. The mind was focused, expectations heightened and accumulating memories embedded. This sustained flow of events shows that arousal was not merely what happened at the beginning of Jesus' teaching in order to attract attention but equally consisted of those words and incidents that caused people to pause, think attentively and consider beliefs and ideas afresh.

His teaching *created new memories* and stimulated and *organized previous memories*. He used established cultural knowledge as a basis for personal identification that evoked a sense of authoritative truth amongst the people. Its novel reality aroused and related to people's expectations and so promoted intensive discussion that ensured that memories were long term. He created a buzz of excitement by his actions and words that arrested their attention by meeting some needs and setting new aspirations and challenges. This was different – even his enemies were aroused and no doubt remembered his teachings. In Capernaum people clamoured to see him, either critically or enthusiastically. The arousal was brought to a climax when after a man was memorably lowered through the roof. There was a theological pitched battle between the religious authorities and Jesus. It was indeed a surprising memorable day. But in the long-term it appears that the established norms may have won through!

Experiential learning

We remember our *experiences* best and Jesus' teaching was normally *interactive and experiential*. Action, objects and situations create memories that are readily drawn back to consciousness and related to ongoing stimuli. Jesus achieved this by involving his followers that yielded sharp visual images, which together with the spoken and kinaesthetic experiences had long-term values and gradually promoted rational generalized norms and continuity. Having watched, heard and participated they reflected and discussed with a sense of involvement, which caused the experiences to enter the long-term memory. This process ensured a high degree of personalisation and identification amongst the followers. This was a memorable form of creative reinforcement that also provided an optimum challenge and a growing sense of opportunity and success. Their actions became memories that were maintained and developed through new compatible memories. The surprises in their learning were probably tempered by a sense of magnitude as they began to realise who Jesus was. His far-reaching and dramatic changes to people's existing understanding was of further significance because major changes are often more memorable than minor modifications when learning.

These first-hand experiences were like a master craftsman working with his apprentices who watched and copied his every move. Each person developed sharp visual images and many had kinaesthetic and tactile experiences that embedded their network of memories. This travelling teacher provided a full array of first-hand experiences to be interpreted. Their personal experiences were infilled and developed by Jesus personally and so they gained ownership of them. There was the danger of situations becoming fused with previous experiences and becoming distorted because memory can imagine and mistakenly recall events that never happened! But these

.2c-102
How did Jesus use language to enhance reliable memories?

intense and repeated experiences minimized that and clarified and regularized their thinking. Memories were secured and heightened!

His deep cognitive processes involved physical, social, emotional senses and mental imaging that interacted to rehearsed and shaped memories. Their personal experiences were especially important to them. When 70 followers went out to replicate Jesus' work, it must have been with fear and trembling and yet they returned in triumph to compare stories gleaned from their experiences and so memories became entrenched and the teaching- learning process was secure. One can imagine Peter drawing upon his sharp autobiographical memories when he related his gospel to Mark or when Mary, the mother of Jesus, talked to Luke. The rich association and clusters of ideas were self-referencing, personal and afforded superior recall.

The use of language

Language heightens powers of memory. Jesus' use of language was probably as memorable as his actions. He spoke in the common tongue that bonded him with the people. His stories such as the Good Samaritan and analogies such as a city on a hill together with numerous metaphors were memorably related to the imagination and personal identification. Also, as we have seen, much of his teaching, like the Lord's Prayer, was poetic and contained rhyming phrases and rhythms that could be easily repeated. Similarly, his teaching statements (e.g. the Beatitudes) were arresting sound bites that could be recalled. He stood where they stood and spoke about things that were pertinent to them. Also, the crowds were unlikely to follow a detailed argument but they could remember and repeat the short significance phrases Jesus used These were not only remembered efficiently but also communicated rapidly.

His sharp concrete, pictorial language such as building a house upon a rock knew no class or theological barriers. One might even wonder whether his Galilean dialect made him more acceptable to the Roman centurion than if he had been a troublesome Judean. Furthermore his practice of silencing his critics through efficient 'question and answer' methods promoted a sense of emotional involvement that gave him added authority and also maximized the possibility of long-term learning and memory retention partly because 'he was one of them'. Overall, Jesus used language attractively which heightened the possibility of it being remembered.

Semantic memories:

Memories are classified into two distinct categories – episodic and semantic memories. Episodic memories refer to *specific events* such as the man whose sins were forgiven in Capernaum. These are striking and personalized but not normally organized. Semantic memories or knowledge are *principles and understandings that are widely shared* and which are meaningful and act as organizers. Jesus had to establish *semantic knowledge and memories* about God and the spiritual reality of the 'Kingdom'. This required that episodic knowledge should be organised to enrich semantic principles. Therefore, he often moved from illustrative episodic knowledge to shared semantic knowledge. For example, the notions of a holy city and prophets could be widely understood.

Peer-group memories

Jesus' followers' memories were enriched as they worked and lived together. As the peer group developed common goals and experiences over a three-year period so their memories became more corporate, deeper and more reliable. One can almost hear them recalling and highlighting the day's events and comparing them with other recent happenings. What might the morrow bring? The small intra-group discussions of events reinforced and regularized their network of memories that were essential later. His message was coherently memorable as together they saw his central teaching elaborated and restructured in different contexts. Parables, messianic teachings, action of all kinds…! The disciples were privileged in their experiential learning A corporate identity and a powerful fund of diverse memories was building up. The memories were generating a sense of ownership. When he travelled, the long-term effects on the crowds were less than on his band of

.2c-103
In what ways are emotions an aid or a hindrance to reliable memory formation?

followers. Whereas the *crowds* may have *forgotten one visit,* Jesus' *followers* would be likely *to remember* it keenly as they compared it with others, each part of which related to previous teachings and anticipated further teaching. This rate and quality of interaction changed their discipleship from isolated experiences to an organic understanding. The process of reporting, responsibility and shared activity made the three-years of varied tuition memorable and ultimately coherent. This was an extreme case but any good peer-group tuition based on purposeful multiple experiences and responsibilities is likely to provide helpful long-term memories and learning,

Flashbulb memories

Sometimes isolated memories 'pop-out' unexpectedly. These *flashbulb* memories are normally caused by powerful events that rise to the surface of consciousness as emotions are stirred or as new stimuli promote fresh memories. On the mind map, the raising of Lazarus is classified as a flashbulb memory but this would vary with the people concerned. For the family it would have been an awesome experience that was relived day after day. For outsiders, however, it might well have become a flashbulb memory that was raised to the level of consciousness by a crisis or by meditation about Jesus. It indicates that whilst memories may be shared, differences between people may be such as to cause them to be varied and have degrees of meaning and consciousness.

A pattern for memorization

It has been emphasized that the brain gathers compatible knowledge into clusters or schemas. Therefore incoming information becomes related to unifying the ideas rather than remaining as isolated fragments of knowledge. The best teaching is likely to be that which achieves a good fit between new and existing knowledge and helps this knowledge to expand, at the same time fitting with the learners' cultural ideas. For example, Jesus' focused and limited network of knowledge had a coherent, dynamic enlarging core and structure about the Kingdom of God. New knowledge was integrated into its existing framework to form these networks of long-term memories. The related stimuli were thereby able to create additional meanings and be used both with established knowledge and new stimuli through deep processing that was 'memory friendly'. He avoided the inefficiencies of relating, retaining and recalling a ragbag of facts or implicit knowledge that may befog learning. And so memories were personalised and became autobiographical and were characteristically interactive and became the building blocks for subsequent understanding.

Memorization and the emotions

Emotions influence what is remembered. The sense of awe on and devotion fostered over near the three years sharpened up and shake memories. The powerful affirmative effect on John can be detected by the claim that 'there are many other things which Jesus did; were every one of them to be written, I suppose that the world itself could not contain the books.' Clearly memory is based on the perception of the knowledge etc being taught.

- Memories are usually enhanced by *interactive learning.*
- Teaching is made memorable by satisfying pupils' *needs and aspirations.*
- Memory is closely related to *performance* and the learning *context.*

.2c-104
Which types of experiential memories have you found especially powerful?

- A role model is memorable when the teacher, message and relationship cohere.
- Is it brief? Remember the principles of primacy and recency!
- The pupils should be given multi-sensory experiences.

Look at Figure 68 and note how it seeks to illustrate why the memorization process around Jesus varied so greatly. It returns to the familiar issue of differentiated priorities. To some the memories contained interesting information, a new awareness, a wide range of opportunities, relevance, empathy and a fine teacher, whereas others could drown the memories as dangerous and a mere novelty that did not comply with their established beliefs.

Summary

It is possible to identify the following memory friendly qualities in Jesus' teaching methods that can promote efficient memorization now.

- Pupils need emotional experiences that involve enjoyment and curiosity.
- There should be opportunities to develop novelty and surprise.
- There were everyday experiences for the disciples to talk about.
- The knowledge should be both organized and incidental.
- Learning is related to observations, established knowledge and experiences and memories to imagination and reality.
- Learners construct meanings around contextually significant stories.
- Pupils create powerful developmental associations and ideas from teaching.
- Knowledge is chunked into convenient learning and memory packages.
- Core concepts are used frequently in different contexts.
- Memory is sharply contextual. *John ch.20 v.16.*
- Memory is improved by rhythm, keywords and visual imagery.
- Initial studies should be intensive and prolonged.
- The learning is constantly reviewed.
- Emotions and memory are linked in learning.
- Memory effectively selects, interprets and makes use of the senses.

As a culmination of this chapter, select six memory aids that Jesus used and which you might use (Fig.73). The purpose of the letters *A-F* and the numbers *1-12* are meant to aid the location of cells e.g. A1, C4 etc.

Jesus' memorable teaching may be characterized by experiential learning, perceived worth and significance, teacher authority/and knowledge, satisfying needs and aspirations, appropriate language and emotional attachment. These elements were integrated into a memorable holistic teaching style.

Personality Factor – 9

What might have been two contrasting views about the personality of Jesus? What are the implications of this for the 21st century?

.2c-105
Select what you think are six major memory making skills used by Jesus.

Figure 73
An analytical aide-memoire of factors influencing memory.

	A	B	C	D	E	F
Teacher	Authority based on memorable actions John ch.20v28	Authority based on new and superior knowledge Mk 7v1-23	Authority based on high goals and values Lk 12v2931	Authority based on recognized compassion Lk14v14	Authority based on strength of input, promise and inspiration Mk11v15	Authority based on strength of vision, skills etc Luke 4v18-22
People and pupils	Memories that create aspirations Luke ch.10v1	Memory – satisfying personal needs Jn ch.6	Memories related to responses Matt. 9v8	Memories related to defying opposition Matt.ch.12v2	Faith generating autobiographical memories Jn .8v1	Personal achievements Mk.6v7
Knowledge	Develop contextually related memories John ch4	Memories related established knowledge Matt.15 v32	Knowledge perceived as worthwhile/ significant Jn13v12 15	Episodic knowledge that contributes to semantic knowledge Mk.9v51	Semantic statements drew Knowledge together Jn .6v48	Patterning memories and knowledge Lk 7v22 Matt. ch.5,6,7
Teaching skills	Memories & chunking process Matt.5v1-11	Using keywords to memories Luke 6v1ff	Memories of special events John ch.21	Using kinaesthetic experiences Jn 9v6,15	Stimulus/ challenge ohn.6v67	Pictorial memories John ch10v11
Methods	Personal memories John3v3, 7v50,19v3	Novelty fosters memories Mark 9v2	Memories related to people Lk 19v1	Memories and Visualization Lk 10	Using rhythm in memories Matt.6v9	Memories based on pithy statements and promises John 10v14
Recall, reinforce and develop	Reinforcement by frequent use of memories Jn.6v5,	Challenges related to memories John.14v1-9	Memories related to places Then go....4v31	Frequent and ongoing memories Acts 20v35	Appropriately spaced reinforcement Matt.16v21;17v22	Regular retrieval of memories Matt. 16v9
Experiences	Associative memories John 13v1ff	Memories related to personal progress John.17v6	Memories related to plans Matt.28v19-20	Using performance memories Mk .5v17	Experiences and anticipatory 'memories 'Lk18v32	Strength of input of memory ch.19v17
Relationship	Distinctive memories Lk 7v11	Shared autobiographical memories John .8v1	Memories related to attitude Matt.9v22	Involvement in demonstration memories Lk 18v35	Emotional memories John ch21 v7	Memories related to affection Luke 7v38
Culture	Using cultural knowledge and practices John .15	Relating the past to the future John .3v14	Identify with tradition Jn.8v58	Personal memories Luke ch.22v61-62	Memories based on appropriate language Matt..6v1	Primacy and recency Matt. 13v24
Environment	Using the environment for teaching Matt. 13	Group experiences and shared memories Luke ch22v7	Enlarging and infilling previous memories Lk 24v13ff	The linkage between related memories Lk9v21,ch.18v31	Memories based on a known locality Matt. 26v69Mk16v7	Privileged memories Mark 9v2
Personal development	Memories related to word and deed Luke ch.24v19	Memories influenced by personal closure Matt9v9Jn6v6	Restructured memories and knowledge Lk.22 v7	Memories based on personal recognition Matt.. 16v18	Personal action and satisfaction Lk15v17ff;Lk .8v43	Surprise and encouragement Matt7v28-29 Matt.14v27

Chapter 9

Socialization

Looking forward

A new society?...A pattern for socialization...Primary socialization. Secondary socialization...Separating paths...A leader socializes...Traditional attitude change...Jesus' role and group dynamics...A four part model of the attitude change...Conclusion

The power of this topic, 'socialization', can be gauged when it is rewritten as 'What do we want the pupils to be like?' It makes a fundamental statement about the nature and function of teaching and learning — no matter whether it is in a formal or informal setting Jesus could certainly answer – that question and state how socialization ought to be achieved – and by this he meant practical spirituality. The dynamism of socialization has similarities with that of memory and perception. All are in a constant state of interactive flux and modification as the uncertain recollections of the past plus interpretations of present experiences and future expectations interact to develop perceived realities. Although they are developmental, personalized and yet shared, they are life's building blocks

Being cultures apart from us, his actual methods are not all applicable today but the essence of his thinking is – but how can his practices enrich our understanding of socialization?

The thematic table of questions about socialization shows that it is not only related to the other six themes being considered but it also asks questions about:

- The issue of socialization and training that implies issues of freedom, control, initiation and identity.
- Differences in the socialization process and outcomes are significant.
- The fact and manner of socialization has far reaching motivational repercussions.
- The effect it has on the teaching process.
- The long-term influence on memories and emotions.

Figure 74

	Issues particular to the theme	Relating the theme to Jesus	Relating the theme to teaching generally
Leadership	How does a leader socialize his followers?	How did Jesus socialize and train people into his chosen ways?	How does a teacher train people appropriately?
Perception	Different perceptions of socialized behaviour between people?	Jesus perception of a person socialized into 'Kingdom' behaviour?	Interpreting patterns of socialized behaviour in T/L situations
Motivation	Motivating people into appropriate behavioural action?	How did Jesus socialize/ motivate people to act accordingly?	How are T/P motivated to be socially active?
Memory	How do we develop common memory patterns?	How did Jesus develop agreed 'social' memories?	Why is socialisation an important aspect of memorisation?
Cognition	How can cognition be influenced by socialization?	How did Jesus use socialization to enhance cognition?	Matching cognition and socialization
Emotions	Influence of emotions on socialization	Jesus and emotional responses as he socialized people afresh?	How can emotions and socialization influence T/L?

.2c-106
Which socializing influences were in common between you and Jesus?

A needs-based developmental pattern of socialization

In every society there is competition for control and to establish a pecking order that can state authoritatively what is permissible and what is not. Often principles remain similar even if the tools for achieving them differ. The stark if unspoken message, rings out, "If you comply we will reward you, if you do not we will control you" which, when supported by a legal system, and a powerful set of traditions and/or the military etc are common sentiments in most nations, societies and groupings. But it also applies at the individual level because just as everybody is a teacher, so we all tend to socialize each other to some degree, which means to modify their behaviour. There is, however, a deep-rooted conflict within many people concerning the pursuit of self-actualisation and corporate acceptance and recognition.

Figure 75

Stage One Primary Socialization 0–5 Approx							
Pre-natal needs	**_Post natal needs_**	**_Feelings_**	**_Watch_**	**_Respond/ Interact_**	**_Imitate_**	**_Personal judgment_**	**_Early norms_**
Nourish Responses	Physical and social dependency Positive interaction/ bonding	Sensitive emotions to be calmed. Loving acceptance	Observing/ Absorbing and copy behaviour/ emotions	People admired/ feared Patterns in sound, reactions, emotions, permissible	Focused aspirations and fears Gross imitation of surrounding behaviour	Choices are made Considers and replicates satisfying behaviour	An emerging pattern of personal behaviour and expectations

Stage Two Intermediate Socialization 6-13 approx							
Early norms	**_Needs_**	**_Feelings_**	**_Watch_**	**_Respond/ Interact_**	**_Imitate_**	**_Personal judgment_**	**_Develop Norms_**
Patterned behaviour. A view of self etc	Stability, success, social links. Respect	Concern / Optimism Emotions? Confidence Pursuit of happiness, mastery, achievement	Skilled individuals/ crowds What is 'good', heroic etc	Group behaviour or withdrawal	The hero/ gang /friend Be like...	Idealisation Dreams	Coherent or fragment Short-term?

Stage Three Mature socialization 14–adulthood							
Develop Norms	**_Needs_**	**_Feelings_**	**_Watch_**	**_Respond/ Interact_**	**_Imitate_**	**_Personal judgment_**	**_Mature norms_**
Growing confidence or uncertainty	Stability, success, social links Respect	Concern Optimism Emotional Adequacy/ inadequacy Future?	Major 'top liners'	Potential power of aspiration/ fear of failure?	Strong attractions or rejections	Decisions of right / and wrong etc	Reality? Safety or aspirations

Fig. 75 is structured to show eight recurring but developing elements in socialization. Each becomes more complex as this socialization process widens and dominant forces change.

> .2c-107
> *Take one of the three age groups – which are the major socializing influences?*

Part 2 Universal positive needs that emerge with varying strengths during socialization and so influence spiritual and behavioural norms.

Figure 76

```
                            Reconciliation
              Identity                    Approval
                    Confidence    Leadership          Forgiveness
    Achievement   Personal                  Stability
                  authority
                Pleasure                  High expectations
    Aspirations                                      Respect    Affection
                Self-Esteem   Which of these universal needs
                              could the Master Teacher meet?
                                                    The heroic
                Good moral norms                              Security
                                              Guilt-free
    Fellowship       Community
                          Emotional safety
                                              Friendship
              Belonging
                          Acceptance
```

Fig.76 lists 25 universal needs and ideals. These are not contentious in themselves but it is difficult to envisage a society in which these are put into practice. Many would go further and say that the flipside can become the reality – for acceptance read rejection, for belonging read isolation, and for respect read disdain etc. Jesus could well have described the Kingdom of God, under the leadership of God, in these ideal terms and so the question here is what as a master teacher he was doing in his teaching to resolve these unrequited needs, and to what extent can these be met in our various formal and informal teaching situations?

Although socialization is a common concept, it has varied on-going developments and applications throughout life. Childhood, employment, marriage, old age etc all display aspects of behavioural and attitudinal aspects of socialization. Whilst conceding this, it must be recognised that Jesus' socializing processes were rooted in spiritual criteria, and so his holistic approach is distinct from humanistic psychological models.

Jesus socialized his followers effectively by:
- Being a desirable *role-model*.
- Showing what God desires and how people are *enabled* to achieve it.
- Promising that the Holy Spirit would develop his work through them.

The pattern was laid down and the socialization process developed with the freewill support of his followers who partly shared his spiritual inheritance, were attracted by the present situation and accepted Jesus' promises with alacrity. This, allied to secure relationships and the sense of personal 'call', provided the basis for establishing their effective socialization. It also contained the general principles of socialization as applied to teaching.

Jesus did not want people merely to have a good opinion of him or to nod in agreement with what he said, but rather, he set out to change people's lifestyle. He required a spiritual change amongst people who had been socialized into alternative life patterns. He would create a new society that required spiritual teaching with distinctive attitudes. A core agreement such as this is fundamental

.2c-108
Which forces are socializing you?

to all social groupings and systems. Even a young pigeon fancier had to learn about routine, work, rules and particular discipline within a pigeon club in order to reap the benefits. But how could Jesus socialize people to adopt his ways? When he said, "Follow me…." nobody could have visualized the implications, nor could they have guessed that it would begin a critical process of socialization. Like all leaders, Jesus realized that he had to teach his followers what was required, because they would be his spiritual builders. They had to *willingly share his vision, lifestyle and attitudes*. In a positive sense, they were being socialized. This is not simply an historical novelty for the 21st century to consider. One only has to glance at the current rival forms of socialization to ask how a harmonious society can be developed?

This leader's aspirations exceeded his needs. He socialized his pupils by being their role-model and convinced them that this spiritual conquest was attainable as they moved from being helpers to being his independent 'reps'. Their values were defined, and provided the rational basis of their actions. The prevailing sensitivity meant that emotions flared and varied between anger and joy and resulted in emotional struggles that could put the socialization process in jeopardy. Such a picture is widely recognizable today.

A pattern of socialization

The mind map (Fig.75) shows that people pass through experiences which determine or powerfully influence their spiritual and behavioural development, some of which match Murray and Maslow's analyses of psychogenic needs. It is suggested that there are similarities at each of the three stages of socialisation which are defined by such key words as:

   need satisfaction   feelings   observing   responding and interacting   imitate

   arrive at personal judgments   norms of behaviour   aspirations achievements

This is particularly noticeable at the infant stage where children quickly develop speech, emotions and make gross imitations of surrounding behaviour. Therefore, long-term patterns of behaviour that develop at an early stage can be difficult to change. Clearly the ancient saying, "Give me a child until he is seven and I will give you the man" has truth in it. Children look for and latch on to a role-model even if that person has no desire or suitability to do so.

Briefly, children and adolescents enter stages 2 and 3 with recognizable patterns of behaviour actively searching for 'need satisfying' situations. When a role-model who might satisfy these demands is recognised there is an attraction and their behaviour is likely to reflect that of the role-model. This process is similar to that of the infants, namely watching, responding, imitating, judging and acting accordingly – for good or bad. Socialization can be partially imposed as shown when Jewish leaders controlled the twin aspects of social and spiritual 'security'. When Jesus challenged them, their spiritual 'security' was imperilled and the greater spiritual 'satisfaction' offered by Jesus came to the fore and became the new socializing pattern for many as they recognised his claims. Coercive socialization is fragile and temporary, as was shown on a grand scale with the demise of the Soviet Union and apartheid South Africa.

The close bonds formed between Jesus and his disciples influenced each other's learning, sense of identity and created a distinct life within a social world. Although they joined Jesus freely, it was a highly disciplined life that separated them from many, but at an acceptable cost. Similar patterns occur in every aspect of life as a few become fully immersed (socialized) in some occupation whilst the rest watch.

.2c-109
When might we find that our aspirations are greater than our needs?

Jesus experienced powerful forms of socialization but he was not its prisoner and questioned many of the practices of the Jewish people. For 30 years he developed his faith in God's character and attitude to man, realizing his own identity, and what that could mean to other people. He knew that it was not enough for people to accept his leadership momentarily. That might be little more than a foundation of sand, whereas he was looking for a rock on which to build. Whilst some recognized Jesus' qualities, others were offended by the cost of discipleship / socialization. Admiration was a vital part of their socialization, but it needed to be deeply rooted in attitude change. Hence, people moved from a sense of awe, to making sensitized responses, often at considerable personal cost. It could be likened to a spiritual entrepreneurship.

The long-term socialization process was through a *role model* who was *warm* and *affectionate, competent and powerful* and *identifiable* to onlookers (Bandura) and who *encouraged* people to *imitate* and *identify* with him. This process required people to *observe, learn* and *model* their behaviour on him (see Fig.70). But first he needed to exemplify it himself. Pre-eminently socialization was based upon memorable relationships whose ideals were seen in an attractive model even if these were seldom attainable. Furthermore, any socializing body, such as a school should be a restoring institution. Socialization is characterized by a degree of failure in the face of prejudice and realities that frustrate expectations and drive people to look for a more satisfying socializing body. This issue is debated by John Bazalgette. He argues that unless pupils first live within a school that possesses a genuinely forgiving attitude, there will always be rebellion amongst some pupils. He illustrated this from the work of three Christian head-teachers who transformed church secondary schools. He concluded that a management model alone is inadequate, but that it needs to be developed through a *relationship* model such as Jesus taught. This requires a value system in which:

- active co-operation replaces teacher dominance.
- achieving mutuality rather than coercion.
- behavioural failure is met by forgiveness and restoration.
- disappointment in pupils is met by fostering pupils 'faith' in themselves.
- The spirit of the school's law is greater than the letter.
- The element of grace is an active ingredient in school life.

This involves a pupil gaining a sense of self worth, that in part reflects the teachers' perception of the pupil's worth. If a teacher fails in this regard, it is likely that a pupil will look elsewhere for validation, even at the expense of compromising particular opportunities. Bazalgette's overriding claim is that attitudes tend to stabilize when people know that they are fully accepted and not merely when they are totally successful or obedient.

Primary socialization

Socialization is in two stages – primary and secondary. The first is concerned with developing social skills and attitudes amongst young children and the second focuses on attitude change amongst adolescents and adults.

If a child lives with criticism, he learns to condemn.

If a child lives with hostility, he learns to fight.

If a child lives with the ridicule, he learns to be shy.

If a child lives with shame, he learns to feel guilty.

If a child learns with tolerance, he learns to be patient.

If a child learns with encouragement, he learns confidence.

If a child learns with praise, he learns to appreciate.

If a child learns with fairness, he learns justice.

.2c-110
What does being a restoring institution signify?

If a child learns with security, he learns to have faith.

If a child lives with approval, he learns to like himself.

If the child lives with acceptance and friendship, he learns to find love in the world.

One could add additional words such as *condemnation, punishment, fear, forgiveness, compassion, care, trust etc* and predict their outcomes. The poem probably reflects the tenor of Jesus' attitude to primary socialization. He was the eldest son in a large family and one wonders how that contributed to his special love and enthusiasm for children. During his primary socialization he had benefited and developed the best traditional religious attitudes and beliefs. He knew that:

- God makes promises and demands.
- A pure religious attitude would be at the heart of everyday life.
- Religious attitudes are characterized by love, righteousness, mercy and justice.
- Social order was important.
- Teaching and learning were of paramount importance.

Socialization was like a spiritual and social language with 'grammatical forms' as he saw parents and other adults show what was permissible, and so he formulated a lifestyle that was the basis of his adult life. Although he grew up in a particular culture he identified important social and spiritual 'universal laws' such as love and forgiveness. Hence, he respected authority when it complied with these values.

The goal of primary socialization is for the pupils to gain ownership of the values and attitudes and for them to be so integral to the individual that s/he wants to act accordingly no matter what the situation. Anything else would be dysfunctional. This expects pupils to see differences and similarities when responding to problematic situations and decide which choices to make in the light of their attitudes.

Aspects of a socializer are usually reflected in the person being socialized. Hence loyalty breeds loyalty. He taught people to be submissive to God and live within the spiritual dimension of life that permeated every aspect of his life and was also the basis of leadership, perception etc. Therefore, his concept of freedom and liberation was significantly different from that of typical humanism. All claim that children should have excellent memorable experiences but Jesus wanted these to evoke faith and expectations in the context of the values of the Kingdom of God, and so all could be 'blessed' accordingly. For example, he recognized that rebellious qualities needed to be harnessed positively. This required teachers' to have a directive function and a sense of commitment and care that was rooted in compassion but the precise nature of this has been a bone of contention.

Secondary socialization

Primary socialization is usually relatively stable as children develop new skills and enter into fresh experiences. Personal and social needs are generally met and the pursuit of happiness and achievement seldom results in long term emotional turmoil as they watch, respond to group behaviour, imitate heroes, dream of future conquests and recognize behavioural constraints. This is the classical model but with the onset of adolescence, secondary socialization gathers apace. Often there is a growing uncertainty, changing priorities and a fresh intensity of emotions as they watch their heroes, respond to the possibility of failure, and are swept along by peer-group passions or feel isolated from them. This becomes a time of personal judgment focusing on moral, social, economic and spiritual issues. This period of relative turmoil is often an occasion when lifelong decisions are made.

.2c-111
What are the limitations of truth in the poem about primary socialisation?

Jesus socialized people into sharply defined knowledge, beliefs, attitudes and values.(see Fig.77), which left little scope for personal opinion. He realised that thinking revolves around attitudes as he indicated by causing his followers to solve problems, interpret his words and reflect on his actions.This minimized the chance of people making hasty judgments that were not rooted securely in the attitudes for which Jesus looked. His followers enjoyed the security of his constant support and also that he fostered positive attitudes by himself having no negative attitudes.

A leader socializes

This strong, purposeful leader provided such evidence of compassion and hope that followers were encouraged to follow paths of faith and risk. They saw and were persuaded results of his spiritual pilgrimage.

Figure 77

Faith in followers Trust Tasks Long term	**Vision** Spiritually driven Personal cost Sacrificial service	**Courage** Exposed to danger Oppose sin Defend his followers Resolute in creating and pursuing initiatives
Truth Jesus the truth (both product and process!)	*The outcome of Jesus' secondary socialization.*	**Teach appropriately** Disciples Crowds Opposition
Lifestyle Simplicity Compassion Responsiveness		**Inclusive care** Outsiders Responding to all needs

Strangely, the more demanding initiation to a group is the more attractive it often becomes. There are innumerable reasons for people being attracted to such a group, e.g.

admiration   promise/reward   personal acceptance   ambition   coercion

cultural norms   fear/ security   conquest   truth   relationships

These are the basis of pro and anti-social attitudes. It is striking that Attila the Hun, Napoleon etc used these qualities and evoked loyalty among people who knew that it would result in death or conquest. Jesus too offered a challenging, if dangerous future that could mean death, but still they followed him and conformed to his pattern of living. But why? Jesus gave them a personal and group identity, and he even gave Simon a new name, Peter, which was an expression of his own authority. They had seen astounding events but they would do even greater! This remarkable promise confirmed their attitude change as they saw his commitment to them! He saw people differently and that was his hope for the angry and impetuous Sons of Thunder. They were sufficiently motivated to be socialized into Jesus' attitudes. Although the teaching was not orderly, it was unselfish, and developed friendships and experiences that enhanced the probability of

.2c-112
Which socializing forces are most likely to influence a tendency for continuity or change?

Jesus' vision being accepted. Their desire to imitate Jesus developed into working aspirations that were bonded through personal relationships. This was never fully achieved during Jesus' lifetime but this socialization had a secure foundation. The teachings of the Kingdom of God were repeated continually in different contexts, and although some found them difficult to understand, as they watched and listened so their attitudes to others such as Samaritans, Romans and 'sinners' were changed. Jesus showed that socialization is unlikely to be achieved by teaching alone. The interactive process extended their abilities and long-term confidence. A working partnership powerfully influenced their socialization.

Jesus' teaching was not purely spiritual, because it encompassed aspects of everyday socialisation that are relevant to current formal and informal teaching. Having seen and heard Jesus at work they were invited to imitate him, which involved understanding and sharing his attitudes and values. The external controls Jesus imposed upon his followers were accepted because the socialization process was complete and motivational needs and aspirations. The personal fellowship with Jesus engendered a fresh and enjoyable mutuality that contrasted to their previous relationship with the religious authorities.

Figure 78

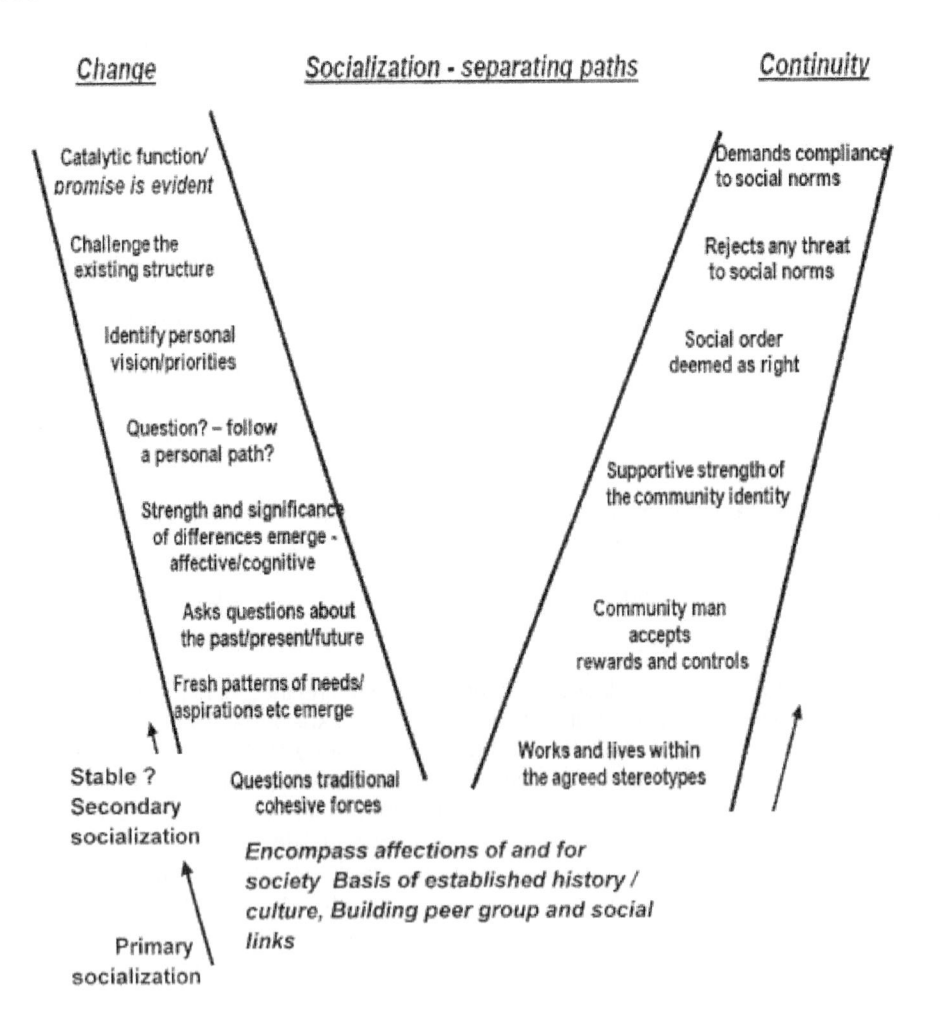

Change — *Socialization - separating paths* — *Continuity*

Change:
- Catalytic function/ promise is evident
- Challenge the existing structure
- Identify personal vision/priorities
- Question? – follow a personal path?
- Strength and significance of differences emerge - affective/cognitive
- Asks questions about the past/present/future
- Fresh patterns of needs/aspirations etc emerge
- Questions traditional cohesive forces

Stable ? Secondary socialization

Continuity:
- Demands compliance to social norms
- Rejects any threat to social norms
- Social order deemed as right
- Supportive strength of the community identity
- Community man accepts rewards and controls
- Works and lives within the agreed stereotypes

Encompass affections of and for society Basis of established history / culture, Building peer group and social links

Primary socialization

.2c-113
Which might be regarded as the most important aspect of socialization?

Confidence in their new teacher grew rapidly as:
- They watched and admired his character.
- They saw him demonstrate his teaching.
- They heard a liberating message of promises about God.
- Jesus skilfully and quickly gave them a core basis of belief.
- The group talked, questioned and worked together as they moved towards an understanding of this new faith and inculcated Jesus' attitudes and lifestyle.

As the disciples watched Jesus teaching and struggling with the religious authorities four distinct but related questions about God and life probably emerged.

- Who and by what authority should decision-makers have their views accepted?
- What authoritative knowledge legitimatized decision-making?
- And which beliefs, attitudes and customs should dominate habitual actions?
- How could people's thought processes and world view be conformed to Jesus?

In modern parlance, they were developing mindsets similar to those of Jesus and their bank of memories reflected Jesus' values and standpoint. It was apparent that though Jesus worked within a culture, he was claiming to establish a new universal 'culture'. His pupils, through sustained association, re-aligned their personal worldview and habitual lifestyles to those of Jesus. A period of gestation was necessary for this range of moral and spiritual obligations to emerge, the cost of which had to be carefully assessed. The significance of the intra-group relations was vital as the emerging group norms developed. Their historic thinking, new image, dignity and freedom brought them into shared tasks with himself and by friendship!

Basis of established history

In this new culture he did not want to lose the best of tradition or to be enslaved by it. The attitudes he expected were respected as part of their historic faith, and were outward looking – after all there was the world to teach! Pupils had time to reflect and develop what was alive in them. This was essential as the cost of the moral and spiritual obligations emerged. They had to recognise the implications of choosing to surrender to Jesus. Could they see and want sufficiently Jesus' visionary creation? Did they share his desire, conviction and courage to make long-term differences? Was their new teacher big enough to hide behind in times of difficulty.

Figure 79

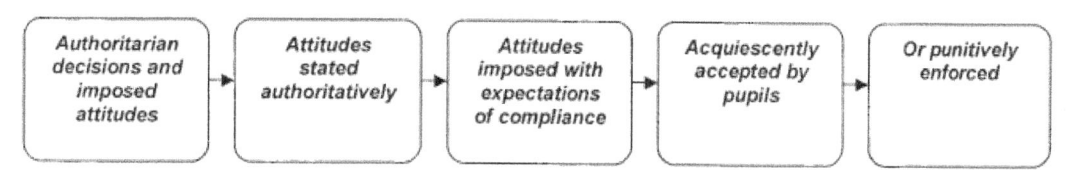

| Authoritarian decisions and imposed attitudes | → | Attitudes stated authoritatively | → | Attitudes imposed with expectations of compliance | → | Acquiescently accepted by pupils | → | Or punitively enforced |

The traditional Jewish approach to socialization and attitude change is common today. Throughout history it has been usual for a control model based on the traditional attitudes of authority to be taught on the assumption that children and adults would comply with traditions. Surely what the children were taught by the authorities would become the embedded truth with some minor changes. A problem was the degree of coercion that needed to be used to maintain the status quo.

.2c-114
What might be the most important attractions to join a group such as Jesus'?

This traditional model (Fig.79) succeeded in suppressing many but was not always successful in achieving long-term, voluntary secondary socialization whereas Jesus' alternative gradually became acceptable to some, but why? He developed confidence in a loving and caring creator who was concerned for their personal welfare. Further, the people were given the opportunity to make personal interpretations of his teaching. Jesus realised that commitment could be inspired, not commanded. These new revelations released and encouraged belief in their new teacher's authority.

Jesus' role and group dynamics model

Although traditionalists could claim that there were certain similarities between Jesus' socialisation process and their own, major differences revolved around relationships, initiatives and ongoing discussions. What is particularly interesting at present is that certain methodologies in modern social education show parallels between the ways in which it and Jesus' teaching were developed. Without wishing to push the similarity too far, the following are found in best teaching.

- An awareness of the problem and its causes.
- An input of authoritative knowledge.
- Group and individual reflection.
- Experiential activities.
- Intra-group discussions.
- A possible response.

There were many differences but the flow chart in Fig.73 accords with many modern expectations. (See Ultimate Teaching Strategy C).

Figure 80

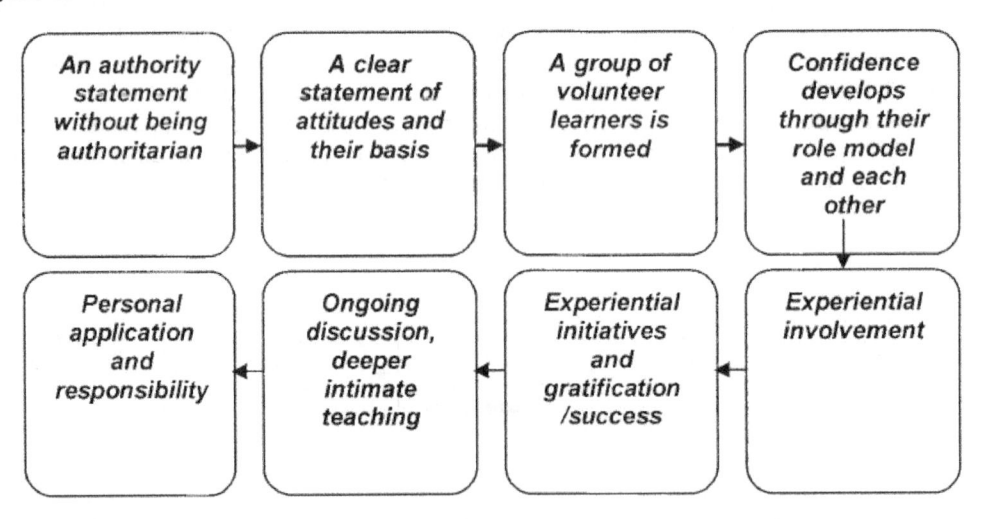

```
[An authority statement without being authoritarian] → [A clear statement of attitudes and their basis] → [A group of volunteer learners is formed] → [Confidence develops through their role model and each other]
                                                                                                                                                         ↓
[Personal application and responsibility] ← [Ongoing discussion, deeper intimate teaching] ← [Experiential initiatives and gratification /success] ← [Experiential involvement]
```

Jesus' followers probably continually recalled and discussed pleasant and dramatic incidents as they travelled with him and as the *quality and frequency of interaction* developed so did their shared beliefs as to what was good and worthwhile. This basis of secondary socialization for the teacher and the learning group had credibility that aroused confidence rather than anxiety. Jesus showed them how fear could be overcome and to see the personal relevance of what he said. The major qualities were summarized by Harold Belben:

- He offered men his friendship.
- He started where they were.
- He listened to what people had to say.
- He got to the root of their questions seriously.
- He asked favours of other people.
- He did not force himself upon people.

.2c-115
How might a person set about changing the attitudes of pupils?

Jesus was taking people from one mind-set to another. This is generally achieved by associating with somebody or something of which a person can be proud. Such socialization by Jesus resulted in increasingly stable mind-sets. Within this process of socialization, faith partnered understanding to shape reason in a particular lifestyle.

Jesus had achieved secondary socialization that encompassed:
- Developing distinctive beliefs.
- Changing their previous world-view.
- Adopting a fresh or superior moral code.
- Entering into a spiritual life as defined by Jesus.
- Confronting the social realities of life.
- Adopting new habitual lifestyle.

Of these, the easiest might be to just believe in him!

This is a major problem today where competing definitions of what are good and legitimate attitudes exist. Knowledge is vital, but not adequate in itself. How can people be persuaded to persevere with certain attitudes? When he asked Peter to follow him, he demonstrated his belief in the unproven potential of possibly disaffected people who could reciprocate his love and faith. The principle he acted upon was that as he served them there would be freewill responses and *willing socialization*. Evidently attitude change requires the following major components:
- The strength of the affective commitment to the attitudes being developed (we feel).
- Stable cognitive comprehension providing rational evidence for desirable attitudes (we know).
- The driving, behavioural force to achieve a required attitude (we do).
- Those crucial aspirations (we hope/ expect).

There are personal and externally imposed drives. What would be their gain /value? For some it was material success but for Jesus it was the *spiritual drive*. Fig.75 illustrates how attitudes can be formed by *affective, cognitive and behavioural* components – that is a *feeling, knowing and driving to do*. Their combined power results in an attitude. A person may have strong affective, emotional strengths but little understanding and so the result might be weak – for example, feeling a desire to help people in Africa. If this affective component is then applied to an improved cognitive strand and an action strand the total attitude may become vigorous. Together these can define goals and plan actions etc. But the power of *existing* attitudes may compete with the three drives and so reduce or enhance them (D or E). The total composite outcome, therefore, consists of $A \pm B \pm C \pm D$.

In Jesus' case his servant attitude was $A + B + C + E - D$.

The differences between onlookers' explanations and the dynamics themselves may be great, but it helps to understand processes influencing attitude change. Jesus was persistent and despite pressures, he was unhurried. He had time for the rejected and gave positive affirmations so that they felt appreciated but he looked for identifiable standards and attitudes. He responded by enabling them to be effective followers. As his disciples watched him teaching aspects of knowledge and attitude formation constantly came to the fore even if they did not realise it and as he struggled with the religious authorities, distinct but related features could be identified.

*.2c-116
Are there any common points between Jesus training his disciples and people being socialized today?*

Figure 81 Which other spokes develop socialization through friendship?

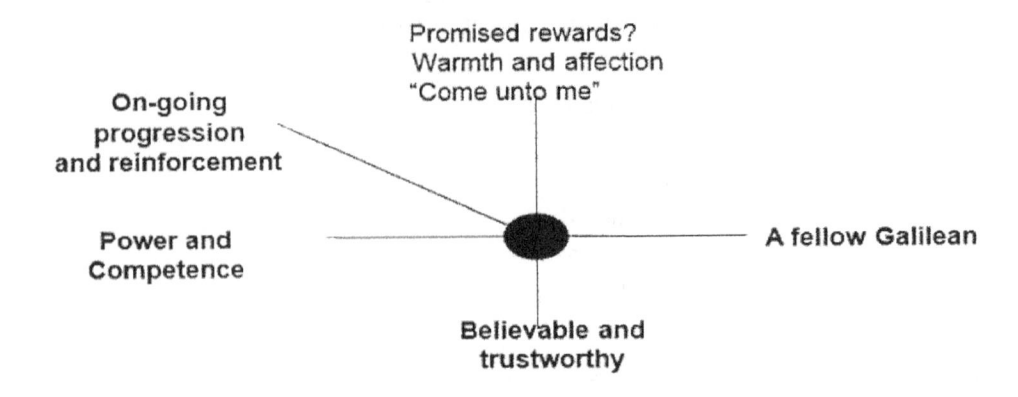

```
        On-going              Promised rewards?
       progression           Warmth and affection
    and reinforcement           "Come unto me"

      Power and                                        A fellow Galilean
      Competence

                              Believable and
                               trustworthy
```

> *Socialization is not primarily achieved by efficient instruction. The mind map (Figs.66a and b) shows the significance of watching, imitating and developing an emotional identification with a role-model. With Jesus as their role model, the disciples were willing to be socialized into new attitudes despite the risks.*

This small dynamic group had two powerful advantages – the first was that they were volunteers who wanted to learn and so had a sense of identity. As a semi closed group they asked questions and discussed Jesus' teaching. Imagine celebration not only of Jesus' work but also their own involvement and so share his reflected praise.

The second was Jesus' decision to choose 12 disciples. This raised many possibilities for him as a teacher. As the quality and frequency of interaction in the group developed, so did their aspirations and beliefs as to what was good, and worthwhile. The internal dynamics within the group raised confidence, worth and self and mutual acceptance that enabled them to explore Jesus' stories and other teachings. Together they developed social and cognitive schemas that increasingly approximated to Jesus' desired attitudes and understandings. This enabled them to become more fully liberated in both their abilities and self-image. This modelling process and growing mutual trust proceeded to the point where they became motivators and teachers. This growing confidence was summed up in the simple words, "Come and see….". It was the outcome of Jesus' belief in co-operative work, even when he had to rely upon ill-prepared people. Active co-operation was at the heart of all he did.

This process of interpersonal and intrapersonal development was characteristic of attitude change and became an attraction in itself. It yielded mutual satisfaction that caused the group to want to be maintained and developed. One wonders if the Judean member of the group, Judas became isolated amongst the Galileans and never felt wholly accepted and at ease. It is reasonable to imagine him being the butt of jokes and not entering fully into discussions about Jesus' and the expectations of the group. And so we begin to see a surprising person who had the qualities to socialize a varied band of unpromising people.

.2c-117
When might it be justified to ensure that traditions are not lost?

Summary

Jesus' pupils reflected and through sustained association developed a sense of wonder and re-orientated their personal world-view and lifestyle so that they became aligned with that of Jesus. This extended period was necessary for a new range of moral and spiritual obligations to emerge. The significance of intra-group relations on group norms should not be underestimated. The social exchanges between them were transforming factors in their lives and sufficient to provide a long-term identity and ability to resist severe cultural and religious pressures.

The process of socialization poses the certain questions about teaching strategies.
- Is the teacher a good role model? Can he/she simply say, "Follow me"?
- Is the teacher seen to be credible?
- Is the pattern of socialization worth the range of cost/benefits it entails?
- Can peer groups provide mutual support and stimuli?
- It is the ethos of the group more attractive than that of alternative groups?
- Are pupils given the opportunity to reflect and re-orientate their ideas?
- Is this socialization process built into the wider teaching-learning?
- Do pupils have time to appreciate that ethos and spirit of the learning situation?
- Does the role-model offer the promise and means of a healthy self-identity?
- Can the pupils see the wider long-term context and issues when learning?
- Is the social process of teaching/learning appreciated?
- How are the quality and frequency of interactions improved to help learning?
- How can the required trust between teacher and pupil be built up?

.2c-118
How might socialization be developed through friendship?

Figure 82 What might such a model for attitude change indicate?

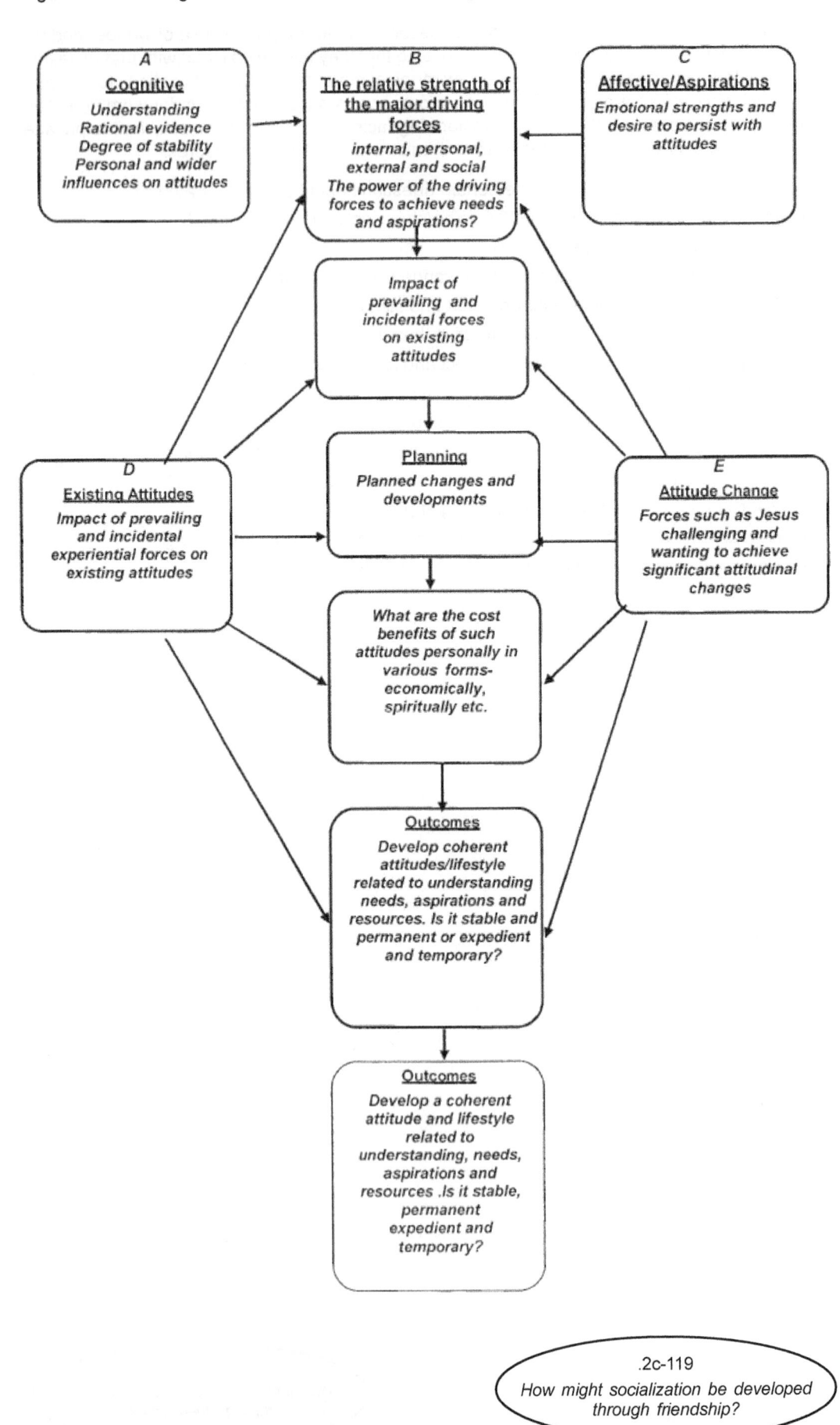

A — Cognitive
Understanding
Rational evidence
Degree of stability
Personal and wider influences on attitudes

B — The relative strength of the major driving forces
internal, personal, external and social
The power of the driving forces to achieve needs and aspirations?

C — Affective/Aspirations
Emotional strengths and desire to persist with attitudes

Impact of prevailing and incidental forces on existing attitudes

Planning
Planned changes and developments

D — Existing Attitudes
Impact of prevailing and incidental experiential forces on existing attitudes

E — Attitude Change
Forces such as Jesus challenging and wanting to achieve significant attitudinal changes

What are the cost benefits of such attitudes personally in various forms- economically, spiritually etc.

Outcomes
Develop coherent attitudes/lifestyle related to understanding needs, aspirations and resources. Is it stable and permanent or expedient and temporary?

Outcomes
Develop a coherent attitude and lifestyle related to understanding, needs, aspirations and resources. Is it stable, permanent expedient and temporary?

.2c-119
How might socialization be developed through friendship?

Chapter 10

Cognition, Creativity and Problem Solving

Looking forwards

The thinking process...Introducing the imagination – Revelation? Assimilation and accommodation – Brain Based Learning...The cognitive basis of Jesus' teaching. A note about knowledge – Creative thinking, the imagination and teaching – Problem-solving – Focus for Thought.

If a teacher's major art is to enable pupils to understand and learn on a long-term basis, then Jesus was a master teacher. But what can we learn from his skills?

Cognition is knowledge gained by experience, reasoning, perception and intuition and is the summit of much human activity. Jesus' reputation was built on his understanding of spirituality but he displayed ample cognitive powers both in spirituality and the other 6 themes in Part B. What light can his cognitive skills cast on these various themes? *What substantial aid can it give when teachers seek to impart information in such a way that it can be learnt efficiently?* Whilst not claiming to make anything approaching a scientific study (if it could be made!) of such a theme we will first pose important 'cross thematic' questions, consider some relevant aspects of his cognitive activities and draw appropriate conclusions.

To achieve this, it is helpful to:
- Highlight the major elements in the thought processes.
- Consider how Jesus implicitly used these.
- Further, consider the place of imagination creativity and problem solving in the learning processes

It is possible to note how Jesus' teaching style enhanced the appropriate cognitive development for that particular situation. The question becomes how far the principles can be adapted to current needs.

Figure 83

	Issues particular to the theme	Relating the theme specifically to Jesus	Relating the theme to teaching generally
Leadership	How does a leader understand the requirements etc?	How did Jesus learn and then teach others essential understandings?	How does a teacher establish procedures for effective learning?
Perception	What is the difference between cognition and perception?	How did Jesus perceive if people understood the teaching?	How can teachers perceive if they are understood?
Motivation	What motivates a person to remember certain knowledge?	How did Jesus motivate people to learn and remember?	How are teachers and pupils motivated to learn and remember.?
Memory	How are memories formed and developed?	What was the basis of Jesus developing memories?	How are memories maximized in the T/L situation?
Socialization	How are people socialized into understanding?	Why did Jesus fail to make some people understand?	How do T/P develop shared understandings in T/L situations?
Emotions	How can emotions influence understanding?	How did Jesus use emotion to aid understanding?	How are emotions both helpful and a hindrance to cognition?

Cognition

Cognition is a major example of where faiths believe that *natural ability* and *development* are co-joined with *insights and understandings from God*. Jesus clearly stated that revelation (and the thought processes) stem from the Holy Spirit. Although Jesus gave priority to the spiritual aspect of cognition, the links between these two functions of the brain are emphasized here.

Figure 84

Teacher Input	*Pupil Cognitive Development*
Preliminary Stage • Clarity of Purpose 　personal goal 　teaching goal • Confident in teaching 　authority relationships • Is fitted for the task – competence • Has a defined teaching message	• The pupil' incoming disposition and existing schemas based an partial / popular knowledge and heroic expectations
• Recognizes pupils' skewed schemas • Has an appropriate pupil-teacher relationship • Can make reliable promises • Knows an appropriate course of action • Can challenge at an appropriate level • Can stimulate with creative approaches	• Traditional truth is recognised • Pupils are arrested by the teacher' competence • Arresting promises are made etc • Stimulating and exciting evidence is produced • Group attention and subsequent development • Differing degrees of response and commitment
Has mastered two distinct strategies • Assimilation – can present new knowledge and skills that are compatible with existing knowledge etc and have an evident validity • Accommodation – can present new knowledge that needs to recreate existing schemas and be subsequently internalised	• Learn and relearn by　Watching　} 　　　　　　　　　　　　Listening　} 　　　　　　　　　　　　Helping　　} • Relates to personal disposition • Pupils enthusiastically gain preliminary mastery learning
• Can create and reinforce new coherent norms and schemas • The teacher is consistent and a problem solver • The teacher's competence and ongoing refinement of material can establish a new developmental schema.	• Adequate stimulus /energy maintained in self 　their teacher /role model • A sense of privilege drives them on • Process of validation of self and their teacher becomes embedded • Schemas gradually approximates to that of their teacher • Ongoing peer reinforcement and refinement • Developmental possibilities emerge

Jesus gave careful consideration to people and situations and although he would not have accepted Gautama's statement that "the mind creates the world" he would have understood its sentiment together with the notion that the mind might be said to make a man. It relates to everything being considered here – human perception, memory, motivation, socialisation, emotions etc and is more than a means of processing information.

The mind is a pattern maker that selects or rejects incoming stimuli that can possibly challenge or make radical changes to existing thought patterns. The ongoing processes of mental elaboration or modification of the mind can link networks of concepts together and point to powerful processes of using existing knowledge as it responds to new information.

.2c-120
Why was the phrase "the mind makes the world" acceptable or not?

The crucial factor, therefore, is not the continual flow of fragmented knowledge but how our minds organize it into meaningful patterns so that is used promptly, economically and efficiently. As indicated earlier, past experiences, competing present situations and anticipations all meet to create and colour meanings which form powerful personalized bases for thought, and this was the characteristic of Jesus' thinking.

Neuro-psychologists describe the mind as a selective pattern-making organism that brings stimuli into coherent meaningful clusters. Jesus, like all good teachers, used a multitude of teaching images that fitted into this pattern making nature of the mind. He was an imaginative, analytical thinker. Whereas the religious authorities tended to think within closed historic religious patterns of thought, his more open mind (and spirit) allowed his Jewish heritage and personal revelations to create changes that illustrate how cognitive processes are active and can respond to new information. His powerful mind developed a recognizable core of knowledge, thinking and understanding about the Kingdom of God.

The delights of imagination

Jesus' teaching was imaginative (see Fig.4). No matter whether he used stories, actions, metaphors or promises, the positive imaginative elements attractively seeded memories to become projected possibilities and related thoughts. These took listeners 'beyond the information given' to enter new realms of possibilities for reflection, Visualization and discussion. Imagination helped to open spheres of knowledge – old and new, personal and social, plus generating the possibility of revelation and creative insights. As it has been emphasised already, the constant activity of the mind is interpretive, creative and imaginative as it makes links between stimuli.

We do not know how Jesus' imaginative thinking developed. Like all Jewish children he was trained in the Prophets and the Law and probably knew the prophecies of Isaiah well and so grew up with the notion of rising on the 'wings of eagles'. He was confident that God was enlightening and revealing this message that demanded obedient but imaginative responses. And as he reflected during those 'hidden years' so his revelation developed.

Jesus changed popular thought patterns imaginatively. He set common situations within new frames of understanding. The drama of the Good Samaritan when compared with negligent religious passers-by must have cut across the enquiring lawyer's existing expectations. Jesus' many imaginative links with the surrounding world involved marriage, flowers, kings and armies etc,- there were always stories to tell that found their parallel in the Kingdom of God and that were not only realistic and authentic but were worth remembering and retelling with imaginative vigour! Their experiences provided novelties that developed into a fresh rationality that gave new answers to the 'whys and wherefores' of life. Expectations grew amidst a sense of awe and probably an amazed laughter in their richly stimulating world. What might happen next? The stories and actions initiated varied responses that contrasted with previous experiences. Jesus was serious, but it must have been fun to listen, watch and learn. No longer were they inflicted with predictable mental processes, but with memorable teaching that provided a basis for truth and stimulated a creative release and an imaginative and refreshing image of God.

Imaginative possibilities generally result from a trained and prepared mind that is activated by an event, situation, memory, need etc. This took two forms in Jesus' situation. There was a legalistic boundary. In this creative imaginative thought is shaped by culture and occurs within prescribed and limiting boundaries. This was characterized by traditional Judaism which could boast of a rich vein of creative imagination, especially in the poetry seen throughout the books of Job, the Prophets, the songs in Psalms and the imaginative wisdom in Proverbs.

.2c-121
Why is reflection important to understanding cognition?

Alternatively the imagination can be seen as life promoting / directing that generates and explores new possibilities. This was illustrated by Jesus' attitude to the world and the Kingdom of God. Although much of Jesus' thought patterning was within the Jewish culture, many possibilities occur in the core that have been a mainspring for alternative developments. Hence, the teaching of Jesus has legitimately taken many forms. This is imaginatively exemplified in such magnificent works as 'The Heliand Saxon Gospel' by an unknown Saxon monk who wrote the Gospel in poetic form using Saxon / Germanic cultural ideas and language to make it more compatible to the people .e.g.

'So the local men did not approve of Him…….They did not want to listen to His message…..He knew that there were no other people among the Jews so grimly hostile….as the ones from Galileeland…..they did not want to devoutly receive His message. Instead the local people, the warriors, began to plot among themselves how they could inflict the greatest pain on the powerful Christ. They called their fighting men together, their warrior companions….His word was of no use to them nor His brilliant spells, and so they began to discuss among themselves how they could throw such a strong man off a cliff, over a mountain wall. (Song 32)

And so the battle goes on between the earls, warriors, thanes etc and the men and their Good Chieftain, the best of all sons of God the Ruler, the Rescuer from Fort-hill Nazareth. The imagination's delight knows no bounds.

There is a rational basis to imaginative thought – no doubt Archimedes 'eureka 'moment had been well prepared by previous thought and experimentation. If we refer back to Figs.79 and 80 It is evident that the 'cognitive webs' provide a wide range of alternative links between the cognitive nodes and so the creative / imaginative possibilities increase exponentially.

Jesus matched his knowledge (*Truly, I say unto you….*) with imagination and developed them through such methods as:

> *Visualization ….as in the Temptations*
> *Observation……as in nature*
> *Interpretation…..the Good Shepherd*
> *Meditation……..withdrawing into the desert to pray*
> *Historical tradition…Jonah*
> *Future prophetic judgements….the sheep and the goats etc.*
> *Human interaction...Nicodemus*
> *Deliberate problem solving….the unique strategy of personal sacrifice*
> *Maturation of thought….the 'Hidden Years'*
> *Extending experiences….Feeding the multitudes and being the Bread of Life*

Therefore, what we see is an imaginative life style and mode of thinking / teaching.

(This is developed more explicitly in Part C)

.2c-122
Why might imagination have been a crucial element in Jesus' teaching?

Although we often consider imagination as most closely related to the emotions and the arts, it is fundamental to all forms of problem solving, projective and interpretive thinking. As Jesus showed, it is a powerful teaching tool when used appropriately (see Part C).

The Thinking Process

Jesus, like all Jews, saw people holistically, consisting of mind, body and spirit. He emphasised this when he reiterated the Golden Rule, "...you shall love the Lord your God with all your heart and all your soul and all your mind and with all your strength, and your neighbour as yourself...". Although such an holistic notion is now commonplace, nobody could have conceived the complexity of the brain 2000 years ago. Then the mind had the dual meanings of understanding and motivation, but since the 1980's neuroscientists have made rapid progress in studying the brain as an organ and the mind as its interactive outworking. One could now imagine him smiling at its wonder and relating it to Psalm 139 vv 13-18 which Jews knew by heart.

The brain is the physical organism and the mind is the dynamic functioning that responds to new stimuli and *attractors* to make personally meaningful connections. As clusters of compatible information form linkages so *conceptual networks /cognitive templates* are formed. These filter and formulate fresh information into meaningful patterns. Imagine looking at a scene and asking, "What is there?" What is seen is partially dependent upon what *one expects to see* and how *trained the person is* to recognise it. The brain's response is likely to be based on previous experiences, to existing or related links and stored memories. These elaborate, confirm or reject previous experiences to form '*conceptual maps*'. Such mental patterns are called *schemas*. This *patterned recognition* was the basis of Jesus' cognitive template of the Kingdom of God. As it has been neatly stated, 'Schemas provide skeletons around which situations are interpreted'. From a Christian perspective this does not take account of the working of the Holy Spirit, which was the basis of both Jesus' revelations and those of his followers. Even so, there is a coming together of the natural processes within the brain and the active work of God the creator.

As the mind identifies and stores meanings it develops *corresponding patterns of knowledge* that are elaborated and confirmed (or not!) by new stimuli. These form bases to aid understanding, and habitual thinking strategies that relate to schemas and so make sense to the person concerned. This cognition is known as being *socially situated whereby one can visualize and relate incoming stimuli to a specific 'home' schema*. Like language, the cognitive process responds to known stimuli and attracts other related material that enriches memories and understanding and extends possible applications. This can lead to prejudices. It is evident that the religious authorities had elaborate schemas predisposed to reject Jesus' teaching. Our mental schemas become established but are not immutable. Change occurs because *cognitive processes are active rather than passive*. Reverting to the context of Jesus, a psychological logic could be as follows.

Jesus shared the Jewish prophetic traditions, but was concerned about attitudes to the teaching of the Mosaic Law. The fact was simple – God's requirements had been revealed in the Law and the Prophets, which were securely treasured for posterity. This wisdom and revelation was the standard against which all thought was measured. Jesus' schemas were described as 'fulfilling the Law'. This was based on established traditions, experiential evidence and spiritual revelation. Psychologists may not dismiss the notion of revelation, but they emphasize the natural creative processes developed within the subconscious mind. That would be an adequate explanation of Archimedes' 'eureka' moment but not all revelations. Also, some see revelation as God bringing existing schemas to fruition that suggests it is born out of reflection and related principles but takes little account of divine initiatives.

There were numerous examples of *logical thought* processing. It appeared that if God was the provider of all blessings and good things, those who were wealthy must have been blessed even more than the poor. This resulted in laws being distorted in favour of the ruling classes. Even so,

.2c-123
Which methods are most generally applied to arouse imagination?

the tradition of prophets such as Jeremiah, Amos, Hosea and John the Baptist protested against this convenient view of God and wealth. Their logic was that God is essentially *moral as well as spiritual* and so their teaching flowed consistently from this premise – sin must be judged and righteousness be rewarded … ultimately.

Jesus' thought processes were logical. He took a limited number of concepts and developed them within common social and spiritual contexts, which the brain developed into spiritual conceptual maps.

Related to this is the fact that the mental processes are related to *rhythms*, by which it is meant that the mind should be given time to absorb, respond and organize new inputs and to show their relationship to previous learning. This means that there is the danger of depriving people of established rhythms and expectations so that they can prepare mentally, spiritually and emotionally for the new knowledge etc. This is not to deny the validity of surprises activating the thought processes, but there is the danger of impromptu responses being ill-considered and so resulting in unintended perceptions and responses. This occurred when Jesus found it necessary to withdraw from people and gradually allow them time to meditate and revise their expectations.

Assimilation/and/Accommodation

The Swiss psychologist, Jean Piaget used two terms to describe how the brain processes new information – *assimilation and accommodation*. Briefly, *assimilation* occurs when new information is accepted into a schema and so confirms and develops it. This information must be sufficiently compatible for the schema to be modified slightly. This is seen within formal planned teaching amongst like-minded teachers/pupils. New stimuli can be assimilated when minimal and possibly predictable changes occur.

Alternatively *accommodation* occurs when incoming information challenges the structure of existing schemas and so is likely to be rejected or at least require radical changes within the existing understanding before it can be accepted, or *adapted*. This was typical of Jesus' demanding teaching about the Kingdom of God.... would the people revise or retain their existing thought patterns? By presenting the teaching as parables upon which the people reflected, their significance gradually became ore comprehensible. Few Pharisees were able to accommodate his teaching, but those who questioned the Pharisees were more likely to accommodate their existing schema to Jesus' teaching. Hence, logically the religious authorities rejected this new teaching, but others such as Nicodemus and Joseph of Arimathea, carefully considered the persuasive evidence. This process of accommodation can be seen where Jesus rejected many accepted teachings and logically developed his alternative schema or revelation. Examples of this creative core in his teaching that required accommodation by other people are:

- Forgiveness is to know no bounds.
- Leadership necessitates a servant's heart.
- Conquer by love and suffering rather than the sword.
- Justice is rooted in mercy.

.2c-124
Which knowledge might you easily assimilate and which might be difficult to accommodate?

As he taught these new realities he knew that people needed time to re-orientate their previously secure knowledge. By so doing he used sound educational principles. This is a common feature in schools where the values of the school and pupils differ significantly.

Once his followers were immersed in his teaching, there was a shift from the radical process of accommodation to assimilating what had become acceptable. This is a persistent struggle as people react in varying degrees to Jesus' teaching. For example, the challenges of Teresa of Calcutta, Dr Martin King and Archbishop Tutu have posed awkward moral and spiritual questions. They had assimilated Jesus' teaching but critical people needed to pass through a process of accommodation before they could assimilate it with ease.

These issues are common. It is seen in churches when people are expected to assimilate the teaching, whilst in reality the listeners may not bother to go through the arduous process of accommodating their present understandings with those of the church, or for a particular church to accommodate itself to outsiders. Thinking is not inevitably stylized into habitual patterns that are shaped by cultural context and social history but it needs to be sufficiently flexible to allow a person not to be confined by previous shaping processes but have the possibility of change. Stereotyped thinking is often prevalent, but it is helpful for people to reflect for the accommodation process to be achieved and creative acts and ideas to be conceived.

Jesus' thought processes were rooted in a stable schema about God the Father and his own unique purpose. We do not know how this occurred, but the outcome was well defined and prompted his rational judgments. His thought processes were interactive – not only with others but also with past experiences, present situations and future expectations. Just as attitude and thinking are closely related, so faith can be the driving force that determines the strength of thought and attitude. This was exemplified when it was said that Jesus set his face as a flint and went to Jerusalem to die. To simplify the matter it could be said that in Jesus' case his fundamental attitude of love regulated the perception and thinking processes that were driven by faith. This produced an harmonious pattern of thought, within his teaching.

Established schemas are not immutable and Jesus expected people to make real choices. To some he made direct challenges, whilst to others he seemed to tell them to consider what they had seen and heard. On other occasions, people such as Peter were so awestruck by shock or surprise that it challenged a schema and evoked a rapid response. Judas possibly never made the complete change. Altogether the cognitive, spiritual and emotional shocks had to be assimilated or accommodated.

Brain Based Learning

A popular writer about brain-based learning is Eric Jensen. The following is a loose but faithful paraphrase from "The Learning Brain", but there is no suggestion that Eric Jensen has a shared view with Jesus' about spiritual purposes.

Although this is a clear cause-effect learning model, it goes beyond such traditionally defined models because the creative brain and the social interaction are always likely to generate surprises. Hope is the basis of learning (page 184) and the best advance indicator of success is the degree of expectancy and the importance of the learning to them (page 60). Goals should be challenging but attainable (page 82) with a high degree of challenge but low stress (page 145). Pupils should have success in short-term goals that enable them to achieve long-term goals (page 60). Success is tied into learners believing in both themselves and the purpose of their studies and having a secure emotional commitment to the work, with the teacher having a strong belief in their capability, establishing an imaginative context for their success and providing them with a sense of self worth (page 187). The pupils will copy the teacher who is seen both as a problem solver and a product maker.

.2c-125
Why are previous experiences crucial to our thinking?

Teachers should provide pupils with clear advance organizers so that they can map out their conceptual journey (page 65). This should provide them with a global overview in which the pupils are freely exposed to the learning with oral previews (page 140). The crucial element is to enable the pupils to be immersed in pick learning (page 71). Problem solving is the brain's favourite activity (page 144) but the problems should be restated in various forms to enhance creativity (page 77). Also the teacher should ensure that the pupils can see that a solution is possible page 186) and that they have the necessary skills and resources to complete the task (page 82). This will also require that the environment is conducive to success. The pupils should be given a positive image of the environment and its dynamic significance (page 105). The pupils will need ample feedback in order to make corrections but they will need to be convinced of their capabilities to sustain pursuit in the face of negative feedback. This will require both support and encouragement but these should not be excessive. The brain thrives on looking for contrasts (page 185) and the memory is aided by novelty (page99). Stories should be developed through concrete images (page 80).

Learners should work on short modules (page 99) with peer tutoring partners who share their experiences (page 71). They need to have some control over their work in respect of content, need to develop positive engaging social contact that is essential to goal attainment (page 145). Pupils should be able to develop habitual multiple perspectives of the problems facing the learning environment and the work process. (page 186). These peer-tutoring partners them. The pupils can work from memory maps in which they see the problems repeatedly in different contexts.

The cognitive basis of Jesus' teaching

Jesus did not impart a complex body of information but rather a series of concepts that is called here his 'Big Idea'. Everything else was an explanatory illustration of this Big Idea. It was incomplete and the challenge was to understand it and prove it experientially. Therefore, he enabled people to explore ideas that required flexible thought. For example, his teaching was based on a network of concepts based on the phrase 'the Kingdom of God is like…' followed by appropriate illustrations. Hence, whilst the religious authorities provided a massive body of precise information based on analytical debate, Jesus provided deep, structured principles. Its transformation was stimulating, memorable and less threatening. He worked from established knowledge and the environment but avoided most religious technicalities. Instead people grappled with distinctions between universal, social and personal knowledge and how these can be learned appropriately. New knowledge had to be consistent with historic core values but open to revitalized knowledge -even if it required a leap of faith! He showed that knowledge can be both evidence and faith based, with the miracles being described as the Kingdom of God in action (C.H.Dodd). Permanent and ephemeral knowledge were combined to support and illustrate the values of the Kingdom.

His knowledge had a philosophical basis. Its rationale was coloured by the cultural background but was universal and absolute in its values rather than relative and idiosyncratic. Debate required the acceptance or rejection of rival absolute statements rather than open-ended relativism that can lead to discussion about the relative merits of the rival unresolved standpoints. Hence it was seen that *God is truth* rather than *truth is God* and that the *truth will make you free* rather than *freedom is truth*. The teaching was confessional and expected to be accepted as a whole. Similarly Jesus emphasized this absolutism by confidently stating 'I am the truth'. The value basis of this knowledge rendered every statement as being obligatory. This knowledge needed to be with the meaning of his stories and the significance of his actions and came to conclusions about the Kingdom of God that may have been right or wrong. They became reflective thinkers who solved incomplete puzzles, using the clues to interpret the teaching. As he taught these new realities he knew that his students needed time and constant involvement as they gradually moved from the previously secure knowledge into the unknown. By so doing he brought together faith, logic and attitude.

.2c-126
When might Jesus' teaching be too difficult to accommodate?

A note about knowledge

Jesus had an *absolutist* view of knowledge and would find many modern assumptions unacceptable. For example, if one starts from the premise that this is God's universe, the logic is that environmental and social issues are spiritual and not merely a matter of economics, politics, expediency or self-preservation. He went beyond knowledge to create wisdom amongst his followers, who might not be clever but could be discerning with wisdom providing the basis for decision-making. This spiritual wisdom stood in contrast to foolishness, as shown in parables such as the wise and foolish builders. Therefore, he emphasized spiritual wisdom in decision-making.

To Jews, knowledge went beyond intellectual facts- it indicated a relationship such as that between a husband and wife. This can be implied in Jesus' words "If you knew me you would know my Father". Hence, knowledge had social connotations. It had a purpose and was not regarded as an end in itself. It challenged both individuals and society as he promoted faith in God's expectations. Although this had a corporate strand, it was more individualistic than say, Muhammad's more socially structured knowledge. It encapsulated ideas and lifestyles that were necessary to change the world! At present it would be necessary to ask:

- What is the *purpose* of the knowledge being taught?
- Is it likely to foster both long-term *personal development* and *social competence* based on the *core values* expressed by Jesus?
- Will it be applied to the *principles* in personal and social life?
- Are the *core values absolute*? If so, do they need to be imposed?
- Are core values based upon *understanding and willing agreement* or opinion and personal preferences?

There was a core of teaching for all that was further developed amongst committed followers. This challenge of knowing the unknown was achieved through a wide range of teaching strategies. The knowledge was rendered intensely *memorable* and became a topic of *conversation* that heightened people's *curiosity*. Jesus related the knowledge to the *people's known past*, their *needs* and *aspirations*. For many, his teaching involved an imaginative *creativity* as they listened and copied him.

Creative thinking and teaching

Human creativity takes many forms but it is normally characterized by novelty and the ability to transform and develop a situation, idea etc. Jesus' creativity was both social and spiritual, but what were its essential features? It might be shown that his creative thinking passed through three stages (Fig.85). He inherited the religious historic tradition (Stage 1) that was filtered through his Galilean family. This was his inheritance and that of the people around him.

He transformed this into a new inheritance for succeeding generations. The critical features of this transformation illustrate the creative qualities of Jesus as a thinker and teacher (Stage 2). Central to his creativity were the four characteristics of *expertise, spiritual insights, a sense of 'destiny' and a driving pertinacity* that are common in creative people. It might be said that these characteristics were revealed in both his personal and social life. These drive and interact with a mix of 16 (or more) personality and character traits of creative people, which means everybody to some lesser or greater extent, although not all are found in all creative people! Jesus shared these characteristics with other major creative people but who manifest them in forms appropriate to their specialisms. These can be summarized as follows:

- He made *independent value judgments* that in turn spawned related teaching.
- He was secure in his self-perception and of others and the world.
- He was *rebellious* where issues could not be justified righteously.
- He displayed a supremely *imaginative dimension* in his thought.
- He had an intuitive grasp of whole issues and their implications.

.2c-127
What might be a "Big Idea" in your life?

- He was fearless to make *novel decisions* even when it resulted in opposition.
- As *a problem solver* he saw into issues that transcended traditional information.
- He had total confidence in *his personal vision.*
- Tasks might remain *unfinished* but were rich in their underlying, principles.
- He persisted in the pursuit of his vision.
- He was a *divergent thinker* who looked for alternative solutions. But he was also a *convergent thinker*, and one could imagine that his convergent thinking predated his divergent thinking when he critically examined the dominant prevailing teachings.
- He was indifferent to the *demands of authority.*
- He continually *responded to problems* with positive solutions.
- He *reinterpreted* established knowledge and *reformulated* accepted principles.
- He was insistent on the superiority of his understanding.
- His vision was more important than any material gains.

This resulted in the creative transformation shown at stage 3 of Fig.85. He was not merely a recipient and conduit of tradition, but looked at situations creatively which enabled him to translate his vision and principles to others which we can replicate. These include:

Can pupils *see creativity* being exemplified. Is there a *stimulus* to create?

Can pupils be inspired to maximize existing expertise and insights to create?

Is the creativity seen to have worthwhile *possibilities*, bearing in mind the *cost?*

Which *values* are incorporated into the creativity?

Few would deny that Jesus was a creative thinker and teacher. He was what Jerome called "the spermatic word" or life giver. Jesus made a "creative leap" as he moved from the traditional teaching about the God of Israel to the wider more inclusive teaching of the Kingdom of God. This creative leap was at both spiritual and cognitive levels and seen in his teaching methodology. This is not to deny or minimize the creative spiritual revelation that resulted in his "Big Idea" (if it can be so called) of reconciliation and conquest through sacrifice and faith in God.

Creativity takes many forms in such disparate disciplines as science, art, music, technology…. and spirituality, but there are common features which were exemplified by Jesus. His first recorded example of creative thinking reached its climax at his temptation and was the foundation of subsequent thinking, activity and teaching. He turned the basis for logical thought around. It was akin to what Edward de Bono has called 'lateral thinking' – that is looking for an alternative, if unlikely solution to a problem. Jesus' answer to enmity was to "love those who hate you" or to use a more recent phrase "destroy your enemies by making them your friends".

His creativity was rooted in aspects of revelation and prayer. But how had he arrived at his revelations? As a keen observer he drew deductions as he reflected on problems based upon the foundational principles of God's character found in the Scriptures. As he asked "What is acceptable to God?" he recognized that God could not tolerate exploitation and burdens imposed upon the poor. Perhaps he generated more fresh meanings than facts.

.2c-128
How do we solve common moral problems satisfactorily?

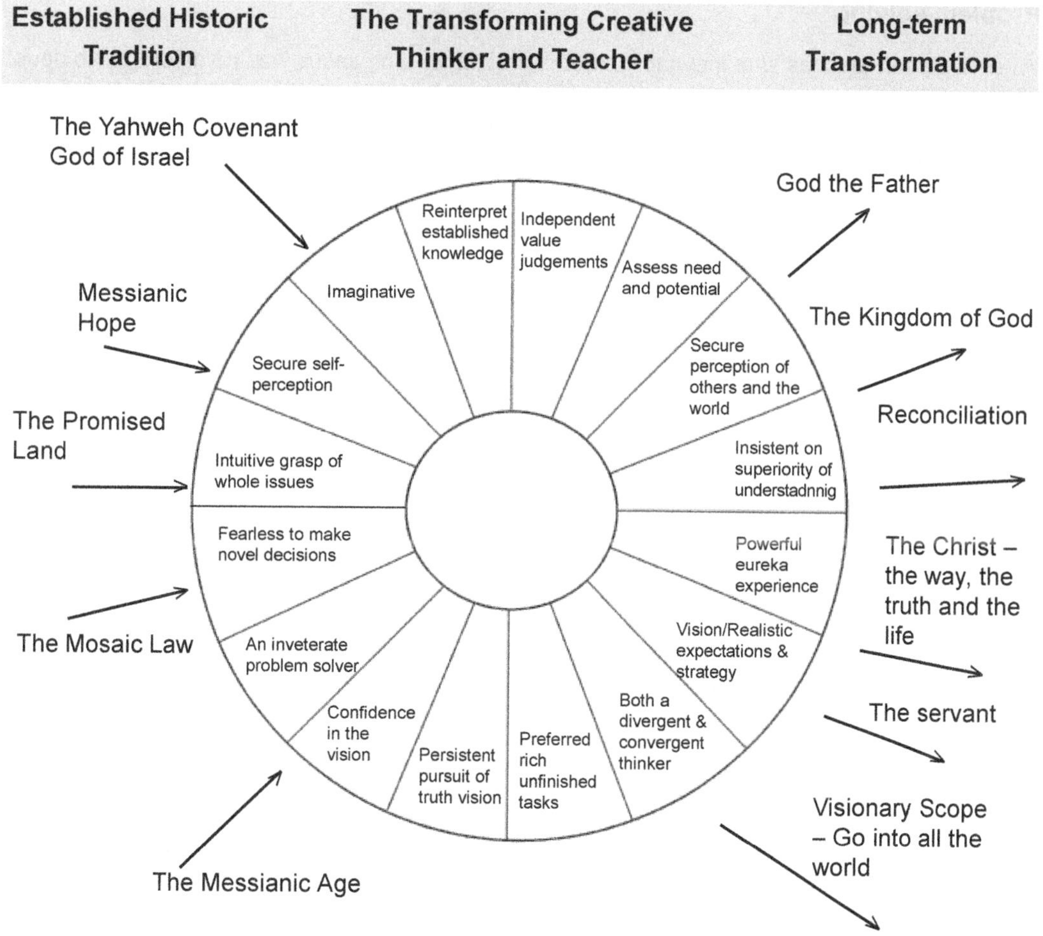

| Established Historic Tradition | The Transforming Creative Thinker and Teacher | Long-term Transformation |

Established Historic Tradition:
- The Yahweh Covenant God of Israel
- Messianic Hope
- The Promised Land
- The Mosaic Law
- The Messianic Age

The Transforming Creative Thinker and Teacher (wheel segments):
- Reinterpret established knowledge
- Independent value judgements
- Assess need and potential
- Secure perception of others and the world
- Insistent on superiority of understadnnig
- Powerful eureka experience
- Vision/Realistic expectations & strategy
- Both a divergent & convergent thinker
- Preferred rich unfinished tasks
- Persistent pursuit of truth vision
- Confidence in the vision
- An inveterate problem solver
- Fearless to make novel decisions
- Intuitive grasp of whole issues
- Secure self-perception
- Imaginative

Long-term Transformation:
- God the Father
- The Kingdom of God
- Reconciliation
- The Christ – the way, the truth and the life
- The servant
- Visionary Scope – Go into all the world

Figure 85

But how did his creative thinking influence his teaching methods? It might be conjectured that his learning and teaching bore similarities so that "as he learned, so he taught!" As he looked at the plight of man, his revelation appears to revolve around parallel worlds – the spiritual kingdom of God and the physical kingdom of man. Normally we think of Jesus converting spiritual ideas into concrete situational images, but he probably initially translated his personal experiences into spiritual truths to give the basis of his teaching methods.

One can envisage how Jesus' attitude reflected aspects of his own childhood experiences. His creative mind and spirit may have reflected on his experiences with Joseph and seen qualities of a trusting provider that he described within the context of his heavenly Father. As he watched and became a builder, he saw spiritual parallels. His creative spirit was interpreting everyday sights and occurrences to a higher plane and using them to transform the arguments of the Pharisees. It was not enough to forgive two or even three times because in the Kingdom of God people can be forgiven 70 times 7 times. He avoided religious technicalities that clouded the real priorities. The incidents from life about sheep, robbers, weddings, court cases, employers, family relationships etc were seen as spiritual parallels. There were always sources available for stories, long talks, discussions of hopes, memories and crises to which he could make creative and meaningful responses, no matter whether the situation was known or changing. His creativity enabled him to develop a creative spirit in others. Indeed, his creativity proved to be contagious, even though his greatest creative act appeared to be destructive.

.2c-129
How was Jesus bringing together understanding and lifestyles?

Problem-solving

When a person teaches s/he inevitably creates problems - and Jesus was no different. No doubt he experienced problems as a builder and Mary his mother expected her eldest son to respond to a problem at a wedding. It was as though she habitually relied upon him. But now his major problems were of a spiritual nature that spread into concerns about God, human interaction and values.

Some problem-solving skills, like thinking skills, can be taught systematically. At this stage it is important to recognise that these, along with intuition, can be primed and respond by systematic and reflective teaching to situations as they arise. It would appear that Jesus had a thorough grasp of elements of these skills. He appears to have used:

- established procedures and criteria using observational thoughts.
- reflection.
- flexible reformulation of problems and situations.
- *differentiated skills* to meet appropriate requirements.
- Match a range of problems with *relevant* 'case studies'.

In addition to responding to problems with fresh spirituality, values and insights, his cognitive templates provided or superimposed legitimate solutions. For example, as an inheritor of the Jewish faith he had the problem of freeing people from the traditional addenda that had accumulated and to establish a fresh set of absolutes to correct a distorted view of the character of God. Jesus retained the essential elements of tradition, but the extent of his radicalism was provocative. His solution to understanding the qualities of God's character appear straightforward now, but not when confronted with the task of convincing people as to its correctness.

He was concerned to resolve problems persuasively and his problems were maximised because he had to overcome prejudice and explain and persuade people to accept what appeared to be unlikely abstract, blasphemous spiritual 'truths' that were beyond their comprehension. He was a problem solver and not simply a co-learner. He claimed authority and that his knowledge was absolute. This was rooted in powerful, stable beliefs that would not be compromised or violated by rival teaching. All solutions to problems had to be compatible with the major solution that he had defined during his baptismal period. Many problems were concerned with the *methods* he used to teach such people. The basis of his problem-solving was to unfold *statements and explanation* - which alone may not be enough, It also needed *evidence* provided by himself and others. Although this met the need for a foundation of action, empirical evidence and words, he knew that spiritual problems could only be resolved through spiritual criteria having priority over social, economic, political and traditional religious criteria.

He recognised that the success of his teaching did not always rest in its absolute truth or their understanding but in their perception of him, the teacher. If this could be achieved he knew that as a result, in purely human terms, this faith in him could cause people to achieve beyond all expectations, or as Jesus figuratively described it, faith could move mountains. He wanted, however, to put this faith on a rational basis and so he told people to *judge him by the outcome of his works*. This was probably the basis of faith that is required in any teacher-pupil learning situation.

Although solutions to many problems are intuitive, his solution lay in giving the disciples time for reflection and participation in his work. He was in fact re-orientating their perceptions of reality and truth. He did not expect them to understand immediately. Instead, there was a period of incubation during which the group could watch, listen, question and discuss reflectively. The problem of persuasion was based upon tangible evidence and a secure relationship. It was only

.2c-130
How can everybody be creative?

after some 17 months into his teaching that he felt he could ask his 3 disciples who they thought he was. Although Peter said, "You are the Christ" Jesus clearly knew that they still did not understand the full implications of what he said. Therefore, it was important for the whole problem-solving process to be continued, using this same process of reflective observation, participation and thoughtful discussion. By so doing he gradually enabled them to accommodate his revolutionary insights. He was justifying his solutions by practical effectiveness in his lifestyle. In his problem-solving Jesus cut through many issues. He avoided unconstructive arguments, any form of condemnation and diversionary questions but protected his friends and followers. Although he willingly confronted his critics he was also willing to withdraw from over enthusiastic crowds who may have prejudiced his long-term goals. By sensitively assessing the situation and facing the real needs he took personal actions, used traditional stories and reduced his opponents to silence by his questions and statements. Ultimately, however, he knew that no matter how he defined the problems and developed selected possible solutions, it was not until the teacher and the pupils had a shared perception that they could understand the validity of his solutions.

Jesus faced critical problems such as:

The *value* position between him and the religious authorities was non-negotiable – the teacher could not be neutral and he was certainly not asking people to analyze and assess which was the better of two alternatives.

This was not like a modern plural society where many values are relative and where the most absolute value is to tolerate differences. Jesus set down a marker, and in a non-coercive way, invited people to respond to his teaching. As we look at rival policies of force and optimal freewill, one can see that this has been a recurring issue over the centuries, with control being the norm. But he was emphatic about each individual's responsibility to respond to learning and decision-making situations. He had to:

- *Demonstrate* the nature of *his teaching.*
- Provide a basis of *faith* in him.
- Provide a basis of *knowledge* and *personal experience.*
- Encourage them to *resolve* and *interpret* the puzzles (or parables) he was setting.
- Provide the basis of *tangible success* in the future.

Jesus faced faith problems from four types of people. There were *professionals* who rejected him on principle, because he was not an official rabbi and was attracting those who were under their authority in the general population. *Alternatively* there were *professionals* who did not reject him, the *crowds* who readily responded to his message and that *small minority* who became his *trusted friends* and disciples. Each posed types of problem that required distinct solutions. One concludes that no matter what the situation and requirements, his response to problem solving was rooted in personal values and the attitudes of the people concerned. He appears to have adopted approximately 12 distinct strategies when responding to problems.

Professional opposition:

When criticized he might:

- Justify his stance from traditional sources or common sense practices.
- Counter the questions with alternative unanswerable questions.
- Reverse the problem on them and so become a problem poser.
- Face extreme opposition in silence believing that God would justify him.

.2c-131
Which particular skills did Jesus use that might be used in the 21st century?

Professionals who are not opposed in principle:

- Quietly provide statements for reflective thought.
- Accept hospitality and teach from the situation.

Crowds:

- Brief ear-catching prophetic statements (sound bites).
- Teaching by identification / puzzles (parables).
- Demonstrations of teaching/ and personal responses.
- Friends and followers respond.
- Informal conversations with a range of respondents.
- Teaching deeper intimate details to followers.
- Assistance in practical tasks.

Focus for Thought – What are the following statements suggesting?

- Jesus' problem solving was unique to him but certain principles remain.
- What is the spiritual/value basis of teaching?
- What are the places of absolutism and relativism when teaching?
- What is the degree of authority of the teacher?
- How might solutions differ according to different categories being taught?
- How might methodologies between groups or different types of problems differ?
- How can quality and frequency of interaction influence spiritual and social problem solving?
- Creative problem solving is simply an informed habit.
- Jesus had a compassionate mind. How do you think that might have developed? How might any person develop this fundamental aspect of teaching?

Personality Factor – 10

Which personality factors were probably influential in focusing the thinking, problem-solving and creative processes of Jesus, and of His close followers

.2c-132
How can, say, a labourer or any worker be creative?

Chapter 11

Emotions

Looking forward

The range and responses to emotions... Emotions in Jesus' ministry... Interaction within his group... Emotions arising out of conflict... Emotion and learning... Emotional intelligence... Analyses of social intelligence... Emotion and achievement... Summary

The impact of *emotions* on human behaviour is as old as mankind and nobody is naturally exempt. Now we try to measure them or at least the emotional quotient (E.Q.). The mass-media are public demonstrations that emotions are primary driving forces that influence formal teaching and many contemporary aspects of learning, but it might be said that we have *two* interacting minds – one is characterized by rational thought, centred on the pre-frontal cortex and the other by emotional feelings in the limbic system. This theme considers emotions in Jesus' lifestyle and teaching., and its effects.

Figure 86

	Issues particular to the theme	Relating the theme to Jesus	Relating the theme to teaching generally
Leadership	How can leaders use emotions constructively?	How did Jesus use emotions to maximize learning and action?	How can teachers use emotions most effectively?
Perception	How can emotions modify perceptions when teaching?	How did Jesus link emotions and perceptions?	How are emotions and perception linked in the T/L situation?
Motivation	How can emotions motivate people?	How did Jesus use emotions to motivate people?	How might emotions be used most effectively in teaching and learning?
Memory	How can emotions influence memory?	How did Jesus use emotions to develop memories?	How are memories related to emotions in T/L?
Socialization	In what ways might emotion and socialization influence the T-L situation?	How did Jesus use both emotion and socialization when teaching?	How might emotion and socialization aid the T/L process?
Cognition	How can cognition be influenced by emotions?	How did emotion hinder cognition in Jesus' message?	What are the effects of emotion on cognition?

Every action relates to emotions to some degree. These range widely across the spectrum from those that are positive and healthy to others that are negative and destructive. They are transitory and tend to flow from root attitudes and personality traits. This final theme considers what place emotions had in Jesus' teaching and lifestyle and how these understandings might help us today especially in the context of formal or informal teaching. Without emotions there would be no compassion, mercy, forgiveness etc. – simply a walking death. Jesus knew that just as he displayed this wide array of emotions so he evoked the full range of emotions amongst individuals, groups and crowds. This was integral to his teaching because both cognitive and emotional strands are essential to learning.

Although Jesus' teaching pre-eminently had spiritual goals that enveloped powerful motivation, socialized behaviour and cognitive understanding, all of this required the transformation of people's emotions both towards him and his radical teaching. Let us consider how his actions can be applied currently.

.2c-133
What effect can emotions have on truth?

Emotions normally have such strong effects on learning that two prime predictors of success and failure are hope and worry. As distress normally clouds mental clarity so emotions can act as determining factors of motivation, and it is not surprising that attention is paid to the effects of emotions on relative achievement.

Jesus did not use the term 'emotions' but if he did so he would have used it in terms similar to those we use today. He was in the midst of emotional turmoil, with himself being the central figure amongst the broad band of emotions listed below. Some are not strictly emotions, even so, all are recognized as influences on 'emotions' that affect learning.

Figure 87

	Jesus and his Transformation of Emotions
The Prevailing Popular Condition	Frustration, anger and crude excitement
The Challenge	To transform emotions of individuals and the group into a positive emotional life style by interaction and achievement through: • Authoritative leadership, action and promises • Vindication • Challenging, achievable worthwhile demands
The Positive Dynamics of Emotional Change	• Build up bonding and group identity at the sight of success • Frustrating the opposition • A sense of personal and group success • A sense of mutual acceptance and appreciation • Immersion in ethos of habitual positive emotions A healthy submission based on security and expectations
The Resultant Emotional Life Style	Evident Improvements • Recognition and hope • Despite doubt and difficulty there is a safety net vindication • Leader's and group achievement generates vicarious authority • Positive emotions become an expression of faith and a life style stimulated by autobiographical memories of success

.2c-134
Why are emotions important in long-term learning?

Figure 88

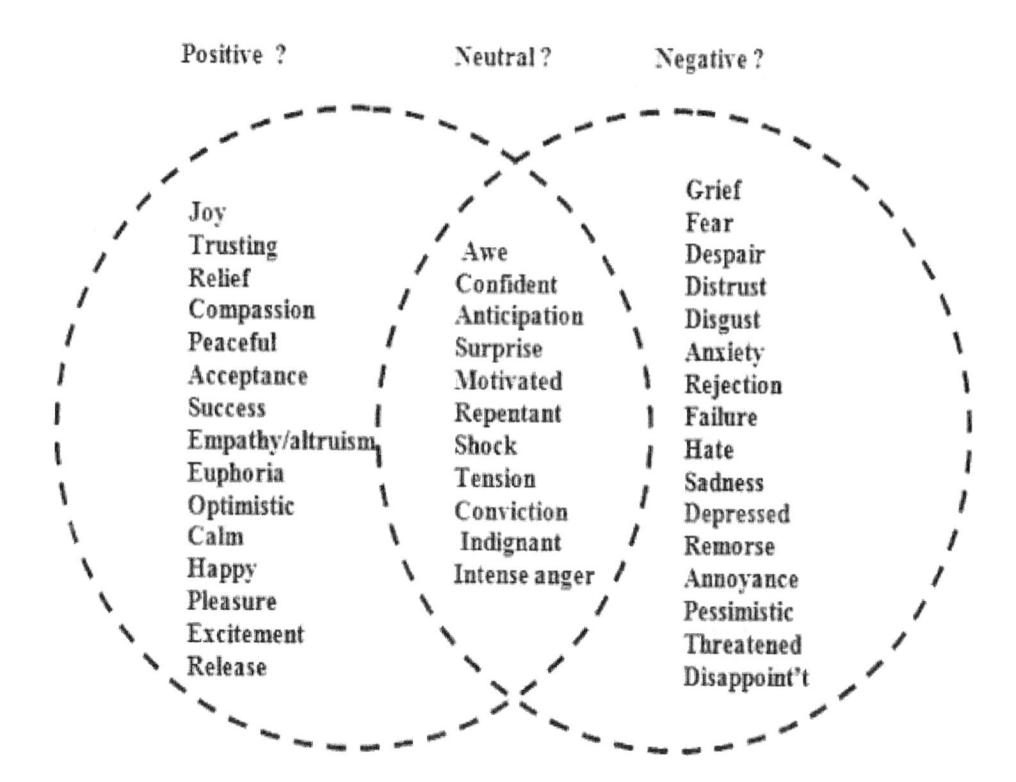

Positive?   **Neutral?**   **Negative?**

Positive:
- Joy
- Trusting
- Relief
- Compassion
- Peaceful
- Acceptance
- Success
- Empathy/altruism
- Euphoria
- Optimistic
- Calm
- Happy
- Pleasure
- Excitement
- Release

Neutral:
- Awe
- Confident
- Anticipation
- Surprise
- Motivated
- Repentant
- Shock
- Tension
- Conviction
- Indignant
- Intense anger

Negative:
- Grief
- Fear
- Despair
- Distrust
- Disgust
- Anxiety
- Rejection
- Failure
- Hate
- Sadness
- Depressed
- Remorse
- Annoyance
- Pessimistic
- Threatened
- Disappoint't

The emotional responses of people who wanted to be free and proudly 'knew' they were 'correct' were powerful! One can visualise the extreme emotions that flowed wherever Jesus went. He knew these were integral to healthy living, learning and faith and that his teaching depended upon them Emotions were related to promises, defending his pupils, involving them in his work and laying bare his own condition. This total emotional scene was central to the situation. Learning was not merely cognitive understanding. Jesus expected emotional responses and recognized that his work provoked these as he asked people to believe him and imitate his actions. Today similar responses occur when pupils see teaching skills that can be appreciated and are beneficial components of learning. We might well consider what Jesus' emotions were in each situation. When he looked up at Zacchaeus the tax collector in a tree and invited himself to a meal, there were powerful emotional interactions.

John Bazalgette made the point that where pupils *feel* accepted and *know* that they can be forgiven, attitudes can change and achievements rise. Therefore, emotions are a practical teaching – learning tool. Just as emotions are commonly used to project pupils into unknown situations to promote empathy and understanding, so Jesus used them when talking about the Kingdom of God. His roller-coaster of emotional challenges affected everybody. His spiritual perspective of his own life experiences released a full range of emotions. It might be said that many emotions can be seen separated as in Fig. 89.

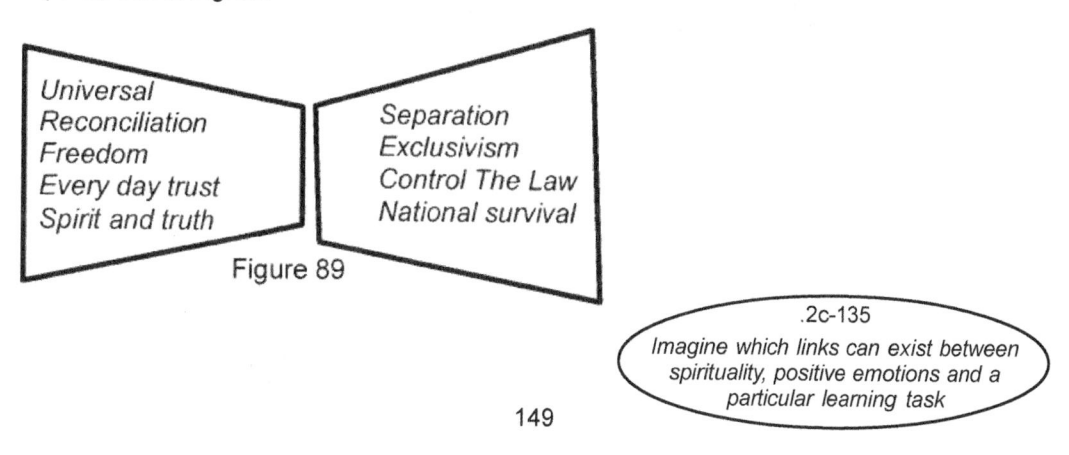

Universal
Reconciliation
Freedom
Every day trust
Spirit and truth

Separation
Exclusivism
Control The Law
National survival

Figure 89

.2c-135
Imagine which links can exist between spirituality, positive emotions and a particular learning task

As the Christian Church developed, there were fewer miracles but a powerful emotional element remained. The bond between Christians stimulated such activities as singing, fellowship and challenges that embedded the emotions. These were inextricably linked to Jesus' spiritual message. For example, the recurring theme of peace was not only peace (reconciliation) with God, but also the emotional peace that generated a flow of elated emotions such as joy that maximized commitment and increased learning possibilities whereas the negative emotions aroused by the religious authorities minimized willing and creative responses. His strategy of liberating people from negative views about God quickly influenced such people as the Samaritan woman. These were both an impetus to such people and the natural outcome of his teaching. Jesus not only knew that the heart (or emotions) was the driving force of man's actions, but that he, himself, was not a mere 'Pale Galilean' but one who experienced the whole palette of life. His teaching could take people from the disaster of being continually judged and subservient, to the hope of having a sense of worth and being called sons and daughters of God with good prospects. Jesus' confidence in them was not merely spiritual but also an emotional drive.

Jesus was a master of emotional self-control. Although he wept, cheered, was angry, was compassionate and responsive to every situation, self-control always prevailed. Even at difficult times he channelled emotions creatively. Stability and faith in his pupils were crucial to his teaching. Even when people left him he refused to be despondent. His motivation, persistence and self-control were essential to his message.

Jesus used emotions in similar ways to us when teaching. He created positive emotions that fostered a creative sense of well-being, and which had a major effect on the working of the brain. Some might even regard him as an early perceptive psychotherapist. His patterns of interaction with and between his learners created positive emotions that contributed to their confidence in him. His calmness together with demonstrations of his teaching evoked an optimum level of emotional arousal. By building a sense of trust, security, success and fresh expectations their attraction to him was confirmed and their anticipation of the future heightened. Imagine the range of positive emotions which were generated as he said, "Look at the fields……," "Come unto me…..," etc. or that resulted when he defended his disciples. The shock he aroused when he cleared traders from the Temple must have been transformed into pride for their leader. The total quality of relationships and rewarding conversations increased the sharpness of their learning and memories but the question as to which came first, motivation or emotion is similar to that of the chicken and the egg. In all probability emotion often gave birth to motivation that then released further emotions. He enabled his pupils to identify imaginatively and emotionally with his tasks that became a major fillip to achievement.

Although Jesus was living in an emotionally charged situation, there were two major aspects that can be related to our current situations. These were:
- The dynamics within his closely knit group.
- The manner in which he faced opposition.

Interaction within his closely knit group

The effects of emotions on the process of attitude change were illustrated by his firm leadership and the group's affiliation. Once a decision was made to follow Jesus there was a group attribution in which they proudly regarded him as a prophet and later as the Christ. The spontaneous communal and personal emotions were heightened as their teacher attracted crowds and their self-esteem rose as they became the link between the people and their master. Acceptance of truth alone was not enough! It required an emotional identity as they moved from anonymity into their privileged position. This required that the bonding within the group and with Jesus was

.2c-136
What did Swinburne mean when he called Jesus a 'pale Galilean'?

secure, with their emotions being an essential component of their discipleship. These interacting emotions were components that generated:

- Bonding/affiliation.
- A compelling drive to achieve fresh spiritual goals.
- Shared perceptions.
- Shared causal explanations.
- Shared intentions.
- Shared authority.
- Shared identity.
- Shared evaluation.
- Collective behaviour within a personal and shared 'community of faith'.

One only has to consider these characteristics amongst this group who at last had something good to talk about and identify with. The emotions of enjoyment and surprise were 'the stuff' of motivated memories and action. Jesus created 'mood effects'. Statements of promise, such as, 'blessed are the pure in heart' and the word 'Father' was emotionally calming. These were not likely to arouse revolution, but rather to inculcate trust and perhaps a certain quietness that was necessary after the excitement of hearing the initial message and seeing accompanying validating signs. He imperceptibly managed the emotions of his followers because emotional arousal affected the processes of perception, cognition, memory and motivation powerfully. As the climax of his life approached so the emotions changed.

Emotions can simplify thinking processes and colour their interpretations. The impact of seeing a miracle and dancing for joy, listening intently to Jesus, or feeling threatened was extraordinary. He had to wean them from impetuous emotions that could do lasting harm but which increased as they shared his rising popularity. Their group emotions with its characteristic language and behaviour, needed to become more like their master. Their privileges, responsibilities and joyful euphoria had to be matched by a growing sense of empathy and responsibility. Imagine the shock when after three years of success, the temple guards arrested their revered leader who had done no wrong. Their emotions boiled over – this was not a time for considered judgment, it demanded action! Would they fight or flight? Would they resolutely stay or run? After the initial impetuosity of Peter and others, fighting was quashed by Jesus' calm acceptance of the situation. They were deflated, fearful and escaped into the darkness. After the Passion they came to share his emotional calm.

Truth alone is not usually sufficient to evoke the type of following that Jesus wanted. His strategy for bonding this close-knit group included the following:

- They might be described as an 'out-group' who lived on the hills and in towns and villages in Galilee. It was crucial to attain a strong group identity that confidently looked to Jesus.
- They appear to have developed roles and built up relationships that survived hazardous experiences.
- They became bonded with a shared spiritual language and ideas, affiliation, collective behaviour and drive that built a sense of privileged group identity.
- Together they stimulated memories as they discussed their experiences.
- They copied Jesus and acquired appropriate social and spiritual qualities and skills such as compassion and encouragement.
- Mutual expectations were established as they considered the past and future.
- Together they shaped their desires, shared their problems and sought to implement Jesus' wishes that led them to emotional self-awareness.

.2c-137
Imagine a link between spirituality and negative emotions.

These generated a profusion of emotions that coloured their understanding and reactions. Positive emotions were activated by their sense of awe, anticipation, and a fresh view of repentance. Their motivation emerged from emotional experiences that included negative emotions such as grief and fear, anger and despair, but which were later transformed into positive memories. Jesus' task of opening worlds of understanding required mutually satisfying emotional links to retain their value.

Emotions arising out of conflict

The power of emotions was similarly evident in the opposition to Jesus. The religious authorities not only disagreed factually with him but they felt that both the nation and themselves were threatened as admiring crowds melted away, which initiated emotions that distorted their judgments. The power of their emotions made it difficult to arrive at rational decisions, because they too had gone through an intense socialization process that established their identity and secure self-concept. Like Jesus and his disciples, they were emotionally bonded and had a collective behaviour pattern, religious language and discipline. Perhaps people such as Nicodemus and Joseph of Arimathea were outsiders who had freedom to consider the validity of Jesus' teaching without excessive pressure to conform.

It is common in emotionally charged ideological groups for members to be blind to evidence or to misinterpret it. Their hostility moved from indignation to outright opposition. Responses between rival groups commonly escalate and attempts to achieve a mutual understanding, often only confirm the status and determination of the 'out group', in this case Jesus and his disciples. Any consensus required submissive emotions as they enquired into the validity or otherwise of this new development of their faith. This did occur several years later, but at that particular time group identity and established knowledge prevented it. This pattern of conflict is a concern in society generally and perhaps especially in schools. Attitudes harden, emotions heighten and the authorities often question and dismiss proposed changes and fail to satisfy the needs and aspirations of the 'lower' group. How could the breakthrough be achieved? The answer from one perspective is compliance to established practices. The alternative is a re-examination of tradition with rational humility. This becomes a philosophical issue that strikes at the heart of both society and individual responses.

Jerome Bruner hypothesized that when people face difficult situations they adopt either coping or defending behaviour strategies. Those who confidently develop successful solutions are *copers* whereas *defenders* take negative attitudes to limit failure. Both involve emotional responses to personal and social situations. Jesus displayed coping strategies when challenged by the religious authorities, whereas many Galileans around him were defenders by withdrawing from or acquiescing to threats. The coping strategy was characteristic of his teaching and transformed many prevailing negative emotions into habitual positive mindsets. Hence the Beatitudes took people from depression to positive expectations, from fear to peace and from rejection to a sense of acceptance and approval. These dramatic shifts in emotions show that Jesus knew the importance of the positive word and how negative emotions stem from persistent doubt and fear. He set the tone for successful tuition. Pupils want a teacher to have the will and the skills to teach and confidently make contact with them. This can create a desire to learn and foster a confidence to make contact with the teacher – and so a two way process based on reciprocal emotions enhances the possibility of learning. If pupils face negative emotions such as frustration, fear can grow and they become *defenders even whilst appearing to be coping with the situation.*

.2c-138
Identify the absolute kernel of teaching in Figure 90?

Figure 90

Memory	Conception	Emotion
Thought Reasoning Perception Language	The world Particular aspects of studies	Personal and corporate attitudes and opinions Long term values

Jesus was tolerant but not passive. In this context tolerance is equated with sustained involvement when a learner fails and passivity indicates a degree of relative indifference. His was seen to be positive and relevant and one which fostered a coping emotional stance.

If the quality of learning is dependent upon *memory, conception and emotion,* that must include the impact of negative and positive emotions. Where emotions are functional to learning, the emotional stamina and consistency shown by their role model, in this case Jesus, enhances learning. Figure 90 indicates how memory can shape for good or ill the thought, reasoning, perception and language processes. Will they be couched in a coping or defending mode? Similarly, memory is applied to a conception of the world and particular aspects of learning. Are the world and learning seen as the copers' opportunities or the defenders' threat? Linking these, what force do emotions exert upon opinions, attitudes and values? As a powerful coper Jesus exerted an *emotional thrust* as he envisaged God's world and will and focused his thought, reasoning, perception and language on that which had developed throughout his life and resulted in a life-vision. For a defender, emotions drive a person into seeing the world negatively and adopting evasive action. This exemplifies an everyday problem in teaching and learning – do emotions liberate or imprison this process? Learners need recognition and praise. Apparently Jesus did not constantly praise his followers but he trusted them for the present and the future. Such trust empowered thought and established personal beliefs that in turn became *capability* beliefs! The emotional basis of the relationship between the teacher and the taught created a climate for new thinking. The process of learning deepened their confidence in shared values, cognitive understanding, their leaders' success and an agreement about the failure of the present system. The increasing power of the positive emotions grew and aided the development of Jesus' embryonic group.

During Jesus' teaching the people's emotional responses apparently preceded significant understandings. As he created expectations so people wanted to learn and hung on every word. They developed an emotional commitment to him, which stood in contrast to their emotional alienation of others. As he took them through the extremes of memorable emotions he remained a secure anchorage. His teaching is often caricatured by solemnity, and that has truth, but in reality the full range of human responses was stimulated. One can imagine the gamut of emotions when people talked about the new rabbi, whose teaching was so effective. He had the ability to meet every situation and evoke a wide range of positive emotions. But it is possible to envisage the disappointment when only one leper returned to give thanks after being healed. The disciples shared Jesus' emotions and so the disappointment probably became positive.

Emotions are not mere impetuosity that should be self-controlled but are possibly a distinct aspect or *form of intelligence* that can be trained to enhance attainment. Indeed, it has entered many school curricula as an aspect of personal, social and health education. Traditionally intelligence was regarded exclusively as intellectual thought but this was found to be inadequate and in the mid-1970s Howard Gardner proposed that there are eight distinct forms of intelligence, namely:

Linguistic   **Logical mathematics**   **Musical**   **Spatial**

Kinaesthetic   **Interpersonal**   **Intrapersonal**   **Naturalist**

.2c-139
What might have been the dominant emotions just before Jesus" arrest?

Daniel Goleman extended this in the mid-1990's when he indicated that emotion might also be a form of intelligence. At the turn of the century Danah Zohar claimed to identify a spiritual intelligence. More recently, in 2006, Daneil Goleman proposed thast there is a spiritual injtelligence. All of these forms of intelligence relate to the ability to adapt to and learn from experience (George Kelly). This, however, does not equate with wisdom, which is the ability to use knowledge sensitively and advantageously in decision-making.

Daniel Goleman's detailed analysis of emotional intelligence, which has a strong relationship to social psychology, highlights the qualities of being able to initiate sensitively, adapt and respond to everyday emotional situations but what does it mean? In view of the social nature of emotions it is not surprising that Goleman stressed social skills. If this is analysed in the context of Jesus the master teacher, it is evident that he would have recognized the qualities as components which he developed in his followers' lives, but he would have couched them in traditional definitions of emotions and added an overtly spiritual component.

Goleman's analysis is based on a framework of five major components:

Self awareness   self-regulation   motivation   empathy   social skills

These were subdivided into a further 23 sections and then refined into a further 85 sub-sections which are fully described in 'Working with Emotional Intelligence'. His major contention is that it is not intelligence as traditionally defined that is the determining factor of a person's success but rather the personal motivation, the quality of human relationships and pertinacity. He widened his analysis of emotions to include social skills because he saw the two sets of skills acting upon each other. Indeed one might say that social skills are given prominence over what might be traditionally regarded as emotional skills. Goleman took most of his examples from the commercial world as one can see from my modified table of his analysis. For example, if one looks at the empathy - service orientation it can refer to a management statement rather than to either teaching or religion. But Jesus' would probably have accepted the four service application priorities, namely:

- To understand the needs of others.
- To seek ways to increase loyalty etc.
- To offer assistance gladly.
- To act as a skilled and trained adviser.

Goleman's analysis contains basic universal applications that would have been recognisable to Jesus, especially when orientated towards:

- Inter-personal sensitivity.
- needs.
- aspirations.
- appropriate responses to others.

This analysis is applicable to both informal and formal teaching and is useful when developing guided enquiry approaches to learning. Although service was at the heart of Jesus' teaching, he would probably have gone beyond Goleman and emphasized emotions related to:

Selfless service, sacrifice and altruism, spiritual motivation and supporting the needy

Jesus applauded the notion of self-control and envisaged emotions being rooted in a *spiritual lifestyle*. Therefore, their development went beyond learning emotional habits and self-control mechanisms through socialization processes. Even so he was their role model who socialized them and set standards. He established emotional habits based on spiritual promises and built permanent emotional bonds with people who learned spiritual and emotional realities as they travelled. He was not anti-intellectual but he recognized the power of emotion to override cognitive rationality on occasions. The reality was that he brought intelligence and spiritual sensitivity to emotions. As people heard his words and saw his supportive actions so the pervasive process of learning was completed at both the cognitive and emotional levels. Identification and faith developed together.

.2c-140
When are emotions likely to change within t group you know? well?

Jesus belonged to a small community that he understood and which accepted him. Knowing them and their culture, he appraised their situation and enabled them to project into his imaginative teaching. This evoked emotional responses to his pictorial language and dramatic actions. His empathy was often reciprocated, thereby producing a virtuous circle of teaching and help, followed by support and attention. Frequently, however, this was only a temporary enthusiasm that could not withstand opposition. Jesus did not often pressurize such people with threatening emotional messages but rather fostered hope.

Figure 91

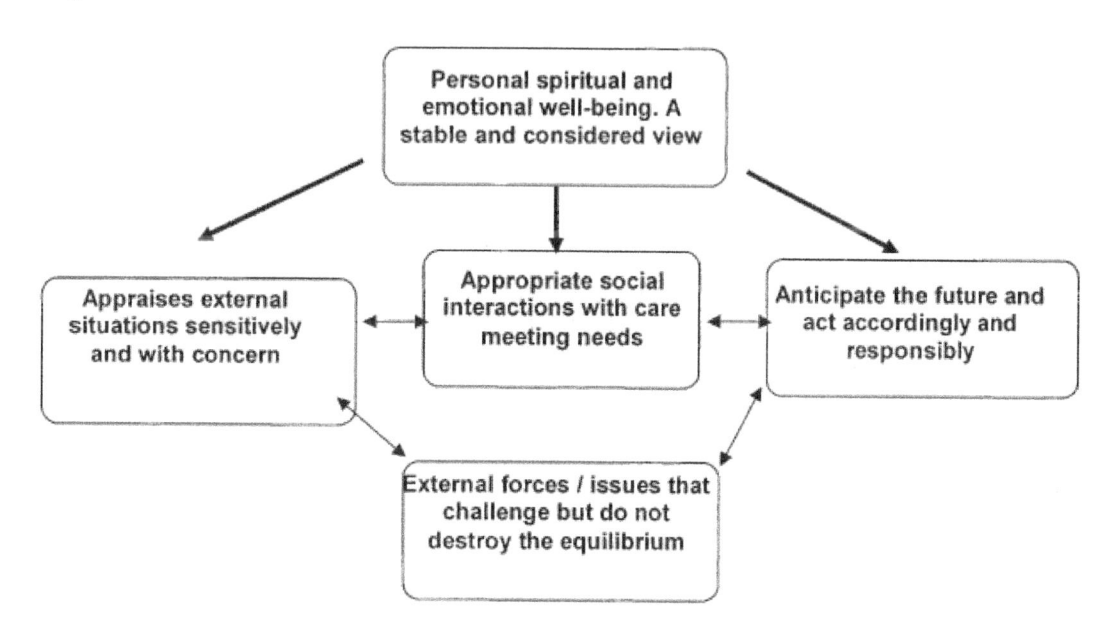

```
                    ┌─────────────────────────┐
                    │ Personal spiritual and  │
                    │ emotional well-being. A │
                    │ stable and considered   │
                    │         view            │
                    └─────────────────────────┘
                    ↙           ↓           ↘
┌──────────────────┐   ┌──────────────────┐   ┌──────────────────┐
│ Appraises        │   │ Appropriate      │   │ Anticipate the   │
│ external         │ ↔ │ social           │ ↔ │ future and act   │
│ situations       │   │ interactions     │   │ accordingly and  │
│ sensitively and  │   │ with care        │   │ responsibly      │
│ with concern     │   │ meeting needs    │   │                  │
└──────────────────┘   └──────────────────┘   └──────────────────┘
            ↘                   ↑                   ↙
                    ┌─────────────────────────┐
                    │ External forces/issues  │
                    │ that challenge but do   │
                    │ not destroy the         │
                    │ equilibrium             │
                    └─────────────────────────┘
```

He entered into the ethos of effective emotional support that made his teaching attractive, at least in the short term. As a teacher therefore, his creative use of emotions resulted in a high level of interest before, during and after events. Small communities felt a sense of well-being and people appraised the external situation confidently. Jesus showed three major emotions with which the people and his disciples in particular could identify. Modern educators would be sympathetic to his model of teaching.

Both Goleman and Jesus understood that the development of the emotions should primarily foster freedom and release and result in a confidence to achieve highly – even if it requires faith and pertinacity. An example of this revolves around the issue of inclusion and exclusion. The development of healthy emotions usually achieves confidence and a desire for inclusion amongst groups. But where fear and distrust predominate, a protective attitude of exclusion may ensue that becomes a major issue in the health of both individuals and society.

.2c-141
Jesus' close followers were typical over achievers – Why?

Summary

1a. Jesus was not concerned with I.Q. – but rather with commitment, values and relationships that encompass aspects of what is termed emotional intelligence and spiritual intelligence, insight and response. Although this does not express Jesus' spiritual teaching, it provides indicators that can maximize learning compared with the prevailing under-achievement of so many. This is summarized in Fig 91.

Figure 92

Maximize of Over Achievement	Under achievement
Hope - a predictor of success A general mood of optimism	Anxiety which undermines the intellect
Enthusiasm x positive expectations	Worry, fear and persistent error which are reliable predictors of failure
Pleasure of performance – approval – discovery – creativity	Non-ownership of what is taught
	Rejection or sense of insignificance
Satisfaction in communal immersion	Threats which endanger future welfare
Develop a non-defensive attitude	No acceptable effective leadership
Accepts secure leadership and a stable role model	

Spiritual faith was the essence of Jesus' teaching methods but what are the significances of the differences between Figures 92 and 93 in respect of emotions and teaching and learning?

Figure 93

I.Q.?	Personal/social	Values	Situation
Discriminate between short and long term goals Rationalization of choices and opportunities	Identity based on: history, current success Prospects: life paths that are open.	Perceived validity of working values to society and individuals	Stability/change - acceptable balance Satisfying outlets Social approval

Figure 94

Organizing realms of emotions	1	2	3	4	5
Intra-personal	Emotional self-awareness	Assertiveness	Independence	4 Self-regard	1 Self actualization
Interpersonal realm	Empathy	Social responsibility	Interpersonal relationships		
Adaptability	Problem solving	Reality testing	Flexibility		
Stress management	Stress tolerance	Impulse control			
General mood	2 Happiness	3 Optimism			

.2c-142
What emotions might have been felt when Jesus called Peter "The Rock"?

2. Stephen Stein and Howard Book devised a test (Bar On EQ-i) for exploring emotional intelligence focused on five major organising 'realms' of emotions. They highlighted 15 areas where emotions are particularly significant. They tested over 42,000 people worldwide and four major areas were found to be those indicated in Figure 94. Which do you think would have been applicable to the major characteristics and priorities of Jesus and his disciples?

3. Identify the following about emotions in the gospels:
   - The leader promotes positive emotions and identifies negative emotions.
   - The leader uses emotions to project pupils mentally into new situations.
   - The leader perceives the characteristic emotions of pupils.
   - The pupils perceived the characteristic emotions of their teacher.
   - Motivation stems from emotions and also promotes emotions.
   - Emotions can both heighten and distort memories.
   - Positive emotions are normally matched to healthy socialization.
   - Emotions communicate unspoken attitudes in this socialization process.
   - Positive emotions provide the freedom to understand and recall.
   - Negative emotions severely hinder understanding and recall.

Note:

1. It is dangerous to equate EQ with self-control, rationality, the development of alternative pathways and the control of emotional impulses.
2. Prior experience includes mental history and related subconscious responses.
3. Emotional patterning results as primary emotions trigger secondary emotions.
4. The relative degree of stress tolerance and responsiveness modify this analysis.

.2c-143
Consider how emotions might be closely linked with memory and conception.

Figure 95. A summary of Goleman's analysis of socio-emotional priorities

Self Aware		→ Understand own emotions	Link feeling thought and action	Feeling affecting performance	Aware values/ goals
	Self Assessment	→ Aware strength weaknesses	Reflective learning of experience	Open feedback self develop perspective	Humour
	Self confidence	→ Has presence self-assurance	Voice unpopular views	Decisive, sound decisions	
Self Regulation	Self control	→ Manage impulsive emotions	Stay composed	Think clearly in pressure	
	Trustworthy	→ Act ethically	Build trust reliability	Admit error confront unethical	Tough principle stands
	Conscientious	→ Meets commitment / promises	Accountable to meet objectives	Organized and careful in work	
	Innovative	→ Multi-sourced ideas	Considers all solutions to problem	Generates new ideas	Takes risks in thinking
	Adaptable	→ Handles multi demands smoothly	Adapts to fluid situations	Flexible perspective	
Motivation	Achievement drive	Drive to → meet goals	Challenging goals/risks	Pursues improvement	Learns to improve
	Commitment	→ Sacrifices to meet goals	Sense of larger mission	Decisions based on core values	Aim fulfil group mission
	Initiative	→ Seizes opportunity	Pursues greater goals	Mobilizes others	
	Optimum drive	Seeks goals →	Hopes for success	Setbacks manageable	
Empathy	Understand others	Notes → emotional cues NVS	Sensitive to other perspective	Help based others needs	
	Develop others	Acknowledge → reward others	Offers feedback meet needs	Mentor timely coaching	
	Service orientation	Understand → needs	Seeks to increase loyalty	Gladly offers assistance	Acts as trusted advisor
	Leverage diversity	→ Relates to diverse cultures?	Understands diverse WV	Creates environment for all	Challenges intolerance
	Political awareness	→ Assesses power relationship	Detects social networks	Understand belief shaping	Accurately assesses realities
Social Skills	Influence	→ Are persuasive	Can appeal to listeners	Strategies to build consensus	Uses the dramatic to teach
	Communicate →	Effective emotional cues	Difficult issues dealt with	Shares information	Open response to news
	Conflict	→ Diplomatic	Spots potential	Encourage	Develops win-win

	Management	/tactful	conflict	discussion	solutions
	Leadership	➔ Shared vision / mission	Leads as needed	Guides performance of others	Leads by example
	Change catalyst	➔ Change/ remove barriers	Challenges status quo	Supports improvement	Models changes in others
	Building bonds	➔ Develop Informal networks	Mutually beneficial relationship	Good rapport	Maintains friendships
	Co'labor'n/ cooperation	➔ Attends relationships	Shares resources	Generates good climate	Nurtures col'borat'e opportunities
	Team Capabilities	➔ Model's qualities	Inclusive	Team identity	Protects group reputation

---

Personality Factor – 11

Which personality factors would lead Goleman to regard Jesus as having high emotional intelligence?

.2c-144
When might emotion be an import aspect on the social scale

Summary of the seven themes

We have seen in Part B that Jesus identified and implemented generic practices that are integral to our contemporary teaching. For example, although he did not teach about perception, he was perceptive and indicated ways of looking at people and the world. Similarly he recognized that positive emotions that stem from compassion and acceptance open the pathway to cognition, and although he did not teach thinking skills he did teach a way of thinking.

All seven facets are inextricably linked and interactive, therefore, the inevitable question arises, "Can seven become one?" Can they illuminate each other? The seven themes have provided a wide range of principles and indicators that can be applied to teaching in many forms. Much within the unifying principles can be summarized in the following two tables.

Table A. T x (P1xP2) = R which means Teacher x Pupil x Peers = Reward.

(All of the themes illustrated that there is a cost before there is a reward.)

Figure 96

Teacher	Pupil	Reward
1 The teacher was not there for himself	The pupils realized there are limits to what the teacher can do without pupil cooperation.	Long term learning power and motivation
2 The teacher had faith in all aspects of the teaching and learning	The pupils went beyond their expectations by being sufficiently motivated.	Ownership of their learning and thinking powers
3 His vision and goals were more significant than the pupils or what anybody realized.	Pupils seldom realized the significance of what they were doing.	Thorough competence in the range of understandings
4 He had the full body of expertise, and was the basic resource and role model	Pupils needed to recognize the teacher's purposes – long and short term	They had the capacity to develop beyond their expectations
5 He was perceptive to recognize the pupils' potential	Pupils needed to reciprocate the faith of the teacher and have a growing vision.	They learned to apply the knowledge and ideas insightfully
6 He socialized the pupils with consistent pro-pupil support	Pupils needed to reflect and organize their cognitive schemas	They had the confidence to use their skills to move into the unknown
7 He provided a wide range of experiences	Pupils needed to show emotional consistency and staying power, even at hard times	Life became a form of experiential learning based on earlier experiences
8 He motivated and surprised pupils by his ability and working with them	Pupil needed to have rising expectations and be surprised by what could be achieved	What had been learned became the basis of interpretive powers
9 He set up memory banks and cognitive scenarios in pupils	Pupils needed to work cooperatively with other pupils as they moved into the unknown	They felt secure in their cognitive scenarios and could respond to new situations
10 He recognized that for the long term he had to teach problem solving and creativity experientially	There were disappointments before achieving their final success	They had total pleasure and confidence in their final achievements

Note that as they succeeded so motivation increased.
- The teacher was fully prepared and committed to the task.
- The teacher was a risk-taker who went into 'unknown territory'.
- The teacher's motivation was the basis of their motivation.
- Pupils had personal responsibilities and normally worked together in flexible groups.

.2c-145
From above, what would appear to be the major strengths of the Teacher?... the pupils?

Leader	Perception	Motivation	Memory	Socialisat'n	Cognition	Emotion
• Confident in role • Defines strategy • Has clear vision • Desires to lead	The leader perceives • Followers' commitm'nt • Develops a world perception • Perceives needs and strategies	• Motivated by providing goals, success, friendship • The surprise of security and higher aspirations.	Evoked memories by • Personal actions • Illuminating Stories/ promises Sense of privilege	Changed people by • Friendship, competence, collaboration and faith in them	Leader developed • A way of thinking • Enabled pupils to develop skills, faith, understand'	• Leader has stable emotions • Pupils feel emotionally safe and optimistic • Does not rush into conflict
	Perception • Self perception is related to one's world-view and psychological health • A person perceives qualities in self and others?	• Motivation can be modified by a perception of the situation - actual or not!	• Memory is related to perception of the situation and significance	• Socialization is shaped by perception of significant others • Perception leads to behaviour	• Cognition related to self perception • Trained people to look for personal, absolute realities	• Recognizes perceptions which are intuitively satisfying to others
		Motivation • Intrinsic motivation sees the long term • Motivation can rise or decline in competition with other motivations	• Motivation shapes authentic memories • Memories are often selected by personal motivation	• Socialization/ motivation mutually entwined • Socialization tends to validate and shape motivation	• Acts on a flow of information within a faith structure Motivation/ learning are linked by VAK and life experiences	• Emotion is a prime mover in motivation • Motivation is a prime mover in emotion!
			Memory • Motivation shapes authentic memories • Memories can be selected by personal motivation	• Socialization validates, colours and selects memories	• Memories enhanced by converging multiple learning paths	• Memories are accentuated or possibly warped by emotional change
				Socialization • Socialization can determine cognitive values • Socialization shapes affective values	• Cognition reflects socializing influences • Thinking stems from a person's realities	• Can use projection to recognize emotions of others
A Matrix of Interactions Between the 7 Themes All of the themes are interactive to some degree, which indicates that teaching is more than efficient instruction. Figure 97					**Cognition** • Can judge intuitive responses • Recognize realistic rational schemas • Can relate to moral and spiritual norms	• Healthy emotions are paths to understand Emotions gateway to the thinking mind
						Emotions • Emotions generate other emotions ...are sensitive to emotions in others

Chapter 12

Ultimate Teaching Strategy B

Jesus' ability to foster long-term learning was remarkable. In Parts A and B various approaches to teaching have been indicated but pupils are not learning machines, they assess the worth of the task put before them – which may seem to be of little value. This can be especially so if there seem to be anonymous forces controlling the content and pacing of the learning regardless of their own priorities. But, can teaching strategies go beyond organizational expediency and compulsion?

Before drawing together certain aspects from Part B to contribute towards Ultimate Teaching Strategy 2 eight questions might be posed. Although the questions will not be answered directly, to raise them implies answers that deserve to be considered.

- Q1. What is high-quality *worthwhile* teaching and learning?
- Q2. What might characterise a good teacher who is also *a leader to learners*?
- Q3. How are *long-term learning prospects* perceived during *current* teaching?
- Q4. What are the most *worthwhile means of motivating pupils*?
- Q5. Which *learning* becomes truly *memorable*?
- Q6. Which *behaviour and attitudes* are likely to gratify pupils in the long term?
- Q7. Which patterns of *understanding* are likely to gratify pupils in the long term?
- Q8. How should teachers be *developing and using the emotions* of their learners?

These highly generalized questions have no agreed answers and yet they are inevitably asked in some form and answers are often assumed to be self-evident.

Learning is often rapid amongst highly motivated people, but Jesus saw the matter differently. He knew that various learners need somewhat alternative exposures to teaching – and Judas showed that even the best teachers do not always succeed. The summary mind map (Fig.9) identified key issues which must have influenced Jesus and which can be translated in principle across cultures. Let us examine these as a series of six decisions about the teaching process might be regarded as self-evident, but the attitude and decisions taken reflect issues in the 21st century and have implications for an ultimate teaching strategy.

Decision 1: Jesus' major focus established a healthy basis for learning in the community. He provided an *ethos and expectations* that showed both what was significant and also his *high view* of people. They saw that although he was rigorous, he 'led from the heart' and worked alongside them as a *servant leader* who talked with them informally. By describing himself as 'the Door' and 'the Good Shepherd' they felt secure. He showed that his was a *restoring, reconciling group* in which the pupils could have total *confidence*. The impression is that rather than criticize their undoubted weaknesses, he fed them with *positive self-images* and *strengthened their strengths*! His first band of decisions covered their *learning atmosphere* – once that was established, learning developed effectively.

Decision 2: He chose some low level pupils and was more concerned about their attitude than their qualifications, because *motivation enhances abilities*! He was not merely looking for people who would believe him but who were motivated to walk with him.

Decision 3: His was a *teacher-centred* situation in which his *expertize* took pupils beyond their awareness and *evoked a sense of awe* but he required *total pupil involvement*. A *pupil-centred* approach alone was limited and inadequate. He would raise them to a level of which they were unaware.

Decision 4: His approach to knowledge was uncomplicated. He focused on core principles such as mercy, justice etc and illustrated naturally and raised levels of awareness.

.2c-146
Add two further questions that you think were crucial.

Decision 5: The *learning environment* was distinctive. He was the authoritative expert (Rabbi) and could be likened to a master craftsman with apprentices who would *see, copy and (make) do whatever the master did. This involved maximizing the use of the senses, solving problems and creating new human situations* and so they had a profound sense of variety and worth. This ultimate strategy for teaching could afford no disagreement but it did reflect six major strategies (see Chapter 14) containing four critical features:

- Restoring the learning ethos
- The influence of the expert teacher
- The response of participant apprentice learners
- The effect of personal experiences. And all within an *indelible hope!*

Many teachers are non-experts and so the authority and scope of the learning is undermined in the eyes of pupils. Teacher ignorance can have serious repercussions. The non-mathematician who teaches mathematics is a byword for pupil failure and non-commitment. Schools need to be flexible, but does it matter if teachers are not experts? They can adopt the role of co-learners but expertise is needed for authoritative teaching to be recognized.

Decision 6: Jesus was more than an expert – he was their *role model or living representation* of his teaching. People *watched* him and knew what he was teaching. It demanded both confidence and commitment but although this made demands it was probably the most memorable aspect of his teaching. This recalls the acronym PACT that, if emphasized, learning should be Positive, provide Authentic experiences, and promote Creativity and be rooted in Truth. Here the notion of truth relates to core values and procedures that include pupil – teacher and pupil – pupil relationships.

In Part C we will look at thinking and cognitive processes in action and his skilful use of techniques, but they all come and go unless we retain those core elements of teaching and learning that virtually have a life within themselves and are capable of new growth as existing processes pass into history. He was showing teaching methods that will live whilst we temporarily adapt them for particular purposes.

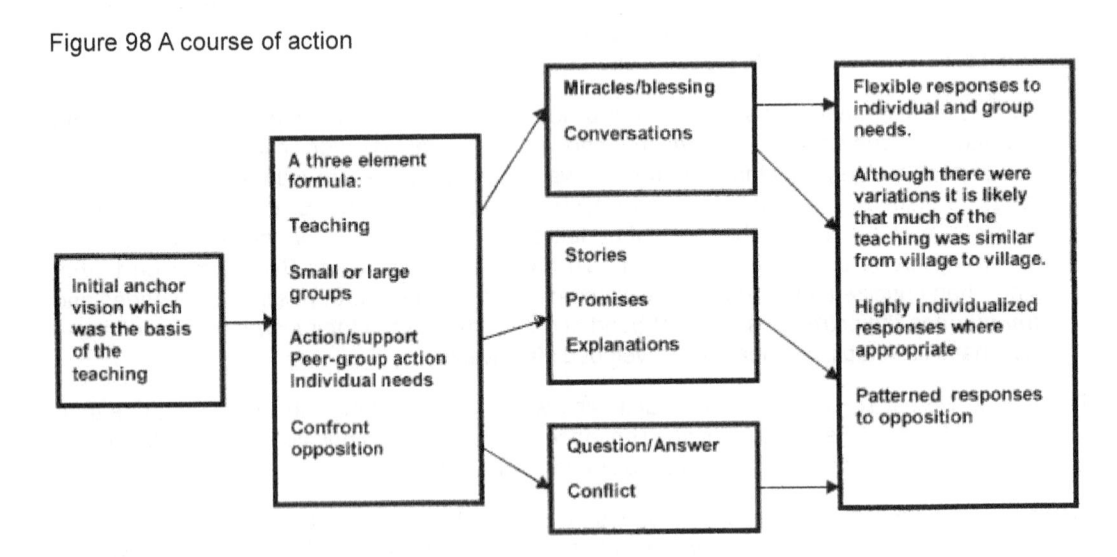

Figure 98 A course of action

The above diagram is a hypothetical representation of Jesus' teaching methods as he travelled around Galilee from village to village.eg.1. Capernaum....2. Nain......3. etc

.2c-147
How did Jesus maximize the effectiveness of his teaching?

This would be a recognizable and repeated teaching package with variations as they moved from village to village. The message remained consistent and many promises, stories and explanations were probably frequently repeated. The major differences would have been conversations, miracles and individual blessings plus the opposition when it occurred. If this was the pattern, the disciples gained a deep knowledge from Jesus' preaching and intense experiential understanding from the activities in which they were involved. It is not possible to have a direct *comparable modern strategy* but it would include the following:

A. The teaching element

- Identify an agreed point of need and motivating purpose.
- Teacher-led initiatives that serve to illustrate teacher expertise.
- Established stories/incidents to illustrate ideas and promote debate.
- Explanations of responses.

B The activity element

- Possible environmental/community involvement or research (Peers),
- Drama- to act communal situations.
- Debate/discussion regarding opposing views,

C The instruction package

- …would examine major common problems, issues and visionary solutions by considering evidence from an authority (e.g. Help the Aged).
- The teacher would both teach and lead.
- Pupils would work together in small groups and report back to the larger group who would discuss of corporate findings.
- Individual pupils would write their own reports with appropriate conclusions.

The assumptions are:

- The teacher is in overall control of direction and goals.
- There is a ready response to personal needs, including spiritual etc.
- The teacher has direct responsibility for leadership and provision.
- An inquiry/peer-group response to needs, including spiritual.
- Pupil development is assessed for future action.

Teaching based on principles

Jesus' teaching methods are generally typified by visual and succinctly memorable narratives and metaphors but Jesus' teaching was based upon *central principles* into which important *concepts* were fed, which in turn had been illustrated by *demonstrations of love and faith and information* (see Fig.3) It assumes, however, that the teaching is based upon the teachers' authority.

Fig.99 illustrates aspects of Jesus' typical pattern of teaching. There is ample scope for imaginative, creative problem-solving in many types of teaching and learning, but certain imperatives remain (see Ch.3). It indicates the scope for teacher led instruction is wide and can meet most situations. This is illustrated in Fig.90 that summarizes questions that were probably assumed by Jesus and which we now examine with great care. Take each of the nine headings and consider what Jesus' assumptions might have been and what ours might be today. Why were the principles which underpinned Jesus' methods appropriate and how can they be applied today in, say for example, the teaching of literacy, which will be further developed in Part C.

.2c-148
What are the effects of teaching based on principles?

Jesus was moving with the tide of expectation. It was seen to be relevant and met people's sense of need and aspiration but could it be made comprehensible? A challenge was issued, rapid initial progress and achievement ensued and people followed him. We then see a hectic flow of activities as summarized above. When considered it becomes evident that these nine (and more) aspects are common to most learning. For example, when teaching language and literacy at an early stage, one is constantly enabling them to use, relate, enrich, personalize and 'fix' language into situational memories, around heroes and others. It is apparent that if one takes the religious message out of Jesus' preaching one is left with a very powerful methodological skeleton. Furthermore, if reflection is taken as a unifying practice it takes on a purposeful dimension, but it does need the input of teacher.

Figure 99

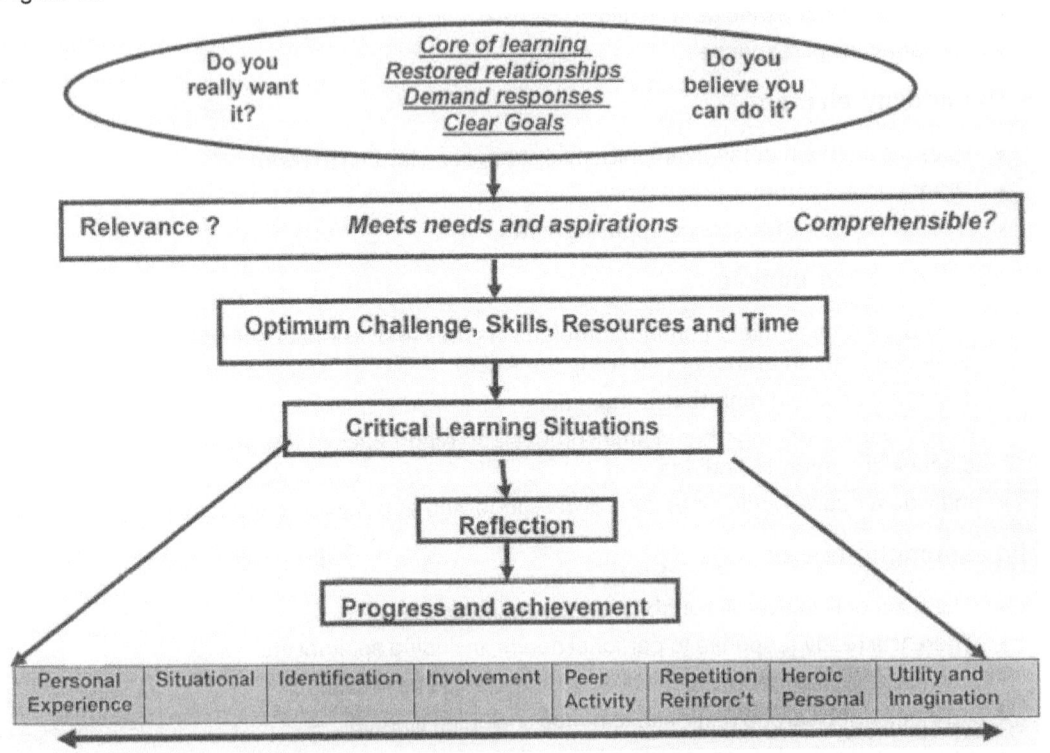

```
        ┌─────────────────────────────────────────┐
        │  Do you        Core of learning    Do you    │
        │  really want   Restored relationships  believe you │
        │     it?        Demand responses    can do it?  │
        │                Clear Goals                  │
        └─────────────────────────────────────────┘
                              ↓
┌──────────────────────────────────────────────────────────┐
│ Relevance?      Meets needs and aspirations   Comprehensible? │
└──────────────────────────────────────────────────────────┘
                              ↓
        ┌─────────────────────────────────────────┐
        │ Optimum Challenge, Skills, Resources and Time │
        └─────────────────────────────────────────┘
                              ↓
              ┌──────────────────────────┐
              │ Critical Learning Situations │
              └──────────────────────────┘
                              ↓
                    ┌──────────────┐
                    │  Reflection  │
                    └──────────────┘
                              ↓
                ┌────────────────────────┐
                │ Progress and achievement │
                └────────────────────────┘
```

| Personal Experience | Situational | Identification | Involvement | Peer Activity | Repetition Reinforc't | Heroic Personal | Utility and Imagination |

But that is only a part of the story. To maximize the effectiveness of teaching it needs to be an example. The well-tested statement that 'it' is both caught and taught identifies a particular characteristic of Jesus' teaching. His followers enjoyed their experiences and entered into the power of his teaching. It was taking the ceiling off life to reveal new possibilities. Its liberating effects touched both their faith and their imagination. These three factors of teaching (expertise x pupil involvement x enjoyment), for example, were well illustrated amongst a class of pupils with a range of special needs who had a reading age of six to seven years at the age of 11. I decided that if they were unlikely to learn a great deal at least they would enjoy it! We began by making educational language games – or rather they did. With the input of teacher expertise and a sense of exploration they produced their own learning materials and proudly made remarkable progress. They could take the games home and play with their parents and siblings and if the games were ever lost or torn, the pupils made fresh and better versions. The point is that it maximized personal involvement and gave them a surprise and freshness as new games were devised and produced. Their productions became a total readings/literacy course that was divided in 100 stages. The pupils produced and stored each stage stocking boxes. The pupils needed to progress through one stage every two days in the year. Again, in common with Jesus' followers, they gained a high degree of ownership of the activities that was motivating and translated them from reluctant to avid learners.

.2c-149
Which decisions were most crucial to his teaching?

Major issues stood out when considering how to develop such a literacy course for low achieving pupils. These can be summarized as follows:

Leadership

What expertise is needed to meet the demands of diagnostic teaching?
What decisions were needed to unify the range of experiences into a coherent course?
How could the reading scene be authentic and personalized?

Perception

What was their attitude to reading? Do they see failure or success?
What perceptual changes were needed after six years of failure?
How could I train pupils to see literacy as friendly and helpful etc?

Motivation

How could the pupils *extrinsic* motivation be developed?
How can pupils achieve *ownership* of their literacy?
How could *intrinsic* motivation be created within the pupils?

Memory

How could literacy be made pleasantly memorable in itself?
How could their memory skills the maximized?
How can memories of literacy be elaborated?

Socialization

How could a fundamental attitude change be achieved?
How could literacy become a non-fearful norm?
How would a fundamental attitude change be achieved?

Cognition

How could the literacy be related to the pupils existing mental scenaria?
Which aspects of literacy would be assimilated / accommodated?
How would the notion of brain patterning be used?

Emotion

How could the pleasure principle be adopted?
How could pupils enjoy the literacy experiences?

In Part C eight teaching styles implicitly used by Jesus will be considered. It is worth noting their particular application to teaching literacy. They will illustrate how pupils make *secure, sequential progress* (strategy 6), use *precise instructions* (strategy 1), have a definitive *knowledge basis* (strategy 7), experience *teaching and learning styles* (strategies 2 and 3), and *attain the path for flexible skills* (strategy 4/5).

.2c-150
When are assumptions listed above are most questionable?

The teacher as a reader (practitioner)

Jesus led by inspiration and example and was a skilled and delighted practitioner. The wonder of converting the shape of letters into an infinite range of meanings and new possibilities can be lost if the teacher is barely proficient. When Jesus said, "I am the Way" he was not merely teaching, he was inviting others to follow him along a path that was greater than they could imagine. No doubt his spiritual characteristics would be revealed in a similar way if teaching literacy. He would use the panoply of emotions from his own experiences and enjoyment as a reader. His teaching of literacy would certainly be characterized by *expertise* but also by *leadership, pleasurable inspiration and ongoing delight* in the literature. Passivity would have no place as he felt the *power and significance* of what he was teaching. He would *reveal new possibilities* that were only limited by the imagination. He *regarded learners highly* and knew that as a leader his specific role was enrichment. He can be seen as a master craftsman with a commitment to quality as he met people's needs and aspirations. He was leading them from a problematic present into an undreamed of future. His pupils or apprentices could watch, observe and copy what he was doing. They proudly identified with him as they learned by involvement, interaction and replication. As they watched him the group could enter into his insights and skills. In such a context as literacy, it would be an ongoing experience as well as enhanced knowledge. With enthusiasm he would 'extend their coasts' beyond functionalism. He would not deny the importance of functional needs but he would show them the possibilities of the treasures that lay before them in literacy. Just as Jesus took people beyond formal belief into spirituality, so he would take them into the world of literacy and all that implies. As he revealed the range of skills, he knew that only by extensive practice could they develop proficiency, but this did not mean the death of creativity. As a participant reader he would extend reading into a new but demanding world of literacy... or of course art, music, science etc.

In Jesus' teaching one senses creative faith sweeping the disciples on and this potent force being replicated in them. And so, perhaps the rapid progress of my pupils in literacy had something in common with a far greater teacher being copied on this personal professional 'pilgrimage'.

And so Part B is concluded with a statement and a question.

Jesus, the teacher / leader had a clear perception of his task, motivated pupils and gave them powerful memories that became their inspiration as they modelled their lives and thinking on him – and it was achieved with a range of identifiable skills that involved many valid experiences and emotions – it was memorable and 'path-striking'. How can something similar be achieved in the 21st century?

.2c-151
How might Jesus have used the natural environment to teach literacy?

Chapter 13

Teaching Methods in the Gospel according to John

In Part A there was a survey of Jesus' teaching methods as recorded in Matthew's Gospel. It included such aspects as those listed below. As you read John's Gospel trace these aspects and note the similarities and differences between them and those in Matthew.

Figure 100

1. Personal preparation	16. Reflections
2. The teacher's faith	17. Secure judgments
3. Attracted attention	18. Trusted and challenged pupils
4. Teacher's authority	19. Enhanced knowledge
5. Cultural expectations	20. Used a variety of methods
6. Core message	21. Faced personal challenge
7. Demonstrations / actions revealed ability	22. Teaches at different levels
8. Character and manner encouraged	23. Faced disappointments positively
9. Invited pupils	24. Persistent
10. Non-coercive control	25. Variable support
11. Promised to meet goals	26. Taught from the "Big Picture"
12. The basis of rules and principles	27. Celebration
13. Acted as a role model	28. Crisis resolution
14. Defensive care of pupils	29. Justified actions / decisions
15. Used participant helpers	30. Saw the long term challenge

Chapter 1

- Having seen and lived with Jesus, John's overriding impression was of his *authority* and *character*. He was seen as the Word who was full of *grace and truth*.
- Jesus *built on existing developments* – the work of John the Baptist.
- Jesus *observed* the disciples – e g Nathaniel – and had criteria for selection which were vital in the long term.
- Jesus partially taught in that the *established prophetic tradition*, and was recognized by his cousin John the Baptist who used a symbolic language – the Lamb of God – which had *relevance* for his listener.

Chapter 2

Verses 1–12. Jesus was *unpretentious* but *responsive* to faith at the wedding.

Verses 13–23. He lived and taught within the customs of the land. He quickly displayed his *courage and standards* when he cleansed the temple. He required that the place be fit for purpose, honesty, order, clarity etc.

Verse 25. Jesus knew what was in man.

Chapter 3

Verses 1–15. An informal conversation with a stranger who might have been regarded as part of the opposition.

1. Jesus *accepted* the Pharisee, Nicodemus and *spoke* to him in *his own terms*. He spoke to Nicodemus in *metaphors* and gave him time to reflect.
2. Note the emphatic I.

.2c-152
To what extent was Jesus both inclusive and exclusive as a teacher?

3. 'born anew' – a typical phrase in an unusual context.
4. 'the Kingdom of God' – a common *aspiration*.
5. the wind – Using a *natural phenomenon* as a spiritual metaphor.
6. The distinction between Jesus' conception of spiritual truth and Pharisaic custom (the Law of Moses).
7. Jesus used established *symbolism* based on Moses.
8. The teacher was *seen* and *recognized* as having *authority*.
9. Verse 22. Jesus referred back to the symbolism of baptism.
10. Verse 35. The great *ongoing theme* of the Father and the Son was emphasized.

Chapter 4

Jesus showed that he had *no prejudices* and travelled through Samaria. Also, he showed his teaching policy had no exclusions.

- He used an incidental meeting.
- He developed a conversation based on their situational context, his needs and her capabilities.
- The conversation was interactive and he spoke into the pupils situation but beyond her understanding.
- The moment of insight was the moment of her recognition of Jesus.
- The questioning process was used by Jesus to enable him to get to the heart of his supreme purpose.
- Verse 29. The people readily recognized Jesus as the Christ but *at their own level*.
- Pupils responded to what they heard/saw/felt/experienced.
- The people in Samaria felt acute needs.
- They had aspirations that they felt might be satisfied by Jesus. Their amazement was real.

Verse 30. Note the *key words* that are taken from *everyday life* and *personal observations*. My food – harvest – reaping, sewing, wages, labour. He was talking in riddles and expecting the people to *reflect* on what he had said. The pupils began to *share attitudes* and *set levels of belief* that became the basis of long-term learning.

Verse 40. The teacher expected to assert his *authority*.

Verse 43. He returned to Galilee where he had a mixed reception.

- An Herodian asked for help – and got it.
- The capacity of the teacher to establish capabilities and expectations that were realizable was crucial.
- Pupils needed to see action to develop belief. Again there was no sense of exclusivity.

Chapter 5

Verses 1–15. Jesus taught by signs and *demonstration*

- He was *helped the excluded*, the helpless and the needy – a person who had been neglected by the religious people – the Good Samaritan in action?
- Jesus *commanded* the man to do what he thought he could not do.
- His teaching was *creating joy and expectations* – such a teacher developed an authoritative position.
- Jesus had a righteous authority – that was recognizable and a challenge.

.2c-153
Why might the principle of using pupils' resources maximize learning?

Verse 17. The *core message* was emphasized.

Verse 18. Jesus recognized that the opposition was strengthened as people felt their position was challenged.

- Here was a direct conflict between conformity and spirituality (v.42).
- Jesus could challenge the Jews with confidence because he was under authority and so had authority.
- He was perceptive in seeing are the motives of other people.

Verse 45. Once again Jesus used Moses and tradition as his authority when talking to the Jews that was *appropriate*. Another example of symbolism being used.

Chapter 6

- Jesus taught in a *practical* way by *meeting needs*.
- He *saw and responded* to the situation and used it to translate the *concrete into the spiritual*.
- Jesus *the enabler* was an attractive aspect of his teaching.
- This teacher *used what the pupils* had and *maximized it*, which was incredibly *motivating*.

The teaching situation was characterized by *orderliness* and in *mutual teamwork*.

- Without performing miracles teachers could still *multiply rather than divide* what the pupils have to meet what they need.
- He was getting the pupils into a habit of being *tidy and wasting nothing*.
- The teacher's working was his evidence and the basis of trust.
- The teacher was *aware* of the *difficulties* and *recognized* that there was a ready helper. The meagre *help of the pupil* was the turning point in a situation.
- Such pupils wanted to follow and inquire to some degree. Although the teacher was going beyond their understanding everything was based upon their *experience and established tradition*.
- The crowd's *response* – they wanted to force him into their own mould. Instead the *teacher decides the direction!*

Verse 16–21. The teacher is always waiting to *help* and is at hand as a source of *continual encouragement* – verse 20.

- He had appeared to leave them to their own devices but the *teacher support was available*.

Verse 22–40. People followed him *because* their physical *needs* had been met. This was no bad thing, but it justified Jesus' attitudes in the temptations regarding turning stones into bread.

The teacher was essentially the *leader of the situation*

- Jesus talked to them in their own terms – Moses and the manna.
- Jesus' greater purpose – the teacher should see a greater purpose than the pupils.
- Note again that the core message was continually mentioned.
- He was a *caring teacher* who would *raise the mark* but ultimately everyone was required to *recognize themselves* and their *long-term learning*.

Verses 41–65. In a synagogue at Capernaum. A critical moment as the Jews looked at him. What might be a typical response by Jesus? But consider the *degree of difference in understanding* between Jesus and the Jews – they did not understand what he was saying.

Verse 66. The harder or demanding saying revealed that the teacher gave his pupils *options* – but did they want to follow them through or not?

.2c-154
Why might Jesus as a teacher make it difficult for people to understand?

- They had a *simple choice* and Jesus did not insist or coerce pupils to become learners.
- The learners had to be *assured* of the *authority, skill and overall abilities* of the teacher – but there were always be those who pretended to be learners and would have a wrong view of the teacher.
- His true pupils recognized that there was nobody else who could *meet their needs and aspirations.*

Chapter 7

- How often the degree of opposition could *divert the work and progress* of the teacher.
- No matter how good a teacher he was, he would not be accepted by all.

Verse 10. The teacher had the sense of being alone.

Verse 15. Jesus' authoritative teaching was illustrated by *involvement, conviction and truth.*
- The issue of authority was at the heart of all teaching.

Verse 19. Back to Moses again! Jesus was being forced to justify the quality and goodness of his work even though it was *self-evident.*

Verse 25. Truth was divisive. There is never total consensus.

Verse 32. Recognize hatred against goodness when tradition and personal standing were questioned.

Verse 37. The teacher was *protected by his works.* Jesus again *taught out of the situational context* – using the *moment* and the *place.* His *wisdom was evident*

Verse 40. Here we see in division a *degree of hope* (Nicodemus) the *seed had been sown* with no apparent outcome but there was the *opportunity for gestation*

Chapter 8

Verses 1–11 *Wisdom and separation* – the teacher will often take a different path than his pupils.
- *Mercy* frustrated critical judgment. Is critical judgment the norm for maintaining tradition?
- Jesus frequently did not enter into a debate or argument but simply *answered critical questions with a simple statement or question.*

Verse 12. Again a statement is based on the situational context. The power of the metaphor!

The opposition seemed reasonable but what was the justification?

Verses 23–30. Unbelievers - critical and non-supporters could not hope to understand Jesus' teaching. Note the allusion to their authority (verse 28).

Verse 31. Jesus would *not compromise* with the opposition.
- Again Jesus alluded to their traditional authority.
- The Jews were *bound* by their own *preconceptions* and couldn't understand the new ideas (or new wine bottles).
- Strangely Jesus made it difficult for the opposition to understand. He had a *sense of mission* but constantly use tradition to confront tradition.
- The teacher needed to know himself.

Chapter 9

Verse 1–12. Jesus used the people's *figures of speech* in a familiar place.
- He healed/taught by using a *kinaesthetic aid*- mud!
- Even those who had been taught barely understood.

.2c-155
In what ways can the Good Shepherd principle be applied in general teaching?

Verses 13–23. The opposition was adamant and could be likened to the traditional versus progressives.
- There was no compromise because of the entrenched positions.

Verses 35–41. Jesus went to *find the person he had helped* – even after apparent separation. This further raised the level of opposition and *ultimately the pupil must stand on his own feet*.

Chapter 10

Verses 1–18. Jesus talked to the Jews. He used his favourite metaphor – the Good Shepherd.
- Is this a discourse or has it been shortened? Jesus tended to have *succinct deliveries*.
- The *complexity of ideas* used by Jesus is partially *simplified* by the use of *common situation* with figures of speech.
- He had been *acting out* in chapter 9 what he was *now teaching*.
- This teacher had both courage and was faithful to those he taught, and his sacrificial lifestyle was evident.
- His authority was based on his actions.

Chapter 11

Verses 1-4. The crisis arose – note that *every teaching situation must be turned into a positive one* otherwise the pupils might collapse.
- The teacher could *see the long term*.
- Pupils could be *disappointed* in their teacher.

Verses 5–16. The teacher had a *clear strategy* that was *unclear to the pupils* – indeed it is beyond their comprehension.
- The pupils were becoming discouraged and disappointed but the teacher had courage and would not be turned back – how often do *teachers give up* especially when everything depends upon them?
- Religious talk was not good enough (verse 11) – *plain speaking* is needed.
- Jesus was *fearless* when faced with a mountainous problem.

Verses 17-27. So often pupils cannot see the full plan and capacity of the teacher that *the seed of hope/faith must be developed*.
- The teacher made *dramatic* hard sayings, *demands* on the pupil and the need for a *positive response was striking*.

Verses 28-37. It was imperative to make the *pupils aware of the capacity of the teacher*.
- We come to the moment of truth!
- The teacher needed to go beyond words and demonstrate his meanings.
- The teacher had to allow for total misunderstanding.

Verses 38-44. The responsibility of an enabling teacher is to give confidence and take a situation in hand.
- He himself had to draw upon the authority of the Father.

Verses 45-57. Teachers were not surprised when even in the face of evidence some maintained or increased their opposition vehemently. *Opposition* is not necessarily produced by truth.

.2c-156
Jesus wanted his pupils to do greater things than he – how are pupils equipped for this?

Chapter 12

Verses 1–11. There was such a *range of pupils* – dedicated students who wanted to be active.
- The learners needed to have something for which they can be really *thankful* and they wanted to hang on to every word.
- Teachers should be thoroughly *appreciative of their pupils*

Verses 12–19. This was most unusual and surprising that *each servant teacher is recognized* even if crowd support is limited in its effects.
- Again, history shows that opposition knew no reason.

Verses 20–36. Let all pupils be included.
- Jesus used a simple illustration to reveal a greater truth.
- Emphatic teaching – certain imperatives cannot be avoided.
- One cannot romanticize. There are hard sayings and teaching can cost a great deal.

Verses 37–43. How often teachers are unable to teach because of opposition.
- Even earnest learners can give away to vehement opposition.

Verses 44–50. The teacher was in his desperate extremity!
- It was true that non-learners ultimately bring judgement on themselves and walk in darkness whereas the *learners walk in degrees of light*.

Chapter 13

Verses 1–20. This is a powerful truth. The fact was that the *good teacher was a role-model*. He was a servant to his pupils and the pupils could then follow in the teacher's footsteps.

Verses 21–30 Some pupils betrayed their teacher and tried to take short cuts etc. – but to no avail – they would walk into the night.

Verses 31–35. The teacher said, "even as I have——-you——-" This was the role model. There was no alternative or short cut from the teacher's way.

Verses 36–38. Pupils meant well but were *prone to failure but can be restored*.

Chapter 14

Verses 1–11. This discourse is peppered with *promises, metaphors, appreciation* etc., all of which makes it memorable.

Verse 1. a *positive and a typically personal* statement.

Verse 2. a common metaphor that Jesus had probably used frequently This was a highly personalized vision of the Father. The *lack of understanding* must have *disappointed Jesus just as it would any teacher*.

There was the problem of taking pupils so far from their initial understanding and making serious demands upon them that it causes them to ask how much are they understand.

Verse 11. The value of *experiential learning* was highly significant. The degree of mysticism may *appear straightforward to the teacher but not to the pupil*.

Verses 12–14 The teacher *encouraged them* by giving a threefold *promise*. In the long term pupils may not rely on the teacher – but they *could move in the spirit of the teacher* and so move on.

.2c-157
When might you teach even though the pupils are not likely to understand?

Verses 15–24. The key issues of the Father, the abiding spirit, the ongoing support were reiterated over and over again, but that would only be *understood later in retrospect*. The manner of the teaching was to *maximize memorisation*.

Verses 25–31. The role model approached the great and final demonstration of all he taught with promises which they still did not understand. The *teacher's long-term faith in the blessing he left was so essential if it is to remain at the forefront of their memory.*

Chapter 15

Verses 1–17. This important passage shows Jesus taught what one suspects was his favourite mode, a *serious conversation* in which *he took the lead*. Again Jesus used a common and favourite metaphor that was likely to be memorable.

- He was talking in conversational terms but not discussing the content of his message – *this was a time of instruction*. His instruction draws upon their *experience* with him, and *uses that past experience to teach a higher truth*. His authority was both that he claimed to be the Son of God but also that he was the role model that he had presented to them.
- His teaching was based on proven trust, love and a settled relationship. He made significant promises as well as preparing them for the horror that was to come.
- He made one serious commandment, namely that they should love one another as he had loved them (the role model) and this commandment he emphatically repeated (verse 12 and verse 17).
- He stressed that they were *a privileged people* who had been chosen by him for a unique purpose.

Verses 18–27. Having said so many positive things to strengthen, Jesus warned them of the hatred to come. This was an *appropriate instructional sequence*. He emphasized the process of *identification* with him and *reiterated an important promise* that they would be enabled to carry on his work. One suspects that he had talked about the Holy Spirit frequently, just as he had spoken of the Father. Note how *the teaching consisted of both the method and an appropriate development of content*.

Chapter 16

In this continuation of chapters 14 and 15 Jesus in effect said that what has happened to him was going to happen to them. One suspects *that he knew that they did not really understand* the full implications of what he was saying that *they would do* as they *experienced* the truth of them.

Verses 4–15. It is almost certain that the disciples could not have understood the significance of these verses about the Holy Spirit, but on Pentecost they would be able to say, 'Ah! Now I know.' Therefore, Jesus was not confining his teaching to a simple system of mastery but he *raised issues, questions, curiosity, challenge and reassurance*.

Verses 16–33. The disciples showed that they did not understand Jesus (verse 18). He recognised this and brought together the unvarnished facts of his suffering together with confidence about the Father, prayer and the Holy Spirit. Note how in true Jewish fashion *he spoke in concrete terms* and used the metaphor of a mother giving birth to a baby. Jesus brings this passage to a conclusion with a stark warning and a promise of peace. The *balance was very neatly achieved as Jesus concludes with a typical encouragement saying,' Be of good cheer.*

.2c-158
What are the most brilliant examples of teaching in John's Gospel?

In these three chapters it is possible to see Jesus' teaching method beginning and ending in *building up confidence amongst his pupils*. He showed them that *he had been a role-model* which *they had to copy*. He used appropriate metaphors. *The ideas were complex* but the *language was simple*. The warnings were stark but *the promises were great for teaching was highly personalized* in terms of his Father (mentioned 46 times with 10 promises), Jesus himself (mentioned 181 times), the Holy Spirit (mention 26 times) and the disciples themselves (mentioned 176 times).

Chapter 17

This is not a chapter that illustrates Jesus' teaching methods, but it does show that *the teacher was totally committed to his pupils and would continue to be so both in the present and the future*. He was also *concerned for the outcome of their work*. The key words might be regarded as *guarded, confidence, keep, consecrated*.

Chapter 18

Verses 1–11. Jesus as the role model, *protected his disciples* (first 8) and showed that he was a *man of peace* (verse 11). *He was emphatically acting out his teaching.*

Verses 12–40. Notice how little Jesus had to say to people who are opposing him for no good cause.

Chapter 19

Verses 1–37. All of the teaching here was a *public demonstration* of his previous teaching

Verses 38–42. What a triumph for Jesus' teaching of Nicodemus. He had *pondered on a difficult concept, gradually came to the truth, talked to his friend Joseph and finally showed a commitment to Jesus*.

Chapter 20

Verses 1–10. The teacher was now beginning to produce the ultimate evidence that he has been correct all along but it was still a mystery to the disciples. *How he persevered.*

Verses 11–18. Jesus *talked to his pupils personally, and appropriately* and led them onto the next stage. It was all done quietly in a spirit of compassion.

Verses 19–32. Despite the evidence that pupils were still frightened he came to them with *words of promise and an authority* to forgive sins that was a sign of their divine commission.
- Jesus considered his disciples/pupils individually and so he treated Thomas appropriately.

Chapter 21

Verses 1–14. This is brilliant *experiential teaching* in which he proved his authority and *brought together memories and sensory, emotional, social and spiritual experiences*.

Verses 15–23. Another piece of brilliant teaching. It was *given personally to the man who denied him and so now he was being asked to confess his love without being criticized*. The pupil understandably had a certain reticence and was only gradually capable of answering Jesus. *The teacher then showed his pupil that he was fully restored and had a commission that would involve a cost. Notice that Jesus treated each disciple differently - this was a good example of individualized teaching.*

Personality Factor – 12

What match existed between the teaching style of Jesus and his personality factors.

.2c-159
What are the implications of "acting out your teaching"?

Part C

Making It Happen

An Overview of Strategies and Methods

Looking forward

A Sketch of Teaching and Learning

Spirituality – definitions,, Jesus Focus, Spiritual Intelligence

Eight teaching strategies considered

Ultimate teaching strategy Part C

Jesus' teaching methods in Luke's Gospel

Conclusion.. A theory of instruction?

A theory of learning?

Their cross curricular application

Personality factors of Jesus

"Teaching is the proclamation of hope."

William Barclay

Parts A and B indicated most of these aspects of this Master Teacher. Part C will now consider certain of these as they might be seen today

.2c-160
Why was Jesus' teaching style suited to his work?

Looking forward to Part C

The ultimate challenge in Part C is not to analyse Jesus' teaching style *per se* but to show the relevance today. Part C is in two sections:

- Jesus was teaching spirituality using forms of what we might regard as eight current strategies and therefore that is a focus.
- To use these insights to indicate how they can be organized into a coherent plans to teach most subjects and skills to a wide range of abilities and age groups.

In Parts A and B the major components of Jesus' strategies were identified. These will now be integrated into his working practice and incorporated into our contemporary teaching. Indeed, perhaps, Jesus' generic methods can promote a freshness for all concerned. For me personally this is illustrated by the fact that at the time of writing this, I have been involved in teaching literacy skills in the UK, RE projects and devising skills for teaching literacy in ill- equipped African schools and all this is rooted in methods related to those used by Jesus.

To simplify this, the following five part overview of the teacher, his pupils and the major teaching strategies and methods (Fig.102) has been drawn up to pave the way for an awareness of links between teaching in the 1st. and 21st.centuries and might be used profitably as an advance organiser and point of reference.

Although much of Jesus' teaching was incidental, using impromptu situations, one can see the dynamic interplay of the eight strategies and related methods being used that can be translated into our contemporary uses in more highly structured forms.

Jesus' priority was not as a code of practice to be enforced but as *a living vision to be encompassed*. But questions remain, for example:

- Has the teacher the will, time and skills to make contact with the pupils?
- Have the pupils the desire/motivation to make contact with the teacher?

Jesus did not impose himself on people who could reject what he said. He convinced them they were significant and so rejoiced through teaching based on *relationships* that provided a sense of *worth with prospects* – a *value* that is still paramount.

Figure 101 briefly highlights the nub of the problem addressed in Part C. Jesus matched the teaching with individual responsibility to learn. He maximized learning possibilities that ensured the pupils would be less likely to wander from the 'flock'. As needs and aspirations were met so they chose to become disciples. He had become their *'significant or knowledgeable other'*. His teaching methods were coherent and maximized learning. We can identify how Jesus used the following:

Figure 101

Personal qualities	The structure of learning
1. Personal development	1. Valid agreed goals
2. Values - religious or not (character)	2. Appropriate strategies for efficient learning
3. A desire to identify with the teacher	3. Effective methods and techniques
4. Allowing generic drivers to develop	4. Ongoing long-term developments
5. Sympathetic insights yield appropriate responses	5. Criteria for evaluating success

.2c-161
What would you consider to have been two major feature of Jesus' teaching skills?

Figure 102

An overview of the Teacher, the student, teaching strategies and methods	
Some major aspects that might be reviewed within a fresh context	
The Teacher	**The Students and Relationships**

A. The recognized authoritative leader- of both self and others
The role model –credible
A distinctive 'value-based' character
An attitude of acceptance, forgiveness and inclusion
A visionary with unique concepts / lifestyle
Personal courage
 	
B. Recognized proven abilities
An ascribed authority
A powerful motivator
A purposeful vision to be achieved
Revealed truth
Values and core concepts are absolute
An interpreter
Evoked personal faith and expectations
An enabler/ established capabilities
 	
C. Fostered new relationships
Taught /generated life qualities-faith, love, hope
A degree of mutual admiration
 	
D. Provided nurture and protection
	A Need satisfaction- spiritual
	    social
	    physical
	    emotional
	    cognitive
	
	B Aspirational satisfaction
	    Continuity- past, present, future
	
	C Shared cultural / community norms
	    Security
	    Clear unequivocal demands
	
	D Deference, submission
	    Similance (imitate), agree, believe
	    Affiliation
	    Faith evokes faith
	    Mutual admiration
	    Growing shared conscience
	
	E Confidence- superiority
	    Faith to copy, build, extend etc

Major Teaching Strategies	**Major Teaching Methods**

A Teacher led decision making
    Option based student involvement
    Disciplined involvement
    Close teacher-pupil living and teaching
 	
B. Master teacher /mentor based teaching
    Apprenticeship learning
    Imitation / role modelling
    Cultural investigation
    Value / attitudinal based learning
    Relational teaching / learning
    Affiliation / cooperative based involvement
 	
C. Meaningful experiential learning
    Peripatetic needs response teaching
    Incidental community care-based teaching
    Practical service
    Range of peer group activities
    Created joyous expectations
    Concept based learning
    Concept attainment
 	
D. Develop established, traditional knowledge
    Central core message developed
    Go beyond established knowledge but within agreed principles
 	
Figure 102 (Part 2-seeFig.39
	A Oracy
	    Instruction
	    Discourse
	    Dialogue/conversation
	    Discussion
	    Aphorism/ symbolic language etc
	    Short stories
	    Illustrative statements
	    Questioning
	    Recall and reinforcement
	    Similarity and difference/ contrast
	    Used tradition
	
	B Thinking skills eg.
	    cause and effect
	    prediction
	    projection etc
	
	C Kinaesthetic experiences
	    Multi-sensory experiences
	    Incidental life experiences
	
	D Visualization /imagination
	    Demonstrations
	
	E Memorable situations
	    Emotional arousals
	    Dramatic and vicarious Involvement

.2c-162
What were the major features of Jesus' teaching style?

Chapter 14

A sketch of teaching and learning

Teaching and learning cannot be equated. Teaching often fails to translate into learning, especially when it demands attitude change! He taught many who agreed with him but how many learned? Teachers seldom *communicate* all they intend, as Jesus found when people were spellbound by their experiences. New horizons were opened amidst the fun and awe, pleasure and surprise, discipline and satisfaction, and personal needs and aspirations being met but there was also anger from those who felt displaced. Ability normally exceeds attainment, but how can potential be maximized? Ideally, the first task is to know *how* people learn and then to *match the teaching and learning* but often learners are matched to general teaching methods that may be inappropriate.

From the drama and interpersonal nature of Jesus teaching, we can clarify his priorities. He met many expectations logically. For example, he developed concepts within social and spiritual contexts as when reconciliation was graphically illustrated in the parable of the Prodigal Son. Similarly the shepherd leader (himself) was clearly committed to restoring the wandering sheep (the surrounding people) from danger. Jesus' process of teaching could be received by those who had 'ears to hear' within an ethos of love and morality.

Jesus' teaching integrated great themes such as God's attitude to the poor that incorporated much of what is now called social, emotional and spiritual intelligences. His guiding principles moved from the *known to the unknown, concrete to the abstract and the specific to the general*. These were enveloped within positive relationships and spiritual discipline. Learning is usually incomplete but he produced long-term learners by including what Jensen has called the three keys to goal acquisition, namely:

- Developing personal beliefs and a sense of their own capability
- Establishing clear goals
- Harnessing their emotions and drives.

The quality of Jesus' teaching is gauged by its *effectiveness* to inculcate lifelong learning amongst unproven followers. He knew that he could not rely upon the crowds who cheered him on! Therefore, he only gave them a general exposure of his message, with deeper teaching to his close pupils... but even that was not detailed. There was an order and methodology in his teaching, but it was not exhaustive. He used that which conveyed his core message. Imagine how he taught the Beatitudes as short memorable statements, akin to the Ten Commandments. In his holistic approach he did not burden them with obscure, detailed ideas as the Pharisees did.

His powerful oral and visual *initial stimuli* attracted crowds. Few grasped the implications of his words, but images and memorable 'sound bites' remained to be discussed later and so his message was reinforced as he travelled. These moments formed the basis of impressions, expectancy and motivation. Memories, though unreliable, were activated and were a basis of faith. To achieve this his pupils needed learning that was:

- experiential (I know because I did it!).
- experimental (personally testing new knowledge).
- conceptualized (understanding the ideas, rather than merely remembering information, and applying them in differing situations).
- providing ample opportunities for reinforcement and reflection.
- evaluative - arriving at decisions about the value of what had been learnt.

Pupils are at least as important as the information being taught. He knew that f*aith and vision* were *caught* and information could be added later. This principle was exemplified as he drew upon what was authoritative to both the listeners and himself, rather than emphasize minor matters. A parallel can be seen today in the significance given to *relevant* environmental matters in schools. It appears that Jesus knew that progress is greater when based upon success and acceptance His teaching, therefore, was adapted to the nature and needs of those concerned as he aroused

.2c-163
Which do you regard as being the three most significant variables shown in Fig.102?

desires and curiosity. It was evident that although teaching methods are usually typical of their culture, many of Jesus' decisions are recognizable today.

As we move into a 21st century interpretation and application of the underlying principles of Jesus' teaching methods a problem that can typically exist is to assume a top-down definition of aims and objectives just as Jesus knew that he should have priority. This issue persists. Should the appointed leaders define the goals or should learners influence goal-making decisions (see ch.2). This poses questions about order, authority, control etc. Jesus could impose this 'top down' process amongst many because he was recognized as having wisdom, expertise / power and an admirable character.

His Product and Process Goals

By the age of 12 Jesus was confident of the Fatherhood of God. Over the next 18 years his conviction matured and he recognized how his work would be achieved. By prayer, observation and reflection / revelation Jesus planned how his goals would be attained. These took two distinct forms that are termed 'product' and 'process' goals'. Jesus announced the Kingdom of God as a *fact* to be recognized (a product goal) and how people would *develop or become disciples* as an ongoing enactment of faith (a process goal).

Product goals are identifiable understandings / standards to be gained whereas the process goals are attitudes, skills etc which develop during learning. This does not imply that one is superior to the other, it is simply a convenient differentiation.

Jesus' specific product goals were taught, learned and developed as the pupils worked together and acquired Jesus' understanding of faith, service etc. Also they caught his faith and attitudes and internalised them into a lifestyle. Likewise, Jesus' teaching required both product and process goals to be at the forefront of consciousness, Jesus' death was his best example of uniting product and process goals.

The notion that understanding is "always under construction" (Brown et al) emphasizes that the two types of goals often overlap. There were defined beliefs and commands (ie product) but there was also the ongoing lifestyle that revealed the process goals. Although these were spiritual product and process goals it is possible to give Jesus' spiritual goals a wider application.

Product goals	*Process goals*
To understand and believe that Jesus is the Messiah	To become disciples who learned to obey Jesus' revelation
To understand and trust in the Fatherhood of God	To have faith in and practise the lifestyle of the Father
To understand the principles of repentance, reconciliation etc	To repent and be in a state of trusting fellowship with the Father
To understand the values of the messianic lifestyle (e.g. to forgive, to love your enemies Figure 102	To live out the values of the messianic life as demonstrated by Jesus (e.g. to forgive 70 times 7)

Personality Factor – 13

Bearing in mind how you perceive Jesus' personality how might he achieve his product and process goals?

.2c-164
Is knowledge always under construction?

Chapter 15

Definitions of Spirituality

This chapter acts as necessary bridge between Parts A/B and ch.16 onwards where modern strategic developments are considered in some detail.

Given that Jesus' major concern was to enhance spirituality, it is appropriate to initially consider a range of his methods in the context of these particular goals and then translate them more broadly into the current scene.

Spirituality has been traditionally perceived and defined in religious terms and especially through prayers, hymns and readings from the Bible. As such it was relatively easy to teach in an acceptable manner. But as society has become multicultural and moved towards post-modern lifestyles, traditional practices have been questioned and deemed to be educationally ineffective and even immoral.

Recently spirituality as a concept has had a revival, but within wider competing definitions. The question is now whether spirituality is anything more than a vague general term related to non-material thought.

The task here is to consider the teaching of spirituality in an educational setting that may or may not include religious education. An analysis such as this seeks to prevent this facet of human experience being reduced to dry forms, and be dealt with sensitively to make it meaningful and accessible to all. This requires adequate definition(s) and answers to the following questions:

Does it meet recognizable criteria for being regarded as spirituality?

What is permissible?

To what degree is it teachable?

What can be taught that is worthwhile and of long-term value and needs?

Can it meet current expectations?

One hesitates to regard spirituality as problematic, but any problems must be met. Here 8 strategies are outlined to promote it as a stimulus rather than an issue. The parameters within which it is written are the three dominant definitions of spirituality.

- *Theistic (notably Christianity, Judaism & Islam) interpretations and religious assumptions.*
- *Non-theistic religious concepts (notably Buddhist)*
- *A post-modern social psychological mode commonly built into school curricula.*

These need not be wholly mutually exclusive. Each has particular characteristics. Whereas Jesus talked about restoring a spiritual relationship between God and man, and Gautama the Buddha wanted man to rediscover his inner self, a typical post-modern blanket statement is found in the Handbook for Inspection of Schools (1994 page 86).

'*Spiritual development relates to that aspect of inner life through which pupils acquire insights into their personal experience which are of enduring worth.. It is characterized by reflection, the attribution of meaning to experience, valuing non-material dimensions to life and intimations of an enduring reality.. Spirituality is not synonymous with religion; and all areas of the curriculum may contribute towards the pupils' spiritual development.*'

This non-religious definition led to an Ofsted discussion paper that stated '*spiritual development is about how individuals acquire personal beliefs and values, determine whether life has a purpose, and how they behave as a result. It is about how pupils address 'questions which are at the heart of existence'. It involves the idea of a spiritual quest, and asking who and where are you going?* This general definition of spiritual development would be expected to involve:

.2c-165
What is spirituality?

- *Beliefs* – the development of personal beliefs including religious beliefs, people have individual and shared beliefs on which they base their lives; they develop understandings of how beliefs influence personal identity;
- *A sense of, wonder and mystery* – being inspired by the natural world, mystery or human achievement;
- *Experiencing feelings of transcendence*, that may give rise to the belief in the existence of a divine being or in the ability to rise above everyday experiences;
- *Search for meaning and purpose* – asking 'Why me?' at times of hardship and suffering; Reflecting on the origins and purpose of life; responding to the challenging experiences of life such as beauty, suffering and death;
- *Self knowledge* – an awareness of one's self in terms of thoughts, feelings, emotions, responsibilities and experiences; a growing understanding and acceptance of individual identity; an ability to build up relationships with others;
- *Relationships* – recognize and value the worth of each individual developing a sense of community; the ability to build up relationships with others;
- *Creativity* – express innermost thoughts and feelings through, for example, art, music, literature and crafts; exercise imagination, inspiration, intuition, insight.

The common factor in these definitions is the motivation to care for each other *and the world* – but what will be the basis of the necessary motivation and sacrifice?

Here spirituality is seen as the essence of religion. This is not to negate other forms of knowledge or definitions of spirituality, but to recognize that a prime function of religious education is spiritual sensitivity, because spirituality is greater than religion.

Figure 103

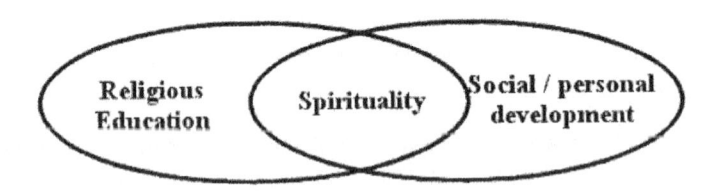

The teaching strategies will be considered within two contrasting approaches:
- Jesus' methods interpreted.
- Spiritual Intelligence and how common teaching strategies and methods can be adapted to teach spirituality within or outside religious education.

Considering a 'Jesus' type focus

Jesus' teaching methods were an expression of spirituality that consist of central tenets of life and understandings. This was based upon five elements:
- Spiritual revelation and relationships.
- Traditional/historic practices that were shared and authoritative (the Scriptures).
- Universal moral laws (Amos 5 v.24).
- Current social situations.
- Personal understandings and revelation.

His generic teaching has been interpreted and applied to contrasting cultures worldwide. The customary 'white' interpretation of Jesus' spirituality is now questioned in black Africa, and by liberation theologians in South America. He was not a white European and these new definitions and those in post-modern Britain etc. require a spiritual core that is transferable across cultures.

.2c-166
In what way might Jesus have planned his teaching ministry around spirituality?

Even so, Jesus' methods were underpinned by certainty and authority rather than exploration and debate. His common goal and norms were embodied in the Kingdom of God, the basis of which was service and sacrifice that became symbolized by a cross, a towel and a shepherd.

Although spirituality was central to Jesus, he never defined it. He described the sacred and the spiritual in everyday language and left listeners to interpret his words, even at the risk of distortion. He provided meaningful mental images but no definition! His concrete terms, provided clear stable understandings, but what did they entail in respect of spirituality and what relevance have they today?

Jesus could echo with all Jews 'the earth is the Lord's and the fullness thereof'. This incorporates within spirituality a vein of responsibility towards the world and the sense that man is securely under authority and in brotherhood with other people. Hence, the traditional God-man conception has been visualized vertically. But post-modernism where spirituality is regarded as a secular expression of emotional and moral responses, has made Jesus' spirituality debatable.

Jesus was confident that people are predisposed to spiritual matters and that God 'put eternity into the heart of man' (Ecclesiastes 3 v.11) and so he lay down spiritual pathways for 'everyman'. To him *what* spirituality is and *how* it is integral to individual and corporate living is predicated on the notion that Man is ultimately under authority but enjoys freewill. This demanded understanding and responses that could be sacrificial. Implicit in this was that spirituality is a process rather than simply a product and is seen in values, meaning making and action. Therefore, rationality is revealed in attitudes to God, self, others and the world. At its best this can be seen as a Christian quest for authentic spirituality to generate a life stance, much of which is commonly recognized within religions.

This traditional belief that spirituality consists of a life ultimately controlled by God was expressed in a modern version of a popular synagogue song from Psalm145.

> *Happy is he.... who keeps faith for ever;*
> *Who executes justice for the oppressed;*
> *Who gives food to the hungry;*
> *The Lord sets the prisoners free;*
> *The Lord opens the eyes of the blind.*
> *The Lord lifts up those who were bowed down;*
> *The Lord loves the righteous.*
> *The Lord watches over the sojourners,*
> *He upholds the widow and the fatherless;*
> *But the way of the wicked he brings to ruin.*

This was later adapted by Isaiah and subsequently Jesus read it aloud in the synagogue at Nazareth (Isaiah 61 v.1ff, Luke 4 v.18-22), Although Christianity has lost much of its simplicity, it has been the implicit definition and visual expression of spirituality. This high view of God and spirituality with such distinctive features as simplicity and restoration was described in Jesus' story of restoration – the Prodigal Son. It emphasized values and a world-view that takes account of the moral plight of man. Hence, Jesus commended actions such as the widow who gave her mite, those who visit the imprisoned, and those who provide a simple service such as a cup of water, Today Jesus' spirituality would insist on continuity with the past, and meeting the challenge of the present and the future selflessly. He spoke into his contemporary culture. Now as we move into a post-modern culture the question becomes how to interpret and carry spirituality into our contemporary culture in a 'Jesus' style by using observations and stories that are applicable to the 21st century.

Jesus' spirituality emphasized the following:
- Foundations – To develop the best of traditions 'founded' by God.
- Share his personal long term vision.
- Apply eternal principles (mercy, justice etc.).

.2c-167
Which of Jesus' goals might appear to be especially significant in the light of your goals?

- Follow the Mentor and his high-quality interaction/ relationships.
- Follow the Mentor's personal example (the definition of spirituality).
- Authoritative and absolute standards and strategies.
- Challenges within defined principles.
- It is integral to individual and corporate living.
- Man, although free is ultimately under authority but accepts it.

Figure 104

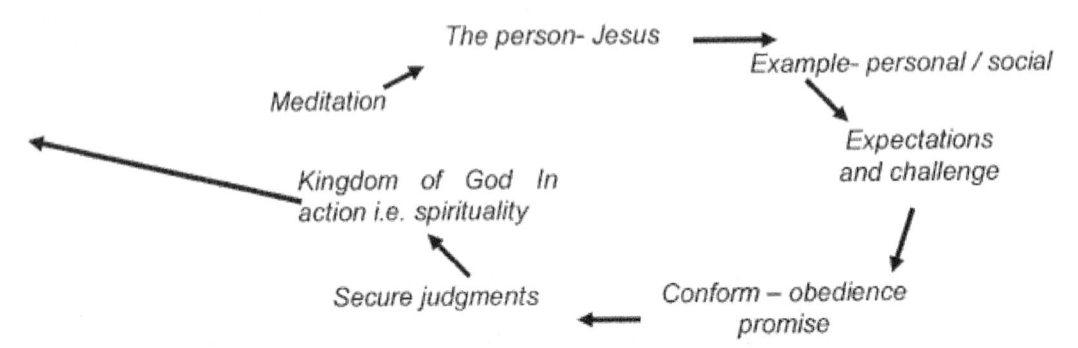

```
              The person- Jesus →
        Meditation ↗                    ↘ Example- personal / social
                                            Expectations
  ←           Kingdom of God In            and challenge
              action i.e. spirituality
                        ↑                      ↓
                    Secure judgments  ←  Conform – obedience
                                              promise
```

The teaching style of Jesus should result in a robust, sensitive view of spirituality that shapes 'the Big Society'. Its questions propose problematic answers. How do we foster care, love, inclusion etc when Jesus conceived leadership as the simplicity of servanthood? He developed his pattern of teaching, actions, and relationships from his conviction about God, himself and the world. This' view of spirituality promoted action and provided the tools to achieve it But how? It is an habitual framework for thinking that can be a basis for everyday living. This, therefore, brings together spirituality and social education. It is worth noting that the contemporary Chinese curriculum consists of four major components:

Learning to know...Learning to do...Learning to live together...Learning to be.
It appears to recognize the need to achieve social-spirituality without God.

Jesus assumed that spirituality can be applied to a conventional setting, but...
- Although he and his teaching about the Kingdom of God (ie. spirituality) can be understood cognitively that is not necessarily authentic spirituality.
- Spirituality can be learned but the role of a mentor, who is himself under authority, should show the worth of the spiritual basis being taught.
- Standards are set and relationships and expectations are established.
- It is necessary for healthy interaction, time for reflection and the opportunity to develop spirituality.
- Needs and aspirations are met in complex situations and people develop an understanding of spiritual realities and how they impinge on everyday life.

.2c-168
What is the difference between cognitive understanding and spirituality?

- There are absolute values even if people rebel against them.
- Jesus passed on the best of tradition but rejected pseudo spirituality.
- He, the mentor, recognized his pupils had free choice and responsibility.
- Spirituality relates to values seen and copied as being worthwhile.
- Much spirituality is intuitive and based on habitual norms of behaviour, thought patterns and judgments.
- Spirituality fosters sensitivity and responsibility to self, others and the world.

It will be noted that spirituality is essentially positive and creative and can be summarized by such words (process goals) as:

service	**sacrifice**	**forgiveness**	**restoration**	**acceptance**	**repentance**
giving	**creative**	**pertinacity**	**challenge**	**response**	**encouragement**

When considering goals one might ask, 'Whose goals - the teacher's or the pupil's?' Ideally they coincide but it usually involves a trade-off between them. Although Jesus responded to opportunities as they arose, he defined the goals. These goals were ultimately for the benefit of the people, rather than himself, or even God. The implications are that the teacher's goals should incorporate those of the pupils and yet exceed them. The quality of teaching is often gauged by whether this is achieved with pupils' goals being seen as relevant and motivating.

Jesus' primary goals

Let us assume that amongst Jesus' many goals the following were dominant:

To *reveal* God's character by *meeting the needs* of the poor, downtrodden etc

To *teach essential knowledge / core understandings* about the Kingdom of God.

To *create aspirations* and the *abilities* to perpetuate his work.

To *develop faith, character, skills and attitudes* to act *effectively*.

His goals varied for himself and for those around him. For example, they differed for Peter, whom he called 'the Rock', for the crowds, and yet again for the Pharisees. Furthermore, all had distinct goals in respect of Jesus. Their competing goals influenced the teaching processes that enabled his pupils to teach others.

These goals can be differentiated into long-term aims and short-term objectives. For example, Jesus' primary aim was to establish the Kingdom of God, but his objectives were, for example, to build faith in his disciples and enable them to understand the principles of the Kingdom. Today a young pigeon fancier's aim would be to win races like adults, but the objectives involved building a loft and learning the basic skills of breeding and training the pigeons, and each aspect had sub-goals to define activities more precisely. The objectives create short-term awareness of *progress, precision* and *permanence* in learning but the question remains,' Do pupils understand what is happening to them?'

One can identify a range of goals within Jesus' teaching. He had what we would call:
- Subject specific goals - knowledge, understanding of his spiritual message.
- Personal goals to fulfil his mission.
- Societal goals.
- Goals to promote skills for service.
- Moral and attitudinal goals.

.2c-169
Some believe Jesus had been a Pharisee but was disillusioned. What effect would this have on his teaching style?

In modern language they might be listed as follows:

To enable the disciples to:
- Understand the character and person of God the Father.
- Understand the nature of the Kingdom of God.
- Understanding the person and life purpose of Jesus himself.
- Understand the principles of living the life that he was stating.
- To have the skills to promote faith in others.
- To act out the role of Jesus himself.
- To be able to relate environmental features to the Kingdom of God.
- To be able to relate tradition to the Kingdom of God etc.

Such goals could then be further subdivided as follows
- To understand what should be the characteristic attitude to money.
- To understand what should be the characteristic attitude to non-Jews.

The inevitable question is, how will it be taught? To answer this we will firstly examine Jesus' teaching strategies and then consider his methods and techniques, but all in relationship to current teaching. These developed the following learning processes:
- To provide learners with *experiences* within integrated learning packages.
- Develop a *broad range of activities* within different settings.
- Foster *affective and cognitive* aspects of spiritual, social and emotional development
- Provide opportunities for disciples to *state* their *knowledge and feelings*.
- Ensure that pupils experience significant *progression*.
- Create pupils' self-awareness of achievements and prospects.
- Plan *flexible varieties* of thinking, lifestyles and experiences.
- *Recognize and understand* the legitimacy of their development.
- To *actively participate* in a learning processes.
- To develop *self-reliance* in the learning processes.
- *To explore* novel faith ideas and practices
- To *grapple* with the *wide range* of answers, ideas and activities.
- To *encourage* appropriate faith *responses* in various situations.
- To enable followers to understand and achieve the *expected standards*.

Above all he created hope and new aspirations even though they appeared to end in failure. He revealed the skill of having expertise and yet remaining in touch with the common man's language and emotions.

To do so he used eight major strategies that possess features which are relevant today.

Common, formal *instruction*/didactic teaching methods.

Sustained training by apprenticeship and situated learning

Maximized understanding by *using all the senses*

Imaginative language

Independent learning based on *socio-cultural knowledge* and the *environment*

Mastery learning to achieve *consistent success*.

Concept awareness.

Concept attainment to *understand ideas* and their *application*.

It will be helpful to relate each section to the summary sheet (Fig.101)

.2c-170
Why might the notion of Spiritual Intelligence be widely attractive?

Spiritual Intelligence

In contrast to Jesus' concept of spirituality an alternative called Spiritual Intelligence has been proposed by Zohar and Marshall. They defined spirituality in terms of *sensitivity* to self, others and the application of key values in the natural and social worlds. This differs fundamentally from spirituality as Jesus would have defined it, and comes from Asian roots, It raises the issue of whether spiritual intelligence can be taught without reference to God. It is related to Gorman's concepts of emotional and social intelligence and also to spiritual/moral aspects of post-modern social development programmes. Just as Intelligence can develop or decline so spirituality is likened to an organism from which spiritual intelligences can be developed through experience and teaching.

They pose six questions in particular:

- Is a spiritual component built into the frontal lobes of the brain?
- Can a person recognise spiritual/social situations with its alternatives and implications for decision-making?
- Can a person reformulate a situation or arrive at a conclusion superior to traditional responses based upon spiritual/social criteria?
- Can a person develop strategies to resolve spiritual/social problems?
- Has a person the insight to identify spiritual /social influences?
- Has a person the ability to learn from and express a sensitive spiritual response to an interactive personal/social situation?

A person who responds sensitively to the last five questions in everyday situations would be regarded as having a high spiritual intelligence.

Zohar and Marshall's arguments cannot be considered here but they assume the ability to:
- Create a high degree of self-awareness.
- Respond to the 'deep self'.
- Use and transcend difficulties.
- Stand against the crowd when necessary.
- Be reluctant to cause harm.
- Make secure spiritual judgments.
- Arrive at logical spiritual conclusions.
- Display inter-personal and intra-personal sensitivity.
- Develop creative personal scenario for living.
- Searching for one's true self.
- To have the ability to pursue moral issues.
- Develop a view of death within that total plight of man.

The basis to develop spiritual intelligence revolves around the following:
- A moral code of duty.
- Nurturing and understanding self and others.
- Personal transformation.
- Accepting the brotherhood of man.
- Accepting certain leadership.
- Make and justify personal responses.
- Problem-solving and creativity concerning personal, social and environmental matters.
- Observing/reflecting to attain insights.
- Reflection based on adequate knowledge.

.2c-171
Which aspects of Spiritual Intelligence would be eagerly adopted?

Jesus could have lived with much of this but the difference would be concerning the dynamic involvement of God. Zohar suggests a problem solving approach to individual understanding through a primary process of calm meditation. This contrasts with Jesus who did not see man as a lonely figure in a vast, often hostile, universe. The concept of spiritual intelligence offers attractive possibilities for teaching that enable secure, reflective judgments to be made.

The application of Spiritual Intelligence might be visualized as follows:

Figure 105

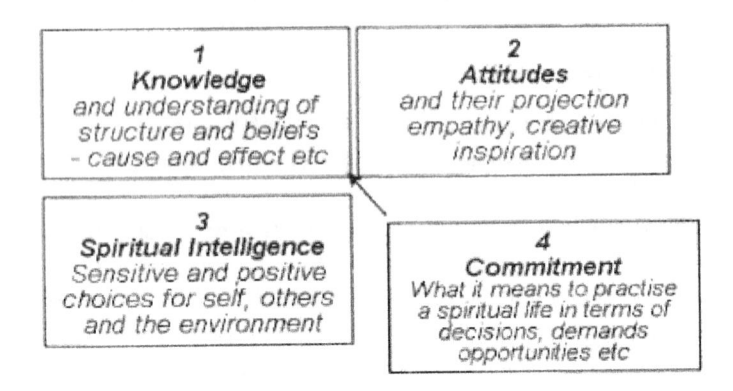

1 **Knowledge** and understanding of structure and beliefs – cause and effect etc	2 **Attitudes** and their projection empathy, creative inspiration
3 **Spiritual Intelligence** Sensitive and positive choices for self, others and the environment	4 **Commitment** What it means to practise a spiritual life in terms of decisions, demands opportunities etc

Therefore, in this context spirituality consists of:
- Not simply knowledge but it must include that.
- Not simply attitude but it must include that.
- Not even simply spiritual intelligence but it will include that!

A useful 'everyday' exposition of non-religious spirituality, together with ample activities, is given in *Spiritual Intelligence* by Brian Draper (pub. Lion Hudson 2009). 'Jesus' type focus and Spiritual Intelligence - similarities and differences'. *The following similarities and differences show typical limits to their mutuality.*

Figure 106

Jesus	Spiritual intelligence
Personal authority, but under the authority of God	Relativity and the logical differences
A spiritual pattern maker - Beatitudes etc	Individual responses to self/meditation
Principles of obedience	Personal insight and sensitivity
Brotherhood of man through spiritual reconciliation	Involvement in the brotherhood of man
Shared visionary purpose, action and restoration	Negotiated personal and social stances
Effect of direct heavenly involvement and spiritual 'tools'- prayer, faith etc	The world's underlying spiritual basis and human responsibility without a divine input

Similarities

Priority of spiritual perspectives	Make secure, sensitive judgments
Moral issues / values	Stand against a crowd
Acceptance of good leadership	Arrive at a view of death
Personal transformation and responses	Wonder of creation and its conservation
Self and community awareness	

.2c-172
What are the significances of the similarities and contrasts to spirituality and their general acceptability?

Spirituality is unique but its methodologies have similarities to most teaching but with appropriate orientations. The following are typical teaching styles found in both the gospels and spiritual intelligence. They are a useful aide-memoire.

- An *Appreciation of environmental encounters*.
- *Aspirations*. The promises and prospects received become more believable in the light of experience.
- *Association/connectivity* between God, man, teachers and prophets.
- *Attitude change*. The ethos, experiences and example of their role-model created an appreciation of attitudes such as humility.
- *Awe and wonder*. The great mysteries of life, the evidence they saw, and the need to interpret these and so result in authority, vision and lifestyle of leaders such as Jesus.
- *Case studies*/exemplars etc- authentic problem solving.
- *Community involvement*. Spirituality was being developed through stable community interaction.
- *Deductive work* based on artefacts, symbolism, art, music, dress etc.
- *Discussion* and dialogue to verify and explore truth.
- *Drama*. Projecting into novel situations to explore and express ideas.
- *Emotion*. The constant emotional responses and movements.
- *Experiential involvement*. Acts of service and spiritual work promoted understanding and insights that motivated disciples and shaped their interpretation of events.
- *Explore and value relationships*. Long-term bonding of those involved gradually create common perceptions.
- *Exploring important questions, organisations* etc.- People need time to ask questions and debate amongst themselves.
- *Expression*. Frequent opportunities to express their convictions reinforced spiritual reality amongst this community of faith – mentally emotionally and socially. The ongoing drama was a vehicle for experiential proofs and facilitating creative activities.
- *Goal based motivation*. Different types of goals were reviewed refined, gradually reinforced and the outcome predicted.
- *Illustrations*. Using the concrete and experiential to answer questions and provide a known parallel to the ideas being taught.
- *Inclusion*. To enhance the possibility of identity.
- *Inductive thinking*. Parables etc. Conclusions based on 'evidence'.
- *Interactive responses* to and between the motivated followers. During a time of spiritual exploration, people recount and examine their daily experiences. This might be called peer- group learning.
- *Knowledge*. This is paced and reinforced in human settings. It may be established, ephemeral, personal or corporate knowledge.
- *Meditation*. To go beyond the superficial thought processes.
- *Metaphor*. Expressions to clarify and make ideas more memorable.
- *Mentoring*. To personalize and deepen the teacher-learner situation.
- *Multi-situational thinking*. Giving ample practice for these varied learning situations can foster multi-dimensional views.
- *Mutuality* of which Jesus spoke.
- *Need satisfaction*. This may promote initial faith but could be short term. For example, many recorded miracles occurred in Capernaum but that town was condemned for a lack of faith. Needs can be hierarchical.

.2c-173
What+ do the methods listed below suggest about teaching spirituality and teaching generally?

- *Observations.* Incidents are watched and translated into spiritual judgments.
- *Oracy.* To enhance personal expression, reinforcement and enquiry.
- *Peer tuition.* For exploring, formulating and organizing evidence and experiences with fellow learners.
- *Problem solving.* Exploring, resolving unfinished business/learning.
- *Projection.* Imaginative drama, creative speech/writing etc.
- *Promoting ample practice* to think within the spiritual dimension. This involved looking for cause and effect, comparisons and similarities.
- *Question / Answer* To recall, reinforce, assess and inquire.
- *Reflection.* This enables the multitude of inputs to be considered, rationalized and become coherent cognitive schemas that promote consistent spiritual judgments and responses. This method is often underrated and needs to be taught.
- *Reinforcement* Consistent reinforcement together with fresh development was characteristic of Jesus' teaching methods.
- *Rhythm and rhyme.* To memorize learning more easily.
- *Situational teaching* (or field work). Spontaneous responses to opportunities.(e.g. Jesus and Zacchaeus, Luke ch.19).
- *Storytelling* To pose and answer problems memorably within contexts to show motivation, cause and effect etc.
- Teaching and learning as a consistent expression of *morality*.
- *Teacher availability.* Their authoritative teacher/ mentor's availability.
- *Template and framing.* To impose a pattern on the learning.
- *Thinking skills* – conceptualising by different thought processes.

Thinking skills should be built into any programme that seeks to promote spirituality. For example, these would include the following:

Comparison	Analysis	Justification	Evaluation
Classification	Synthesis	Contrast and Similarity	Meditation
Projection	Judgment	Cause and effect	Interpretation
Inference	Prediction	Visualization	Perceptive awareness

It cannot be assumed that these skills are naturally employed / developed and so alternative thinking strategies need to be readily available. Without it thinking can become captive to popular, habitual thought patterns and predispositions. It is implicitly evident that Jesus had such a framework (as part of his world view) within which he developed major principles and illustrated them by word and action. Ideally this enhances the quality of thinking by providing varied study tools.

- *Using the past, present and future.* The authority of historic heroes and experiences were seen as relevant to the present and validated hopes and expectations. Therefore, related methods are worth exploring, despite difficulties, as in specific spiritual methods such as prayer.
- *Visualization.* Seeing and extending possibilities mentally.

Personality Factor – 14

What might there have been in Jesus personality that would make him a good teacher of spirituality?

.2c-174
Consider which of the following strategies. may be particularly effective ton develop spirituality?

Chapter 16

Teaching Spirituality through Eight Strategies

Understanding alone is not synonymous with spirituality. That requires sensitivity of thought, will and action, of which knowledge and understanding are a part.

Although spirituality is more than a set of concepts or projection skills (strategies 1and 2) succeeding strategies build upon them. Once they are handled with ease the scope for teaching spirituality extends rapidly. They are tools to be used selectively with various types of learning experiences for studying Jesus' approaches to teaching. This is extended into other aspects of teaching at the end of Part C

The list above indicates priorities around which teaching will be organized in the following sections. Their development into a coherent working model (Fig.5) enables various approaches to be taken. The outer circle indicates twelve strategies that can be used to examine spirituality and lead to eight major areas of study. The two circles are meant to be independent of each other and could be rotated in a three-dimensional version. Hence creativity/problem solving could be related to any of the inner eight segments. The terms. below the cyclical model are aspects of teaching

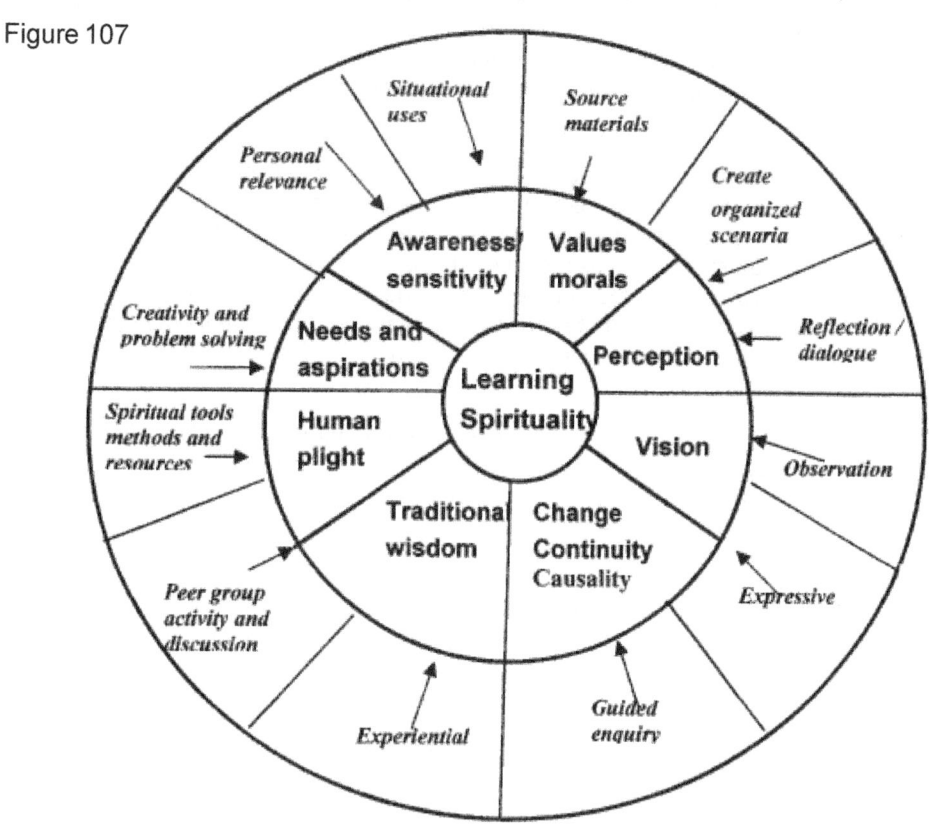

Figure 107

An aide memoire to develop Figure 107and Strategy 7 is useful

experiential — environment — needs based — interactive — expressive — evidence based — recognise diversity — celebration — mutuality symbols — authority — story telling — conceptual patterns — Q and A — listening — shared understandings — ownership — evident development — envision — achievement based — clarity — explanation — understanding/imagination — truth and validity — ritual — principles plus illustration — shared priorities — inquiry — responses

---

.2c-175
Why is reflection a vital part of the teaching/ learning process?

A Strategic Approach

The following is not a philosophical study of spirituality as such. It is a convenient and appropriate setting to illustrate briefly eight working strategies that can act as frameworks. The dynamics of spirituality exceeds its religious *concepts* but these do provide coherent bases for study. They help students recognize elements of spiritual life and their impact on personal motivation and social priorities. Concepts can be related to lifestyle, interpreting situations and decision-making. They spawn further understandings and perceptions of actions, reflecting on truth and allow fresh revelation, insight and interpretation. Indeed religious concepts (prayer, worship, faith etc.) can shape relationships, rationality and decision-making. These enable a host of comparisons and judgments to be made, and act as a suitable means for studying people or situations, At the conclusion of each of the eight strategies are eight boxed diagrams to summarize the ideas and to indicate examples of Jesus' use of that particular strategy. Typically, spirituality consists of some form of inspiration, identification and interpretation of issues. Figure 107 provides a preview of the strategies being considered.

Strategy 1 A didactic approach

Spirituality has been traditionally taught through didactic instruction. Preachers expect people to hear, be persuaded, remember and act. But memory is patchy and often short-term and the will is closely related to perceived self-benefit. It is interesting to note how often at the end of a lesson or church service how little has been remembered, unless there is some reason to do so. Therefore, formal teaching that should result in predicted actions (i.e. spirituality etc.) can be unreliable. But it has its place.

Although the attitudes of crowds can be spectacularly influenced by charismatic didactic teachers, it is often less effective unless it is highly personalized. The function of this style of teaching is to impart information but if the pupils' schemas are not adequately prepared to assimilate new knowledge the gains can be short term. Jesus faced this problem but persisted in re-organising their understandings by using other means of teaching, one of which was to allow a degree of emotional engagement to occur to promote identity and learning. Although it may have limited uses with extraverted pupils it does provide the more introverted with their preferred security, continuity and defined learning paths.

Therefore, didactic teaching is especially useful when the teacher has expertise and authority, the listeners are motivated, the teaching is illustrated memorably, and if it develops schemas based on existing knowledge that can assimilate new ideas that can be established through emotional engagement. But that was just one of Jesus' strategies!

Didactic teaching assumes that the listeners both want and can learn but severe problems can occur when the teacher's vocabulary (or register of speech) is significantly different from that of listeners, or when there is little continuity between the teacher's thought processes and those who are being taught.

Briefly, this consists of an *'expert's formal instruction'*, which Jesus often did. As a boy he spent hours being taught by rote in a synagogue, learning scriptures and structured facts that enabled him to readily recall traditional stories and pithy statements. That gave him a link with people who had also learned traditional knowledge – but didactic teaching exceeds rote-learning. Didactic teaching is convenient and can be replicated economically, often using precise pre-planned material. Ideally, listeners respond to the authoritative voice and image of their teacher who should be a charismatic 'expert'. At its best didactic teaching can be powerfully effective. Although typically likened to a formal lecture procedure, this is not necessarily so. A good example of didactic teaching is the Royal Society's science lectures for young people that are shown each New Year on television. Jesus did not have technological resources available but he was an effective didactic teacher. He demonstrated that such a strategy should contain the following qualities and methods.

Qualities: Ideal didactic teaching is economical and contains a shared body of stimulating knowledge that is controlled by the teacher but focuses the listeners and takes account of their limited attention span and possibly knowledge. The objectives are clear and attainable and the clarity of delivery and

.2c-176
In which particular ways can Fig.107 enhance spirituality?

synthesis of sequential knowledge should promote interest and greater awareness of the study area that is seen to be relevant.

Methods: Whilst good active teaching retains the essential teacher – listener format, it uses a variety of visual aids, demonstrates the ideas with memorable illustrations and seeks to involve the listeners to some degree. This was typical of Jesus and encouraged a grounding in shared understanding and later reflection. Commonly, however, a didactic teacher is neither an expert who can take students into fresh areas of knowledge nor is sufficiently charismatic to hold people's attention and create memories, which can result in negative perceptions. Pupils frequently question its relevance, time, interest and need satisfaction as they evaluate general didactic teaching and its motivating powers. Memory and learning are inter-related but both can be distorted by didactic learning. Rapid memory fade and the difficulty of transferring knowledge from the short-term to the long-term memory frequently result in ill-digested, partial memories that are distortions of what was taught. Jesus avoided this by using sharp, pictorial, short sentences that had little need for extended causal explanations. Also, *reflection* is an aspect of memorization that often does not have a sufficient place in didactic teaching.

The listeners may agree (or not). This was typical of Jesus and encouraged a grounding in shared understanding and later reflection. Commonly, however, a didactic teacher is neither an expert who can take students into fresh areas of knowledge or is sufficiently charismatic to hold people's attention and create memories, which can result in negative perceptions. Pupils frequently question its relevance, time, interest and need satisfaction as they evaluate general didactic teaching and its motivating powers. Memory and learning are inter-related but both can be distorted by didactic learning. Rapid memory fade and the difficulty of transferring knowledge from the short-term to the long-term memory frequently result in ill- digested, partial memories that are distortions of what was taught. Jesus avoided this by using sharp, pictorial, short sentences that had little need for extended causal explanations.

Its *instructional* purpose is to *set a scene*, *equip* people with essential *knowledge* and guide their use of *study tools*. It can introduce spiritual intelligence by demonstrating examples and providing an overview or advance organizer. Many of these skills are used in everyday life and literature. Didactic teaching needs to be authoritative and recognized by listeners as significant. Where teachers have insufficient specialist knowledge they are not usually authoritative. This is particularly noticeable in mathematics where few students remain in its domain. Similarly, the exposure to spiritual matters is seldom elevated to spirituality, unless the learning is characterized by the elements shown in Fig.107. These are found in the gospels where some criteria for didactic teaching are met.

Figure 108

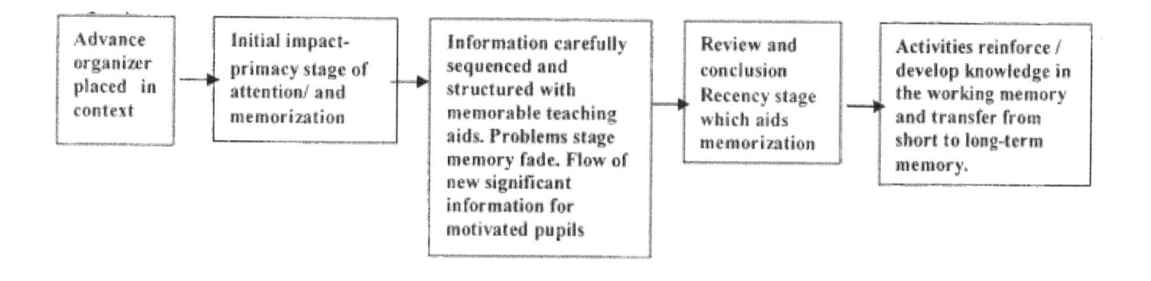

| Advance organizer placed in context | → | Initial impact-primacy stage of attention/ and memorization | → | Information carefully sequenced and structured with memorable teaching aids. Problems stage memory fade. Flow of new significant information for motivated pupils | → | Review and conclusion Recency stage which aids memorization | → | Activities reinforce / develop knowledge in the working memory and transfer from short to long-term memory. |

.2c-177
What probably made Jesus a good didactic teacher?

Figure 109

Didactic: Instruction/ Information						
Efficient, Authority Knowledge Structure Large group	Sound bites Memorable Coherent Information Patterned	Sequential developing concepts Reception learning	Clear goals /knowledge check Question / answer	Ongoing consolidation/ connectivity Formally planned	Thinking skills High prediction Cause and effect etc	Advance Organiser/ principles &concepts based on experiences Bread John 6
Didactic: Examples - Information / Instruction						
Knowledge Fresh Authoritative E.g. Moses John ch.3v14	Soundbites Memorable Relevant Matt.ch.5 v3-11	Using senses Visualisat'n Kinaesthetic John ch5	Question/ Answer Friendly Jn.ch.14 Opponent Luke5v21	Consolidate Connectivity 2 disciples walking to Emmaus Lukech24	Thinking skills Prediction – Lazarus/Dives Cause- effect Lk.ch.16v19f	Advance organizers Principles concepts Nazareth - Isaiah 61 Lk 4v18-22

Strategy 2 Situated cognition and apprentice tuition

Spirituality is not fostered by any single approach. Even so, both Jesus and advocates of spiritual intelligence would see apprenticeship as the most effective teaching strategy. This was exemplified by Jesus' choice of disciples and Zohar 's emphasis on interaction with guru like figures. The notion is straight-forward. Learning is powerfully linked to the learning *situation* and being taught by an *acknowledged master* who one might wish to emulate.

In the context of Jesus' teaching, spirituality might be described as being taught authoritatively by the master in the midst of living, relevant case studies. Therefore, his pupils were:

- In a significant and memorable situation.
- Taught by the Master who could be likened to a master craftsman .
- Projecting themselves into the Master's world as his apprentices .
- They obediently perceived needs, copied and interpreted situations.
- Learned to predict, and act like the master craftsman. It was consistently meaningful.

Jesus did not teach haphazardly. Everything was matched with his central purpose and was appropriate to the people and the culture. Therefore, Jesus adopted different strategies for teaching his disciples, the crowds and the opposition. A critical factor was he trained a few disciples. To do so provided deep essential information and the means of implementation, which required demonstrations in a wide range of settings. He acted as a master craftsman with apprentices rather than a religious instructor with his students. They watched, imitated and became involved with him. Jesus did not proceed in a strictly orderly way, but he developed the apprentices' process goals by demonstrating practical skills. He wanted his apprentices to have understanding and a robust bond of trust between himself and them and also amongst the disciples. From the outset he provided a feel-good factor. As they watched the master their expectations rose. They discussed what they had seen and heard, came to conclusions and helped and copied him. By so doing they received privileged teaching and were motivated. When problems and weaknesses did occur Jesus offered opportunities for restoration that resulted in effective long-term learning. Jesus successfully took the apprentices from being common Galileans to 'master craftsman' upon whom he would rely to change the world.

Jesus probably had apprentices in his workshop and recognized that spiritual learning was an apprenticeship that could lead pupils to become independent learners who not need his support, and who would, like him, rely on the Holy Spirit for guidance. This classical pattern was applicable whether he was a carpenter or a prophet, but his apprentices were adults who became apprentices by invitation. As they followed, watched, listened and worked together so that they became imitators

.2c-178
What is a usual shortcoming in a didactic teaching strategy for spirituality?

of Jesus. The pattern aided their resolution and memory retention and lessened the danger of them being vulnerable lonely learners with skewed understandings.

This common practice is still the basis of much every day teaching, although it has been replaced in schools by a more fragmented approach that allows a wide range of subjects to be taught independently and economically. In recent years the notion of apprenticeship training has been reinvigorated and is still the practice where expertize is passed on from older to younger or less skilful aspirants, dare we say ranging from surgeons to jockeys! This approximates to the following pattern used by Jesus.

- The skilled master clearly had a special knowledge and evoked a sense of awe.
- The apprentices wanted to be with him and learn his special ways and skills.
- As unskilled apprentices they watched and helped him on a small-scale.
- These apprentices shared each other's knowledge.
- Their master explained and demonstrated his special skills and knowledge.
- He set them contributory tasks.
- They helped to an increasing degree.
- Their understanding improved over several years.
- Later, their proven skills were fully recognized by others.
- Where appropriate, the apprentices entered a special group of established 'masters'.

As their master teacher worked so the apprentices' contributions increased and their skill level rose. The learning was interactive with the expert teacher 'on the job'. This type of relationship was apparent when Jesus fed the 5000 and at the entry into Jerusalem on 'Palm Sunday'. This was powerful pre-vocational activity and guided discovery as they *watched, listened, helped, copied and developed Jesus' work*. This process of peer education was vital. They were learning revolutionary ideas with and from others and gained confidence in speaking to the group about their new faith. As they talked so each person learnt and discovered something about Jesus and gained acceptance from the group. Overall important gains were made as they increased their sense of self-worth and increasingly saw the world from their master's viewpoint.

The validity and re-emergence of apprenticeship teaching has been linked to 'situated learning' as it emphasizes that the *situations* in which *personal interactions visual images and identification* occur are powerful and memorable bases for learning. Similarly, peer groups provide a frame of reference and understanding over a prolonged period of time.

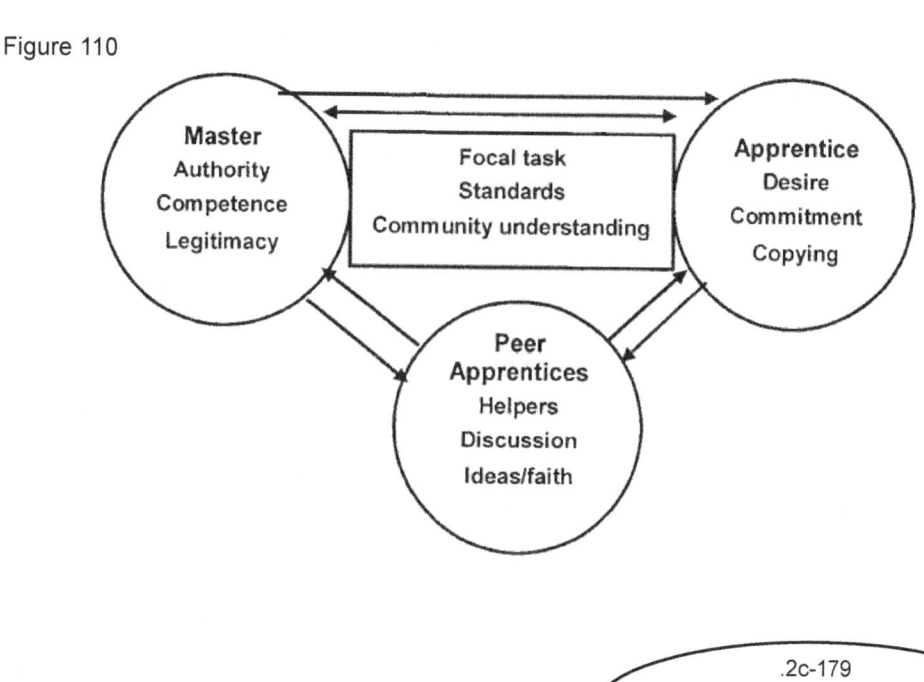

Figure 110

.2c-179
What is a strength of using a didactic strategy when teaching spirituality?

Figure 111

The Master Craftsman / Mentor	The Pupils as Apprentices
• He possessed demonstrable recognized skills • He possessed authoritative knowledge • He was in overall control • He worked within cultural understandings • He exceeded the expectations of his apprentices • He represented his apprentices' interests • He was responsible for guided participation • As the role model he was the arbiter of standards	• There were agreed and controlled teaching and learning responsibilities of established knowledge and skills with desirable outcomes • The apprentices learned to mastery level and combined to produce worthwhile tasks • Their work was related to goals and processes and involved intensive reflective thought • Memory retention was maximised through varied applications of learning experiences • Social life was fundamental to learning • Learning was interactive between the apprentices, the master and learning situation

As they observed and entered his innermost thoughts, emotions and actions, they modelled themselves on him. They knew that they were privileged and had access to deeper secret knowledge than the crowds. When they saw him weep over Jerusalem, pray in the Garden of Gethsemane and when three of them saw him transfigured on Mount Tabor /Hermon, they knew that they were entering into his 'sacred space' – a privilege that had a long-lasting impact. Imagine their pride and the bonding effect of being identified with Jesus and being 'legitimate peripheral participants' or helpers! Furthermore, this master – apprenticeship relationship provided motivating benefits of an immediate feedback, a positive self-image and anticipation of success, after all Jesus had promised they would achieve greater things than he had! The dynamism undoubtedly enhanced their intrinsic motivation, maximized their own beliefs and enabled them to progress from watchful experiences to ownership. Although he only had a handful of apprentices he estimated that their reliability and faith would be more vital in the long-run than the crowds who wanted to make him king. As they moved with Jesus, so their accomplishments became the basis of a faith to achieve ventures of which they had never dreamed and so make progress more likely.

The teacher was not just organizing and demonstrating special revelations with them – both he, the master, and the apprentices had creative roles. Their master teacher may be the originator, facilitator and enabler but the apprentices represented the future. When looked at from a 21st century standpoint it is apparent that Jesus' methods of training his apprentices were and are still valid. Figures 109/ 110 itemizes those major characteristics that can be directly applied to Jesus working with his disciples.

The value of apprenticeship and situated learning was and is dependent upon the teacher possessing *recognized skills* and a degree of *cultural continuity* with the apprentices who were 'just plain folks' (J P F). The master teacher adapted to and *reinterpreted social expectations*. This required *adequate time and commitment* by the teacher, a *learning environment* with a *reinforcing positive ethos and meaningful experiences.*

A further component was their developing community of practice, which was led by their master and provided a group identity and collective learning. A current example would be an orchestra for a musician or a doctors' group practice. This process of situated learning allows scope for pupils to take leadership roles and to make important practical decisions both in respect of fellow apprentices and the area of study being pursued. This style of leadership can be limited in subjects where relatively few teachers are specialists with a deep love for the subject. Such teaching can be debased to become bureaucratically simple and may not develop experiential work that is regarded as authentic and worthwhile. The apprentices, however, may anticipate good prospects.

The Master/Mentor and Apprentice/Pupil strategies

.2c-180
Jesus' followers were not simply pupils who were being taught – they were apprentices. What is the difference?

Figure 112

Learning by association	Peer Groups	Ample Practice	Continuity	Public Recognition	Anchor
Association with the Master/ mentor

Observation of the Master

Replication of the Master

Replication of set skills and knowledge | Constant interaction

Mutual discussion

Interpretation and helps

Partners

Shared language and poetic rhythms | Ample regular practice

Associated memories

Reinforcing situations

Development situations | Honed skills In various situations

Long term goals and achievements

Using occasional demands | Public recognition of skills and knowledge | Long term and novel practices

United celebrations

Anchored to knowledge and skills |

The *knowledge was culturally significant* to enhance its *impact* and likely *memorization*. As the apprentices *looked, reflected* and became *involved* they not only saw its *relevance* but it also promoted an *imaginative leap*. It is surprising the high degree of expertise which people attain when they share their experiential knowledge and are highly focused on what they consider to be *worthwhile* e.g. bird-watching, music, tactile and auditory skills of blind people. The *teaching removed negative blocks* and provided *active/experiential involvement*. This *interactive learning* was characterized by the *relationship* between the *expert* and the *novice group*. Although the *curriculum* may appear limited it constantly *revisited ideas in various forms* and took them to a *greater depth*. This learning brought together *ongoing interaction*, a degree of *structure*, a *developmental process* and *distinct roles*.

Briefly, the development can be related to Spiritual Intelligence as follows:

- Within a case study pupils focus on a **role model**, gather **evidence**, look for **motivation** and possible **outcomes** to make secure **judgments**. To achieve this they probably:
- Choose a **meaningful situation** or topic and look for appropriate role models involved.
- **Identify the core values** to be applied to social and personal situations that develop a stable world-view.
- Teach pupils to methodically work through the **listening, observation, projection, perception, interpretation, judgment and prediction process.**
- **Human settings**. This is achieved by opening, analyzing and passing sequentially through the 5 spiritual intelligence stages mentioned (p.7).
- **Identify the core values** to be applied to social and personal situations that develop a stable world-view.
- **Display** the problems, evidence and judgments until the likely outcomes are achieved.

.2c-181
How would the master have taught the apprentices?

The sequence above is useful once pupils have acquired the habit of using them. Allied to this, pupils use the moral criteria Jesus expected, such as mercy, forgiveness etc.

The difficulties of fostering spirituality in a non-spiritual environment or with a person who is either not sympathetic or an acknowledged master can be immense and counter-productive. To limit this, older pupils have often made use of a wide variety of charities. Full preparation is required with a structure which makes observation, interviews / questioning, interaction and reporting back meaningful, but apprenticeship learning requires sustained personal contact. The mentor (s) resolves difficult problems amongst the group.

Group and peer work can be regarded as merely a useful methodological vehicle – but Jesus saw it as an essential component of long-term learning. He understood the wisdom and the power of teaching in small groups even though he did a great deal of mass teaching. In recent years the value and influence of peer group education has been increasingly recognized as a means of reinforcing and developing what has been taught. He could see the internal life within the group that was evoked by their shared enthusiasms.

Jesus frequently withdrew from the group of disciples to pray and reflect on his work, and we know very little about what happened amongst these enthusiasts whilst he was away. It is reasonable to assume that they talked with an emotional enthusiasm about what they had seen and heard. Their joint responses would have filled out the corporate body of knowledge, given them fresh insights and a renewed sense of purpose. In fact Jesus wanted to know what they thought and on some occasions they revealed their uncertainty and ignorance, which appears to have been somewhat exasperating for Jesus. Even so, they did discuss vital issues and arrive at important conclusions that were central to their whole purpose. Their experiences were being interpreted in the light of their traditional knowledge, which was often inadequate. Therefore, on some occasions it was necessary for Jesus to teach the whole group whilst on other occasions they worked in twos and encouraged each other and developed enabling skills and faith. Their shared successes must have caused them to value each other as they worked together in a similar way to their master. They thereby developed the mutuality that would prove to be increasingly vital when Jesus left them. This is not to suggest that it was an ideal group because there was a degree of sustained rivalry amongst them, so much so that Jesus had to demonstrate his own teaching by washing their feet which appalled them at first. Also there was an individual who had responsibility but who finally splintered off with tragic consequences.

As the group watched and heard Jesus, so they gathered the central tenets of faith and moved towards a degree of guided discovery about their leader. As they interacted a leader emerged who is likely to have influenced the outcomes of the group's enthusiastic discussions. These group experiences produced opportunities to recall, refine, reinforce and reflect on the significance of what was happening.

This small group was essential to Jesus because he needed helpers but as he gained in authority so their sense of privilege grew. They confidently used his phrases, which was a vital aspect of achieving attitude change. Each person knew that he was close to the leader and yet they interacted with each other meaningfully. As a result, their evaluation of the teacher was both individually and corporately positive. They began to see in a way what the crowds could not, that the message of the Kingdom of God must result in a changed lifestyle. This unique peer group was being prepared to become educators by a process that incorporated the leader and the followers and yet which allowed a degree of freedom. The group developed a pride in being linked with this new unconventional rabbi and so felt a degree of responsibility and focused on the highlights of his teaching assiduously.

.2c-182
How Is this model of the master and the apprentice applicable generally?

In our current terminology, Jesus was the mentor of each of his close followers. This form of individual supportive teaching can be significant in shaping people's attitudes as indeed it proved when Jesus approached the crisis of his life. Mentoring involves more than goal setting and establishing procedures for study, it is both relational and enables the pupils to consider their own understanding in greater detail. Ideally, a mentor should use personal coaching skills that enable each pupil to learn from their personal situation and develop optimism and confidence as a state of mind.

As their mentor, Jesus was helping his followers to make sense of this complex experience and be involved in a joint engagement. He was helping them to pattern information into similarities and differences and process that information into representational thought. He was modelling every aspect of their lifestyle and understanding. As he observed and reflected on his and their experiences, he emphasized the importance of relationships as between God and man, Father and Son, master and servant, himself and them etc. As a mentor he did instruct but he also left his followers to make real decisions. He was supportive, fostered curiosity and increased their self-awareness as they progressively became more distinctive. It is particularly interesting that if one looks at Jesus through the eyes of a mentor or coach it is possible to see a template for training and action.

Like any good mentor or coach he worked alongside people but when asking whose purposes and values would be given priority, it was undoubtedly his! It was a form of initiation which was being made acceptable and comprehensible to the pupil and resulted in a progressive understanding and also a sense of responsibility which enabled the mentor to say that he had protected each of his pupils (John ch.17).

This mentor taught the pupils to transform the information given into universal and yet personal values that were absolute. In other words, he had to enable the pupils to go 'beyond the information given'. The mentor, in this case Jesus, had a responsibility to:

- Identify potential, give timely advice and help pupils to gain a shared perspective.
- Be prepared for a task.
- Become committed to the pupil even to the extent that it puts himself at risk.
- Become accountable for his pupil to some extent.
- Give quality time and opportunities for dialogue, reflective and developmental thought.
- Re-evaluate pupils or when they failed, discreetly supports them.
- The mentor sets goals and tasks. As an enabler and role model the mentor provides an example and sets standards for success, and so the mentor's own authority increases.
- That they imitate as they see the mentor demonstrate skills and support them.

From this one can see that the crowds and the group had different experiences of what it meant to be taught by Jesus. There is ample evidence to show that the crowds were equivocal, and although it might be said that this was also true of his pupils, in the final analysis they were sorrowful and wanted to succeed.

The process of mentoring a small group can be shown to be a productive strategy of teaching both in terms of attainment and attitude change. The power of this teaching, together with the internal dynamic of the group, raised the level of expectations and the quality of interaction so that every aspect of teaching could be developed profitably. We have situations in which Jesus is both a teacher and a mentor and pupils become both learners and peer-group educators, which is a powerful mix! It led to a *committed response, clear recall, and reinforcement* of what had been taught and valuable *opportunities for reflection* about implications of what had been learnt and what their personal and corporate *responsibility* would be in the future as they watched their master.

.2c- 183
Why is this well proven model seldom used?

Figure 114

Mentor x Pupil	Knowledge x values	Enquiry	Observation	Experience	Spiritual action/ decision making	Outcome
Authority Interaction Listening/ Receptive Fellowship Appropriate demands/ goals	Established Knowledge Ephemeral Knowledge x Values Personal Values x Social knowledge x	Personal Rooted in values 1st hand shared process	Mentor Case studies Needs Motivation Demonstration	Sense of wonder Sense of worth Challenge Success Learn 'how to' skills	Reflection Prayer Faith Positive action towards others / self	Recall Commitment Reinforcement Reflection Flexibility/ Projection Generalization

Strategy3 Accelerated Learning Systems

If the basic structure and organization of Jesus' teaching was akin to the situated learning / apprenticeship strategy mentioned above, the actual teaching process approximated to what is now known as Accelerated Learning. This focuses on the relationship between thinking processes and the brain's efficient use of all the senses. Although there is no precise parallel between strategies 2 and 3, Jesus intuitively shared ideas that have emerged over recent decades. These are summarized in the mind maps below where the importance of using the senses and emotions to build memorable images and patterned knowledge are shown. This emphasizes total pupil involvement as follows:

- Jesus' goals led the disciples to build long-term scenaria as they moved forward.
- Their learning was varied with visual, auditory and kinaesthetic experiences.
- Their learning was limited to relatively few themes that were built upon vivid mental images and emotional engagement.
- Their knowledge was chunked down/simplified, patterned and related to the situation.

This range of appropriate experiences and materials were the basis of their emerging spirituality. These were crucial because they would move into unknown 'spiritual territory' (Acts ch.2 onwards). This was in contrast to the limited practices of many official religious teachers. The diagram below emphasizes the importance of using the senses and emotions to build memorable images and patterned knowledge.

The assumption of accelerated learning is that people learn most effectively through multi- sensory activities involving visualization, auditory reception, plus kinaesthetic and tactile experiences. It is said that we remember 20% of what is read, 30% of what is heard, 40% of what is seen, 50% of what is said, 60% of what is done and 90% of what is read, heard, said, seen and done Although these figures seem 'convenient' they do indicate the need for total learning. This was characteristic of Jesus' teaching methods, in contrast to those of Pharisees. He made learning memorable by constantly using the senses and the environment appropriately. One only has to glance at the gospels to see his experiential and experimental teaching. Traditionally schools have given priority to the printed word that may have produced distorted results in favour of pupils with higher literacy intelligence. One wonders what the disciples' preferred learning styles were and whether they would have been as successful in the 21st century as they were with Jesus. Now methods enable pupils to use other forms of intelligence, and particularly maximize the use of the senses to aid the memory.

Jesus began with his Big Picture of the Kingdom of God and then 'assembled the parts' in the form of parables, miracles and promises etc like a jigsaw puzzle. Everything was contextualized that made the memories powerful. Similarly the language was developed through strong, simple concrete images. The brain was sharply activated by his arousal of attention, sharp imagery, emotional engagement and physical stimuli. One can imagine that when he cried out, 'Have I been with you so long…' that he must have made constant connections during his interactions with his disciples and others. But he was creating a sense of awe, expectations, posing challenges and giving the notion of unfinished business. He anchored their understanding with patterned and associated

.2c-184
Why was Jesus so efficient in his teaching?

memories and reinforced learning as he went from village to village where no doubt his followers repeatedly heard some of his stories. He not only set goals but he framed expectations for the future. But he did not wait for total understanding before progressing, Instead, he gave them rich experiences, after which they still argued as to who was the greatest! Instead of giving extended information and explanations he *chunked* the knowledge into its simplest form and presented it as a simplified, coherent picture which most could understand. These living, experiential and visual communications were in essence a pre-technological version of accelerated learning.

The mind map (Fig.115) indicates eight major strands within Accelerated Learning Systems and all can appreciate to some degree its power when related to Jesus' teaching ministry. If you refer back to a similar mind map (Fig.6) it is possible to see similarities between the nature of his teaching and those systems being developed today. Similarly Fig.6 shows comparable ideas but with a more specific emphasis on learning.

Figure 115

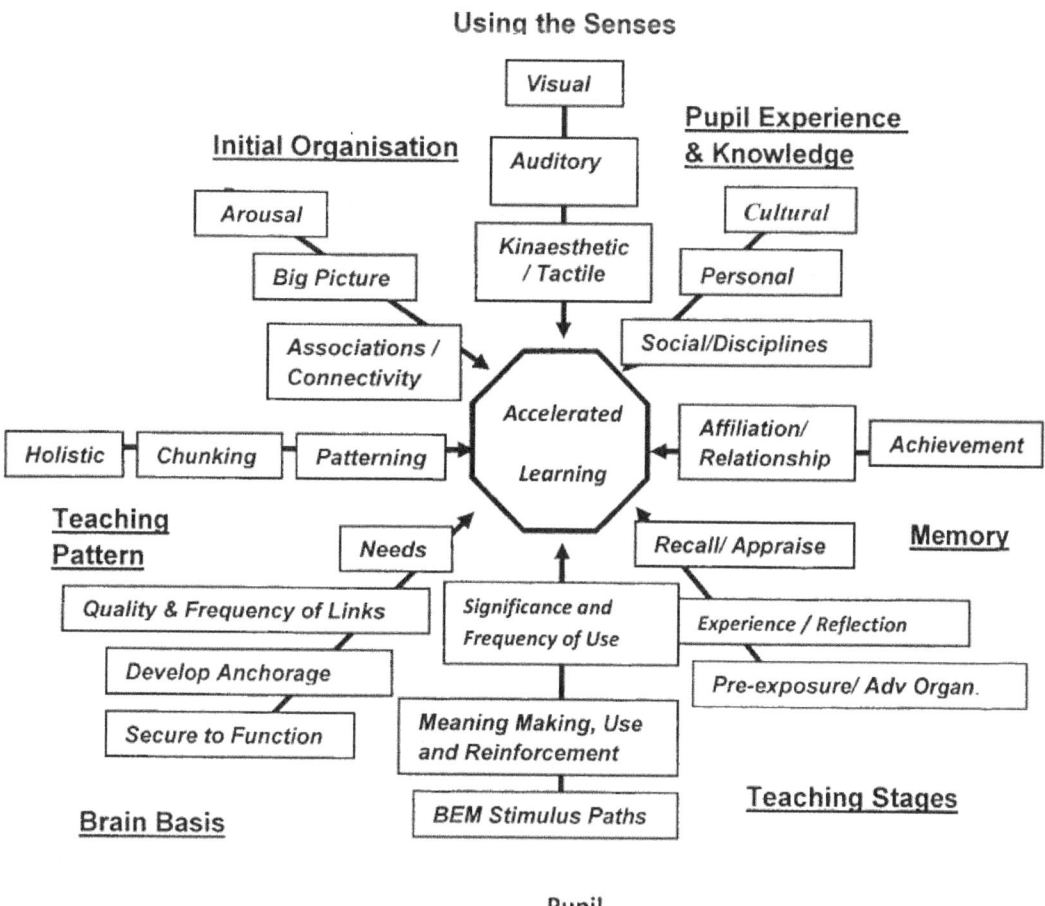

Using the Senses

- Visual
- Auditory
- Kinaesthetic / Tactile

Initial Organisation

- Arousal
- Big Picture
- Associations / Connectivity

Pupil Experience & Knowledge

- Cultural
- Personal
- Social/Disciplines

Teaching Pattern

- Holistic
- Chunking
- Patterning

Accelerated Learning

- Affiliation/ Relationship
- Achievement

Memory

- Needs
- Recall/ Appraise
- Experience / Reflection
- Pre-exposure/ Adv Organ.

Brain Basis

- Quality & Frequency of Links
- Develop Anchorage
- Secure to Function

Teaching Stages

- Significance and Frequency of Use
- Meaning Making, Use and Reinforcement
- BEM Stimulus Paths

Pupil motivation

.2c-185
Why might Jesus' life and teaching be suited to accelerated learning?

Consider the following description of accelerated learning as applied to Jesus' pupils.

Jesus activated prior knowledge and explained his goals and his Big Picture. He set them in a positive emotional state and gave them ample active learning opportunities. They could tell others of their experiences and this confidence and pride reduced their stress. This constant exposure embedded their particular thinking skills. They appear to have enjoyed **good working** relationships and gradually moved from 'what's in it for '*me*' to 'what's in it for '*others*'. Their confidence and expectations grew as they experienced Jesus' varied teaching styles that involved using all their physical senses. The chunked knowledge was accessible and memorable, especially as they felt valued. The interaction between them and the promises they received maximized their learning.

A fascinating example of using this as an aspect of spirituality was when a class of Y9 pupils (14 y.o.) with no prior background started a study of Buddhism using Accelerated Learning Systems. They used of a range of senses and skills to develop patterned schemas. There was a didactic introduction that included part of a DVD. This was an advance organiser that provided the pupils with a 'Big Picture' of Buddhism and brief pattern of knowledge. The class was divided into six groups, each of which studied one of the following topics:

historical foundations **major ideas**

important places **people and their religious customs**

symbols of faith **stories**

As a frame to develop their studies. There were replica artefacts, varied computer programs, frame to develop their studies. There were replica artefacts, books, DVDs, IT online and a tape containing an interview with a Buddhist. Also, there were addresses of appropriate organizations. The pupils posed questions, reflected on possible answers and then, with the teacher as an adviser, they refined and recorded their findings. Each group reported back to the class. Questions were raised and the groups returned to refine their findings. These were combined into one project, printed, reviewed and displayed. They had asked some of the questions that Zohar regards as typical of spiritual intelligence. Also they achieved ownership of their studies. This was not the conclusion. They presented their findings to a parallel Y 9 class who further developed their work and reported back to the originators who evaluated their report critically. In particular this involved reflection, enquiry, reinforcement and meaningful communication that required standards of presentation.

The effects of this teaching in respect of spirituality are unknown, but it certainly contained appropriate elements. The process of reflective thought continually recurred and one gained the impression from this multi-dimensional learning that the pupils paused and gave spirituality serious thought. This pattern was later replicated in other contexts.

Using the full range of senses

It has been shown in this teaching strategy (Accelerated Learning) that the most evident feature of Jesus' teaching was his use of all the senses or the assumption that people were using their full range of senses. This multi-sensory approach to methodology has coincided with major aspects of all great traditions in teaching (e.g. Montessori etc). When he said, "Look unto the fields which are white and ready for harvest" he was telling people not merely to see but to remember and interpret by retaining that visualization. When he instituted the Holy Communion he combined the senses when he spoke and the disciples handled and tasted the bread and the wine. At the same time he taught humility by actually washing his disciples' feet. He kept everything identifiable and clear with his uncluttered visual and auditory pictures. Each had a potent message that was memorable in its own right and yet was related to others. Typical of Hebrew teaching methods, he did not talk about understanding as much as saying, "he that hath eyes to see and ears to hear....", or as William

.2c-186
In what sense are we are all storytellers?

Barclay expressed this, "If you will not listen, then see!" Similarly, those who resisted his message were described as being "blinded by the God of this world". All of his parables were auditory pictures. The Good Samaritan was a shocking story, but one that could be visualised, discussed and easily repeated. The processes by which the disciples participated in Jesus' activities were further examples of experiential learning being experiential. Many of these examples were incidental and capitalised on a momentary happening whilst others were deliberately planned by the teacher for a specific purpose. The notable contrast between the typically concrete Hebrew style of teaching and the relatively abstract explanations that are often given in the European situation is salutary.

Figure 116

Accelerated learning VAK Build scenaria	Maximize senses Visualization Auditory Kinaesthetic Tactile	Organised schemas brain based learning	Mental memory Maps Imagery	Emotional engagement	Chunking down knowledge etc	Patterning knowledge and memories	Using the occasion and situation

The fascinating array of symbolisms, such as a shepherd, was memorable and thought provoking, although it must be said that they were prone to mistaken interpretations. But the power of visual symbols can be gauged by the shared confidence of the people in the bronze serpent on a pole that had been an instrument of healing since the time of Moses. The nature in which virtually all learning was multi-sensory and emotionally evocative has been increasingly rediscovered in schools during the 20th and now the 21st centuries. This has its limitations but it is the norm of apprenticeship and accelerated learning.

He often aroused people by briefly telling them what they wanted to hear. His brief initial statements were readily recalled and reported amongst the people. One can only imagine the excited anticipation that swept through the villages. As people gathered to hear him teach, he used short statements that might now be called 'sound bites'. He could look at the crowds and see the poor, the sorrowful, the meek, the righteous, the merciful, the pure in heart, the peacemakers, and the persecuted and give each an unforgettable promise that they could latch on to. It was like a series of short mission statements of promise in schools for those who had been under achieving, bullied or were simply working hard. The distinctive promises were in effect like a contract between the school and the parents. They were organizing principles upon which his ministry could be based. This can be likened to good practice in all teaching situations.

Figure 117

Accelerated Learning Using the senses Building scenaria	Moving into the unknown Transfiguration Mark ch.9v2	Activity Help John 6	Meeting problems Storms Matt.8 v24	Imagery True vine Shepherd Door John 10 v1	Mental memory maps Matt. 26v75 John 2v22	Challenge Unfinished business Awe Expectations	Emotional engagement Lazarus Jn.11v35 Wept over Jerusalem Lk.13v34

Strategy 4 Imaginative Language

Perhaps Jesus' best known strategy was his imaginative use of common language which took various forms but all were characterized by brevity and the familiarity of everyday topics and structure. Let us consider two related aspects and their application.

.2c-187
Banking would be a likely topic for contrasting modern parables. Why?

- Jesus, the storyteller in a world of metaphors.
- His imaginative use of similarity and difference, contrast.

Of course, many of his stories were not stories at all as we know them, but were simply shafts of 'metaphorical light' such as a shepherd looking for a lost sheep. The parallels which he constantly drew between the physical and spiritual have become embedded in our language even when there were no cultural links with camels, wine skins etc. What could have become culturally specific has become commonplace.

Jesus was an influential storyteller, but he was not alone – in fact we all do it, although perhaps not as effectively! The traditional storyteller's role ensured the continuity of the cultural heritage and provided an awareness of their identity that was in contrast to many modern stories whose purpose is simply to entertain the listeners or readers. Although Jesus had heard the traditional heroic stories such as Moses crossing the Red Sea, he did not generally follow this historical rabbinic style of storytelling. This may be because he knew that it would result in a pointless debate with the religious leaders. He was doing something that was relatively new. Although we can see that the rabbinic style of teaching influenced him, he may have drawn upon their stories such as the parable of the sower, the seed and the soil. His stories, however, were contemporary, interpretive, thought provoking, based upon recognisable situations and many required completion or solution by the listeners These were living incidents pregnant with possibilities. Also, they were short and appropriate for the open-air where they had to be sharply memorable in view of the frequent movements and disturbances amongst the crowds. He provided few details and the listeners were expected to fill in the use from their own experiences. Unlike our modern stories they contained no plot, no names and little dialogue but there was an identifiable setting (e.g. the road from Jericho to Jerusalem), action, a climax and a conclusion - all in a few verses!

Jesus knew what he wanted to teach, but would not give them a consumerist agenda of information. The *learners were at the heart of the teaching together with the Father and himself,* with the teaching presented in appropriate emotional and spiritual environments. Although the person of Jesus might be said to be the real story, we can see how the pattern of stories and metaphors were developed. As a teacher, I ask pupils about what they would like me to tell them an impromptu parable. If even I find their attention fixed and the parable remembered, how much more might it have been so with Jesus and the crowds! It might have occurred as outlined in Figure 118. Jesus had a core message (see column 1) containing essential features of the Kingdom of God. These were applied to any situation and were developed by his fertile imagination and observations (see col.2 and 3). He had seen shepherds looking for lost sheep and sleeping at the door of the sheepfold. Therefore, out of his life experiences, which he shared with other Galileans, he built realistic stories and metaphors that were integral to his greater spiritual message. . As he identified with the needy and saw a parallel between the Kingdom of God and the natural world, so a rich stream of illustrations emerged. He confidently used this physical view of God to take people from concrete to abstract spiritual understandings as they lived in the midst of a great unfolding creative drama. Similarly his miracles can be called 'metaphors in action'. Modern parables can take the same principles and apply them to modern activities and situations (column 5). When pupils raise what they think is an unusual topic (e.g. wrestling) they seldom realise that it can be related to a general parable about motivation. As he watched life he saw living incidents that were pregnant with possibilities and that helped him to formulate his spiritual and moral teaching. Also, he knew and used oral traditions and recognized the power of the binding word because he was amongst people who believed covenants should not be broken. It would appear that he was a calm, good conversationalist who was a ready listener. Not only does he appear to have enjoyed people's company, but it also enabled him to gauge their relative attitudes, priorities and expectations.

.2c-188
Parables can be powerful but are relatively seldom used now. Why?

Figure 118

Core message	Jesus' stories	Jesus' metaphors	Metaphors in action	Modern topics
Ambition	Lost sheep Rich fool	Father Son	Consider these from the other 4 columns	Architects
Celebration		Counsellor		Celebrations
Caring	Lazarus/Dives	Light		Crisis and needs
Choices	Good Samaritan	Shepherd		Engineering
Differences	Prodigal son	Lamb		Environment
Forgiveness	Mustard seed	Door Vine		Family situation
Forward looking	Flowers	Vineyards		Farms and food
Growth	The King's army	Wind		Fishing
Helping	The wise and foolish builders	Birth		Financier
Humility		Wine		Gardening
Judgment	The talents	Bread		Hobbies
Pertinacity	The seed and soil	Candle		Home care
Priorities	Treasure in the field	Celebration		Invention
Provision	Talents	Flowers		Nature
Repentance	Prison visiting	Fields		Newspapers
Responds	The wise virgins	Fishing		Sporting achievements
Restoration	The Wedding Banquet	Servant		
Rewards	The Lost Coin	Salt		Tourism
Seeking	Cleaning the nets	City etc		Driving
Truth	Workers in the vineyard etc			Exploitation
Wisdom etc				Music etc

He often aroused people by briefly telling them what they wanted to hear. His brief initial statements were readily recalled and reported amongst the people. One can only imagine the excited anticipation that swept through the villages. As people gathered to hear him teach, he used short statements that might now be called 'sound bites'. He could look at the crowds and see the poor, the sorrowful, the meek, the righteous, the merciful, the pure in heart, the peacemakers, and the persecuted and give each an unforgettable promise that they could latch on to. It was like a series of short mission statements of promise in schools for those who had been under achieving, bullied or were simply working hard. The distinctive promises were in effect like a contract between the school and the parents. They were organizing principles upon which his ministry could be based. This can be likened to good practice in all teaching situations where pupils are given assurances of what they are likely to achieve during the course of study... and enabled to fulfil them.

It was essential for everything to be memorable and therefore much of his teaching was poetic and couched in rhythmic patterns. For example, the central prayer that was clearly designed to be remembered and passed on, reflects the simple Aramaic poetry and uses a remarkable economy and simplicity of language to express powerful and repeatable ideas.

The techniques he used have proved to be hugely effective. For example, the unexplained parables required closure/completion by the people. That meant it gave people a degree of ownership of the parables, although no doubt many came to the wrong conclusions! His teaching was like parallel universes of the spiritual and material, and heaven and earth. Therefore, God could be likened to an affectionate Father who could be totally trusted. His teaching was characterized by a constant flow of metaphors and similes as he likened the Kingdom of God to mustard seed, corn, farmers and any contemporary life situations that could give spiritual significance and meaning.

Some of his most powerful teaching was brief and almost terse. For example, epigrams about

*2c-189
Why might reflection be regarded as particularly important?*

leadership and servant-hood neatly summarised what could have been a long explanatory text. Similarly, his use of hyperbole halted people in their tracks and forced them to consider what he meant by such ridiculous statements as having a plank of wood in their eye. Hence, over the centuries people have remembered such phrases as, "If you're right eye causes you to sin, pluck it out and throw it away….."

It is impressive and surprising to see how well pupils in primary schools are able to do something similar to that of Jesus if they are given a 'frame' and a purpose. They fill the frame with the relevant words related to an unknown situation and either write or tell a story or poem to illustrate the point.

Given that we too are surrounded by such illustrations that can be applied spiritually, compare the following parable written by the Rev. Eric Challoner with that of the Prodigal Son. It is evident that both had a spiritual purpose. There are similarities such as the forgiveness and acceptance but whereas Jesus' story is virtually closed and we know of most of the outcomes, Eric Challoner's story is open and poses questions about the human response and we are never told whether the daughter 'came to herself' as the Prodigal did.

John and Mary were not wealthy but they loved their daughter, Sharon, very dearly. They made sure that she had virtually everything she wanted and even sent her to an expensive private school where she did well. But when she came home and saw her parents' poverty she was embarrassed to invite her friends there.

When she left school she wanted to travel and reluctantly they allowed her to do so. She chose to go to America and promised to write regularly which she did it for a short time, but then she met a man and decided to live with him. He turned out to be very cruel and treated her badly and eventually turned her out of his home. For months she did not write to her parents. Her father died broken hearted.

Her mother decided to go to America to find her daughter. She went to the last place from which she had received a letter, and showed the picture of the girl before she had left home and enquired if anybody had seen her lately. They said that she had called several times, but not recently. However, the lady invited Mary to leave a message for her daughter in case she did call and suggested that by the message Mary should place a picture of Sharon before she left home and picture of herself now. The picture revealed the pain and suffering that had changed her life. By the picture, the mother put this message. "Sharon come home. Mother loves you. All is forgiven."

Pupils can become adept at converting every day news items and personal interests into spiritual parables. These foster reflective thought and cause some to enter into spiritual issues that they had not previously considered.

Jesus did not see spirituality as an easy option. His taught that it encompasses practical situations such as the inclusion of outcasts, and the moral requirement of justice and social righteousness. Just as the lepers posed unspoken questions to Jesus' followers, so hard questions are to be answered by criteria such as empathy, justice, forgiveness etc.It is apparent that spirituality can be taught where there is the will to learn, and the methods of Jesus applied in any situation, no matter whether it is spiritual or not – although of course it could be said that everything is spiritual! But can it be taught where there is no faith? Perhaps the major point however, is the quality of the role model and the confidence of the relationships together with the tools that Jesus left to be used.

Although the person of Jesus and spirituality might be said to be the real story, the pattern of his stories were like extended metaphors. As a teacher I asked pupils about what they would like me to tell them an impromptu parable. Their attention was fixed and the parables remembered. How much more it was with Jesus and the crowds!

It might have occurred as outlined below. Jesus' core message (see column 1) contained essential features of the Kingdom of God. These were applied to any situation (see col.2 and 3). He had seen shepherds looking for lost sheep and sleeping at the door of the sheepfold. Therefore, out of life experiences he built stories and metaphors that were integral to his spiritual message. As he identified with the needy and saw a parallel between the Kingdom of God and the natural world, so a rich stream of illustrations emerged. He confidently used this physical view of God to take people from concrete to abstract spiritual understandings. They were in the midst of an unfolding creative drama. Similarly, his miracles were 'metaphors in action'. Modern parables take the same principles and apply them to modern activities and situations (column 5). Spirituality is alive and authentic! When pupils raise an unusual topic (e.g. wrestling) they seldom realise that it can become a general parable about motivation etc.

'Show stopping' words and actions evoked a growing spirituality amongst some – and perhaps that was typical. His short statements might now be called 'sound bites'. They were like short mission statements of promise in schools for those who were under *A formal comparative conceptual approach*. A common approach is a cognitive study of contrasting practices in representative 'faiths'. An enlarged chart (Fig.12) is useful to consider factors such as perception, motivation etc . But is this spirituality?

Major faiths are studied under, say, six themes as shown or conversely take these themes as the organising tool and examine how the faiths illustrate them. As a cumulative chart or frame is gradually filled it becomes a focus to identify similarities and differences between faiths and develop branches that highlight features within them.

Jesus' use of similarity, contrast, symbols and imagery

Like any good Hebrew teacher, Jesus taught in a pictorial language that was memorable and communicable. We probably only know a few of his parables but all were forms of extended similes and metaphors, ranging from images of the Father, himself, the Holy spirit, the Kingdom of Heaven - in fact every aspect of his teaching. The point to be made here is that Jesus was not doing anything extraordinary because we all talk in verbal pictures. He did not use an extended register of speech/ vocabulary but he animated the environment spiritually. Even when the subject being taught is not spiritual, one only has to habitually say to oneself, "it is like…." and a repertoire of similarities, contrasts, symbols and imagery build up. It is as though this was Jesus' standard style of thinking. The point of contrast is indicated by the word 'but'. He frequently said, 'but I say unto you' which was a contrast between him and the religious authorities. This occurs 10 times in the Sermon on the Mount..

Jesus used similarity and contrast to indicate a sharp degree of difference and promote a sense that people had to make a choice. For example, two sons were commanded to work in the vineyards, but only one did.

Symbols and imagery were possibly the most powerful tools that Jesus used when teaching. These were rooted in traditional mind sets and assumed that listeners could interpret his allusions. Minimal explanations were required and listeners would often expand the imagery imaginatively which resulted in different degrees of understanding.

.2c-191
We tend to talk in metaphors and similes. Does it matter if they are true?

The varied images were powerful. Some simply make a statement and the hearer is left to interpret it in the light of tradition and imagination. Jesus could say that he was the Good Shepherd, the Bread of Life, the Door, and the True Vine and expect people to have a degree of understanding, although this was not always so. Other images were more extended metaphors, some of which almost have a touch of humour about them. When he used phrases about a camel going through the eye of a needle or taking a beam out of your eye they hardly needed any explanation. His metaphors were especially powerful in silencing the opposition, such as when he declared them to be whitewashed. He was a person whose literary skills were allied to a vivid imagination

Using the Imagination

Pre-eminently Jesus was an imaginative teacher! But all of his imaginative images and ideas were rooted in reality rather than fanciful thoughts that might be called creativity. He would have recognized *The Lion, the Witch and the Wardrobe* as an extended meaningful parable but other traditional stories would probably be re-cast to contain a spiritual, moral or social/economic dimension. Therefore, if imagination is an essential ingredient of teaching and learning, what might that mean in this context?

Imagination takes many different forms – both positive and negative. It can evoke pleasure, expectations, curiosity, exploration, anxiety and fear. Although Jesus did use fear on occasions (e.g. Lazarus and Dives) his teaching and action were normally positive and evoked wide ranging physical and spiritual imaginative responses. No doubt his teaching today would be highly imaginative and spark outcomes that went beyond the standard levels of understanding. His stories, promises and actions all achieved these responses.

Let us assume for convenience that imagination is powerfully stimulated in the situations.

Figure 119

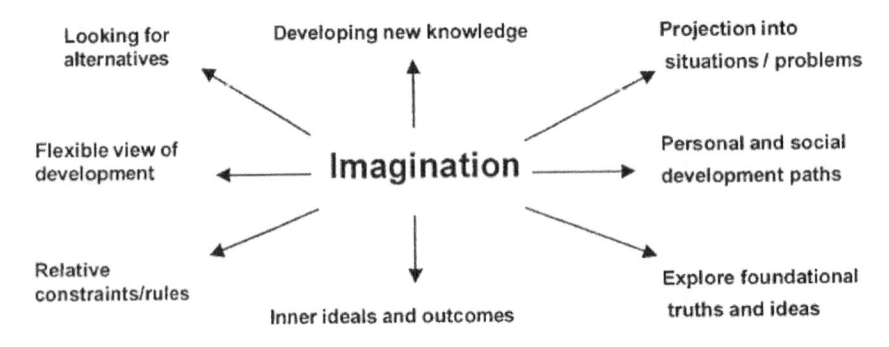

```
        Looking for         Developing new knowledge        Projection into
        alternatives                                        situations / problems
                    ↖              ↑              ↗
Flexible view of                                            Personal and social
development       ←——————  Imagination  ——————→             development paths
                    ↙              ↓              ↘
        Relative                                            Explore foundational
        constraints/rules   Inner ideals and outcomes       truths and ideas
```

Whilst imagination can be planned and developed, in the case of Jesus' followers it was the outcome of total life experiences that led to heightened expectations. They were gradually transformed from 'under' to 'over achievers'. It was not based primarily upon efficient instruction or structure but upon the ethos of the situation. As Jesus created aspirations they watched and copied him and so it fostered imagination and celebration. They were being trained into different perspectives and released into fresh possibilities. This might be seen to be the basis of developing imagination in any aspect of learning. It required their willingness to lower traditional defences and characteristic thought patterns and venture, with growing confidence, into a new range of possibilities such as those shown in Fig.119 /120.

.2c-192
Why is visualization important in teaching/ learning?

Figure 120

Personal situation and drive etc	Established social situations and requirements	Forward looking stimulation
• Intense personal desire • Habitually poses questions and looks for alternatives • Willing to break the mould • Aware of relevant knowledge • Successful past experiences • Standing on the shoulders of previous generations • Habitual reflection • Reaction to novelty • Identification/relationship • Personal surprise/ excitement	• Problems studied /resolved with others • Established group expectations and group suggestions • Watching excellence • Developing a process • Completing the unfinished statement or task • Impact of visualization and sensory experiences • Responding to the unexpected	• Planning goals to meet expectations • Looking for structured alternatives to a problem • The overriding vision • Technical excellence • Pursuit of interests • Urgent demands • Based upon traditional stories, occupations, organizations, social activities, hobbies

Spirituality can be an intensely personal dramatic force on which emotions and intellect are focussed. At times a person or group's spirituality cannot be understood... without entering into this sphere of awareness and action. The intense spirituality of Frederick Handel can be seen in his masterpiece 'The Messiah'. Imagine his emotions and devoted actions as he shut himself away for 11 days and emerged with this expression of his spiritual faith. One can hardly imagine what the atmosphere in his study was like! This notion of projecting oneself into such a spiritual biography with its emotions and driving motivation that yields such creativity is the stuff of dreams, even so it covers all types of human behaviour and spirituality. Consider the spirituality of Cicely Saunders and Mother Theresa of Calcutta. Both were concerned with the welfare of the dying and yet so differently. Archbishop Tutu and Nelson Mandela had a common cause in South Africa but their spirituality differed.

For most, spirituality does not revolve around problems but is a life orientation that colours attitudes and answers to everyday situations, namely what to approve and advise or situations to avoid / reject. It enters into the flow or frenzy of life and identifies the strength of motives behind actions. But what is the source that shapes this life stance? Is it a pattern to be instinctively followed or one based on an authoritative source such as a religious faith?

Let us consider a form of projection that typified Jesus....the storyteller in a world of metaphors – from observation to parables that illustrate *truth*. Jesus was not alone in being an influential storyteller – in fact we all do it!

The traditional storyteller's role ensured the continuity of the cultural heritage and identity that was in contrast to modern stories whose purpose is to entertain. Jesus had heard traditional heroic stories such as Moses crossing the Red Sea, but he did not generally follow this historic rabbinic style of storytelling. Possibly he knew that it would result in a pointless debate with the religious leaders. His purpose was the Kingdom of God and spirituality. He did something relatively new. He did draw upon rabbinic stories such as the parable of the sower(Mark ch.4). His stories, however, were short living incidents pregnant with possibilities, sharply memorable and appropriate for the open-air. He provided few details but listeners recognised the sense from their own experiences. Unlike our modern stories they contained no plot, names and little dialogue but there was action and a conclusion, all in a few verses!

Although the person of Jesus and spirituality might be said to be the real story, the pattern of his stories were like extended metaphors. As a teacher I asked pupils about what they would like me to tell them an impromptu parable. Their attention was fixed and the parables remembered. How much more it was with Jesus and the crowds!

It might have occurred as outlined below. Jesus' core message (see column 1) contained essential features of the Kingdom of God. These were applied to any situation (see col.2 and 3). He had seen shepherds looking for lost sheep and sleeping at the door of the sheepfold.

.2c-193
Why might imagination have been a crucial element in Jesus' teaching?

Therefore, out of life experiences he built stories and metaphors that were integral to his spiritual message. As he identified with the needy and saw a parallel between the Kingdom of God and the natural world, so a rich stream of illustrations emerged. He confidently used this physical view of God to take people from concrete to abstract spiritual understandings. They were in the midst of an unfolding creative drama. Similarly, his miracles were 'metaphors in action'. Modern parables use the same principles and apply them to modern activities and situations (column 5). Spirituality is alive and authentic! When pupils raise an unusual topic (e.g. wrestling) they seldom realise that it can become a general parable about motivation etc

'Show stopping' words and actions evoked a growing spirituality amongst some – and perhaps that was typical. His short statements might now be called 'sound bites'. They were like short mission statements of promise.

Equally important, would he be likely to enable them to see *new horizons* to which they felt instinctively drawn. But perhaps the distinctive language could be essential to the message itself. He demonstrated the value of clear unambiguous instruction and also frequently talked to people as confidants as shown in John chapters 14 -16. This prolonged discourse emerged out of an informal conversation and questions and answers. One can visualize the sequence of events as his followers fell silent and he began to speak with his acknowledged authority. Conversations operate two ways and it would appear that Jesus was not only a good talker but also a *listener*. We do not have clear indications of how Jesus used this skill. He had a small listening group of which he was dominant member but which was surely interactive. In fact, it is plausible to suggest that he developed some of his illustrations from their comments. Such situations are normally received with perhaps a rueful smile and approval. If so, the group had a role in generating informal teaching amongst each other.

But so often the skill of listening is neglected and its creative function unused. If the question, "Can a person go through a whole course without being listened to?" is asked, the answer is undoubtedly yes, which can be a hugely damning observation. Jesus' followers were not unusual in the development or their Idiosyncratic understandings. Learners views and understanding must be clearly ascertained. They may have a germ of a concept that can be developed *if the teacher is aware!* Conversely the person may have flawed concepts that need to be corrected. Listening is the basis of interaction and teacher awareness, which aids the development of pupil understandings.

Listening is commonly lightly assumed and consciously limited to such aspects of learning as:
- Accurate/corrective answers to closed questions.
- Accurate recall of information.
- Pupils making brief unambiguous statements.

But often sensitive coherent listening (and speaking) is interrupted. Any observer is likely to note how informal dialogue is frequently broken up by those who anticipate its outcome with such familiar words as, "Yes, but…" etc. So much conversation is left undeveloped and this multi-dimensional activity can remain undeveloped.

Listening is essential but can become problematic for teachers and learners. It may decline into 'little more than a sound passing by'. The importance of genuine listening is fundamental to people's self image, acceptance and self-worth (Bazalgette). Being listened is liberating (Long, p.33) and takes pupils beyond formal learning to develop a commitment to further enquiry. The teacher is seen to be available through sensitive listening and self discipline that then can transform the mundane to a creative level. This listening strategy is apparent in all these eight general teaching strategies. No doubt Jesus' own listening skills involved body- language, eye contact and emotional responses that resulted in mutual interpretations between himself and his listeners. These combined to form a listening ethos that set a high value on the process of listening which is a key to interactive speech and ideas.

.2c-194
Why might listening be regarded as a language skill?

Some occasions were planned whilst others were incidental and some were individual whilst others were group related, but the overall pattern was likely to involve the listening teacher appreciating, enhancing responses, and turning them into questions to foster reflection that promoted meaningful thought processes. Obviously his responses promoted the quality of thinking that influenced the quality of decisions

Despite our lack of precise knowledge about Jesus' interactive speaking and listening techniques, one gains the impression that he stimulated listening with fresh, meaningful knowledge that could be open ended. This posed questions and required reflective thought and for which he may not demand answers. His developmental teaching fed in relevant information that cumulatively built up his 'Big Picture'.

Questions and answers were staple elements of his interactive language and in the gospels we find over 100 questions being asked, and some being answered. Some of Jesus' first words were apparently questions. Many were rhetorical and really statements that caused people to think and arrive at appropriate answers. An example was when Jesus answered a question by telling a story such as the Good Samaritan. His stories both captured the attention of listeners and caused them to ponder and possibly re-orientate their understanding. These involved no threat but were releasing which was in contrast to other sharp instructional approaches. The stories provided opportunities for forms of reflection that enhanced the possibility of attitude change, whereas bare statements could provoke automatic rejection by those who were unsympathetic to his teaching.. The stories and his other metaphors, therefore, were not only memorable but deflected much opposition and sharpened the attention of followers. An example of Jesus answering a question with a question that promoted reflection was when he told Nicodemus that he must be born again. One can imagine this Pharisee going off into the darkness pondering on this strange statement and discussing it with trusted friends.

Questions and answers normally have six purposes:
- To promote thought "I wonder how..."
- To recall knowledge "Can you remember...?"
- To promote inquiry "Could you find out if...?"
- To inquire. "Would you be able......?"
- To defend oneself or somebody else "You're not going to try.... are you?"
- To attack a person's claims/attitude etc . "Do you really know....? "

Answers normally take the form of:

Facts.....Opinions......Promises......Question the question......Feelings......Asssertions

What type of answer would Jesus be likely to use most frequently?

Jesus recognized that a question often concealed its true motives. Therefore, he refused to be sidetracked into pointless debate. His response was simply to answer a question with a question that was effectively unanswerable. He knew that he was changing people's habitual thought processes and developing new frames of enquiry. Jesus astutely differentiated between the self-justifying question, the genuine enquiry, the request for truth posed as a question, and answering unspoken questions.

.2c-195
In what ways is the notion of 'scaffolding' fundamental to all teaching?

Figure 122

Basis of Communication - interaction/ and listening Matt.26v50	Setting the quality of relationships John 15v13	Trigger the imagination/ and questioning Luke 15v1ff	Links with past, present and future Mark 2v25ff
Instruction mentoring- similarity / contrast John 13v1ff	Enabling knowledge organised / demonstrate John 6v12... v47	Variety of emotions - emphatic brevity John8v12	Basis of Instruction and experience Luke 10v1ff

Strategy 5 Using the community as a basis for study

Spirituality is often regarded as a highly individual characteristic but it is also a community phenomenon. People are shaped to some degree by their *community,* and so too are their concepts of spirituality. Therefore, it is an essential tool of learning generally and spirituality.

Jesus organized his teaching around his band of apprentices (strategy 2) and accentuated people's learning by using their multiple senses (strategy 3). But what would be the basis of the teachers' awareness of pupils and how they acquire knowledge? This has been the focus of sustained psychological debate. A Russian psychologist, Lev Vygotsky, developed a seminal system to explain how people learn, and which Jesus would have recognized, indeed many of his practices imply a common approach to Vygotsky's central ideas. The Russian rejected the notion of efficient teaching through didactic instruction. Instead he insisted that learning is essentially *socially situated* and that learning and teaching should stem from pupils' *socio-cultural basis.*

Four of Vygotsky's major ideas were:

- A person learns within a *social context* and concepts and reality are rooted in the pupil's *social setting*. A person is not a prisoner of the parent society but the *shaping of learning and rationalization* are linked to it. This was at the heart of Jesus' methodology.

- Children *talk to themselves* as they learn and ongoing *'inner speech conversations'* make learning meaningful and enable them to develop or link current situations with emerging core principles. Jesus recognized that spiritual learning as well as cognitive development depends upon its *social context*, initial *supporting guidance of the teacher and 'self talk'* or *expressing their thoughts to others*. This justifies Jesus' emphasis upon ongoing interaction and the willingness *to listen to their 'self talk'.*

- Pupils move from vague recognition of elementary concepts to the systematic development of multiple aspects of understanding, which means they may be idiosyncratic. Bruner and Wood (1976) later developed the notion of a need to be given *a structure to assist learning* or *mental 'scaffolding'* around which ideas and skills can be built.

- This scaffolding provides pupils with close support and *rescues them from their own errors*. This, however, sees instruction not just as logical explanations but rather as an *interpersonal network* in which the pupils and teacher describe the logic of their thinking. As pupils develop their skills so this scaffolding is gradually withdrawn.

A teacher makes skilful inputs to *support and interact* with pupils, which assumes that there are time and skills *to prepare and pull the pupils along to construct meanings* and *transform the developments* in pupils' learning. This requires positive engagement, social contact, high challenge but low stress and an interpersonal network. As in the apprentice model, pupils' peers also act as *social facilitators and peer teachers*, and skills that are developed in this social context often exceed those gained formally or privately and so Interpersonal work enables thoughts to be developed and refined. The total learning situation *extends their 'learning zone'.* and their learning is established.

.2c-196
Where might Jesus be seen to maximize/ minimize community involvement?

The social context often exceed those gained formally or privately and so Interpersonal work enables thoughts to be developed and refined. The total learning situation *extends their 'learning zone'.* and their learning is stablished.

Vygotsky's stress on the socio-cultural basis of learning was not new - indeed all of Jesus' teaching practised this. Therefore, how might people/pupils use their own culture to learn about aspects of spirituality? It can be done through studies of faith groups in the area.... But let us consider a hypothetical situation.(see Fig.123)

When Jesus taught his generic prayer, the overriding principle was in the opening phrase, "Our Father, who is in heaven". That was central to his teaching and required an expression of faith by the person praying. But where people's spirituality does not accord with the notion of a personal god, the prayer still offers a *structural* basis for teaching certain aspects of an alternative view of spirituality. It reflects contemporary thinking about social education.

If the prayer is replaced by community awareness and sensitivity, it might be rewritten in similar succinct terms that allude to forms of spirituality but which do not require the faith basis of Jesus' prayer. The two share common features. Both can be outward-looking, expressions of faith, recognise authority, have a community basis, and understand that aspirations, needs and frailties cannot be resolved independently but need an authority greater than themselves. The differences between the two stances are evident in their many absolute and relative values and priorities and so result in powerfully different outcomes.

Despite the obvious limitations both aspects can be developed within characteristic teaching methods that are sympathetic to both those of Jesus and Spiritual Intelligence. Churches nowadays lay great emphasis on their responsibility to the community and to take on the role of servants where possible. The opportunity to understand what the distinct spirituality represents needs to be grasped. The norms of our multicultural society and the multi-faith religious education render the different significance of spirituality ever more critical. Vygotsky would have said to understand spirituality pupils should go into the community.

The dominant ideas were that a pupil moves into what might be called authentic community evidence. The teacher as an enabler provides essential scaffolding and then gradually withdraws it as the pupil makes progress. The stages are based upon existing pupil knowledge, self-talk, planning and having appropriate scaffolding, talking with select people in the community and evaluating the evidence. The dynamics of investigation not only satisfy Zohar's criteria but creative thinking is establishing long term ownership of the emerging concepts, but is there a danger of 'correct knowledge' of spirituality being sacrificed to powerful processes of enquiry.

Vygotsky (and others) asked who is a pupil's *'knowledgeable other'*? This means, who is regarded as authoritatively knowledgeable? Is it a teacher, parents, friends, or hero etc.? Where there is dissension about this, learning can be hindered. This was seen by Jesus' followers who had regarded the religious authorities as their *'knowledgeable others'*. But conflict ensued when Jesus took this role and provided different scaffolding to support their learning in a newly defined zone of development. If didactic teaching is particularly appropriate for introverted people because it is safe, linear and clearly defined, this strategy is more high risk, and even with agreed goals and teacher scaffolding, is more suited to those with extravert tendencies who thrive on uncertainty and exploration.

.2c-197
How is optimum scaffolding achieved?

Figure 123

Our Father focus/ faith	Outward Faith Possibilities Social Personal application	Authority Friendship Aspiration Needs Frailty	_Our community focus/ faith_
2. Who is in heaven		2. *that surrounds us* Humility beyond self, emphasis on corporate	
3. Hallowed is your name		3. *how we appreciate you* Reverential attitude to life, Positive life view - fragile earth	
4. Thy kingdom come.		4 *may you prosper* Aspiration for good, Identify high aspirations	
5. Thy will be done		5. *may all be done*	
6. On earth as in heaven		6. *with the joy and peace we desire* Examine moral and social order Personal practical expressionless of goodness	
7. Give us this day		7 *meet our every need* Shared welfare provisions food and resources	
8. Our daily bread		8. *and are not mine alone* Simplicity! Community awareness.	
9. And forgive us our trespasses		9. *Help & support friends & neighbours* Restore us to each other; honest, repentant spirit & desire for good. Self examination & corporate peacemaking	
10. As we forgive those who trespass against us		10. *as I restore those who offend me* Open confident relationships & pathways	
11. And lead us not into temptation		11 *Do not lay heavy burdens upon us* Aware of our frailty	
12. But deliver us from evil		12 *But liberate us into peace* Dependence on others Community and interpersonal support	

The emphasis is that *learning is social/cultural, and that self-talk is vital to the process of structuring ideas* that are rooted in *changing degrees of teacher-pupil interaction*, with the teacher aiming to gradually reduce his involvement with the pupil. This core skill is frequently seen as an ideal professional ability and something with which Jesus would have agreed.

Vygotsky believed that a teaching skill is to recognize when a pupil moves outside of his/her *'Learning Zone' or existing understanding*. If so learning can become fragmented and unreliable. Instead, a pupil should remain in the *'zone of development'* and fully integrate the understanding as the scaffolding is brought down, at which stage the scaffolding is re-erected to provide a new boundary or area of learning, which again was Jesus' style.

Taking some liberty with Vygotsky's theory, how might it be applied to Jesus' pupil, Peter? Fig.124

.2c-198
What does it mean for teaching to be contextualized?

- Peter lived within the social context of Galilee, with all that implies.
- He began his discipleship in an explosive sense of awe but he lacked any knowledge or skills that would be required to understand this new kingdom.
- As one of Jesus' apprentices he watched, thought (self talk) and listened to the master both in public and private and talked with his peers within his relatively mistaken ideas. Jesus provided the scaffolding of which Vygotsky, and then Bruner spoke.
- There were opportunities to explore Jesus' ideas with others and progress to a rudimentary understanding of this fresh message. Jesus not only instructed Peter, he was also assessing the support needed, which could be reduced as understanding increased.
- Peter showed his growing understanding by stating that Jesus was the Christ. Even so his knowledge and skills were inadequate to undertake independent work. But Jesus gradually withdrew his support and prepared him for 'independent learning'.
- After the intense experiences of Jesus' passion, Jesus' support was withdrawn, although replaced by the Pentecost experience. They became relatively independent learners and had to resolve issues in the light of the principles they had learned.
- Peter advanced from an awe inspired onlooker, to partial understanding and on to a decision-maker who reflected the mind of Jesus. He had the mind of a Jew but his personal religious exploration had changed him from total teacher dependency, to growing confidence to move forward into the unknown.
- Mutual expectations were established as they considered the past and future.
- Together they shaped their desires, shared their problems and sought to implement Jesus' wishes that led them to emotional self-awareness.

Figure 124

1. A pupil lacks skills and understanding but is within a social context and a process of inquiry and exploration begins.	2 The pupil explores and develops ideas personally using self talk in the inner conversation to achieve awareness and rationalization	3. A teacher provides conceptual scaffolding upon which the pupil can build. It must be close but just extend existing abilities. The pupil describes the logic of the ideas.
4. The pupil achieves effective performance when supported directly by the teacher, 'self talks' and is indirectly helped by the peer-group.	5. The support is gradually withdrawn by the teacher, leaving the indirect support from their peers. Teacher dependency is avoided!	6. The pupil's secure concepts develop further and ideally s/he becomes an independent long-term learner and zone of development is extended.

Figure 125

Social/cultural based learning Develop skills and knowledge from locality	Shared language – self and peers. What do they really know?	Optimum degree of support – scaffolding	Learning based on cultural knowledge	Support at all levels and in all situations
	Use of everyday encounters In the community etc	Use of cultural symbols, social identification	Problem solving / creativity based on familiar cultural and social setting	Edging the learner forward within his capacity

Figure 126

Interpreting universal spiritual truths into local and social understanding	Everyday encounters Widow of Nain Luke ch.7v11 Peter's mother-in-law Mk.1 v29	Application Going out in pairs Mark ch.9v7	Using the environment Fields white and ready for harvest John ch.4v35	Symbols City on a hill Light of the world Matt.ch.5v14
	Problem solving and creativity John ch13v1 with Luke ch.22v24	Conflict The temple Matt.ch21v12 Pharisees in the field Mark ch2v23	Revelation Transfiguration Mark ch.9v2 And ch.9v30	The caring Shepherd Jn 10

.2c-199 Looking at Figs.124-126 which principles might be at the forefront of Jesus' thinking?

Strategy 6 Mastery Learning

The priority was unquestionable! Jesus' work must succeed! The prognosis was not good. Failure might seem inevitable – but is it? Certainly not! The psychologist Benjamin Bloom claimed that virtually all learners can succeed to a high level of social competence if…… He claimed that all can achieve a working competence in any aspect of learning, if given the appropriate situation. When he was asked if that could apply to spirituality he was confident that his claim is true. He was probably correct. Spiritual sensitivity/intelligence is for all and not the few. Although the question was asked before the term spiritual intelligence was popularized his conception would have related to Zohar etc rather than a Jesus Focus.

Many people fail, not primarily for lack of ability, but because they must *learn in a given time and in competition with others*. In such circumstances only a limited proportion can succeed, whilst others 'fail' and motivation and ownership are reduced. But with the common human experience of people being free to practice with minimal time controls, mastery can usually be achieved, as such wide ranging occupations and pastimes as archers and musicians can vouch.

Success is often tied to a SMART management model in which goals are *specific, measurable, achievable, relevant and TIMED*. If the time element is deleted from the equation and one is only competing with one's self-failure is of little importance – it is simply a case of trying again… many times over if necessary! But 'time out' requires 'time in which means providing a sense of continuity with ample related reinforcement and every aspect being developmental and mutually supportive. The conclusion becomes…

- a promise of success.
- flexible timing.
- small learning units.
- assured success-re-learn with similar material if not successful.
- an appropriate programme of learning / reinforcement /reflection.
- enhanced motivation.

This is normal when teaching music, chess and most everyday activities. It was probably regarded as 'the son of programmed learning' and a considerable amount of work was done to show its application in mathematics, science and engineering… but what about spirituality? It is ideally designed for spiritual intelligence and even be applied to certain criteria within the Jesus Focus, after all he was the mentor who must have assessed his close followers and then taught them, provided experiences of working with himself and then tested them informally. But Bloom had nothing to say about sacrificial service, and simplified motivation as the product of success. Let us assume that the study topics fall within the matrix shown below.

Although Jesus was concerned with spiritual 'mastery' involving service, attitude, truth, motivation etc., the same basic issues are applicable. By training his disciples for three years, based on a limited curriculum, Jesus could reasonably expect them to listen, talk, help and experiment until they achieved mastery. He repeated his teaching in many forms. For example, the Sermon on the Mount is stated in a similar form in the Sermon on the Plain. Further, they possibly heard similar words and met similar problems as they moved amongst 80 or so Galilean towns and villages. If they had to learn everything quickly they may not have achieved the degree of mastery and ownership that they did. Jesus recognized that he needed to teach them in short motivating stages that involved minimal failure. It is interesting that the major characteristics of 'teaching for mastery' are found in Jesus' teaching. He used *short words and sentences, explicit terms, stressed the importance of the concepts, short term goals, adequate practice, positive relationships, sequencing, visual imagery and gave ample reinforcement* etc-which promote mastery at personal and social levels.

.2c-200
What level of mastery might Jesus have expected?

He gave them the Big Picture and core ideas and then in various contexts broke it down into bite-sized portions. Although it was not highly structured, it was cumulative and led to personal acknowledgement and recognition of his message. He required competence so that they could work unsupervised with new beliefs. This raises a question as to whether the tendency to insist on time-based learning is misplaced and reflects the values of a society that is overly concerned with economy and sorting pupils into ability groups.

Figure 127

Mastery Learning Universal competences Delete time constraints	Universal basic competences	Giving time to learn	Closely developed practice	Motivation by continued success and mastery
	Time element deleted from equation	Periodic tests to ensure not building on pupil error	High degree of teacher control and formal planning	Selected forms of reinforcement

Figure 128

Mastery learning Giving pupils time/ practice to learn	Arrest attention Arousal at Nazareth Lk.4v18ff ?	Enquiry Parables etc Mark ch.4	Discussion Jn.14	Posing problems Parables Matt.ch.13 Confrontation Matt.12v22ff
	Contextualize Visual Memories Jn.21v14ff	Chunking; Patterns Coherence; Congruence	Reflection Jesus in the hills Lk.4v1	Being sent out at least 3 times

Strategy 7 A Conceptual Approach

From the outset it has been stressed that whereas teachers have traditionally provided considerable information and detailed instruction, in contrast Jesus highlighted principles and key concepts which he illustrated with stories and actions – which proved a highly effective, reliable tool for teaching about spirituality (or any other 'subject'). How might this be commonly used now at the planning and operational stages? Jesus probably developed his teaching around principles and concepts intuitively which adds weight to its value. A modern four part conceptual analysis that covers spirituality and across subjects is shown in Figure 128.

Level 1 indicates those high level general principles that stretch across all areas of learning ranging from the sciences to the arts (including spirituality). These are focal organizers. Levels 2,3 and 4 are related specifically to forms of knowledge. For example, in religious terms what *caused* the happenings on the day of Pentecost and in the post-modern definitions of spirituality what *caused* Bill Gates to undertake his philanthropic work?

Alternative social principles (e.g. boundaries, needs, aspiration and interdependence) yield a different focus on spirituality. These four principles can highlight experiences of early monasticism, and yet also indicate the work of say, Christian Aid. It goes well beyond descriptions of religious structures and procedures and enters into the dynamics of human life. This might be contrasted with focussing principles such as growth / decay, stability /change. But what does this contribute towards personal spirituality? At levels 2,3 and 4 an orientation can be applied more specifically to religious education and traditional spirituality.

.2c-201
Did Jesus succeed in taking his pupils to the point of mastery?

Level 2. In the 1960s Professor Ninian Smart and his team emphasized seven universal features of religions' faiths. This categorization of religious phenomena, beliefs and practices was at a high level of abstraction. It has been an influential means of systematizing planning in religious education and promoting discussion but what does it contribute to personal everyday spirituality?

Level 3. Also in the 1960s I devised what I called 12 middle order concepts that are at a lower level of abstraction than those at Level 2. They provide ample scope for illustrating common and recurring features in any religion both thematically and within discrete faiths. It proved to be very useful in providing developmental understanding and unifying studies but I was still left with the question whether it promotes spirituality?

Level 4. At about the same time Attwood produced a set of concepts which were highly specific features within a faith. They are of general use and by generating an understanding of the significance of say, Holy Communion within Christianity could be highly personalized and take us closer towards achieving the expectations and practice of spirituality. Religious education was setting a mark for tangible spirituality and giving examples of inspirational personal and corporate spirituality. Also its agreed expectations, processes and responses can bring a powerful sociological perspective to the studies and provide comparative and developmental frames. One sees the rationale of dominant and formative ideas and practices, how they recur and what their influence might be. A good example of this is monasticism in its many forms worldwide. In fact it can be adapted to major themes such as truth, revelation, sacrifice etc. or minor topics such as dance, songs etc. or by loosely coordinating concepts as Jesus did.

Figure 129

Level 1. High level general principles				
Causality Power /authority Structure /function Conflict /consensus Adaptation Community Values /beliefs Stability /change Growth /decay Similarity/difference Boundaries Needs Aspiration Interdependence Dominance/ Submission				
	Geography	*History*	*Religious Educ.*	*Social Studies*
Level 2	Location Connectivity Determinates Networks Centralisation Spatial structures Resources etc	Civilization Nationalism Legitimacy Government Temporality Law Politics	God Doctrine Ethics Confessional Ritual Experiential Mythological	Socialisation Culture Control/ order Role Society Institution Elitism
Level 3	Accessibility Specialisation Mobility Region Settlement Demography Site/Situation Geog. Inertia Commerce Cost/Time/Soc.Dist. Pollution Cartography	Monarchy Succession Democracy Revolution Conquest Alliance Patriotism Exploitation Republic Capitalism Communism Empire etc	Mystery/Purpose Interpretation Sacrifice Holy men Signs &symbols Prayer Good and evil Faith Revelation/reform Mission Worship Holy books	Mobility Norms Anomie Sanctions Hierarchies Groups Deviance Status Sponsorship Dominance Ritual Working class
Level 4	Valley Port City Exports Route Cyclone etc	King Guilds Middle ages Statues Castle Renaissance	Baptism Cross Judgement Forgiveness Repentance Sabbath etc	Groups Reference Pressure Peer Contest mobility Bureaucrat

.2c-202
When would Level 1, 2, 3 and 4 each be particularly appropriate tools?

No strategy or method is sacrosanct but all need to reflect the nature of the subject itself. Of course religious education has replaced religious instruction with its particular qualities reflecting the wealth of knowledge, values, expressive opportunities etc and which entails asking questions about:

- Which knowledge and concepts will provide the basis of this aspect of education?
- Which values, moral imperatives and attitudes will be the bed rock of the study of religion?
- How might an ethos be generated that reflects religious ideas and lifestyles?
- Which general learning experiences will be provided?
- How will appropriate skills be used to enable enquiry/investigative learning to occur?
- Which experiential opportunities will be provided?
- Which opportunities can be used which reflect the wealth of religious expression?

Jesus recognized that effective instruction incorporated change of attitude, projection, empathy something valuable in confined situations etc as people moved into what he was teaching, something to which this total working strategy can contribute.

Figure 130

Concept awareness	Concept Debate	Conceptual statement	Conceptual Development
I am the Good Shepherd John ch.10	Why do you eat and drink with sinners? Luke 5v30	No man can serve two masters. Matt. 6v24	For as yet they did not know John 20v9
Conceptual proof Put your finger here and see my hands John 20v27	Conceptual demonstration And when he saw their faith he said, Luke 5v20	Conceptual Instructions Pray like this: Our Father Matt.6v9	Conceptual Expression – feelings He saw the city and wept over it Luke 19v41

Strategy 8 Concept attainment

It was vital that people should not only be followers but that they should thoroughly grasp his teaching. He would not be with them long and his vision extended far beyond Galilee. This was urgent! Their understanding had to be sufficiently flexible for it to be understood and applied in various situations both old and new. They would go beyond their personal knowledge of Jesus and recognize, at least in the long-run, that as the people of the Way they were more than a sect within Judaism. They had to develop the revolutionary all encompassing *concepts* that Jesus was teaching.

They watched Jesus, gained knowledge and responded with him to a wide range of needs. Every incident illustrated differences and yet underpinning them were generalizations about faith, forgiveness, repentance and compassion. Could they take common features from these situations and grasp the total conceptual network of Jesus? This is in accord with the normal functioning of the brain, which gathers similar features together into schemas to form generalizations and also possibly rejects information that is incompatible with the schema. When Jesus said, 'the Kingdom of God is like...' that would also indicate what the Kingdom of God is *not* like. As concepts clustered together, understanding developed which were applicable to situations far beyond Judaea. His language and characterisations were sharp and concrete with no misunderstanding as his apprentices pondered over what the metaphors and similes meant in totality. But how could this thorough, flexible understanding that we call *concept attainment be achieved?*

.2c-203
What are the possibilities of normally achieving mastery?

It is said that people need to over-learn concepts, which means that it is necessary to exceed mere linear concepts and be able to apply a flexible multi-dimensional understanding to any fresh situation. This was seen by Jerome Bruner as the criterion for achieving concept attainment. Although he never dealt with spirituality, he assumed that it was necessary to be able to generalize and use a concept to many situations. Therefore, by attaining concepts such as spirituality within Christianity and Judaism, a person should be able to apply them in meaningful studies amongst other faiths, such as Islam. Although this would be an over statement his demand for flexible understanding which can be applied widely is fundamental to teaching spirituality. This principle would apply even more directly to Spiritual Intelligence.

Jesus had a sound and balanced approach to teaching. On the one hand he provided established statements that were authoritative and illustrated by powerful metaphors. On the other hand people were constantly seeing examples of the Kingdom of God in action and tentatively arriving at conclusions, for example through the unexplained parables. Jesus demonstrated his wisdom by *not* telling people that he was the Messiah, not simply because of the excitement and fallacious ideas it would have aroused, but also because it forced people into intense discussions after which they came to conclusions. He generated a creative encounter that gave people the chance to pose questions, use their intuition and hypothesize as to whom he was and the significance of what he was saying.

Items of factual information have value but unless they are it linked with similar ideas and applied to fresh situations they are of limited use. Jesus' pregnant statements were multi-dimensional. He generated more powerful ideas than the information he taught as he guided and enabled them to 'discover' the Father for themselves. During the high teacher-pupil interaction they saw concepts from different perspectives as he illustrated them through stories, miracles, teaching statements etc and so developed them into multi-purpose concepts that could be used widely. Concept attainment, like the six previous teaching strategies mentioned, was an essential and powerful aspect of learning which has been built into most modern teaching and learning., and was certainly vital to early Christians.

During the latter half of the 20th century two major teaching strategies came to the fore – *inductive and deductive teaching and learning*. Jerome Bruner, developed the principle of inductive learning that has parallels with some of Jesus' teaching methods. With many traditional practices in schools pupils are provided with a set of rules and then asked to develop further examples. This is sometimes called *Ruleg* (rule followed by example). Bruner, however, suggested that we should firstly identify the key principles that were being taught. The pupils are then exposed to as much experiential or quasi-experiential material as possible so that by guided discovery these principles are further identified. This is called *Egrule (examples leading to the rule or principle)*.

Bruner started from the well-worn position that 'people tend to like that which they are good at, or interested in'! Like Jesus, he was not suggesting that pupils should have their studies based on tightly managed sequences. His system of inductive learning gave pupils a rich body of anthropological case studies in which were embedded examples of the concepts and principles he was teaching. The pupils examined the study materials, and identified the generalisations and rules that linked certain facts that fed into concepts that could be used to examine further related case studies. Jesus did something similar. Although he briefly introduced his ideas, his major thrust was for people to watch the process of his work and gradually convert the information into concepts. Although the disciples were not always fast learners, they were left to reflect on certain crucial principles (e.g. forgiveness, service, repentance etc.) and apply them to fresh situations. In other words, Jesus was not so much giving them information, as enabling them to acquire the deep structures of knowledge that gave them powerful understandings. Both Jesus and Bruner wanted people to grapple with ideas, solve problems and formulate conclusions. Of course Jesus used the Ruleg procedure when he made statements about forgiveness of sins etc but as a general rule he wanted people to come to conclusions and apply them to the established patterns he was illustrating. This was a significant feature of Jesus' teaching methods because fundamentally his

.2c-204
Concept attainment is the flexible mastery of ideas, Why was this of so important to Jesus?

pupils had to become problem solvers quickly and develop solutions consistent with the concepts they had 'discovered'. With a thorough grasp of his varied teachings they could pull them together and take his vision far beyond Galilee. They would even go beyond their personal knowledge and recognize their new identity as people of the way.

Although the disciples were not always fast learners, they were left to reflect on certain crucial principles (e.g. forgiveness, service etc)and apply them to fresh situations. In other words Jesus was not so much giving them information, as enabling them to acquire the deep structures of knowledge that generated powerful understandings. Both Jesus and Bruner wanted people to grapple with ideas, solve problems and formulae conclusions, This was a significant feature of Jesus' teaching methods because fundamentally his pupils had to become problem solvers quickly and develop solutions consistent with the concepts they had 'discovered'. Even those who do not believe what he taught generally accept that Jesus had a sound and balanced approach to teaching. On the one hand he provided established statements that were authoritative and illustrated by powerful metaphors. On the other hand people were constantly seeing examples of the Kingdom of God in action and tentatively arriving at conclusions, for example through the unexplained parables. Jesus demonstrated his wisdom by *not* telling people that he was the Messiah, not simply because of the excitement and fallacious ideas it would have aroused, but also because it forced people into intense discussions after which they came to conclusions. He generated a creative encounter that gave people the chance to pose questions, use their intuition and hypothesize as to whom he was and the significance of what he was saying.

A common application of concept attainment in the style of Jerome Bruner is to collect visual material from aid societies showing how, for example, they re-establish people after a tragic natural event such as a tsunami. Pupils note the different strategies and also the common principles governing each stage of the recovery programme. These principles are then formulated into action plans that might be used in a hypothetical situation. It is then assessed by an aid society.

Figure 131

Concept attainment Apply concepts in various contexts	Guided Enquiry based learning	Deductive learning - Ruleg	Inductive learning – Egrule	Gleaning generalisation and concepts from related situations
	Using concepts in new related knowledge areas	Experiential learning and field work where possible	Testing through previously unlearned material	Moving into fresh areas of application

Figure 132

Concept attainment Develop and apply concepts in various contexts	Demonstration The paralysed man and his friends Mk ch.2v1ff	Point of contact Legion Mk ch.5v9	Conversation and dialogue Nicodemus Jn3 John 14 -16	Story telling Imaginative Realistic Prodigal Son
	Historical authority Jonah Prophets The Law Matt.ch16v4	Sequencing Teaching about the Law Matt ch.5v21f	Discourse End times Matt ch 24 - 25 Luke 9v46ff	Going into all the world Mk ch.16

.2c-205
Why is Ruleg used more than Egrule in everyday teaching?

A pointer to the use of the eight strategies

Although teaching strategies are often considered in isolation they are usually combined so that appropriate features can be used beneficially, as Jesus did.

Let us assume that a teacher wants to achieve:
- Flexible understanding of principles that have wide-ranging applications.
- Independent learners who gain ownership success by using flexible methodologies.

One could envisage the following pattern of teaching emerging.

Stage 1: An *advance organizer is presented* within a short, clearly established framework that identifies organizing goals and elements in the learning (Strategy 1).

Stage 2: Major concepts are identified to be examined / explored / developed (Strategy 6).

Stage 3: A *group ethos* and sense of worthwhile investment of time is built by demonstrating what the pupils will achieve and its relevance to them (Strategy 2).

Stage 4: Pupils are involved and lessons contain experiential and expressive work to learn through the senses. Begin a display of the pupils' achievements (Strategy 3).

Stage 5: Apply the learning to their social and cultural environment. Provide them with a high degree of support that is gradually decreased. Expect pupils to work at varying paces and require differing degrees of guidance. Allow scope for individual work. Pupils gradually become self-sufficient and gain ownership of that area of study (Strategy 4).

Stage 6: Prevent the pupils from multiplying errors by giving them relatively short units of work that provide tangible success and can have a remedial function (Strategy 5).

Stage 7: Identify major principles and concepts that have been taught and illustrate them from previously learnt lessons. See whether the pupils can apply the principles and concepts into short, fresh and relevant case studies.

Stage 8: The final display enables pupils to gain an overall appreciation of personal and group achievements and recognize how it relates to previous and future work. Problems can be reduced by ensuring that the pupils can see a pathway to success and that made units of work and instructions are available when pupils hit a problem.

Examples of this type of planning and development are presented in chapter 18.

.2c-206
In which aspects of his work would Jesus regard concept attainment as imperative?

Figure 133. A resumee of the eight teaching strategies considered – Where might they be of particular use?

Didactic Information Instruction	Fresh Knowledge	Soundbites Memorable	Using senses Visualisation	Question/ Answer Friendly – Jn.ch.14 Opponent – Lk 5v21	Consolidate Connectivity Two disciples walking to Emmaus Lk 24	Thinking skills Prediction – Lazarus/Dives Cause-effect Lk.16f	Advance organizers Principles concepts Nazareth - Isaiah 61
Apprentices Copy Master Observe, Replicate	Peer education Learners as partners Lk.9v1ff	Interpretation Reviewing the law Jn.8v1-11	Contrast, similarity Jn.8v12	Using situation Lk.19v1 Passover Lk.22	Projection Go into all the world Matt.ch.28v19	Language Poetic rhythms Lk ech.6v20ff	Anchors Associated memories reinforcing situations
Accelerated Learning Using the senses Building scenario	Moving into the unknown Mark .9v2	Activity Help – John6	Meeting problems Storms Matt.ch.8v24	Imagery True vine; Shepherd; Door John.10v1	Mental memory maps Matt.ch. 26v75 John ch.2v22	Challenge Unfinished business Awe Expectations	Emotional engagement Lazarus Jn.11v35 Jerusalem Lk.13v34
Language and imagination	Instruction and impart precise information	Stories for cultural continuity	Stories to impart ideas	Express emotions	Facilitate interaction/ relationships	Enquiry Q-A	Imaginative explanations and expressions
Social knowledge Interpreting universal spiritual truths into social understanding	Everyday encounters Widow of Nain Luke.7+ Mk.1v29	Application Going out in pairs Mark.9v7	Using the environment John 4v35	Symbols City on a hill Matt.ch.5v14	Problem solving and creativity Johnch13v1with Lk .22v24	Conflict The temple Matt.21v12+ Mk.2	Revelation Transfiguration Mark.9v2 and.9v30
Mastery learning Giving pupils time/ practice to learn	Arrest attention arousal at Nazareth Lk.4	Enquiry Parables etc Mark.4	Discussion	Posing problems Parables Matt.ch.13 Matt.12v22ff	Contextualised Visual Memories Jn.21v14ff	Chunking, Patterns Coherence Congruence	Reflection Jesus in the hills Lk.4v1and
Conceptual awareness, know main ideas	Revealing the Big Picture Matt.6-7	State principles of the Kingdom of God Matt.5v1-11	Describing long term concepts E.g. Lk.4	Demonstrate major concepts Lk.10;ch.15	Promises for conceptual continuity / development	Past related to present and future Matt.25	Principles of relationships Jn.20
Concept attainment	Multi-dimensional understanding	Application of principles to varying situations	Apply concepts to novel situations	Evaluate outcomes and cause- effect of change	Resolution of problems	Creative projection into past, present and future situations	Relate change requirements to new situations

Many varied issues have been considered. Therefore, to conclude this section Figure 134 identifies 19 issues.

a. The two central columns indicate those that illustrate aspects of Jesus' teaching style.
b. The two columns on the left reflect degrees of traditional approaches
c. The two columns on the right show problems raised by reluctant pupils who need support from teaching exemplified in the two central columns.

.2c-207
Consider how the 8 strategies in Fig 133 were supportive to Jesus.

.2c-208
Which of the 19 issues listed below(Fig.134) are of particular importance?

Figure 134

Issues Priorities	Extreme Teacher Issues	Significant Teacher Issues	Jesus' Kingdom Ideals	Disciples Teaching / Learning Ideals	Significant Pupil Issues	Extreme Pupil Issues
Agreed Values	Coercive / Imposed compliance	Rule based situation	Love, respect, generosity in authority	Agreed love based mores	Generally cooperative when felt appropriate	Dysfunctional pupils
Attitude	Withdrawal from initiatives	Formal pressure to constrain	Creative pupil orientation and free involvement	Teachable and creatively involved	Negatively compliant	Obstructive
Authority	Maximally coercive	Follows decreed pattern of order and legitimacy	Based upon ability, character and vision	Responsive and contribute to positive authority	Compliant when supervised	Self-regulatory
Purpose	Complete formal requirements	Limited to an authorized task	Clarity and strength to achieve	Strength of needs and aspirations of self and others	Restricted purpose	Lack of agreed purpose
Leadership	Dictatorial, desire to control	Formal task leadership even if ability is limited	The Good Shepherd	Follow 'right' principles	Follow due requirements and no more	Rebellious to authority etc
Motivation	Passivity	Limited involvement	Creative resolution to progress and achieve	A willing determination to succeed	Motivated when supervised	Motivated to suit oneself
Agreed Roles	Controller/ Imposition of role Instructor	Limited to formally recognized and restricted roles	Creative development and role fulfilment	Creative learning pupils		Rejection of the teaching / learning situation
Ambition	Limited to the authority's directives	Limited to formal recognition and success	Serve, uphold and develop others	Communal and personal abilities maximized		Idiosyncratic or no ambitions
Ability	Those aspects recognised by the authorities	Abilities formally recognized by society	Wide knowledge converted to wisdom	Wide range of personal learning skills recognised	Confined to working the social system	Personal and group recognised abilities
Relationships	Imposition of sharp formal distancing	Formal acceptance of distanced position	Liking and commitment to others' welfare	Confident respect for righteous(?) others	Compliant learner	Rejection of relationship - isolation
Restoration	Ambivalent and distrustful of change	Reinstatement on control terms	Active moves for restoration by leader / teacher	Active moves for restoration by follower / learner	Working for personal short term opportunities	Total divorce and isolation
Responsibility	Rigidly responsible	Responsible to required situations	Corporate encouragement rewards etc	Responsibility to the leader and wider groups-2	Acts responsibly under supervision	May be irresponsible and self-centred
Knowledge understanding	Perpetuates established knowledge	Teaches formal knowledge as required	Creative approach to enhancing and develop knowledge	Responds positively to new knowledge		Rejection and non-involvement in formal school work
Inclusion /exclusion	Practices exclusion and separation readily-stereotyping	A limited formal acceptance of pupils	Total acceptance of all willing pupils / others	A willing response to inclusive principles	Acceptance on tight all limited terms	A sense of rejection
Protection /care	Care through control	Formal restricted care/ protection	A supportive enabler of all pupils	Pupil action/involved co-operation	Formal requests when required	Withdrawal from the situation
Freedom/ control	Strict teacher control	Freedom within the system as decreed	Non-coercive, provides options for pupils	The prodigal has the choice to obey - follow the shepherd	Freedom relative to the situation	Demands unrestricted self chosen activities
Long term continuity	Irregular periodic task involvement and provision	Major pressures on consistent involvement	Full and consistent concern over long-term	Faithfulness to the teacher	Short-term interruptions to the learning process	Long-term irregularity due to self and others
Interaction	Total separation of the teacher and the task/pupil	Controlled and limited interaction	Contribute to all types of learning and support	Fully co-operative	Formal involvement as required	Non or reluctant involvement
Order	Meets legal requirements and official demands	Responds to detailed rules	Imposes a few fundamental laws	Willing compliance with requirements	A neutral response to requirements to comply	Non-compliance or anarchy

226

Chapter 17

Analyses of Jesus' methods in Luke's gospel

This follows the analyses of Jesus' teaching style seen in Matthew and John but aspects are quite distinctive. Jesus is seen as a wise model teacher. The key principles can thereby be drawn out to our benefit. We will see the impromptu teacher, the man of action, the traveller, this storyteller and manner of metaphors. His character, goals and methods were demanding of those who could be demanded and a comforter to those who could not. He was a resolute opponent to those who rejected the outcasts etc and his teaching.

Chapter 2

v.41 As a young lad he showed an early interest in his historic faith and was a learner before he became a teacher. He inquired and interacted with the most knowledgeable.

Chapter 3

He watched his cousin humbly but made a decisive start and knew his goals. He built on his predecessors moral teaching and expectations and was supporting the prophetic voice.

Chapter 4

v.1–13. Jesus' extreme self discipline resulted in a strategy of rejecting physical power, sensationalism and meeting his personal needs. His decisions were based on traditional sources and he went out with his vision of a Kingdom and people's needs.

v.14–15. His initial teaching was open, showed promise to the listeners and was attractive.

v.16–22. The teacher knew his role - he fulfilled and met established needs and raised the hopes of the rejected. He took traditionalism to its highest level with a prophetic vision.

v.23–30. Courageous teachers are always likely to be rejected.

v.31–37. The teacher had an authority that was used to discriminate in accordance with the context – straight opposition that may or may not be confronted.

v.38–39. He met needs informally as they arose.

v.40–41. The teacher aroused confidence by his ability and so made people want to come for help

v.42–44. Teachers must take the opportunity to reflect and develop themselves.
  Will pupils recognize the qualities of the teacher sufficiently to seek him?
  A formula is emerging of teacher aspirations and capability meeting needs and motivation.
  The teacher used the pupils' own resources which probably had a preliminary bonding effect.
  The value of contrived impromptu teaching may be seen here.
  The teacher made an offer after showing his ability to which the aspiring could respond.
  The need for long-term teacher/pupil interaction, but note the continued degree of freewill.
  Teachers need to be on a journey themselves in order to reach their goal.

Chapter 5

v.12–16. Crises are always likely to rise, even in times of success.
  People quickly acknowledged the teacher's competence.
  The teacher himself needed constant renewal and growth.

.2c-209
Luke's Gospel was probably written in c.75CE

v.17–26. The teacher recognized the importance of peer-group support.
> There can be calm even when amongst opposition.
> The teacher got to the root of the situation.
> The teacher looked for and recognized faith/involvement in pupils.
> Good teaching involved optimum challenge and pupil response.

v.27–32. The teacher recognized the motivation of others even if it surprised everybody else.
> Pupils can find such a change very costly.
> Teachers look for a radical change in outlook.
> Not everybody wants pupils to make radical progress and change.

v.33–35. The approachable normal teacher.

v.36–39 He did not rise to opposition with a like for like responses. His Illustrative metaphors were eminently reasonable and calming and promoted reflective thought.

Chapter 6

v.1–5. There is no suggestion that this sequence described is as stated originally.
> Note the influence of context on learning – e.g. the Sabbath.
> The teacher protected his followers.
> The teacher was able to use traditional authorities.
> The teacher was not afraid to use his claims of authority.

v.6–11. Teachers may well be viewed critically when they are radical.
> The teacher responded to needs.
> The teacher destroyed critics with logic and evident actions.
> Critics may well not be persuaded by evidence.

v.12–16. Jesus recognized that all of his followers were not equal.
> He was not afraid to differentiate between them.
> The teacher's and major decision was based on quiet reflection.
> He took a risk in choosing Judas.

v.17–23. Teachers who meets real pupil needs will attract pupils and be ascribed with authority.
> He made strong promises to the needy and courageous.
> He had a strong encouraging message and was confident of moral and spiritual authority.

v.24–26. The teacher stated moral principles based on the prophetic tradition – clear unequivocal statements.
> He spoke to the crowds simply and clearly in everyday language.

v.27–36. He turned moral spiritual criteria upside down – he left the crowds with a puzzle which must have seemed ridiculous – but this was the Kingdom requirement
> There was no playing to the crowds.
> His new spiritual morality was problematic to the listeners but not totally novel.

v.37–45. He made a promise of a logical blessing based on judgment, condemnation, forgiveness and generosity.

.2c-210
Luke was reputed to be a sea faring physician who was also an artist who painted a portrait of Mary, the mother of Jesus

The memorable pictures were self-evident but required interpretation and demanded an effort to understand.

Strong moral/spiritual alternatives were laid out.

The logic of inner motivation was clear.

v.46–49. He made a constant referral to the visual picture and its unerring logic.

Chapter 7

v.1–10. This breaks through all barriers.

We can see that cognition was built on experience, surprise and the teacher's word being fulfilled. These enhanced his authority and supported the logic of his teaching. He spoke and it was done.

v.11–15. Incidental teaching 'on the hoof' to meet sorrow and problems head-on is vital.

Note how the teacher responded to a learners faith and also to a person who exhibited no faith.

The teacher was always going towards various needs expecting to solve them.

v.16–17. The pupils needed to see that the teacher was greater than they were and so they were halted in their tracks and given something to talk about.

v.18–35. Teachers always question pupils and the main answer was evidence of the teachers work was where it was transformative.

Our teacher appreciated the wanderer who presented variety and similarity in its basis.

The teacher must recognize who he himself is and requires evidence.

These were difficult phrases to ponder upon – wisdom is justified by all her children – short and succinct but puzzling and demanding, considering the audience.

v.36–50. The teacher was always available to all – top and bottom! There is always scope for restoration – but it is always a two way reconciliation /restoration.

Let the pupils answer their own questions but with a teacher there to respond.

The teacher was always there with the promise of having needs met.

Chapter 8

v.1–3. The teacher moved towards people who may not have recognized their needs.

The good teachers offer high aspirations to those who recognise the quality of the goals, the work and the words.

v.4–15. He showed the art of successful long term teaching using common situations

He posed questions and activated curiosity.

He stated problems that were relevant and demanding to the pupils.

He was available to provide answers for those who would hear.

He made relevant and believable promises

v.16–18. These simple statements must have seemed self evident but they contained hidden meanings to be mulled over.

.2c-211
Luke, a Gentile, laid an emphasis on non-Jews.

v.19–21. There was always a word of appreciation for his pupils.

v.22–25. The teacher took decisions and was a participant.

They shared their dangers and difficulties but he resolved their problems.

The teacher needed to evoke faith

v.26–39. There will always be some who have serious problems and feel rejected but the teacher must not run away from the problem. He confronted problems with costly results! But the individual was worth more than the crowd believed.

The man was both healed and restored – that had been the double challenge.

v.40–48. In one sense the teacher is always travelling and encountering surprises.

His abilities encouraged the people to approach him.

He willingly moved towards inconvenient problems.

A person with a long term-problem took a desperate initiative and was encouraged to have a personal and private faith. Her private action was rewarded, but so was another public action!. People from all backgrounds were recognized and rewarded.

v.49–56. He always had other people to help- but what a contrast! People believed the worst but that was hopeless. He generated hope despite the ridicule. The personal touch made all the difference.

Chapter 9

v.1–9. The bold instructions were COPY ME. What a challenge! He had inspired them sufficiently for this to occur.

v.10–17. They had something to say about what they had done. They had watched, listened, learned, acted, succeeded and reported back with a glow.

One would have expected celebration but reflection was the order of the day!

Crowds were welcomed but with distinct and limited purposes – and he met to their needs.

The amazing economy of reporting!

Face the impossible in a calm, orderly manner.

He could do so because he was well prepared himself.

There was always enough and more.

v.22–27. They were challenged in the light of his demonstration.

Pupils have insights that are important.

The teacher had to face up to his personal destiny.

It is difficult to take pupils from knowledge to understanding.

v.28–36. Every teacher has special moments that pupils can barely understand, and which surprises and even stuns them to silence.

v.37–42. Even top pupils can exasperate a teacher who has to bail them out.

v.43–45. A problem – can the pupils progress without conceiving the significance of his words?

v.46–56. He demonstrated humility from the strength of being who he was.
He received all – even the child – and also the man who was not a follower.

v.57. He was determined and went beyond the pupils' understanding.

.2c-212
Luke emphasised prayer and mentioned Jesus at prayer nine times

Some would not receive the teacher – that was their loss!

v.58–62. The pupils had to face up to the cost of being with such a person.

Chapter 10

v.1–24. He gave pupils responsibilities even though many were unproven. He had encouraged and demonstrated his ideals….now he became a risk taker. He trusted and challenged them. He equipped as far as he could. Would they, with scant knowledge let him down?

This demanding teacher provided support.

The teacher was wise – he asked them to work in pairs. This gave them courage, interactive benefits, mutual visualization, hearing and seeing each other at work which promoted understanding,faith and courage.

His instructions were accompanied by promises and warnings.

He was justified in his wisdom that brought great pleasure.

Pupils who act have privileges.

v.25–28. The teacher wisely let the questioner answer his own question.

v.29–37. Teaching by story and questions led the enquirer to his own answers'

v.38–47. The teacher had varied pupils and recognized their differences and hindrances to learning.

His whole strategy brought together the key principles – talk, observe, visualize, interact, defend, overcome, compassion, evident wisdom.

Chapter 11

v.1. He made time for prayer and reflection.

v.2–4. Note the rhythmic prayer – it contained essential truth, was succinct and easy to learn.

v.5–13. Again we see a memorable story to illustrate a human point

v.14–28. Every teacher is liable to criticism – even when not justified.

There was recognition that he had to keep to his fundamental goal.

v.29–32. Who would go on after a cheap crisis?

v.33–36. The challenge was generic and had scope for interpretation.

v.37–53. He was courageous, faced wrongdoing and saw people's motives.

Chapter 12

v.1–12. He encouraged pupils but did not avoid problems.

v.13–21. The teacher had adaptable skills to get to the core message.

v.22–34. He encouraged them but had to be believed. This was based on his previous work and their experiences.

v.35–40. He mastered the challenge of his work being memorable and worthwhile..

v.41–48. He was building a coherent theme.

.2c-213
The unbounded love of God has never had a better exponent than Luke
–H Balmforth

v.49–59. His teaching was based on common experiences.

Chapter 13

v.1–9. These were stiff lessons of warning based on observation.

v.10–17. He was a person who met needs and caused rejoicing despite difficulties.

v.18–21. Eager brief snippets of wisdom which were uncluttered but demanded interpretation.

v.22–30. Self discipline was essential to success.

v.31ff. Even the greatest teachers can have deep sorrow!

Chapter 14

v.1–6. He met people's reason by answering questions that were morally right.

v.7–24. His stories were simple but memorable and reinforced fundamental concepts.

v.24–35. He would not explain the obvious.

Chapter 15

A series of short parables that may or may not have been originally linked by Jesus. The first three stories illustrate reconciliation in different forms. Absolutely typical.

Chapter 16

v.1–14. He met the opposition with a simple phrase, 'God knows what is in your heart.'
- One cannot help but notice the different types of stories and their effect. This one illustrated observation (the Pharisee and the tax collector at prayer).
- Imaginative spiritual stories which one could imagine had been developed both during his 'hidden years' or incidents as he watched the crowds and the gross inequalities.
- A few extended metaphors.
- Longer illustrated stories.

He was constantly looking for and interpreting situations into spiritual teaching about character and the demands of God. Every day there could be new stories with clear moral and spiritual possibilities.

Chapter 17

v.1–10. The core message of forgiveness and faith cannot be diluted. This was the basis of the message. There is an essential core that cannot be diluted in all teaching / learning.

v.11–19. Practical incidental teaching on the road – faith and thanks.

v.20–21. An old question, a new answer but left unexplained.

v.22–37. Visualization. tradition and warning brought together.

Chapter 18

v.1–8. A parable with a purpose (persistence) assumes knowledge.

v.9–14. Observation with a sharp characteristic point.

v.15–17. The contrasting incidental situation again illustrates an aspect of the core message.

v.18–30. An interpersonal meeting showing Jesus' typical use of a language.

v.31–35. The teacher was open about his goals, but there were no shortcuts. Shocks were not hidden and there was little understanding.

> .2c-214
> *In what ways were both the teacher and the taught risk takers?*

v.35–41. His pupils had not quite understood. Within it there was a typical formula for teaching.

Chapter 19

v.1–10. High motivation is rewarded – costly but worthwhile.

v.11–27. Back to everyday parables – commitment, rewards / vice versa

v.28–40. Teacher's purpose was paramount. Enthusiasm alone wavers

v.41–44. The real sorrow over missed opportunities.

v.45–48. The people wanted him to be authoritative and open.

Chapter 20

v.1–8. Some challenge the teacher's authority even when he is correct.

v.9–18. A concrete, puzzling but understandable parable in the long run

v.19–26. A sharp opportunistic answer to differentiate values.

v.27–47. Seeing through efforts to confuse the situation!

Chapter 21

v.1–4. The poor are appreciated but the elite are not rejected. Acceptance, appreciation based on motives.

v.5–36. A long didactic discourse full of information as you might expect.

Chapter 22

v.7–30. The Passover used tradition, symbolism, artefacts, visual and full of information that would only be understood later.

v.30–46. Disappointment – Yes but criticism No.

Chapter 23

He was proved right - the demonstration and vindication of what he said.

Chapter 24

v.1–12. The teacher's total authority was established by events.

v.13–35. This long informal conversation must have been important to Luke, even if to few others. Related by one of the two travellers?

v.36–50. He entered into pupil doubts and troubles'
   He verified all he had seen and done.
   This moment contained a long-term challenge and promise.

.2c-215
What were the essential ingredients of Jesus' teaching methods which are likely to be used today

A summary prior to the development of theories of Instruction and learning

Jesus was well prepared and had the skills to teach his vision. Following this consideration of his teaching strategies and methods and prior to developing theories of instruction and learning for the 21st century it is appropriate to summarize the findings that will provide a useful framework to enable a reasonable conclusion to be developed. Therefore, see summaries A and B below and anticipate the structure of the instruction and learning models.

Figure 135

Goals	Clear identifiable goals Luke 4v18	Short term goals -meeting needs	Long term goals - shared, inspired	Meet expectations of good/ righteous authorities and self	Creating a serving, united people
Basic Issues	Do people want to be taught?	What hinders them being taught?	Persuading them of the value and truth of teaching	Foster positive learning attitudes of faith and hope?	Develop lifestyle attitudes of love sacrifice, humility
Radicalism?	Is teaching based on a central vision of goodness?	Promote vision, WV and faith akin to Matt.5- ?	Can the teacher question and recast tradition?	The teacher's perception of pupils /students?	Can pupils see an integrated ideal of al life and community?
Knowledge What shall we teach?	Can teachers and pupils see the difference between relative and absolute truth?	Can teachers re-interpret knowledge spiritually, ethically etc?	Can knowledge be based on key principles from which information is related?	Can the knowledge differ with the needs motivation and attainment of pupils?	Does knowledge meet the everyday needs of community social relationships; personal aspirations
Method-How shall we teach?	Teacher as role model - character	In the light of Jesus' attitude to children, pupils etc	From the known /seen to the unknown	Use succinct attainable promises and instructions	Appropriate varied experiential at a personal level
Who shall we teach?	Inclusive of all! Note the types of Pharisees etc	Where ever there is a degree of personal response – including crowds	Response to individual personal need, interest	Intensive small groups	Where there is personal commitment
Likely outcomes	Varied response, including opposition	Some will listen and leave	Life change for respondents	Individual faith , identification etc	Fellowship between mutual growth/ development
Primary expectations	Spiritual / moral qualities - kindness, Enter new areas of knowledge Present new vistas/ opportunities	Enter new areas of knowledge and understanding	Present new opportunities and vistas	Generate security and stability for growth/ development	Make mastery and attainment a possibility

.2c-216
To what degree was the teacher always the vital element in the learning process?

Summary B

Consider which of Jesus' skills were especially important to him and which are still particularly significant.

Aims
- To establish a core of understanding.
- To establish commitment to himself, his values and spirituality.
- To establish secure relationships.
- To develop intrinsic motivation as the drive for learning.
- To arouse/motivate people effectively on a long-term basis.

Teacher's stance
- He was a transparent role-model.
- He had an holistic approach to teaching.
- He protected his pupils and there was no coercion.
- He regarded the material as an expression of the spiritual.
- He recognized needs and aspirations.
- He celebrated his pupils' achievements.
- He had no self-pity when his pupils failed him.
- He recognized differentiation by culture and attitude, but not by ability.

Strategies
- He presented clear advance organizers and 'Big Pictures' of teaching.
- He controlled the cluster of concepts and promises he taught.
- He provided evidence to support his value-based principles.
- He encouraged peer tuition.
- He encouraged experiential work with himself.
- There was structure and he responded to opportunities as they arose.
- He provided an optimum degree of challenge and choice.
- He used encouragement and emotional responses in his teaching.
- He shared his achievements with his pupils.

Methods
- He sent learners on to fieldwork.
- He demonstrated what he taught.
- He observed people and situations sensitively.
- He used rhyme and rhythm to make memorable statements.
- Reflection and prayer were significant aspects of his teaching.
- He was skilful at conversations, oral descriptions and Q-A.
- He provided templates/frames for learning (e.g. the Lord's Prayer).
- He maximized pupils' experiences.
- He presented pupils with memorable case studies/characters.
- He provided short illustrated stories and real-life dialogue.
- He used everyday knowledge of the past, the present and future.
- He attempted to rescue pupils from errors.

He reinforced his teaching through a wealth of methods. He kept the Big Picture before the people and did not extend his teaching beyond the central principles that were within his plan.

.2c-217
List six aspects from the review which were and still are crucially important

He recognized that his ideas were difficult to understand, therefore he worked on the principle of teaching from the concrete to the abstract as exemplified in the story of the Prodigal Son.

At the heart of his teaching were ongoing creativity, novelty and surprise. The people always had something to discuss and so a short story would probably be repeated many times within the crowds or his friendship groups. One feature was that he allowed people to interpret his stories privately or individually at the risk of error. But the people gradually understood some of the value basis and visionary elements of parables, miracles, discourses etc. His apprentices had the privilege of being able to reflect and explore meetings and consult the master. Although Jesus was a traveller there was order and development in his teaching but his conversational methods seldom changed, and he retained the principle of demonstration as when he washed the apprentices feet. A further related facet was his willingness to allow himself to depend upon his apprentices to some degree.

.2c-218
Why is truth alone not likely to be the major determinant of long term learning?

Chapter 18

Ultimate Teaching Strategy C

The following is a consideration of how aspects of Jesus' teaching strategies and methods can be applied to our contemporary scene. It refers to Parts A and B but mainly focuses on Part C.

It is surprising how 'normal' Jesus' teaching was, except for the miracles, and how supremely well it was done. If we assume that we are not likely to perform many miracles, what are the implications of his teaching methods and how might they be built into general teaching?

His teaching was not a study of any discipline, even religion, but rather it moved into everyday situations to demonstrate and promote faith in God's way of living. Now, if he was to teach biology in the 21st century one assumes that it would be *principle led, purposeful, practical and value* based. The manner in which most subjects have since the 1980's become re-orientated to consider major value issues / crises etc would be in accord with his perception of teaching and learning generally but with everything revolving around the quality of *relationships* and his concept of leadership. At the risk of repetition, the following aspects were critically important.

- Jesus' teaching was arresting.
- He realized that 'tired knowledge' is the enemy of learning. We might compare the diligent and learned teaching of the Jewish religious authorities with that of Jesus that was fresh and illuminating.
- His pupils watched, listened, copied and so cumulatively learned.
- He met aspirations, needs and what was relevant to their situation.
- He provided security, appreciation and friendship.
- His competence raised expectations that his promises would be met.
- He developed possibilities beyond their dreams as they followed him.
- He laid down optimum challenges that led to achievement.
- A clarity that was also thought provoking and bemusing.
- He maximized involvement and gave opportunities for reflection.
- He knew that reciprocal relationships are at the heart of successful teaching. This was based upon the sustained faith of the teacher in the pupils that enabled them to respond with faith in the teacher, and which remained even when the pupils faltered. Such a situation instilled such confidence in them that the promises and prospects given by the teacher were seen as reliable and they possibly knew that there was always a way back without any 'loss of face'.

Jesus' teaching had pre-eminently a spiritual function, but a prominent feature was its open practicality. Although he was in the midst of religious issues he did not, for example, teach about worship procedures or even religious doctrine. He was unremitting as he presented a faith that was alive, relevant and practical. He knew that the study of religion was not an end in itself but simply the means to achieve something far greater. Hence, it is realistic to consider that this world-view could be applied to all types of teaching but it does not suggest that all learning would be exclusively 'practical'. His religious teaching had social, moral, personal, cultural and spiritual connotations and one would assume that reflects his attitude to all types of learning ranging from science to plumbing. The teaching brings together the process and product goals referred to in Chapter 14. Every subject is not only a source and focus of knowledge but is also capable of being life-changing. His knowledge illuminated, illustrated and generated something greater than itself. This does not suggest Jesus was a philistine in outlook but he did recognize the sanctity of man and the created world.

The question arises as to what type of religious education (or history or geography etc.) the teacher Jesus might be. Although Jesus' teaching was of a confessional nature we must assume that religious education would be taught in a non-confessional manner - in other words it would seek to teach the fundamentals of religious faith, ideas and actions without distortion or using the teacher's privileged position to persuade children to adopt a specific stance, which is beyond the scope of a state school.

.2c-219
Which a major aspects will Jesus' teaching methods were particularly normal?

A structure for teaching

This is not the place to discuss the basis of content that might be taught in religious education. Instead, consideration will be given to two major aspects of the teaching process:
- Teaching based upon principles.
- An overall strategy for teaching.

Principles

In recent years this has modified and emphasis has been placed on *attainment targets in most areas of study*, a version of which can be related to religious education generally, and also to Jesus orientated teaching. This development can be illustrated in contemporary achievement targets, AT1 and AT2 in so far that they focus on key words such as understanding, comparative explanations etc that Jesus used to teach six major areas of faith:

- *He defined his beliefs, explained* his *teachings* and *referred* to three major sources – the *Torah* and the *prophets*, the *environment* and his *personal revelation*. He *indicated* clearly the *practices* and way of life expected.
- He vividly *expressed* his *meanings aurally* and by *actions* which provided evidence.
- He *emphasized* the sense of identity with him and the father and sense of *belonging* amongst his followers.
- He presented *clear meanings* and purposes of discipleship and that he was the embodiment of truth.
- He *described* the *Kingdom of God* and expected long-term commitment.

Of course, these are remarkably familiar as a revised version of six targets laid down by the QCA. Also, we should take into account the following skills that can be seen in Jesus' teaching methods that also relate to AT1 and AT2.

- To recount/recall, retain knowledge and recognise features of the Kingdom of God etc.
- To retell and identify/know/suggest meanings of parables and the Passion etc .
- To describe and make links between stories and incidents (eg. feeding the masses).
- To realise difficulties and reasons for responses such as Nicodemus the Pharisee.
- To go beyond information to understand and apply principles such as servant hood.
- To explain the structural network of the Kingdom of God and compare it with the prevailing Judaism and Christian traditions.
- To explain how his teaching 'works' in practice of individual responses.
- To relate knowledge to both self and others historically and now (e.g. reformations).
- To analyse/ask questions, give informed accounts and evaluate outcomes (e.g. the Cross).
- To make long-term investigations and interpretations during development.

A combined strategy for teaching

The next consideration is how these principles and concepts can be incorporated into the eight fold teaching strategy described in Chapter 15. Although no strategy or method is sacrosanct they do need to reflect the nature of the subject itself. Having replaced religious instruction with religious education, the particular qualities must reflect this nature of the subject which contains a wealth of knowledge, expressive opportunities etc and would entail questions about: subject which contains a wealth of knowledge, values, expressive opportunities etc and would entail asking questions about:

.2c-220
Consider any aspect of something you have taught recently. Identify any major product and process goals in your teaching

- Which knowledge and concepts will provide the basis of this aspect of education?
- Which values, moral imperatives and attitudes will be the bedrock of the study of religion?
- How might an ethos be generated which is compatible with and reflects religious ideas and lifestyles?
- Which general learning experiences will be provided
- How will appropriate skills be used to enable
- enquiry/investigative learning to occur?
- Which experiential opportunities will be provided?
- Which expressive opportunities can be used which reflect the wealth of religious expression?

When learning is reduced to hearing and comprehension it is out of tune with Jesus' attitude and provision, because he recognized that effective instruction incorporated change of attitude, projection, empathy etc as people moved into what he was teaching. This fuller range of concepts and attitudes means that religious education is distinct from religious instruction. The same principles would apply to other subjects within the humanities and social sciences. The factors and procedural principles which one notes in Jesus' teaching in one form or another consist of.

Figure 136

Knowledge/ concepts	Values, morality and attitudes	Learning skills
Effects of aspects of religion	The ethos of faith	Experiential religion
Expressive faith	Projection to faith	Lifestyle of faith
Demands and disciplines of faith	A degree of sacrifice	A degree of creative exploration

The essence of religious education is to attempt to enable pupils to stand in other people's shoes. But teaching styles might contribute towards achieving this goal? Let us consider six of the eight strategies described in Chapter 15, all of which are relevant and have their place.

Didactic: Provides clarity of purpose and sets the scene. Poses active questions and is essentially forward looking. Poses stimulating information and plan the direction and pace of the study. Provides an identifiable situation that encourages initial projection amongst the pupils.

Figure 137

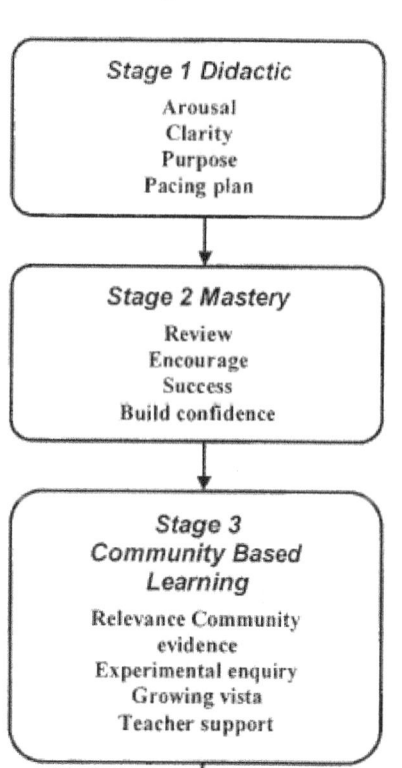

Stage 1 Didactic
Arousal
Clarity
Purpose
Pacing plan

Stage 2 Mastery
Review
Encourage
Success
Build confidence

Stage 3 Community Based Learning
Relevance Community evidence
Experimental enquiry
Growing vista
Teacher support

Stage 4 Socially Situated Learning
Observation
Projection
Inquiry
Role play

Stage 5 Accelerated Learning
Big Picture reviewed
Multi-sense inquiry
Organised schemes
Plenary review

Stage 6 Concept attainment
Apply findings to parallel case study
Express total findings

.2c-221
In everyday considerations when different levels of principles and concepts have been particularly important to Jesus, and now to you?

Mastery learning: This reviews previous work and ensures that the pupils have confidence and sense of previous success that generates positive expectations upon which everything can be built.

Community Based Learning: Following Vygotsky's perception, other interactive community and culturally based learning, one might ask how far the curriculum and learning can be localized so that it can be seen to be relevant and enable guided discovery to be authentic. This acts as an important corrective to some of the previous statements because religion is not primarily conceptual but rather it should be looked at in the context of people, their needs and aspirations.

Socially Situated Learning: This follows the notion of apprenticeship learning and the fact that learning is not abstract but is socially situated in people's minds so that they can envisage and memorize a situation in which the learning occurred. Pupils are constantly assessing teachers and expect them to be the equivalent of master craftsmen and demonstrate what is being taught. They expect to watch, listen, practice and learn by being participants. It is helpful where the teacher has inadequate expertise to incorporate somebody who has, because there is validity in the authentic experience. It is interesting to see how pupils respond to pupils of another faith from another school who describe and demonstrate their religious experiences. As with strategy 3 it has the virtue of constantly seeking to use the occasion and the situation as a valued teaching situation that is precisely what Jesus did.

Accelerated Learning Systems: The pupils learning paths are maximised by using visual, auditory and kinaesthetic senses, which was Jesus' common practice. This helps to build authentic experiences that have long-term value. Also, these experiences help to build up schemas so that they are ready to receive new knowledge that might be assimilated and then later respond positively to new knowledge that might need to be accommodated. Another important feature is that principle based teaching helps the brain to form coherent patterns that are relatively efficient to both recall and develop.

Concept Attainment: As pupils look at issues and principles from different perspectives, they recognise similarities and differences and so the process of reinforcement takes place and future understanding is more likely.

Although Jesus did not have a systematic formula there was a pattern in his teaching, and the characteristics of this strategy that contains elements that are sympathetic to those of Jesus

This style of teaching affects the message itself, and one can recognise that the methods would not be incongruous to Jesus, even though the content may be. For example, initially he would

Figure 138

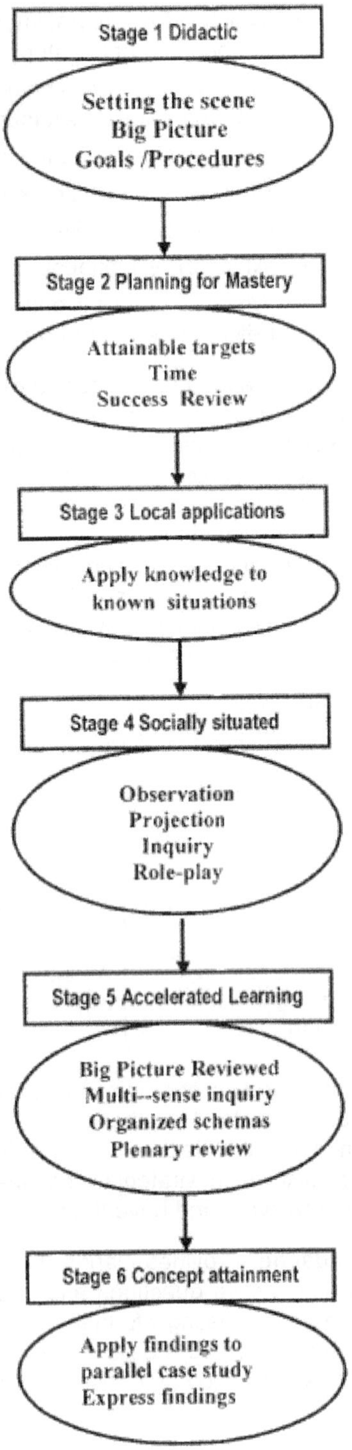

Stage 1 Didactic
- Setting the scene
- Big Picture
- Goals /Procedures

Stage 2 Planning for Mastery
- Attainable targets
- Time
- Success Review

Stage 3 Local applications
- Apply knowledge to known situations

Stage 4 Socially situated
- Observation
- Projection
- Inquiry
- Role-play

Stage 5 Accelerated Learning
- Big Picture Reviewed
- Multi--sense inquiry
- Organized schemas
- Plenary review

Stage 6 Concept attainment
- Apply findings to parallel case study
- Express findings

.2c-222
This has been pointing to a multi method approach to teaching. Did Jesus really have one flexible strategy but many methods?

probably look forward and develop the topic before reviewing the past to establish anticipation and rising expectations. The pupils would be surprised by his fresh relevant knowledge. He would make the link with the past and thoroughly involve every pupil. His specific information and stimulus material would be community-based and be relatively short but contain the basis for concept attainment, supported by memorable illustrations. His groups would explore his initial information and persist until they have reflected and seen the significance of what was being taught. Once this was achieved he would further develop it by a range of methods designed to move beyond the information given to achieve deeper understandings. The pupils might then be asked to discuss and state their conclusions so that the class has a shared body of knowledge and each individual has a personal understanding based on his or her work. The pupils would then apply the knowledge to a new situation to ensure that they had a flexible and long-term understanding. Underpinning it all is the fact that Jesus saw people in the image of God and so helped them with appropriate regard.

One should not exaggerate the compatibility between Jesus' teaching methods and those commonly used now. What we can do is to latch onto the common principles that have been noted within his teaching style and profitably use them when planning teaching, bearing in mind that if he was teaching today he would use all modern tools such as the internet.

Figure 139 indicates a methodological package for a project lasting four to six weeks. It shows the scene and raises expectations about the relevance of the study. Previously learned principles are renewed and related to the new situation and provide introduction springboards for the next stage of learning. The class or group then undertake a corporate task that stems from the teachers initiative. After reporting back they undertake group tasks by which they gather fresh information and develop it through appropriate methods that foster reflective inquiry work that may take many forms. The purpose is to cause them to pause and think until they make the "Ah, now I see" response. The groups return and report to the teacher who has been helping them. The reporting session helps to establish a common body of knowledge especially when it involves ongoing discussion.

The specific information taught at Stage1 would be short but contain memorable illustrations to develop the core religious principles and concepts. The groups explore this initial information through books, personal contacts, visits or the internet and persist until they had reflected and recognised the significance of what had been taught. Topics generally have historic roots, but the studies move rapidly to the contemporary scene and future prospects. Once this has been achieved it is developed further by methods designed to 'move beyond the information given' to deeper and wider understandings and applications.

The pupils then apply the knowledge to a new problematic situation to ensure that they had a flexible and long-term understanding. There is nothing extraordinary about these methods, especially as most of it looks classroom-based but it follows the spirit of the outlines strategy mentioned above but with one major emphasis.

Types of work were designed to cause pupils to reflect and prevent them rushing ahead or coming to thoughtless conclusions. The notion of fostering creative responses individually, in groups or as a class is certainly a method that Jesus used.

.2c-223
Consider any one of the 8 factors of teaching mentioned above and how it might be used when teaching?

Figure 139

Stages of tuition	Types of teaching and learning	Issues- Jesus and general
Introduction	Look forward before reviewing back Establish anticipation Set the stage, the scene	Will it create: Rising expectations? Self review? Growing involvement?
Didactic opening Corporate task	Establish positive expectations Show relevance to pupil needs and aspirations Surprising and fresh knowledge Making the link All involved	A degree of surprise? A desire for continuity
Group A Group task Information and relevant starters	Specific illustrative information of limited duration containing the basis for concept attainment. Relevant starters:	Can a teacher provide the fresh stimulating information? Scaffolding for the pupils?
Group B Group task information and relevant starters	Comprehension - have they grasped the essential point? Deduction - can they see the implications? Looking for evidence - local, internet, literature etc	Pacing? Manageable? Can disappointments be turned around?
Group C Group task and relevant starters	Short units of work with instructions A balance between illuminating information, establishing and applying previously learned principles and concepts. Effective reflection	The "Ah now I see!" response
Group D Group task and relevant starters	Group review work – "What is it all about?"	
Reflective inquiry work	Build on the initial group work to foster reflective thought and enquiry work. Charts, maps, language (written, oral , drama etc), personal enquiry, library work, personal investigations, discussion, observations etc	The "Ah now I see!" response
Review and conclusion	Plenary and presentation Material from the group and reflective for corporate and individual folders. Corporate folder's ongoing review function	
Evaluation	Apply knowledge to a new situation? Pupils aware of the emerging problems? Testing of pupils? Pupils see the way forward?. Expectations?	Establish the framework of understanding and keep it before the pupils who will develop it!

Part C has been highlighting the fact that Jesus had a repertoire of priorities, strategies and methods that were appropriate to changing situations. He was bringing everything alive and in it we could see the values in action. For example he knew that words can create and destroy, and he emphasized this by using memorable phrases in his teaching to 10 characteristics (excluding miracles!) it is possible to see that he developed a framework for teaching in any or every generation.

.2c-224
What is the rationale of each stage of this series of lessons?

He was persistent in the development of his values and aims.

He was a consistent role model who could be trusted. He was eminently believable.

He had a 'story to tell' and was knowledgeable.

He used life and environmental situations imaginatively. He flexibly responded to needs.

He raised aspirations.

He defended his followers.

He was an enabling friend who was authoritative.

He would no doubt be a fine teacher of maths, English, and plumbing and……. wouldn't he?! No doubt you know why.

Towards a Jesus style theory of instruction

Whilst there is no 1:1 match between Jesus' teaching methods and current expectations, he did provide ingredients for a modern methodology. This conclusion uses these to illustrate this, despite his different purposes and culture. Cast your mind back over the previous chapters to gain an overall impression of Jesus, the master teacher. How might his distinctive 'tools' and practices be adapted to our benefit?

In Part A it was evident that Jesus had to learn before he could teach and to grow in wisdom as he recognized the alternative path of the Kingdom of God. It was a pilgrimage during which he saw the futility of coercion and the priority of love, even if that involved ultimate sacrifices. That was a basis of his teaching methods.

In essence, his teaching focused on the human plight as people pursue their needs and aspirations, influenced by personal and controlling forces, demanded the insight, wisdom and vision to make certain long-term decisions that are applicable today. Take Part B. What sort of leader/teacher was he and how would that be perceived now? How could he motivate and make learning memorable? How could he make difficult concepts comprehensible? How would patterns of behaviour and emotions be used or modified to enhance learning? Jesus had answers but not everybody would want to meet their demands. Part C emphasized his use of various strategies and methods, but within the context of historic values and goals.

It is worth converting these findings into coherent **theories of instruction and learning** that can be applied widely. The first question is *do the pupils want to learn* rather than *can they learn*? A paraphrase of one of the most ambitious phrases in the 20th century was - *anything can be taught to anybody at an appropriate level given the appropriate teaching and learning situation*, and Jesus would probably have agreed. He never questioned, as we do, whether pupils had the ability to learn the abstract concepts and lifestyle of the Kingdom of God. Were they sufficiently motivated to learn and want to be good teachers themselves? Would they see it as an acceptable challenge? Would they seize this opportunity or would they turn away? Jesus knew that the major issues were confidence in him and their own personal priorities. His teaching methods took account of the *immediate cultural situation* and also the *permanent learning traits of mankind*, which is likely to be the permanent foundational basis of successful teaching generally.

The learning process itself

Jesus appears to have typically considered how to match the *motivation* of people and *capitalize on their needs and interests* with *his central purpose*. Furthermore, could he create positive expectations and provide grounds for achieving them? As Jesus found, there are always reasons for people choosing to learn or not!

.2c-225
From the characteristics of Jesus' teaching methods listed above, identify five which appeared to be of particular importance?

For some, instruction may seem intrusive into the major issues of life both in terms of time and place. The visits to the official learning centre may promote a feeling of entering somebody else's territory to do something which is difficult and regarded as being of doubtful relevance. These questions and undeniable observations appear forbidding but we can usefully look at what will be called Jesus' 'theory of instruction'. This can only be done if we take into account the following.

Figure 140

| Situational requirements | Teach self-preparation and priorities | Pupil expectations and hopes | Appropriate methods to the content and learning |

An ideal model for all?

The 14 stages shown here are an outline of Jesus' teaching of his disciples, but the stages are not meant to give the impression of an harmonious and ideal development, because it was nothing of the sort! We can, however, pick out any characteristic cost/ benefits that indicate aspects of teaching now. These can be traced as follows:

Figure 141

Teacher confident of position
...value based goals... possessed expertise.
Onlookers arrested by initial stimulus - words and actions... marginal
Teacher gathers willing pupils.
General recognition of his role model function - sense of progress amongst the pupils.
Pupils watch/ copy/ co-operate with teacher as he shows expertise and responds to need.
Growing recognition of the teacher's person and authority as he teaches openly.
Relevant and memorable teaching promising good outcomes

Teaching has value based goals rooted in a vision involving servant-leader relationships which was recognized because of its evident qualities and which was relevant, memorable and gave a sense of worth and promise. The expertise of the teacher involved cost but was motivating for pupils who accepted him as a role model and recognized their own responsibilities and long-term independence. They responded to the range of stimuli and had a sense of progression as they observed the teacher demonstrating what they had to learn and practice. The reciprocal responsibilities between teacher and pupils involved crisis and decision points that had to be resolved

This picture may appear too idealistic but it begins to provide an initial course of understanding to the process that is being discussed here. The 25 keywords were typical of Jesus as a teacher in that he made demands but offered much to the discerning

The pupils develop into fully capable and responsible practitioners.
Pupils' growing independence - they copy the teacher - apply the learning to new situations - despite differences they have shared vision/ responsibilities.
The teacher takes difficult initiatives at personal cost.
The teacher has care/ concern for his pupils and provides detailed teaching and promises.
Both the teacher and the pupils reach crisis and decision points
Teacher makes growing demands, challenges and raises aspirations amongst pupils
Pupils given individual and paired responsibilities as they learn and practice basic skills.

.2c-226
Can an ideal model become a working model when teaching?

Pupils have expectations

On entry to any teaching and learning situation the pupils have justifiable expectations. They will hope that it will enhance their personal enablement, promote their prospects for the future, provide points of interest, and for them to have felt to be successful and ultimately lead to extrinsic rewards. As they learn they may ask if it will provide valid examples that are applicable to life. Also some will ask if there is an ethical basis to the learning or recognize whether they are being taught efficiently and effectively.

As the learning process emerges one will look to see:
- Whether the pupils have become engaged in their studies and are working – individually, small groups, or large groups.
- Will it include everyday encounters with which they can become identified?
- Will the pupils feel extended?
- Will it expand their vision for the future?
- To what extent will the pupil be enriched?
- Will they do so well that they emerge with excellence?
- Will the experience be dull or enjoyable or even extraordinary?
- Will the explanations be clear and lead to further involvement?
- Will it energise them into future activity?
- How will the pupils' conduct an enquiry?
- To what degree can they be experimental?
- To what degree can the involvement be experiential?
- How will the findings or conclusions be expressed?
- In what way will their study be of effective use?
- How will the teacher and the pupils evaluate their work?
- Could this study in any way be regarded as essential?
- Will the exploratory work be guided to ensure maximum benefit?
- Will the pupils be motivated to make them eager to do more?
- Will this teacher and his ways become established or enter into obscurity?
- Will this holy enterprise elevate them to new levels of faith?

All but one of these questions could be answered in the affirmative by Jesus followers – but that one issue was quite distinctive. By these expectations Jesus was an effective teacher.

Designing a theory of instruction and learning – A theory of instruction based upon eight teaching strategies (ch.16) and Jesus

In ch.12 we briefly focused on literacy and that will be further developed in a way that contributes towards the theory of instruction and learning.

1. The expert controls the overall literacy programme. An attention-grabbing stimulus leads to a sense of practical relevance and interest. Instructions are given about requirements and how these will be achieved. Anticipated problems are defined. The stages are displayed so that the requirements and basic study procedures are clear.

2. The expert sequences materials that develop essential skills and these can be continually referred to. A range of exercises will insure that the fundamental skills of word recognition sentence building etc are cumulatively developed. The expert/teacher has defined the situation and ensured that the pupils can make progress and have a sense of success.

.2c-227
Which aspects of the ideal model shown above would be applicable today?

3. Pupils are constantly living amongst socio-cultural literacy. Following Vygotsky's thesis of culturally based learning, the programme draws upon the surrounding culture and environment for its major literacy inputs. The teacher/ 'knowledgeable other' sets up scaffolding to enable pupils to explore potential literacy sources and develop them into coherent literacy skills. This provides the pupils with a sense of ownership and ongoing exploration, but the teacher must ensure there are clear directions in the work. As the pupils become more competent the scaffolding/support is reduced but the pupils' frontier of study is expanded and the zone of proximal development is revised and the scaffolding set out so that by the pupils can extend their literacy work and pursue their learning in conversation with others.

4. This is compatible with the apprenticeship strategy. The teacher is the master practitioner whose job is partly to continually refresh the pupils' literacy from their own ongoing experiences. The pupils copy the master practitioner and work in joint participation with their peers. In both of the last two strategies the teaching is essentially corporate and literacy is seen in experiential terms. The teacher is the expert who is ultimately in control.

5. Virtually all literacy programmes now follow fundamental aspects of Accelerated Learning Systems. The teacher provides the Big Picture that focuses the direction of the literacy work whether it is corporate and experiential or individual and following the mastery programme. The literacy skills are developed by maximizing the use of the visual, auditory and kinaesthetic senses that require yet more experiential work. The teacher has two main tasks at this stage – to ensure that the *materials are chunked down or simplified* and that this new *knowledge is clearly ordered so that the brain's schemas can process it efficiently.*

6. Pupils should gain a multi-dimensional grasp of literacy skills rather than a somewhat fragile sequential knowledge. Therefore, the basic idea behind concept attainment is that pupils should have a consistent core of literacy skills and develop them in a wide range of contexts so that they become enriched with progressive explorations.

As intimated in Chapter 14, this follows the spirit of Jesus' pattern of teaching where we see the distinct role of the expert. Jesus gave precise instructions and facilitated corporate work that had been constantly expanded and refreshed from his own experiences. He taught them from the Big Picture which was simplified and he maximized the use of the senses to achieve increased understanding and competence. All of this was done over a prolonged period of time in many contexts so that it was multi-dimensional.

A value, skills and goal based contribution to the theory of instruction and learning

Jesus purpose was spiritual but here one must redefine the word in terms of values. These are the basis of tuition and create an appropriate teaching and learning ethos.

Look back at Figures 137 and138 and then at 142 that indicate a multi-stage models reminiscent of Fig. 3. Many pupils fail because the situation does not appear to be conducive to success. They are aware of and lay great store on fairness, relationships, acceptance etc. These become the fabric upon which everything else is developed. In this case four major types of values are established and provide the conditions for learning. Although there will be questions as to what these values actually mean, they are quickly recognized and form parameters of life itself. These major values generate others such as acceptance, worth, restoration, and achieve clarity of purpose that enhances the conditions for maximizing their personal capacity for achievement. This perimeter on the diagram enables other aspects to flourish such as the second stage where the pupils have the confidence to develop and use personal and study skills. The 8 rectangles indicate what might be regarded as essential learning tools, but to some degree they are coloured by the values within which they are used. Both of the outer ellipses bear down on the central goals. This provides the purpose, conditions and skills to achieve it. Although some consider that this is more suited to the social sciences, with some modifications this model is useful across all teaching and learning. A frequent problem is the lack of priority given to values. Even if not, it will exist in some form that may be both severely distorted and distort other aspects if it is implicitly based upon undesirable values which give rise to many problems.

.2c-228
Which of the pupils' expectations are likely to have the greatest influence on their learning?

This is not a Christian model *per se* and is applicable by all people of goodwill, Jesus would probably have recognized it as being useful generally in teaching and learning. Without an appropriate ethos for learning pupils are unlikely to have the mental, emotional and spiritual freedom to develop and use the range of skills indicated as they interact with others. The words can be changed but the principle remains.

Figure 142. An ideal model based on a development of the Prophetic and Jesus' lines of thought.

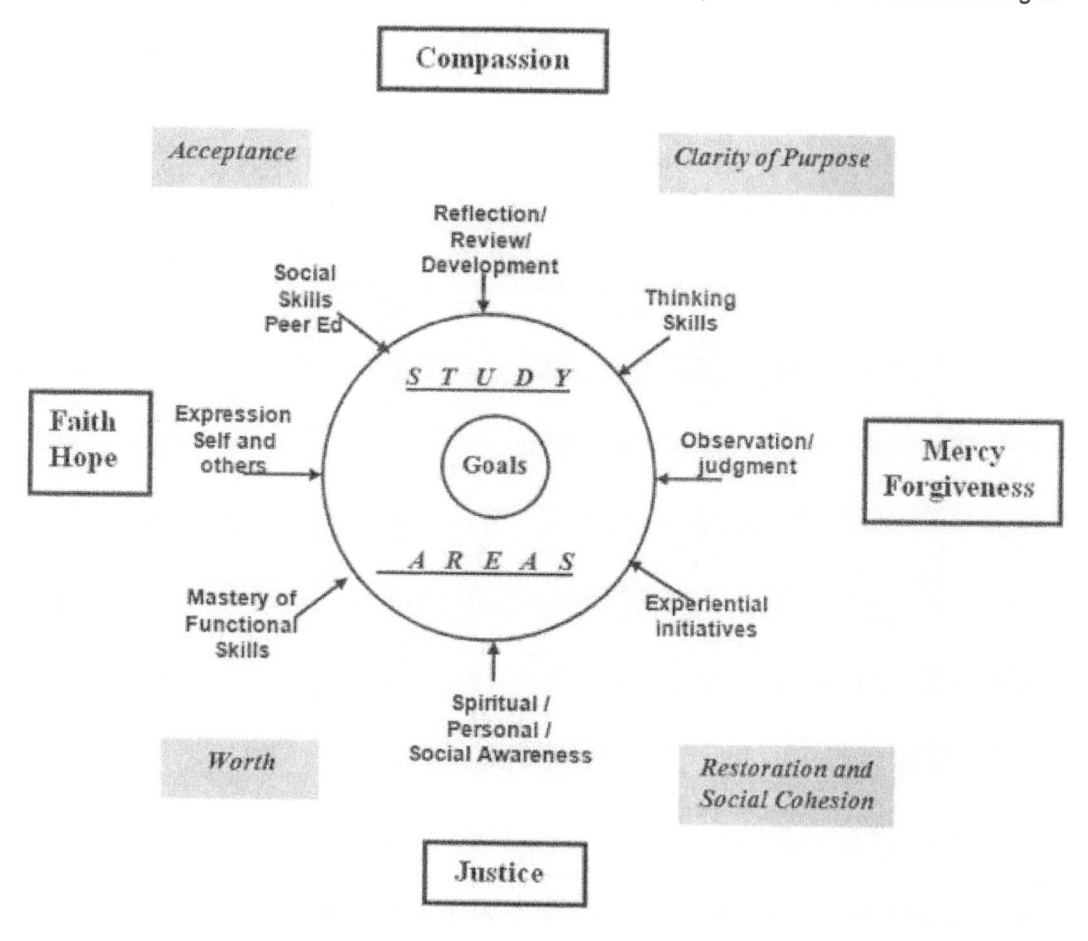

```
                          ┌─────────────┐
                          │ Compassion  │
                          └─────────────┘

     Acceptance                              Clarity of Purpose

                        Reflection/
                         Review/
              Social   Development
              Skills              Thinking
              Peer Ed             Skills
                       S T U D Y
  ┌───────┐  Expression                Observation/   ┌─────────────┐
  │ Faith │  Self and       Goals       judgment      │    Mercy    │
  │ Hope  │   others                                  │ Forgiveness │
  └───────┘                                           └─────────────┘
                       A R E A S
              Mastery of          Experiential
              Functional          Initiatives
                Skills
                        Spiritual /
                        Personal /
     Worth             Social Awareness    Restoration and
                                           Social Cohesion

                          ┌─────────┐
                          │ Justice │
                          └─────────┘
```

What might appropriate theories of instruction and learning contain?

We do not often think of Jesus using theories of teaching and learning to achieve his spiritual goals but, implicitly, he did. We have considered how Jesus taught and how the principles can be applied to general situations. Now look at it as a coherent overview so that it can be handled with ease and be sufficiently uncluttered with detail to enable his pattern of teaching to generate ideas and be of general application.

.2c-229
How are Jesus' and Vygotsky's insights into culturally based learning at the heart of much authentic understanding?

These can be briefly considered in the following five part format because:
- There were core elements around which all of his teaching was structured.
- All of his teaching was rooted in spiritual and moral values.
- His teaching was characterized by certain methodologies.
- People learnt from him in distinct ways.
- People responded to him variously according to their priorities.

Figure 143

Spiritual priorities and values	Compassion Forgiveness Mercy Faith etc
Means of instruction	Clear authoritative statements of prospects and requirements Using historic faith, the culture and environment Actions to meet needs Stories to arouse interest Personal interaction Promises, enablement etc
Core elements	God the Father The Kingdom of God Restoration The servant Messiah Universal care etc
How they learned	People watched, listened, helped, copied, talked together, reflected, asked questions and remembered! Etc And some refused to learn.
Responses	Ready respondents Interested crowds Religious people who paused to reflect Religious opposition

Using the design criteria described on previous pages we will consider how a theory of instruction and learning that was originally derived in principle from Jesus' teaching methods can be related to conventional everyday teaching. The model in essence is transferable between religious and non-religious situations. Therefore, working from Figure 143, which is virtually self-explanatory, it is possible to identify the following.

Row 1 – Values

Values are cumulatively developed and those people concerned should recognize that this is a major aspect to be explicitly borne in mind. Further, it needs to be explained to pupils so that they too can be involved in the spiritual and moral ethos of which they are part. Such a development may be defined by the authorities, although in some places the possibility of ownership is maximized by involving the pupils in its formulation. The critical issue is that it is fundamental to everything else and does not just quietly emerge.

Row 2 – Towards a theory of instruction

This is in accord with the spirit and characteristics of Jesus' teaching methods but without trying to replicate them. The instruction process can vary considerably but the underlying principles remain. Pupils need to know that, as Jesus taught, they are significant and an early task is to implant confidence and direction. They will need to have an unequivocal sense of purpose and awareness of

.2c-230
Why might learning be most efficient when taught in the context of values shown in Fig.107?

what is required. As this develops before them (cells 1 - 5), the pupils acquire skills, an understanding of requirements and likely achievements. Again, like Jesus, although there was no immediate rush and there was time to set the scene and establish work there was an immediate sense of purpose and progression. This provided a sense of good prospects and confidence in the teacher. It is built around an awareness of the Big Picture and an orderly sense of experiential knowledge that creates mastery and expectancy. Although the early stages are short they set the tone for the established process (cell six onwards) that has been described previously.

Row 3 – Core elements

The core elements in respect of Jesus around which everything revolved, were fourfold.

- The major ideas and features of his teaching.
- His major aims and how they would be achieved.
- His characteristic practices that defined all that he did.
- The nature of the progression and what the outcome would be.

Although these were Jesus' core elements, that is only part of the story because one has to take account of the perception of his followers and others.

Row 4 – Towards a Theory of Learning

Instruction and learning are fundamentally distinct, because what has been transmitted is unlikely to be faithfully received. Past history, motivation, cognitive schemas, perceptual differences and emotional states are but a few interpretive influences likely to effect what is learned but one should not totally individualize learning. Common factors such as initial mastery, anticipation and confidence, that grow out of achieving competence at an early stage, link instruction and learning.

But self-image, rival social forces, alternative priorities render the process complex. Jesus recognized the similarities and differences between his disciples but he taught a common message. We do not know the degree to which he personalised teaching amongst his followers but he understood that by teaching in certain ways he could bridge the gap and leave the interpretive process to the Holy Spirit. In other words, by thorough experiential work, acting as a role-model and demonstrating his ideals, providing clear memorable instruction and drawing upon the cultural background, he could trust that the link between instruction and learning would be bridgeable.

Row 5 — Responses

Throughout Part A it was emphasized that the responses to Jesus differed greatly for a range of reasons, which were legitimate to the people concerned. Therefore, because responses vary considerably, the words in this column are simply an aide-memoire of healthy responses.

Simplification

This model of a theory of instruction and learning may appear somewhat cumbersome and too generalized to be of specific application, but it can be simplified and used as a working model across many forms of learning. This staged pattern in Fig.115 illustrates how Jesus' style of teaching can typically be related to seven contrasting areas of learning. Central to this is a concern that reception learning is often de-motivating and inefficient. Instead, the six-part model suggested in Part C, is at the heart of the illustration.

The pre-instruction stage: Jesus assessed the situation and his purpose and made defining decisions. He met people and developed a programme approximating to the following structure that is presented as if it was a modern situation.

.2c-231
In what ways were other means of instruction and learning different and yet related?

Stage 1. He immediately evoked an *interest* by presenting material which was both *relevant and purposeful* and which in itself posed a question/problem.

Stage 2. He then promptly *explained/justified* why his teaching was *worthwhile*.

Stage 3. He showed that it was motivating as it satisfied their *needs / aspirations*.

Stage 4. At an early point he introduced the notion of the teaching/learning *contract* to highlight *commitment* on both sides. If you....... I will.

Stage 5. The overall goals were evident to show:

product goals – knowledge and understanding to be attained

process goals – what they will be capable of doing after following him.

This took place in the context of the material being taught.

Stage 6. Expectations raised by explanation and practical applications.

Stage 7. The *aims and objectives were clarified* and would remain a constant *point of reference*. In modern teaching they would form part of an *ongoing, cumulative working display* that is developed as part of the teaching process.

Stages 8–14. form the core of the teaching process. The essential characteristics show that whilst reception learning has its place, the priority is given to forms of *experiential learning*.

Stage 8. This requires some *didactic* teaching that was preparatory to ongoing action. It was stimulating and offered *good prospects* for *worthwhile study*.

Stage 9. The first part of *mastery learning* is where pupils *review their existing knowledge* (here the teaching of John the Baptist). Pupils began to realize that they had much to learn.

Stage 10. Experiential learning is based upon the *everyday community* using the local situation and contemporary media. The teacher, as the expert, facilitates the pupils' *practical experiences*. opportunities for *reflective thought* can be *provoked* and *structured* or developed *incidentally* from the learning experiences

Stage 11. The teacher as a *participating expert demonstrates* and his apprentices *watch, co-operate, imitate and work together* to make decisions.

Stage 12. The teacher states the *Big Idea*, makes maximum use of the *senses*, achieves a *cumulative coherence* to what was being learnt and applies these to the major principles and concepts that had been initially stated

Stage 13. The teacher ensures that his apprentices gain *concept attainment* and are not fixated to one application by applying his teaching to *past, present and future possibilities*. They gained a body of evidence that could be used widely.

Stage 14. Mastery learning (2). The pupils pose questions as to what they *now know* and *have gained*, and how they have moved towards *achieving* the *aims and objectives* and *what still needs to be done* to attain understanding and skills.

Stage 15. The whole experience is reviewed and pupils further *develop their own work independently* or *with others*, but the teacher input is reduced.

Stage 16. A review using the experiences to pose future problems and patterns of learning.

.2c-232
Were Jesus' pupils aware of the significance of what they were being taught?

The matrix (Fig.144/145) indicates the following:

- The teacher is the participating expert / leader who promotes the direction of the studies.
- The clarity of purpose and ongoing development highlight the overarching principles and concepts that are running threads between succeeding topics.
- Reception learning is ultimately related to experiential/ expressive learning.
- Illustrative knowledge enables developments to achieve the aims and objectives and understand principles and concepts rather than being an end in itself.
- The learning facilitates flexible understanding of the greater world around them.
- For every situation, but it is a working proposition which co-ordinates and intensifies the learning processes. By so doing the total force of the learning process is increased whilst allowing ample flexibility to meet individual needs of peer-group involvement is a primary aspect of learning.
- Identifies how what the pupils learn becomes a springboard for further studies.
- The studies are seen to be worthwhile and to meet needs and aspirations.

Using the Theory

The ultimate test for any theory is its match with truth and reality. A striking feature is how Jesus' teaching elements can be applied, with modifications, to any area of learning. Whilst it does not suggest that Jesus had provided a blueprint for the *structure* of modern teaching and of a curriculum in particular, we can tease out clues that are useful and provide reasons to pause for thought. As we have seen, his main purpose was to explain and demonstrate a particular message effectively that would engender a compatible faith and lifestyle.

Figure 144

Stages	A Generalized Teaching Structure	Jesus' Typical Pattern of Teaching
Advance organizer stated Pupil anticipation	Arousal and expectancy Introductory, forecast and preliminary instruction of learning programme and demonstration	Jesus' initial impact His motivational promises and actions An explanation and demonstration of his goals
First hand in community Second hand interviews Third hand sources Books / internet sources	Pupils plan, explore and examine using familiar cultural basis Teacher assists pupils (scaffolding) Pupil activity Reflection on findings/ tentative conclusions	Practical, group and community based learning Jesus and apprentices work together

This can be illustrated by looking at aspects of the curriculum for pupils in Y7 and above as illustrated in Fig.144. This indicates that the process can be developed through most areas of the curriculum and so it could be chosen for any part applied to any part of curriculum. It can be applied equally well to any other subject. It is not the ideal solution for every situation, but it is a working proposition that coordinates and intensifies the learning processes whilst also allowing ample flexibility to meet individual needs.

Column 3 shows how the *structure* in columns 1 and 2 might be usefully converted into a stable organizational structure for teaching a wide range of curriculum areas.

This is not meant to be anything more than an indicator that the issues raised can all be implemented efficiently across a wide spectrum of teaching and learning.

.2c-233
What range of questions might Jesus ask today that are related to the ideas propounded here?

Summary

1. It has been emphasized that this it is not an attempt to pretend that Jesus was a modern teacher, with all the modern demands and support systems, but he did possess the generic skills to provide valuable pointers which enable us to gain insights about contemporary teaching and even indicate the bases for theories of instruction and learning which can be applied across a wide range of teaching. Which of the following are still valid?

- His central teaching was illustrated by words and actions that were rooted in core values and principles.
- Relationships were an essential aspect of teaching and learning.
- The teacher was a consistent role model.
- He promoted promise and hope that was achieved through a high degree of enablement by the teacher, Jesus.
- Teaching was sharply goal directed.
- The teacher possessed the knowledge and expertise to demonstrate the subject in many forms authoritatively.
- The teacher used appropriate and flexible strategies and methods.
- The teacher was an opportunist who responded to needs and created aspirations.
- Most teaching and learning had an historic basis and flourishes in a meaningful way within the pupils' cultural and environmental context.
- The teacher had a wide range of skills and interests that captured the imagination.

2. In the 21st century Jesus would have to make a range of decisions that were not dissimilar to those he made in the first century (see Figs.4, 9, 104). In conclusion, it is useful to remind ourselves which major features in his teaching might be shared by all people of goodwill, even though the teaching would have different priorities, structures and functions and would not be conceived and designed for purely spiritual/confessional purposes. Using Fig. 105, how might the application of Jesus' teaching priorities remain similar or be substantially changed now?

Personality Focus – 15

To what degree does the effectiveness of any theory of learning or instruction depend upon the PF's of those concerned? Can this problem be avoided, while should the instruction and learning be made to compatible with the PF's of the teachers and learners involved?

.2c-234
Which of Jesus' teaching strategies and methods might be most reliable...or most effective?

Figure 145. Towards a Theory of Instruction and Learning

Values	Towards a Theory of Instruction	Core elements	Towards a Theory of Learning	Responses
1 Moral, spiritual developments • Appropriate acceptance of self and others • Positive attitude to authority	• Basis teacher- role-model/ expert • Worth - attitude and regard to pupils, expectations • Establish expectancy and implant seeds of faith • Clarity of purpose • Promise for the future • Established goals/ Big Picture • Indicate anticipated cost benefits • Leading from the heart	• Entry attitudes and expectations • Initial stimuli • Advance organizer • Relate to the past - present - future	• Pupils' attitudes and learning readiness • Worth - self validation and validation of the teacher's relevance and value of work • Entry it abilities, interests and experiences • Arousal - memorable specifics • Anticipated cost benefits	Basis • Motivation • Needs so • Security • Positive expectations
2 Establish rational moral standards • Recognize strengths and weaknesses • Develops stable norms • Interpersonal restoration	• Stilling/calming exercise • Factual introduction with illustrated material • Pacing with short/long variables • Planned rate and flow of knowledge • Basis of central principles stated	• Working rules stated • Pupils identify with tasks • Operating the pleasure principle	• Pupils at recognize the ongoing support • Pupils establish learning habits • They acquire a sense of personal mastery leading to confidence	• Emotional health • Growing confidence and interest • Recognition of the worth of studies
3 Persistent, copes with failure/success • Operates within the principle of forgiveness • Recognizes the range of qualities in other people	• Source the rate and range of flow and delivery of knowledge • Pupils see the organizational structures • Teach and provide ongoing support • Foster ready recall of knowledge	• Progress and development • Change and a novelty • Awareness of progress	• Growing involvement and competence • Increasing personal input • Cumulative memories begin • For over it recognition of the validity of the work • Assimilate new/ related material	• Responds to a sense of acceptance • Communal harmony • Rising aspirations
4 Boundaries • Established behavioural norms	• Corporate work sequences to establish key principles and sense of mastery • A relatively changing degree of teacher control	• Peer-group interaction • Appropriate experiential opportunities • Review early work	• Growing confidence to respond to and cope with existing and similar situations • Confident to be a contributing co - worker	• Growing faith in the leader • Growing creative harmony within the group
5 Recognition and acceptance of social differences • An acute sense of fairness	• An increasing choice of learning materials and experiences • A growing scope for increasing pupil variants	Teaching ↓	• Awareness of their rising higher skill and understanding levels • Pupils begins to accommodate new problematic materials	• Positive it responds to being a participant helper • Share in peer achievement

Figure 145. Towards a Theory of Instruction and Learning

		Learning ↑	
6 Tolerance of others	• Six teaching strategies planned appropriately • Didactic • Vygotsky's social/community based learning • Apprenticeship / situated learning • Accelerated Learning Systems • Mastery learning • Concept attainment	• First-hand learning experiences • Rising and pupil involvement • Pleasurable choices • Growing identification • Personal awareness of mastery	• Positive affective personal and group responses
7 Recognize wrong when it occurs in self/others	• Develop pupils new knowledge and learning skills • Generated settled confidence to use/develop understandings	• Reflection to develop • Reinforcement to retain • Experiment to verify • Conceptualization and understanding grasped	• A growing confidence to respond with a novel ideas
8 Recognise the value and the cost of restoration between people	• Challenge and develop understandings/skills in fresh situations	• Clear resultant and coherent schemas • Exploration/initiatives and intuitive leaps undertaken to achieve problem-solving and creativity • Verify the work output	• A growing personal awareness of personal capability and a desire to solve problems
9 Appreciating qualities in others and their work	• Attainment is verified • Celebrates a degree of success	• Using the schemes etc on new materials • Attainment • Satisfied with new expectations and long-term rewards • Accepts that virtuous activity and prospects cost but a worthwhile	• Confidence self evaluation and appreciation of co-operative work
10 Altruistic creative help	• Recognition of achievement • Display the learned material • Develop the learned material in similar and contrasting contexts	• Plenary session • A shared personal sense of worth etc • A desire for continuity • Aspirations enhance and forward looking • Has a secure or self esteem • The product and process goals realised and appreciated	• Success • A sense of ownership • Long-term learning • Learning is seen to be worthwhile

2c-235
What is the fundamental logic of the 'Model Format' and a Jesus style application of it?

Figure 146a. Examples 1-4 Fundamental to the process are motivation / values and worth / relationships / clarity / involvement / concept attainment

Model Format	Jesus Application	Sociology	Art	Religious Education
1 Initial novel stimulus evoke interest, and attention.	The big surprise - the Kingdom of God is here	Sociology's surprises can help you - for example..........	What we like. .Imagine an artless world. Types of art. Textiles etc	What is Christianity in the local community? Surprising activities et
2 Why should we learn this?	You had been sitting in darkness and will now be in the light – Matt ch. 4	Who would have guessed? An insight to arrest attention- now/ the future?	Man has always loved art. Helps us to understand and enjoy ourselves without being an artist!	We ought to know what it is that causes these actions
3 Motivation needs - personal/shared aspirations	Temporary / permanent needs and promises for the future – Matt ch 4,5	Casts light on needs. There is permanence and change. It opens future possibilities	We decorate rooms and ourselves- our eyes and brains are attracted We love people enjoying OUR art	We can see how it influences such a wide range of people, and why it does not
4 The Contract My promise - I can deliver	Follow me and I will make you Fishers of men – Lk5	My promise is a contract that we can deliver is.....	You are going to design a pattern that will be good enough to....	I have relevant sources that will open minds to ideas and questions.
5 The Goals product – understanding process - wider skills	To understand the nature of the Kingdom of God and its practical deeds	You will understand the impact of ideas on life and interpret situations sociologically	You are going to decide what makes textiles attractive or not. How you can apply textile patterning skills	You will understand why people act as they do ...and develop enquiry and analytical skills and make judgments
6 Explanation - this is how we will do it	Explanation and demonstration Matthew ch.4 and 8	Principle / concept framing explained/ demonstrated. Methods applied to a case study showing relevance	This is what we will do. We will look at these textile books and go around the town make a display discuss and make	You will construct a case study based on interviews and resources of four organizations and report your findings in a systematic form
7 Aims and objectives displayed	A clear demonstration of aims Luke ch.4v18	Principle and concept based teaching and learning moving towards detailed answers with exemplars	Aims and Objectives- Identify and group textile patterns. Examine qualities, suitability. Design, display your design and its uses	More specifically you will look at: Principles Concepts
8 Teaching Strategies a. Didactic	Organized instructional knowledge presented to prepare for ongoing action. Luke ch 6 etc	sociological Stimulating new materials. Question - Is it true? What implications? A study plan . Injections of knowledge	I will show you. Mini display by the previous year. What makes it good in their estimation. Study plan developed.	Constructing the case study. Questions that shape the enquiry and those that are likely to arise from it.

Figure 146a Examples 1-4 Fundamental to the process are motivation / values and worth / relationships /clarity /involvement / concept attainment

	People's existing knowledge - John the Baptist	Present knowledge - mini test /expectations. Surprise and challenge - prospects	Mini test before we start.	What do you know already? Accumulating existing knowledge in various forms
9 Mastery Learning				
10 Vygotsky's - community based learning -	Jesus in Capernaum - memorable knowledge within the community.	Sociology in the community. Situated inquiry based learning. Scaffolding	Textiles in the community. Situated learning in carpets, furnishings, clothes. Peer groups, scaffolding	Pupils explore community using their own enquiry plans and the scaffolding provided by the teacher.
11 Apprentices - watch and help. Complete Master's tasks. Peer-group decision-	Jesus the master craftsman demonstrated what is expected	Watch, imitate teacher doing small-scale ongoing sturdy. Pupils contribute	The teacher as a master craftsman leads a group who watch, help and complete tasks. Discuss process	Pupils are investigators, the teacher is the master craftsman who demonstrates and facilitates etc
12 Accelerated Learning. State Big Idea Max. use of senses. Orderly brain based learning. Cumulative coherence	Kinaesthetic experiences Emphasize and develop the Big Idea other than the Kingdom of God	They experiential learning is maximized	A experiential and expressive work is maximized. Order any decisions appropriately -	Pupils use the full range of skills as they go through the process of making contact, meeting, listening and recording, reporting.
13 Concept awareness and attainment. Applying the past and the present to future	Moving from Galilee	Parallel sociological study t. Gathering evidence related to concepts	Comparative designs within an ace structure and function suitability	Pupils assess findings. Organize into a structure highlighting principles, concepts motivations
14 Mastery Learning (2)	Summary of new knowledge John 14 – 16	What do I now know? What did I know? Gains?	What do I now know about textile design? What have I gained	What can be evaluated ? What new knowledge has been gained?
15 Goals principles and concepts reviewed.	Promises and enablement confirmed	What can we interpret into other similar situations	Can the designs be used or rejected in other situations?	How might the conclusions be generalized or not ?
16 Conclusion - total review pointing the way forwards	The commission to go into all the world	The total conclusion relating principles and concepts to the knowledge of social dynamics	And the total conclusion relating the principles and concepts of textile design to various uses	Display findings and invite the religious organizations to evaluate the findings and the implications for future developments.

.2c-236
Examine the matrix on page 00 and the 8 bullet points above. Select the 4 most significant features of the outline theory

Model Format	Literacy (5/6yrs)	English (12yrs)	Maths (10yrs)	Environ. Studies (14yrs)
1 Stimulating opening	Reader and attractive story containing important Keywords	What have you have you read recently? I have read persuasive adverts	Angles and rotary distances - radar - the ship at sea or aircraft.	Going 'Green' - power. Critical issues in a case study - future implications
2 Why learn this?	You would love to be able to read this for yourselves	Let us see how this aspect of literacy can effect us.	This is maths with a purpose!	We must understand because……. We know, expect, can do
3 Motivation	You need to read, you want to read and so let us read	It is important to you and me that we recognize their power	Lifestyles change with or without it. See the difference it makes	You need to understand and make personal decisions
4 Contract	I promise that by next Friday you will be able to read this story, if ,……	Over the next 2 weeks you will understand the language of persuasion and write adverts.	Over the next 3 weeks you will develop maths skills used to plan holidays	Over the next 6 weeks we will look at a major aspect that requires decisions – power / waste.
5 Goals (general)	Show what they will be able to do. You can take a paper home to show your parents.	You will collect, analyze and assess adverts to examine consumer responses	Measure angles to 180deg. Measure twice that and track movement in angular movement	3 goals- do we know but do nothing? Or act based on evidence and use knowledge to solve problems?
6 Initial explanation	…and you will be able to read other stories as well!	Firstly, let us see what we know and what we need to find out.	Collect key words and procedures. Begin to compile a wall concept board.	We must examine (or collect) the following facts and possibilities
7 Specific objectives	You will be able to do this – display.	And so let us define precisely what we expect to achieve	You will be able to calculate and predict changing positions.	Build and display objectives to show issues to be considered in some detail.
8 Teaching strategies Didactic	Explain / display key phonic words. Read the Big Book to the class –use flash cards	Adverts may do not convey the true meaning of the words they use.	Teacher shows / explains 360 degree compass and the major segments	Explain decisions and values and which controls and changes are needed
9 Mystery learning 1	Phonic use of words and letter games	Starting to collect common words	Pupils locate positions and conceptualize directions and angles	Pupils select positive and negative actions from evidence and in a game
10 Community based learning	Find common key words related to the story. Where were they seen and heard?	Go to the community and see the uses of adverts- discuss planning / design.	On a local map mark compass points identify direction to locations	Look at the Green Issue locally. Research by Q/A, observation key issues.
11 Apprentice tuition	Work with teacher to use / copy key words from the story and findings in 10/	Teacher /craftsman shows pupils what is to be developed. Pupils initiate work.	Teacher and pupils develop journey and write task cards like the teacher's model	Teacher/pupils note developments and research it by Q/A, interviews etc
12 Accelerated learning VAK	Infilling words, develop key words into sentences, include gaming to reinforce	Pupil initiatives, multi-sense development of adverts	Groups prepare and present their work to other groups.	Gather evidence and record findings by appropriate medium
13 Concept awareness	Use key words to compose a new story with parental involvement	Evidence collated. What is learned about language and visualization?	Inter-group task cards used to assess direction/distances based on angles	Use findings to frame future possibilities / probabilities
14 Mastery learning 2	Read key words based on look /hide/ point /say	What have we gained in our understandings and abilities?	Teacher uses blank map – pupils complete tasks	Draw together a report for the local newspaper
15 Objectives reviewed	Class and individuals red the first story and their story and use the words afresh	To what degree do we understand and attained our objectives?	Pupils use a concept chart / group tasks to ask if they have attained their goals	Pupils assess which objectives have achieved understanding and action.
16 Conclusion / forward	Can we read our books? Yes! Let us make them into songs.	Well, how true are adverts? What do people think? The next language issue	These principles will be developed further for campers and…..spies	Which challenges remain to save the planet.

Figure 146b. Examples 5-8 The Application of the Theoretical Model in Various Situations

Personality Focus – 16

Consider Jesus' personality factors, what types of product and process goals would he have? What place might they have in our contemporary education?

Could Jesus have not compromised his strategy but compromised his methods?

2c-237

Conclusion: An Advance Organizer or a Problem Solving kit

I have been writing materials for Religious Education based on the total package of ideas in this book, but of course they can be applied to many aspects of teaching. The following can be used as an advance organizer or an ongoing development tool. If the following ideas are combined with those in Part C various working formats can be developed. It is interesting to go through the strategies and methods and consider how they can be related to Jesus' teaching in one form or another.

Developing a summary exercise

Given the purpose of this book, a valuable review exercise is to pose the issue of transposing Jesus from the 1st to the 21st century.

> *What would he be like?*

Picture his 'hidden years', his work, his revelation and decisions.

> *What would be his focus of concern?*
>
> *How would he respond to this?*
>
> *How might people respond to his preaching?*
>
> *What might be his outcome? etc.*

Review the book for clues and the framework below as a structural advance organizer.

Figure 148

A	B
• The worth /significance of the topic is.....	• He goals are...
• The major relevant issues are........	• The organizing principles to be chosen are...
• The challenge is appropriate because....	• The structural concepts to be used are....
• The particular qualities of the participants are....	• The strategies and methods to be elected are..... (see following pages)
• The background of the learning is...	• The major skills and resources that will be required will be...
• The teaching priorities are...	
• The prime teaching /learning model will be...	• There will be opportunities for Creative expression, discrete thinking skills, language uses, enquiry based learning, interactive learning
• The likely short / long term outcomes are...	
• The main form of knowledge development likely to occur is...	
• It will be assessed and evaluated as follows	

.2c-238
Did Jesus implicitly have a Model Design Format that could be exemplified?

Figure 149

Strategic choices

A/B	Achievements-measurable Aspirations relate to pupils' Attitude change appropriate Association of ideas closely linked Arousal is appropriate	Authenticity is readily apparent Accelerated learning possibilities Assimilate or accommodated knowledge Boundaries (personal /social) recognized
C	Currency of issues Core ideas related to pupils Challenge is appropriate Choice is appropriate Celebration – opportunities Creative opportunities Pupil care adequate	Cultural difference illustrated Corporate validity recognized Community of learning promoted Non coercive control Counselling possibilities as appropriate Commitment of pupils recognized Concept attainment strategies Crisis resolution
D	Diagnostic basis is defined Didactic strategies used appropriately	Teaching /learning responsibilities defined Demonstration of ideas
E	Emotional responses developed Ethos of security and exploration Empathy promoted	Enabling process evident to pupils Experiences that are replicable Expectations are satisfied
F/G /H	Generic qualities are evident Goals are valid and stated	Hope is created Holistic – contributes to this
I	Identification with the learning fostered Inclusion facilitated Interaction promoted	Immersion as allowed by time/situation Interest and involvement promoted Inspirational element present Integration of knowledge and skills
J/K	Knowledge increase apparent Knowledge that is fresh and paced	Knowledge is cumulatively assessed
L	Learning – promotes a desire for Leadership generates knowledge / enquiry	Learning – spiritual, Learning experience has evident worth
M	Motivation – intrinsic / extrinsic? Memory patterns developed Mentoring possibilities	Memories- link episodic and semantic Multiple methods Mastery learning achieved Memories associated
N/O	Needs met Needs – Societal needs met	Novelty and surprise facilitated Norm related / recognized Ownership achieved by pupils
P	Perceived worth to pupils Perceived – degrees of mutuality Promises – attractive and motivating	Progression- optimum rate Pupil potential recognized Pleasure principles validated Prospects are established and clear
Q/R	Relevance of learning Responsibilities appropriately recognized Revelation/ inspiration can be valid Reviews- ongoing and appropriate	Qualities of learning seen as valid? Risk level calculated Role model can be imitated
S	Success - Aware of personal – celebrated Strategies relate to methods Spirituality – defined and fostered Scholarship is recognized as valid Standards are built into studies Stimuli- power of everyday	Self referencing facilitated Situational differences acknowledged Self esteem promoted Shared schemas identified and used Structure is orderly and relevant Social enquiry- opportunities
T/U	Truth and its' values recognized Teacher competence to teach strategy Time – Quality and worth Teacher- ready availability	Universal concerns – awareness Universal principles linking studies Understandings – long term? Team building facilitated Traditions recognized
V/	Value issues defined and identified in action	Variety of learning evokes surprise

.2c-239
Could Jesus have compromised his methods but not his strategies?

Figure 150.

Methodological Choices

A/B	Advance organizers developed Artefacts used Anchorage points identified Big Picture developed	Aspirations as guide to teaching Autobiographical memories used Anticipatory knowledge developed Brainstorming
C	Cartoons Case studies developed Chunking Comprehension tasks Character studies	Conflict resolution exercizes Conversation Curiosity pursued Cues /Clues
D	Deductive thought (Ruleg) Descriptive accounts Dialogue Didactic presentations Discourses	Discussion Displays Drama Drawing and patterns
E	Elaboration Enquiry work Environmental/ community Ephemera for charts/ enquiry Episodic illustrative materials/ memories	Evidence collection Expanding facts- before (cause) and after (effect) Experiential learning Explain and express ideas Extending ideas Evaluating ideas, arguments & materials
F/G /H	Fieldwork Formal instruction Gaming Graphs Frame / display key concepts	Haptic boards Grids Group research Heroic actions
I	ICT materials Internet Identify relationships Inductive learning (Egrule) Interactive learning	Interpreting symbols and motifs Interview Interpreting text Imaginative leaps
J/K	Jigsaws Keywords	Knowledge insertion Kinaesthetic experiences
L	Letter writing	Library research
M	Maps Memory mind maps Mastery practices Meaning exploration Meditation and reflection	Metaphors Modifying world views Music Develop memory bank Multi choice rationalized responses
N/O	Need identification Newspaper reports Observation	Opportunism Oral descriptions
P	Parables Past experiences recalled Peer tuition Personalization Problem solving and analyses Posters PowerPoint Prioritization	Programs for mastery Project construction Photography Pictograms Plenary reports Poetry Patterning knowledge and performance
Q/R	Questionnaire Q and A Recall facts Record facts Record information for experience Reflective statements Rationalization of knowledge	Repetition in various forms Reporting Resource development Rhyme and rhythm Rote learning Reformulate information Develop retrieval systems
S	Schemas formulated /organized Self assessment management Semantic memories developed Sound bites Storyboarding	Using varied senses appropriately Sequencing Similarity and differences identified Supported self studies Stories told/ written/ interpreted
T/U	Template frames for recall & progression Using traditional sources	Thinking skills- Classification /prediction /projection /justification / contrast etc
V/Z	Visualization Word association	Z or concertina books

.2c-240
What would have been the likely features of Jesus' 'theories of instruction and learning'?

Appendix Jesus and Personality Factors

The quality and success of teaching is not solely based on devising appropriate methodologies and resources which match the content been taught. Equally important are the personality factors of teachers and pupils. This is not the place to compare personality theories, but it is worth considering how personality factors (P.F.) might influence the most effective teaching and the learning styles of teachers and pupils

This must have applied to Jesus and his followers but it is dangerous to try to rigorously tie Jesus' personality down to certain types – indeed the lapse of time and our ignorance prevent this, but it is helpful to consider dominant features that might help us to understand how he both learnt and taught. This may be questionable to some but it has the effect of sensitizing us to both the person himself and his teaching.

When teachers with a dominant set of personality factors are asked to teach in a style more conducive to a different set of personality factors they may seriously under-perform. Hence, a teacher who is relatively introverted may be thoroughly ineffective in one style and yet successful if allowed to teach in a compatible style. The same issue occurs with extrovert teachers and also with pupils.

Appendix C contains an outline of over 200 personality factors which are largely taken from theorists such as Eysenck, Cattell, Rogers, Kelly etc and which might have differing degrees of relevance throughout this book. At the end of each chapter there is a section headed Personality Factor 1 or 2 or 3 etc. These pose issues relating to the personality factors listed in Appendix C and the dominant ideas of that chapter. Hence, by considering Jesus' teaching style we can grasp some notion of his personality, or conversely, by considering his personality we can judge what his most effective teaching style was likely to be.

The P.F.'s are listed both alphabetically and also *some* as they might be related in clusters appropriate to this book. Not all factors are exclusive to one group and not all words are used specifically in formal descriptions of personality, but they are descriptive and can be readily recognized and applied in this context.

This clustering of personality descriptors can be helpful when considering any possible match between teaching and learning styles and which were evident in Jesus' teaching and can be related to the theories of instruction and learning on pages 253-257. Although one hesitates to make a full-scale retrospective personality analysis of Jesus, the significance of the issues encapsulated by this might be judged by the ongoing references. These can help us to appreciate both the person and his teaching styles more sensitively and apply aspects to our current situations.

How can this type of self-analysis help any teacher?

.2c-241
To what extent might a person's dominant teaching strategy be tied to his/her personality?

Figure 151

He was.........				He was not.........
Achiever	Decisive	Happy-go-lucky	Nurturer	Secure
Active	Demanding	Harmonious		Self-assured
Adaptable	Destructive	Healer	Open	Self-discipline
Adverserial	Determined	Hearty	Optimistic	Self-sufficient
Affable	Dictatorial	Helper	Organized	Sensitive
Affectionate	Dignified	Honest	Organizer	Serious
Aggressive	Diligent	Hopeful	Opinionated	Server
Agreeable	Discerning	Humble	Opportunist	Shaper
Ambitious	Discriminating	Humorous	Outgoing	Short-term
Amiable	Dominant			Shrewd
Anxious	Dutiful	Idealistic	Passionate	Sober
Appreciative	Dynamic	Idiosyncratic	Passive	Sociable
Argumentative		Imaginative	Peaceable	Specialist
Arrogant	Easy-going	Impulsive	Protective	Steadfast
Aspirational	Eager	Industrious	Prudent	Stimulating
Assertive	Emotional	Intelligent	Patient	Spontaneous
Authoritative	Empathetic	action	Pessimistic	Stable
Autocratic	Enabler	Independent	Perceptive	Strong willed
Avid	Encouraging	Inquisitive	Perfectionist	Studious
	Energetic	Insecure	Persevering	Suave
Benevolent	Excitable	Initiator	Persistent	Submissive
Benign	Enterprising	Isolate	Persuader	Supportive
Bully	Enthusiastic	Insensitive	Pertinacity	Suspicious
	Even tempered	Integrity	Planner	Sympathetic
Calm	Experimenter	Introspective	Possessive	Systematic
Careful	Explorer	Introvert	Practical	
Caring	Exploitive		Pragmatic	Tactful
Carefree	Extravert	Joyful	Pride	Talkative
Cautious		Judgmental	Principles	Teachable
Changeable	Facilitator	Just	Proactive	Tenacious
Change- Desire	Faithful		Problem solver	Thoughtful
Charismatic	Fearful	Kind		Timid
Charming	Feelings/priority			Tolerant
Cheerful	Finisher	Laissez-faire	Quiescent	Tough-minded
Combative	Focused	Languid	Quiet	Trusting
Companionable	Forgiving	Leader		Truthful
Committed	Forthright	Learner	Reasonable	
Conceit	Fortitude	Lively	Reformer	Unsociable
Confident	Forward	Logical	Relaxed	Uncontrolled
Conformed		Long-term	Reliable	
Conscientious	Generous	Loving	Restless	Warm
Contemplative	Gentle	Loyal	Repetitive	Welcoming
Contented	Goal orientated		Reserved	Withdrawn
Conservative	Gracious		Resolute	
Confrontational	Gregarious	Magnanimous	Resourceful	Vain
Compassionate		Materialistic	Responsible	Venturesome
Co-operative		Mentor	Rigid	Visionary
Courageous		Merciful	Responsive	Vitality
Courteous		Methodical		
Creative		Motivated	Righteous	xenophobic
Cruel		Moody	Rigorous	
Curious			Risk-taker	zealous

Bibliography

The following references/bibliography indicate a wide range of perspectives. As a mainstream Christian, I have found them all valuable when used selectively. Therefore, such books may not be consistent with each other, but each sheds some light on the total picture. For example, as Jews, the books by Vermes and Maccoby provide excellent insights, as does the tome by Alfred Edersheim. A further example of this is Rudolf Bultmann's *Jesus and the Word* in which aspects of chapter 3 were valuable. This eclectic mix should not prove to be a hindrance to the theme of the book as a whole.

Introduction

Alexander H, Editor, *Spirituality and Ethics in Education* (Sussex Academic Press 2004)

> (See Ch. 'Jesus as Teacher' by Nicholas Burbules and Ch. 2 'Jesus as Teacher' by Terence H McLaughlin.)

Prelude

Seligman M, *Flourish* (Nicholas Brealey 2011)

Chapter 1 – Establishing the Scene

Duquesne J, *Jesus* (Arthur James 1996)
Edersheim A, *The life and times of Jesus the Messiah* (latest edition)
Fletcher B, *The Aramaic Sayings of Jesus* (Hodder and Stoughton 1967)
Gladwell M, *Outliers,* Ch1&2 (Penguin 2008)
Grant R, *A Historical Introduction to the New Testament* (Fontana 1971)
Grollenberg L, *Jesus,* (S.C.M. 1978)
Macobby H, *Jesus the Pharisee* (S.C.M. 2003)
Rihbany A, *The Syrian Christ* (Melrose 1920)
Sanders E P, *The Historical Figure of Jesus* (Penguin 1993)
Theissen G, *The Shadow of the Galilean* (S.C.M. 1986)
Vermes G, *Jesus the Jew* (S.C.M. 1994)
Vermes G, *Who's Who in the age of Jesus* (Penguin 2005)
Watts F, Editor, *Jesus and Psychology* (DLT 2007)

Chapter 2 – Tradition or Progress

Barclay W, *The Mind of Jesus* (S.C.M. 1960)
Bultmann R, *Jesus and the Word* (Fontana Books 1958)
Gardner R et al, *Educating for Values* (Kogan Page 2000)
Holt J, *How Children Learn* (Pelican 1983)
Horne H H, *Teaching techniques of Jesus* (Kregal 1971)
N and M et al, *Curriculum & Pedagogy – Inclusive Education* (Routledge Falmer 2005)
Perkins P, *Jesus as Teacher* (Cambridge 1990)
Smith D I and Shortt J Stapleford, *The Bible and the Task of Teaching* (Centre 2002)
White E G, *Christ's Object Lessons* (Stanborough 1993)

Chapter 3 – Ultimate Teaching Strategy A

Part B General

Aronson E, *The Social Animal* (Freeman 1994)
Aronson et al, *The heart and the mind* (HarperCollins 1994)
Argyle M, *Social Psychology of the Everyday Life* (Routledge 1992)
Atkinson R and Hilgard et al, *Introduction to psychology* (Thomas Wadsworth 2003)
Eysenck M W, *Psychology* (Psychology Press 2001)

Eysenck M and Keane M, *Cognitive Psychology* (Psychology Press 2005)
Gross R, *Psychology 5th edition* (Hodder Arnold 2005)
Hayes N, *Psychology* (Routledge 1994)
Hewstone M et al, *BPS text books Psychology* (Blackwell 2005)
Hewstone M et al, *Introduction to social psychology* (Blackwell 1996)
Fontana D, *Psychology for Teachers* (Br. Psychology Soc)
Kincheloe J & Horn R (Editors) *Praeger H'book of Education & Psychology Vol 1-4* (Praeger 2007)
Meldrum C et al, *Psychology* (Collins 2009)
Smith E et al, *Social Psychology* (1995)
Stianton Rogers W, *Social Psychology* (Open Univ 2003)

Chapter 5 – Leadership

Adair, John *The leadership of Jesus* (Canterbury 2001)
Bazalgette, John, *Leading Schools from Failure to Success* (UIT Cambridge 2006)
Covey, Stephen R, *The Seven Habits of Highly Effective People* (Simon and Schuster 1992)
Dorr, Donal, *Spirituality of Leadership* (Columba 2006)
Greenleaf R K, *Servant Leadership* (Paulist Press 1977)
Greenleaf R K, *The Power of Servant Leadership* (Berrett- Koeler 1998)
Hooper A and Potter J, *Intelligent Leadership* (Random House 2000)
Kouzas J and B.P *Leadership – the Challenge* (Jossey Bass 2002)
Lawrence, James, *Growing Leaders* (CPAS 2004)
Roberts W, *Leadership secrets of Attila the Hun* (Warner 1985)

Chapters 6 – Perception

Bagguley J, *Doors of Perception* (SUS press 1987)
Watts, Nye and Savage, *Optical Illusions – Psychology for Christian ministry* (Routledge 2002)
Watts, Fraser (Editor), *Jesus and Psychology* (DLT 2007)

Chapter 7 – Motivation

Please see general introductory books listed above.

Chapter 8 – Memory

Baddeley A, *Your Memory – A User's Guide* (Carlton 2004)
Iddon J and Williams H, *Memory Workout –* (Thunder Bay 2003)
Beike R et al (Editors) *Self and Memory* (Psychology Press 2004)

Chapter 9 – Socialisation

Goleman D, *Social intelligence* (Hutchinson 2006)

Chapter 10 – Cognition

Jensen E, *The Learning Brain* (Turning Point 1995)
Gardner H, *Intelligence Reframed* (Basic Books 1999)
Gardner H, *Development & Education of the Mind* (WIE 2006)
Robinson K, *Out of Our Minds* (Capstone 2001)
Rogoff B, *Apprenticeship in Thinking* (OUP 1990)
Solso R et al, *Cognitive Psychology* (Pearson 2006)

Chapter 11 – Emotion

Ekman P, *Emotions Revealed* (Pheonix 2003)
Goleman D, *Emotional intelligence* (Bloomsbury 1996)

Goleman D, *Working with Emotional Intelligence* (Bloomsbury 1998)
Stein S and Book H, *The EQ Edge* (Kogan Page 2001)

Chapter 12 – Ultimate Teaching Strategy B

Chapter 13

Entwhistle N (Editor), *Handbook of Educational Ideas and Practices* (Routledge 1990)
Leach J & Moon R, *Power of Pedagogy* (Sage 2008)

Chapter 14 – Teaching strategies

Spirituality

Alexander H, (Editor), *Spirituality and Ethics in Education* (Sussex Academic Press 2004)
    (See Ch. 'Jesus as Teacher' by Nicholas Burbules and Ch. 2 'Jesus as Teacher' by Terence H McLaughlin.)

Erricker C, (Editor), *Spiritual Education, literary, empirical and pedagogical approaches*
(Sussex Academic Press 2005)

Ota C, Erricker J, *Spiritual Education, culture religious and social differences*
(Sussex Academic Press 2001)

Adams, Hyde and Wooley, *The spiritual dimension of childhood* (Kingsley 2008)
Best R, *Educating Spirituality & the Whole Child* (Cassell 1996)
Drane, OM Fleming, *Spirituality to Go* (DLT 2005)
Draper, Brian, *Spiritual Intelligence* (LionHudson 2009)
Pickering, Sue, *SpiritualDirection* (Canterbury Press 2008)
Savage, John, *Your Spiritual I.Q.* (Abingdon Press 2010)
Zohar D and Marshall, *Spiritual Intelligence* (Bloomsbury 2000)
Hyde, Brendan, *Children and Spirituality* (Jessica Kingsley 2008)
Worsley H, *A Child Sees God* (Jessica Kingsley 2009)
Wenger E, *Communities of Practice* (Cambridge 1998)
Rose C, *Accelerated Learning* (Accelerated Learning Systems 1985)
Wise D and Lovatt M, *Creating an Accelerated Learning School* (Network Educational Press 2001)
Chapman C, *If the shoe fits* (Skylight 1993)
Nicholson K, *Developing Multiple Intelligences* (Nelson Scholastic Press 1998)
Lave J and Wenger E, *Situated Learning* (Cambridge 1991)
Block J, *Mastery Learning* (Holt Rinehart Winston 1971)
Ginnis P, *Toolbox for Teachers* (Crown Pub 2005)
Moore E, *The Good Teacher* (Routledge 2004)
Pollard A, *Reflective Thinking* (Continuum 2005)
Pollard A, *Readings for Reflective Teachers* (Continuum 2004)

Chapter 16

Jesus, the Middle Eastern Storyteller - BurgeG M   Zondervan 2009
Listening - Long A   DLT 1990
Practising the Sacred Art of Listening - KayLindahl   Wildgoose Pub. 2004

Chapter 17 – Ultimate Teaching Strategy C

Apprenticeship in Thinking - Rogoff B   OU P 1990

Chapter 18 – Constructing a theory of instruction and learning

Towards a Theory of Instruction - Bruner J   Cambridge 1966
The Process of Education - Bruner J   Cambridge 1960

Appendix – Personality Factors

Goldsmith M andWharton M, *Knowing Me, Knowing You* (SPCK 1993)
Gordon, Claire, *Personality Profiler* (Caroll and Brown 2005)
Plus Curriculum Journal R E source Journal

Index

21st century teaching models 38, 39, 51, 244, 255

Accelerated Learning 202
Accommodation 138
Achievement 140, 156
Affiliation 38
Apprentice 196, 198
Aramaic 18
Arousal 112
Aspiration 41
Assimilation 139
Atkinson 107
Attention 213
Attitude 123
Attribution 22
Authority 30, 34, 35

Badderley 108
BarOnEQ-1 (test) 156
Bartlett, F 108, 109
Bazalgette, J 149
Belben, H 40
Barclay, W 19, 177
Big Idea 10, 47
Big Picture 42, 44, 187, 189
Bloom, B 218
Bonding 150
Bottom up 74
Brain based learning 139
Bruner 152, 222

Capernaum 23
Chunking 203
Community based learning 216
Concentric strategy 12
Concept attainment 221
Conflict 152
Contextual learning 316
Continuity 41, 191
Contract 218
Contrasts 11, 35, 37, 39
Conversation 212
Copers 152
Covey 71
Creative thought 141, 143
Crises 213

Deductive learning 222
Defenders 152
Decisions 36, 163
Demonstration 192
Didactic teaching 194

Emotion 147, 157
Empathy 246
Episodic memories 114
Ethics 29
Ethos 191
Experiential 113, 191

Flashbulb 115
Forgiveness 12

Galilee 9, 22
Gardner, H 153
Goals–product 26, 46, 181, 182
Goals–process 149 ...., 182
God 12
Goleman 154, 158

Halakhah 20
Herod 18
Hillel 20
Historical roots 17, 18
Holistic 78

Imagination 136, 210
Inclusion 30
Inductive 222
Influence 9
Inner speech 214
Instruction 10, 164
Israel 22

Jensen 139
Jesus, Background 17
Jesus, Characteristics 25, 36, 50, 185
Jesus, Cognitive basis 140
Jesus, Decision making 20
Jesus, Education 20
Jesus, Effectiveness 13, 30
Jesus, General teaching effects ... 9
Jesus, Influences 17, 18
Jesus, Meditation 19, 20
Jesus, Motivator 99

Jesus, Multicultural background 18
Jesus, Perception 84
Jesus, Progressives 37
Jesus, Radical 34
Jesus, Role model 9
Jesus, Self preparation 12
Jesus, Situational relevance 12
Jesus, Teaching qualities 22
Jesus, Teaching qualities, model 47
Jesus, Teaching qualities, principles .. 54, 184
Jesus, Teaching qualities, processes 33
Jesus, Teaching qualities, strategies 154
Jesus, Teaching qualities, style 15, 41,49
Jesus, Teaching qualities, world view 19
Joseph 18

Kerygma 44
Kinaesthetics 87
Kingdom 12, 211
Knowledge 141
Knowledgeable other 216
Koinonia 45
Kouzes 73

Language 114
Law/Torah /Talmud etc 21, 23, 24
Learning zone 215
Learning sequences 166, 205, 253
Leaders 39, 70,71
Leadership priorities 70
Learning characteristics 34

Maccabbeus 20
Maslow 31
Mastery learning 218
Meditation 191
Memory 105
Mentor 199
Message 22
Metaphors 207
Methods 8, 11, 14, 24, 25, 41, 48
Mind maps 15, 39, 51, 70, 94, 106,
.... 117, 120, 121, 169, 180, 203, 225,
.... 253, 255, 257, 258, 262
Models 12, 26, 247
Motivation 39, 93
Morals 185
Mutuality 36
Murray 100

Nazareth 18, 22,30

Needs based 31, 41
Neisser 85

Objectives 29
Observation 14, 18, 19
Olsen/Torrence 153
Oral ....
Organisation ....

Pact 71, 72
Parables 19
Perception 33, 81
Peer group 114
Pharisees 18, 30, 34
Pollyanna 112
Principles 12, 40
Problem-solving 14,144, 145, 146
Progressivism 33, 36, 38, 39
Prophetic 19, 22, 26
Projection 191
Pupil based learning 37, 245

Question - Answer 213

Rath 101
Reconciliation 12
Reflection 14, 18, 119, 191
Reinforcement 191
Relationships 22, 29, 30, 191
Repentance 12
Retrieval 107, 113
Revelation 18
Rhyme 114
Rhythm 114
Role-model 18

Schema 24, 138
Scribes 20
Scaffolding 214
Self-actualisation 32
Semantic 114
Senses 204
Sepphoris 18
Servant leader 75, 77
Shepherd 18
Similarity/ difference 11
Socialisation 119
Spiritual 23, 32, 76, 183, 185, 189
Stein/Book 156
Story telling 207

Strategies 8, 15, 19, 30, 196, 247
Summary statements 14, 26, 40, 54,
........................55, 116, 156, 160, 161, 224,
.... 225, 234, 235, 252
Symbolism 206, 207
Synagogue 22

Teacher 9, 13, 36, 48
Teaching style 37, 49, 52, 75, 191,
.... 235, 244, 251, 255
Teacher qualities 37, 167, 180
Template 46
Thematic matrices 69, 119
Theory of Instruction 243, 245
Thinking process 137
Toolbox 11, 12
Top-down 74
Traditionalism 30, 34
Training 52
Truth 18

Ultimate Teaching Strategies 53, 163, 237

Values 29, 30, 185, 247
Vision 12, 20
Visualisation 11, 191
Vygotsky 214

World View 83

Lightning Source UK Ltd.
Milton Keynes UK
UKOW06f0037070214

226056UK00004B/6/P